Reclaiming the Dark Feminine

Other Titles From New Falcon Publications

Cosmic Trigger: The Final Secret of the Illuminati
Prometheus Rising
    By Robert Anton Wilson
Undoing Yourself With Energized Meditation
The Tree of Lies: Become Who You Are
    By Christopher S. Hyatt, Ph.D.
Eight Lectures on Yoga
Gems From the Equinox
The Pathworkings of Aleister Crowley
    By Aleister Crowley
Neuropolitique
Info-Psychology
The Game of Life
    By Timothy Leary, Ph.D.
Zen Without Zen Masters
    By Camden Benares
Condensed Chaos: An Introduction to Chaos Magick
    By Phil Hine
Breaking the Godspell
    By Neil Freer
The Complete Golden Dawn System of Magic
The Golden Dawn Tapes—Series I, II, and III
    By Israel Regardie
Buddhism and Jungian Psychology
    By J. Marvin Spiegelman, Ph.D.
Astrology & Consciousness: The Wheel of Light
    By Rio Olesky
Metaskills: The Spiritual Art of Therapy
    By Amy Mindell, Ph.D.
The Mysteries Revealed
    By Andrew Schneider
Beyond Duality: The Art of Transcendence
    By Laurence Galian
Soul Magic: Understanding Your Journey
    By Katherine Torres, Ph.D.
Carl Sagan & Immanuel Velikovsky
    By Charles Ginenthal

And to get your free catalog of *all* of our titles, write to:
New Falcon Publications (Catalog Dept.)
1739 East Broadway Road, Suite 1-277
Tempe, Arizona 85282 U.S.A

Reclaiming the Dark Feminine

The Price of Desire

Carolyn L. Baker, Ph.D.

NEW FALCON PUBLICATIONS
TEMPE, ARIZONA, U.S.A.

Copyright © 1996 by Carolyn L. Baker, Ph.D.

All rights reserved. No part of this book, in part or in whole, may be reproduced, transmitted, or utilized, in any form or by any means, electronic or mechanical, including photocopying, recording, or by any information storage and retrieval system, without permission in writing from the publisher, except for brief quotations in critical articles, books and reviews.

International Standard Book Number: 1-56184-088-2
Library of Congress Catalog Card Number: 96-68642

First Edition 1996

Cover art by Denise Cuttitta

The paper used in this publication meets the minimum requirements of the American National Standard for Permanence of Paper for Printed Library Materials Z39.48-1984

Address all inquiries to:
NEW FALCON PUBLICATIONS
1739 East Broadway Road Suite 1-277
Tempe, AZ 85282 U.S.A.
(or)
1209 South Casino Center
Las Vegas, NV 89104 U.S.A.

Dedication

To Meg Pierce for giving me my second birth.
Your love and commitment have allowed me to
reclaim my soul and my life;

and

To my clients and students whose healing journeys have
profoundly transformed me;

and

To Spirit for sparing and inspiring me and to Whose honor
I dedicate my life and work.

Acknowledgments

I wish to acknowledge my parents; Grandma Ada; Shana; Michael & Mikie Dines; Delfina Ramirez;Emma Bowser; Virginia Amundsen McKane; Marian Kinget; Norman Pollack; Jean Dockery; Margaret Sanchez; Joanne Grieb; Joan Marsh; Nancy McCollum; Nancy Wilsted; Noel Black; Katherine Anderson; Richard Wunderli; Dennis White; Donna Moore; Sheryn Scott; Denton Roberts; Robert Phillips; Pam Levin; Robert & Mary Goulding; Annabelle Westling; Carl Gustav Jung; Marion Woodman; Marie-Louise von Franz; Sylvia Brinton Perera; Clarissa Pinkola Estés; Edward Whitmont; Jean Norelli-Whitson; Michael Whitson; Robert Bly; Thomas Moore; Michael & Erica Meade; David Whyte; Sam Keen; Aaron Kipnis; Elizabeth Herron; Malidoma & Sobonfu Somé.

Miguel Rivera; Bert Hoff; Jack Kammer; Jed Diamond; Susan Loughan; Wende Williams; Ralph Blum; Annabelle Westling; Rio Olesky; Angeles Arrien; Deborah Collins; Billy Rogers; Beloved friends from the Hopi Nation including Patrick & Eva Lomawaima; Michael Kabotie; Gwen Dyer; Joy & Raymond Sequaptewa; Loretta Navasi; Elsie Youyetewa; Janice & Joseph Day; Debbie Hood; Members of the Sonoma County, California Gender Healing Community; Zann Erick; Stephanie Schmitz; John & Gerri Shanteau; Archie Fire Lame Deer; Jamie Sams; Robbie Saunders; Francis & Julia Weller; Fred Engbarth; Peter Morfin; M.J. Papa; Shepherd Bliss; Hari Meyers; Larry Robinson; Steven & Carrie Greenberg; Gordon Pugh; Michelle & David Keip; Malcom Miller; Susan Stewart; Jaci O'Shun; Janis Dolnick; Diane Smith; Foley Benson; Susan Adler— and to all who have participated in shaping my life and therefore this book, I am deeply indebted.

I thank my editor Nicolas Tharcher for engaging with me fiercely and playfully and Denise Cuttitta for her cover art.

Table of Contents

Introduction 8
Sweet Darkness, by David Whyte 24
1. The Price of Desire 25
2. Feeding the Hag 32
3. Under the Spell of the Hag 42
4. Leaving the Mother's House 56
5. In Exile 72
6. The Reunion 85
7. The Tears of the Feminine 102
8. Breaking the Spell 128
9. Coming Home 139
Epilogue 153
Glossary of Terms 157
About the Author 160

Introduction

On a chilly, foggy, typically summer morning in San Francisco, I entered one of Nob Hill's posh hotels and registered for a conference called "Tough Guys, Wounded Hearts". I was there because the conference was open to women and because I was curious. The event had been going on for two days prior, but I was only able to attend on this day.

The first workshop I signed up for, "Healing Our Masculine Selves", was for women only and focused on becoming conscious of one's internal masculine energy. The female facilitator led us in a visualization process which helped me connect with my feminine self, my inner male and an image of the divine within me. About thirty women sat in a circle sharing intimately their reasons for attending the conference. My experience with personal development events is that they are usually under-attended by men. One woman remarked how delightful it was for her to attend this conference and be outnumbered by men. Many of us expressed profound joy and relief in finding each other — discovering other women who were drawn to a men's mythopoetic event, not to "save" their husbands, boyfriends, sons, fathers, brothers or male friends, but to feel and experience the healing of their own inner male.

A few months earlier I had been surfing through the channels on my TV remote control device. I happened to pause on a PBS channel where Bill Moyers was interviewing Robert Bly. I was mesmerized by the interview and by Bly's presence and words. By the end of the program I was in tears, and I didn't know why. I immediately bought *Iron John* and read it twice. Later I caught an interview with

Sam Keen and read and re-read *Fire in the Belly*. Through all of this I felt as if I were the only woman in the world who felt a kinship with the men's movement. Suddenly, here in this room with these women, a dry, parched, lonely, aching place inside me felt watered and nourished.

Throughout the day as I traveled the hallways, elevators and stairwells of the conference hotel, as I sat with men in workshops or at lunch, there was a unique quality of intimacy in my interactions with them. Sometimes we hugged; sometimes we looked courageously into each other's eyes and shared very personal stories of healing; sometimes we just smiled at one another without words. At two different times, men approached me and said, "You are a very beautiful woman, and I'm glad you're here." They weren't hitting on me or fulfilling a "workshop/therapy assignment." Their conveyances were genuine, sincere — innocent yet incisive.

That morning I shed, but for the most part, held back, a reservoir of tears. The part of me I had come to identify as my "inner male" was delighted that I had taken him here, but he was also needing to grieve all the inattention he had gotten throughout my life. Yes, I had been and continued to be a strong and powerful woman, but something had been missing. I hadn't come to know my masculine self. Small wonder.

My father loved me very much, but was nowhere present emotionally for himself or for me. As the conference took me deeper into this new territory of the soul, the little girl inside me wanted to scream to the top of her lungs: "Where the hell was my daddy?!" The grown woman was moved, softened, empowered, intrigued, honored, validated and very much in awe of the entire event. At lunch I sat with men and women who had been complete strangers, but after leaving the table, I felt a huge lump in my throat and remembered a familiar Twelve Step saying: "There aren't any strangers — just friends you haven't met yet."

As I approached the huge ballroom where the afternoon's final closing exercises were to be held, I decided that things couldn't get any more intense than they already were. (Hadn't I learned by now in my healing journey that I never know what's going to happen next?)

I entered the ballroom amid the reverberation of drumbeats that began reaching into my internal organs while I was still a hundred feet down the hallway. In a daze, with tears streaming down my face, I wandered into a vacant seat.

One of the conference facilitators spoke softly and gently for awhile then asked another facilitator to join him up front. He asked one of the drummers to begin a slow, soft drum accompaniment. The two men began moving very slowly and sensuously back-to-back without words or any other sounds besides the tender, powerful drumbeat. One of the men invited others in the audience to join in similar dyads. I was unable to move or speak and shuddered to hold back sobs that were welling up from my stomach. Through my tears I saw men dancing back-to-back with men, women with women and men with women. I had never witnessed anything like this in my life.

After the dancing ceased, one of the facilitators asked all the women to come up front and sit on the stage. I could no longer contain my sobs. For over twenty years I had been attending conferences for women only where, if a man had entered the room, he would have been at least verbally, if not physically, assaulted. I could not believe that these men wanted us to come forward and speak. For about half an hour, several women, some of whom had been in the women's workshop I had attended earlier, shared their feelings and experiences regarding the conference. The open microphone never came my way, nor did I reach for it. It was just as well because I couldn't talk.

Along with the other women, I returned to my seat. Several women and men came forth and recited poems and shared experiences of the conference. Finally, one of the drummers stepped to the microphone and asked that the women come to the front again. As we returned to the front, the drummer asked that all the men in the room form a circle around us so that he could lead them in an African male chant in praise of the Goddess. Some women might have felt intimidated being surrounded by men. I did not.

The thunderous roar of all the drums commenced, resonating through the floor, walls and chandeliers of the ballroom. Twenty years of scenes of myself at feminist, separatist events flashed through my mind. Outside this ballroom in the hotel lobby, dozens of San Francisco Police Department SWAT Team members patrolled the hotel and adjacent streets in an effort to protect an Asian dignitary and his entourage. Outside this room, what Sam Keen calls "the war, work and gender-role ethic" prevailed. Inside this room some three to four hundred men and some fifty to seventy-five women danced and chanted in a tribute to each other's humanity. It was a roomful of recovering alcoholics and addicts, survivors of childhood abuse, single people, married people, divorced people. Some were parents, some had never had children. Some were heterosexual, some lesbian and gay. We were European-American, African-American, Asian-American, Native American. We were coming together not only in love but in fierceness — as warriors for the sacredness of the feminine and masculine in all of us. Through my tears, with the drumbeat piercing my heart, I saw a vision of how it could be — for one sweet moment we were united in heart, soul, mind and body, women and men turning gender wars into gender peace.

In the years following this conference I have become deeply convinced that the crux of whether or not we will survive as a species, given our toxification of the planet, our bodies and minds, lies not in eliminating nuclear weapons, racism, hunger, poverty, cleaning up the environment or finding the cure for cancer. As urgent as all these crises are, that which underlies, supports and feeds all of the life-threatening issues our species currently confronts is the patriarchy — a way of life based on power, control, and the constant battle it perpetuates between women and men. The patriarchy, although primarily engineered and executed by men, dishonors men and the positive masculine as much as it dishonors women and the positive feminine.

As this book is being written, women are being burned at the stake in Bangladesh for committing adultery, and men in America are having heart attacks and committing suicide four times more frequently than women. Patriarchy "permits" women their equality as long as they either: 1) Secure their equality in patriarchal ways by not journeying deeply into their feminine selves, adopting the methods and "equal opportunity " diseases of patriarchy such as lung cancer and other stress-related illnesses; or 2) Do not ask to know who their male friends, partners, husbands or lovers really are. Patriarchy says: "That's just the way men are. They don't talk about their feelings, they "do" love in order to get sex, and loneliness and lack of intimacy is the price you have to pay for having a husband, financial security and children." On the other hand, patriarchy encourages some women to believe: "Men *are* the patriarchy, and none of them can be trusted. They are incapable of love and can't talk about their feelings. Who needs them? Bash them, trash them, relate only to women, and maybe you can have enough peace in this lifetime to survive and have a reasonably sane life — or you might find a male 'soft' enough to become as womanlike and politically correct as you are, in which case, relating to a man is no threat." (For example, one woman I know proudly refers to her husband as a "male lesbian.")

Patriarchy assures men their "privilege," if it is, in fact, privilege, by perpetuating the intergenerational premise that little boys should not have feelings, that they should be needless and grow up as soon as possible seeking only to work hard, make lots of money, go to war when "necessary" and use women as nurturers and sexual objects. Most threatening and despicable of all the for patriarchy is the possibility that a man should look deeply into his feelings, his masculine self and his inner feminine and question or reject his patriarchal programming. If he dares to do so, patriarchy, through the media and women who have been hurt very deeply by men, may angrily and bitterly call him a wimp or challenge his right to work on himself at all. After all, what is he whining about? Men own the world, and women are their victims. How dare they think they need a "men's movement"! Right? Wrong.

Riane Eisler, pioneer teacher and author in the area of gender awareness, invites us to enlarge our perspective in relation to the roles of women and men in our culture. She notes that both genders are passengers on a sinking ship in which men, because they occupy first-class cabins, are labeled "privileged." Michael Meade in *Men and the Water of Life* remarks that the surest way to perpetuate male violence is to deny that men need a mythopoetic movement to deal with their grief and rediscover intimacy with one another. Only through grieving one's past trauma whether it was growing up in an abusive family, the Vietnam war or some other soul-murdering experience, does one feel safe enough to begin dropping the armor of machismo and other defenses developed for survival.

In his foreword to Thomas Moore's book, *Dark Eros,* Jungian analyst, Adolf Guggenbuhl-Craig notes that, "if somebody is successful in completely splitting off or apparently eliminating his or her dark side, he or she becomes empty, bloodless, and — in the end — not connected to any kind of eros."

Eros, the god of love, passion, vitality and life-force is a critical component of human creativity. His presence is also required in the healing process — especially in the healing of the soul. In Greek mythology, Psyche (the soul) and Eros (impassioned masculine love), encounter and are transformed by one another in reaction and response to Aphrodite (the goddess of feminine love). I have noticed that wherever soul healing occurs — in a therapy office, in a workshop, in an intimate conversation between lovers — not only is Psyche there, but so is Eros. The only thing which excludes Eros is a human being's refusal to acknowledge and relate with the dark side.

While volumes have been written on the shadow and the dark side of the human psyche, not enough attention has been paid, in my opinion, to the feminine aspect of it. As essential to our healing and to our creative ardor as "the feminine face of God" is, we cannot restore our souls nor reclaim the taproot of our creativity until we have struggled with the feminine face of evil. After two years of sitting with and revising this book, I find myself feeling even more passionately about some of the ideas I have articulated here and perhaps less passionately about others. My feelings and perceptions regarding these issues continue to shift and change and are by no means etched in stone. I do not have the "final word" but only my piece of the truth.

My intention is not to shame or demean women. On the contrary, my hope is that the issues I have raised here will inspire and compel women to question some of the assumptions we have held sacrosanct for over thirty years without realizing how damaging they might be to ourselves, humanity and the ecosystems. Ultimately my vision for women in the modern world is that we become whole human beings who can experience the full spectrum of our extraordinary healing and creative power BECAUSE of examining our dark side, not in spite of it. In this book, I am challenging women to begin taking the next step in our transformation of consciousness, namely developing a relationship with the dark feminine aspects of the female psyche as well as the disowned masculine self within us so that while we are unilaterally honoring sacred womanspace and honing our quest for equality, we will join with evolving men in a bilateral struggle to heal many millennia of culturally-induced gender wounding.

I am also aware that the shadow side of feminism must be dialoged with, as any energy in the psyche or in the world must ultimately be dialoged with if we are to find a way to live with it. Whether the dialog takes place in the inner world with images of internal hags, witches and ogres or whether it happens in the external world in dialog with political feminism, there is always much more possibility and hope for relationship when dialog occurs than when it doesn't. And dialog surely must take place in both venues.

Nor do I wish to idealize the men's mythopoetic movement or imply that it has no dark side either. However, responsibility for examining the shadow of the men's movement, I believe, is best left up to men.

I do not apologize for the fierceness of my tone or the disturbing nature of my conclusions. These are disturbing, and in my opinion, life-threatening issues. If the two genders cannot live together in peace, how can we hold any hope for nations living in peace or human beings living in harmony with the ecosystems? The farsighted, visionary poet and author, D.H. Lawrence, expressed a similar urgency when he wrote:

The future of the world will not be determined between nations but rather in the relationships between men and women.

More recently feminist Naomi Wolf in *The Beauty Myth* suggests a stunning scenario of the transformation of relationships between women and men:

If women and men in great numbers were to form bonds that were equal, non-violent, and sexual, honoring the female principle no less or more than the male, the result would be more radical than the establishment's worst nightmares of homosexual "conversions." A mass heterosexual deviation into tenderness and mutual respect would mean real trouble for the status quo since heterosexuals are the most powerful sexual majority. The power structure would face a massive shift of allegiances: From each relationship might emerge a doubled commitment to transform society.[1]

Men and women need to leave the house of the dark mother but, at the same time, somewhere in that process, it becomes necessary to develop a conscious relationship with her. Such a relationship can heal and empower any woman or man who is willing to stay with and face her awesome, irrational, chaotic, frightening, potentially devouring presence.

The ancient Grimm's fairytale of Rapunzel is a saga of encounters with a grotesque, horrifying hag, and the tale is as relevant to our time as when it first appeared in the Middle Ages. To dismiss the story as "anti-woman," as some feminist writers have, is to oversimplify and thereby disregard potent pathways to healing and creativity so longed for by women and men in the modern world.

Let us now explore the story...

THE STORY OF RAPUNZEL[2]

A husband and wife who were childless found themselves desiring a child more than anything else in the world. The woman brooded continually, longing for a child and never ceased saying to herself, "I wish I had a child," even one day crying out, "I hope the gods will give me a child!" But still no child came. And it happened that the house the man and woman lived in had two levels, and at the back of the second level was a window. This window looked out over a

---

[1] Naomi Wolf, *The Beaty Myth: How Images of Beauty Are Used Against Women* (NY: William Morrow & Co., 1991), p.143
[2] A glossary of terms can be found at the end of the book.

garden that was surrounded by a wall. The woman sat at the window from morning until night gazing at the things of beauty growing in the garden. In the garden were luscious fruit trees in all the different seasons, and there were flowers coming up in different groups and colors all about the garden, and the thing was a delight to look upon. And as the woman sat looking at the garden, her eye fell upon some lettuce that was growing up out of the ground, showing itself in a fresh, green, vibrant color that only appears on plants that come out early in the spring.

And the woman gazed from morning until night upon that lettuce, that rampion, that green that is called rapunzel, until finally she began to desire some of that rampion to eat. And once the desire to eat had begun in her, it kept growing until soon enough she could think of nothing else at all except the beauty of that lettuce growing in the garden, beyond the wall, outside the window of the house she lived in with her husband. Soon enough she was wasting away because inside of herself she could find no appetite except for that very green thing growing in that garden, and she would eat nothing else. Finally, her husband said to her, "Why are you wasting away like this?" And the wife said, "It is the desire for the rampion, the rapunzel, in the garden beyond the wall there. I wish to have some, and if I had some of it, I would be quite satisfied."

Seeing the insatiable desire his wife had for the lettuce, and because he loved her so dearly, rather than see her waste away, the husband decided he would go into the garden and get some of the rampion.

So that night when the dusk was still in the air and the evening was neither light nor dark, he climbed over the high stone wall and dropped down into the garden on the other side. For some reason, it seemed darker on the other side of the wall. But he walked carefully over to where the rampion was growing, reached down and picked up a bunch, scurried back to the wall, and went over the wall right up to the top of the house to the second floor where his wife was sitting by the window. He gave the lettuce to her and she began to eat. When she was finished she said, "That rampion was inexplicably delicious. It is just what I wanted." No sooner had she said this than the desire to have more began to grow in her. Then she said, "There's only one more thing. If I don't have more of the rampion, I will surely waste away entirely." So the husband agreed that that evening he would go over the wall again.

When dusk came and brought grayness into the sky, the husband climbed the wall, dropped down into the garden and turned and was just about to go in the direction of the lettuce when he sensed somebody near him, and he turned around, and there standing before him was a woman — or so it seemed. This creature had the appearance of a hag, that is to say, a witch, that is to say that when the man looked at her, he was not sure what he was seeing. The hag's appearance was grotesque, for she had only one eye, and where the other eyeball should have been was an empty socket. Her matted hair was sticking out in all directions and the skin on her face looked more like the skin of a chicken than of a human being. Wiry black hairs stuck out of her nose, and a few jagged, broken teeth appeared to float in the seemingly endless cavern of her mouth. This witch-like creature was a terrifying sight to behold, and as the husband kept blinking his eyes in disbelief, a shrieking voice pierced the air with the words, "Why have you come into MY garden? Why have you taken from my garden things that do not belong to you at all?"

Shuddering and shivering the husband replied, "It was out of need that I came. I had to come. If my wife had not had this rampion, she would have wasted away and died. So would you please be merciful and spare my life?"

The old hag said, "Well, if that is how it is, that's fine. Take as much of the rampion as you like. Load your arms with it and take it to your wife. But there is just one condi-

tion. The condition is this: When your wife gives birth to the child she is certain to give birth to, that child is mine."

The husband replied, "If that is the condition, then I must agree." And he began to load his arms with the rampion, climbed over the wall, brought it to his wife who again was delighted to have it and who ate great quantities of it. Soon enough, she found herself carrying a child and soon enough, she gave birth to the child. When the child was born, it was obvious to both the husband and wife that the child should be called after the name of the lettuce, and so the girl child was named Rapunzel. And on the day that Rapunzel was born, the old hag arrived, picked up the baby in her ugly, bony hands, claimed her for her own and walked out of the house with the child.

The old hag took the newborn child, whose name was Rapunzel, to live in the forest with her; and the girl grew rapidly and straight and fine and graceful and beautiful. And when she had reached the age where the body of a girl gives way to the body of a woman, the hag took her deeper and deeper into the forest. And deep in the center of the forest was a tower, and the hag took her up into the tower and left her there. The tower had a window that looked out over the forest, but it had no door whatsoever. And the hag, when they had climbed into that tower said to Rapunzel, "This hair that has grown so finely from your head which is such a long and thick growth of hair that it reaches far, far behind you, I shall show you how to braid it, and after we have made the two braids from it, I shall show you how to throw it out of the window so that it can drop all the way to the ground. You will live here in this tower, and I shall come and visit you every day. When I come I shall call out your name, and only when you hear that name will you throw down your braids, and then I shall climb up the tower and visit you here in the tower and bring you the things that you need, for only I know what you need."

So the hair was braided, and every day the hag came to visit Rapunzel. She called up from the base of the tower, "Rapunzel, Rapunzel, let down your hair." When Rapunzel heard the call she went to the window and threw the braids out the window, and the hag grabbed the braids and climbed up the wall. The hag spent the better part of each day alone in the tower with Rapunzel. No one knows what they did together but, when the hag was not there, Rapunzel sat by the window and looked out over the forest.

As she looked out over the forest, she realized that she was looking upon many branches filled with singing birds. And so Rapunzel, sitting alone, began to sing along with the birds as if she were a bird herself.

And one day a prince, a young man whose father may have been a king, happened to be passing through the forest, looking up into the sky as he rode along. Suddenly, the sound of a beautiful voice fell upon his ear. The sound of the singing stopped his heart and captured his soul. The prince dismounted his horse and stood there among the trees listening to that lovely sound for a long time. Then he followed the sound and eventually saw the tower, but as he walked around the tower many times, he could find no door — no way to get to the top of the tower. When he went back to his home, he could not rid his heart from the feeling and sound of the beautiful voice. And he determined that the next day, he would go back to the tower and listen again to the voice.

And so the prince returned to the tower the next day, and it happened that on this day, he arrived at the same time as the old hag whom he saw before she saw him. And he hid in the bushes and watched as the hag called out, "Rapunzel, Rapunzel, let down your hair!" And the prince saw the braids come out of the tower and drop along the wall, and he saw the hag climb up the side of the tower and climb into the window of the tower. As he watched and waited, a plan occurred to him. He waited until he had seen the hag climb down the tower and go off into the forest. And now it was slightly dark as the sky was turning to the grey of evening. So the prince went to the base of the tower, and he called up, "Rapunzel, Rapunzel, let down your long, beautiful hair." And Rapunzel, thinking it was the hag because that was the only person she had ever seen, let her hair down. The prince grabbed the two long, thick braids and began climbing the wall. Somehow Rapunzel noticed that the tug on her hair was greater in this case, but still she waited. Then up through the window came the prince. Rapunzel was numb with astonishment. She was terrified because she had never seen a man before, and now one was standing there in front of her in the tower. She moved back quickly, her eyes wide with fright. But the prince said, "Do no fear me. I do not come to harm you. The look that I cast upon you has the hunger for beauty in it. I will not harm you. I was drawn here by your song."

Rapunzel felt a little more at ease now. As she looked upon the prince she saw that he was very handsome, and she began feeling feelings she had never felt before. And she found many ways to enjoy his company after her fear subsided.

Then the prince said, "I wish to come here each evening and be with you.

Rapunzel replied, "Please come."

So each evening, the prince came to her and called her, and Rapunzel dropped her beautiful braids from the tower, and each day, the hag came and called Rapunzel, and she dropped her braids and pulled the hag up. And in the daytime, she did those things in the tower that a young woman does with a hag, and at night, she did those things in the tower that a young woman does with a handsome man, and such were the days and nights of Rapunzel for a very long time.

In the evenings when the prince came to Rapunzel, he often spoke to her of his desire to take her away from the tower. He wanted her to come and live with him. Rapunzel replied, "I would love to go away with you, but you come up and down by way of my braids. I cannot climb down by way of my own hair." And once again, as the prince thought upon the matter, a plan occurred to him. The prince told Rapunzel that they could make something like the braids — ropes made of silken threads. So when the prince came to visit Rapunzel every night, he brought silken threads, and in the daytime when the hag was not there, Rapunzel wove her threads into ropes. And it happened that as the ropes of silk were becoming longer and the day was approaching when Rapunzel could leave the tower with the prince, she heard the voice of the hag from below crying out, "Rapunzel, Rapunzel, let down your hair!" Rapunzel let down her hair, and when the hag came through the window of the tower, Rapunzel blurted out, "You know, it's odd. You are much lighter than the prince. It is much easier to pull you up and doesn't hurt my head as much as when he climbs my braids."

The hag was horrified and flew into a rage. "So!" she shrieked, "You have been pulling other people up here, and a MAN of all things!! You think you can have anything you want in this world. You think your beauty is so great that nothing can harm you or take away the beauty you have. You think you are just like the birds in the trees outside the tower and you can sit up here and sing your whole life away. Well, I'll fix you once and for all!! Now you will go down from the tower, and you will go out into the desert, and you will learn the other side of living!" And the hag took the silken ropes which she discovered in the tower and cut them in pieces. Then she took a pair of scissors and with one scissor in each hand, she cut away the braids of Rapunzel's beautiful hair and tied the long braids onto the windowsill. Then the hag took Rapunzel out of the tower and out from the forest and into the desert where she was left all alone.

Back came the hag to the tower, and she lay in waiting for the prince. That evening, which was just like all the other evenings, the prince came to the tower and called out, "Rapunzel, Rapunzel, let down your beautiful hair." The braids came down, and when the prince came up over the windowsill, instead of a beautiful young woman, before him stood the same sight that Rapunzel's father had seen in the garden — the hideous, horrifying, treacherous hag.

Suddenly the hag screamed in rage, "So! You thought to play with the bird again, eh? Well, this time it's the cat you'll play with." And she began to scratch at the prince and claw his face and threaten to throw him out of the tower, shrieking the news that Rapunzel had been taken to the desert. The prince was so shocked and horrified that he jumped from the tower of his own accord and fell to the bottom where there were very sharp, vicious brambles. The brambles scratched his eyes so badly that he lost his vision, and when he pulled himself up off the ground, he could not see where he was going but began to wander about as if the whole world was night.

And it happened that the prince wandered about the forest blind for a number of years, in blackness and despair, unable to see the grayness of dusk or the red dawn of morning. He wandered alone until one day when he had lost all hope, he wandered into a desert place and coming out of the forest into the barren land, he began to hear a sweet song like that of a bird. He recognized the voice, the softness, the music, the sound, and he cried out, "Rapunzel, Rapunzel, is that you?" And Rapunzel saw him and picked up the child which she had given birth to in the desert, and she ran to the prince and showered him with kisses as they all wildly embraced. As Rapunzel wept uncontrollably, two of her tears fell upon the prince's eyes and restored his sight, and he took Rapunzel and their child away, back to his home where they all lived together.

Sweet Darkness

David Whyte

*When your eyes are tired
the world is tired also.*

*When your vision has gone
no part of the world can find you.
Time to go into the dark
where the night has eyes
to recognize its own.*

*There you can be sure
you are not beyond love.
The dark will be your womb
  tonight.
The night will give you a horizon
further than you can see.*

*You must learn one thing.
The world was made to be free in.*

*Give up all the other worlds
except the one to which you belong.*

*Sometimes it takes darkness and the sweet
confinement of your aloneness*

to learn

*anything or anyone
that does not bring you alive*

is too small for you.

CHAPTER 1
The Price of Desire

With every good there comes a corresponding evil, and with every evil, a corresponding good. Don't run too fast into one unless you are prepared to encounter the other. — Carl Jung

One of the first issues in making sense of the Rapunzel fairytale is the meaning of the name "Rapunzel" which is another name for the rampion after which she is named. The word *rampion* comes from the Latin root prefix *rap* which has the same root as the word *rape*. The word is also closely related to the word *rampant*. Rampion is a plant similar to dandelion that grows very close to the ground and also grows wildly and out of control. It invades or overruns its surroundings. The rampion symbolizes our life force energy, our vitality, our creativity, our thirst for living. It is the creative force of erotic love, sexuality, reproduction and desire of any kind.

Indigenous people know well that if life-force energy is not contained in some way, it can become an out-of-control, intrusive, destructive thing. Traditional cultures contain desire through ritual where desire is re-enacted and blessed. The tribe or clan gathers to celebrate all kinds of desires — the desire for a husband or a child or a successful hunt.

There is nothing wrong with desire. Without it, human beings could neither love nor create. The poet Kabir says that "if you make love with the divine now, in the next life you will have the face of satisfied desire." Desire has a spiritual, numinous quality. Yet it wakes up hags and villains in the psyche that insist on being dealt with.

The story begins with a childless marriage, the first clue that something is missing in the relationship. Inevitable in the development of any marriage, regardless of sexual orientation, is the desire for a child of some sort, be it literal or symbolic. Two people in any loving relationship desire to co-create something — another human being, a work of art, a joint-career, a beautiful home. The desire of Rapunzel's mother is insatiable, and without the rampion, she is convinced that she will die.

This fairytale echoes its origins in the Adam and Eve myth which Christianity has traditionally used to "prove" that Eve's desire was the reason for the fall of humankind from its favorable relationship with God. In mythology, desire is associated with the feminine principle, and desire, in any human being, can be a force of either the light or dark side of the feminine. In this story, the mother's desire set off a chain of events that sacrificed her child, handed that child over to a hag and confined her to isolation in a tower. However, the same chain of events, activated by the mother's desire, offered an opportunity for Rapunzel's transformation which might not have arisen otherwise.

In her two-leveled house, the mother wasn't longing for apples from a tree. She desired from up above, looking down. That which she desired was not in the ethereal, mental plane, but very close to the earth, and in order to fulfill the desire, it was necessary to go down. Of all the plants and trees and flowers the mother could have desired, she longed for the low-to-the ground, bitter-tasting rampion. Myths and fairytales are replete with themes of descent as a pre-requisite for renewal. From Inanna to Persephone to Jesus to Iron John, there is a need to descend into the territory of the underworld and encounter dark forces which terrorize and dismember, but also give birth to some new aspect of development.

Desire is a dangerous thing. That which Rapunzel's mother desires is in someone else's garden behind a wall. She has neither a garden nor a child. What is so very significant in this part of the story is the reality that all of the abundance, fertility, life force and vitality are on the other side of a wall in the domain of the negative feminine. When we choose to feel the fullness of our longing for anything or anyone, we are sure to wake up the hag! And here's the dilemma: If we don't desire, we waste away and die. If we do desire, we stir up the dark feminine and often end up paying for our longing with that which is dearest to us.

Some feminists criticize fairytales for being sexist, pointing out that they portray women as having insatiable desires that get everyone into trouble and that the Rapunzel story is just one more example of Christian misogyny's *femme fatale* perspective. To believe this is to miss the inner, symbolic meaning of the story. In the inner world to which the story speaks, no one is at fault, and everyone is at fault. The woman carries the desire, and the man chooses to satisfy it for her. Everyone has some responsibility for their suffering, and at the same time, suffering is an inescapable reality of the human condition.

For the feminine to access the fullness of the life force, it is necessary to do so through the masculine principle. It is a woman's animus who assists her in fulfilling her desires. The agreement between husband and wife in the story speaks to the union of the feminine and masculine principles within, specifically to a woman's inner "marriage" with her animus and a man's inner "marriage" with his anima. It takes both to create and make life happen. The feminine carries the desire, and the masculine goes forth to fulfill it.

In the outer world, women often carry the desire in a relationship, and men don't. Men in our culture are taught doing, not desiring. Thus they often ask their wives "What do you want?" yet remain unaware of what they want. Most men know well how to "go get things," but in the process, they often lose their desire. Rapunzel's father was quite capable of "bringing home the rampion," but the story does not tell us that he had any desire, nor taste for it himself. We are left to wonder what *he* desired, besides staying alive in the presence of the hag. When men are not connected with their inner feminine, desire dies or is never discovered, and it remains for the women in their lives to carry.

The story doesn't tell us if the man could have temporarily escaped the hag. Perhaps he could have bolted and quickly hopped back over the fence. Perhaps he could have said, "Gee, you know, I guess we really don't need the rampion after all. Sorry. It will never happen again." Maybe he could have sent someone else in his place who might have been a more clever negotiator. He could have even tried to "talk some sense" into his wife and get her to see that her belief that she would die if she didn't get the rampion was irrational. In any case, what is clear in this story and every other story where hags, witches or ogres appear, is that the hag keeps showing up. Either she is attended to, or she possesses the unconscious mind of the person or culture who tries to ignore her. In a culture where the dark side of desire is ignored, desire which always wakes up a hag or two, can wreak havoc in peoples' lives and in the ecosystems. The rape of the earth, and of our bodies, says Jungian analyst Marion Woodman, is a result of the unholy marriage of the patriarchal negative masculine with the dark feminine.

We might also ask how it was that the couple in the story had lived in their house all that time and weren't aware that the hag was nearby. No one spoke about who owned the garden, yet the man assumed that he needed to steal the rampion from it. Still another question: Why didn't the couple have their own garden? If the woman needed rampion, why didn't she grow her own? It is here that the story becomes as modern as it is ancient. The issue of denial did not originate at the end of the twentieth century. However, in our modern *technocorporarchy* (see glossary), we desire, lust, envy, achieve, produce, and profit endlessly without consciously dealing with the hag. Sooner or later, she must be dealt with. Buying up other gardens and installing sophisticated security systems does not keep the hag out. Even the hint of desire causes her to stir. She can smell it in the air, and then she's wide awake, ready to devour and make offers that we dare not refuse.

When a man falls in love with a woman, the hag shows up sooner or later and in some fashion, threatens to destroy him. When a woman is swept away by a man, the hag is waiting in the wings to imprison her and injure the vision of her beloved. When a couple (of any gender or sexual orientation) desire a child, the hag is lurking in the shadows ready to take the child and make it her own. That means that the "child," of a relationship, whether literal or symbolic — whether it is an embodied child or some other creation of the couple, is also desired by the hag. Eventually the hag will show up and demand the "child." When any of us accesses our deepest dreams, hopes or aspirations, the hag is there, exacting a price and mercilessly insisting that something has to be exchanged for whatever portion of our life force we desire this time.

When human beings do not face the hag, they act her out and do her treacherous work for her. The hag can always be counted on to try to steal that which is dearest to us. When a culture ignores the hag, children suffer. In fact, we now live in a whole culture of missing children.

On the night of October 1, 1993, a sociopathic man walked into a house in Petaluma, California and stole twelve year-old Polly Hannah Klaas. A few months later, her body was found, and the nation, at least for a while, became outraged at the statistics regarding the violation of its children. For a few days, the culture came close to asking itself why this is happening. The conclusion: We need more prisons. "Three strikes and you're out." Once again, the hag isn't being dealt with, and the wrong questions lead to ever more hag-driven ways not to address the real issues.

Who would not wish to steal rather than encounter the hag? What person in our culture has NOT stolen something in their lifetime? Stealing in the Rapunzel story is not about morality but about life and death. A woman is going to die if she doesn't have a child, and a man is going to die if he doesn't promise that child to the hag. No one in this story, or any other human being, can escape encountering the hag.

The story begins with an impossible choice: Stop desiring, and you die; follow your desires, and you wake up the hag which is also sure to bring about some kind of death. Rapunzel's parents must have died a thousand deaths when they lost their child. Did they have the courage to begin desiring again, or was the longing for a child killed forever? Rapunzel's natural childhood was destroyed by being locked up in the tower until she was a young maiden. The prince was almost killed by the hag, and the story doesn't reveal the extent to which he was able to regain his vision. Surely, it would be naive to believe that even though the prince and Rapunzel's love for each other was not destroyed and they were reunited, the hag did not show up again as they rekindled their love and raised their children, requiring some price that precluded living "happily ever after."

The hag is always undesirable to look upon, but so are the aspects of ourselves and our relationships that we disown. The hag demands that we look at her, the eternal dark feminine archetype. This is no small task. To view her opens one up to the devouring, dismembering Old Woman Nature depicted in the following poem by Gary Snyder:

OLD WOMAN NATURE

Old Woman Nature
naturally has a bag of bones
tucked away somewhere.
a whole room full of bones!

A scattering of hair and cartilage
bits in the woods.
A fox scat with hair and a tooth in it.
a shellmound a bone flake in a streambank.

A purring cat, crunching
the mouse head first,
eating on down toward the tail —

The sweet old woman
calmly gathering firewood in the moon...

Don't be shocked,
She's heating you some soup.

CHAPTER 2

Feeding the Hag

...the hag is bitter and brooding; she is easily insulted, never forgets, and demands an offering, a sacrifice to set things straight.
— Kat Duff, *The Alchemy Of Illness*

Rapunzel's mother and the hag represent two similar but very different aspects of the feminine. Rapunzel's mother holds the desire for a child and then for the rampion. The hag is a devourer. Desire, as we see in the story, can be satisfied whereas the energy of devouring is insatiable. Desire says, "If I don't have this, I will die." The devourer says, "If I don't have this *you* will die!"

Whenever desire is present, there is always the potential for its shadow, devouring, to occur. When the dark feminine energy of devouring is present, it is almost always connected with the belief that there isn't enough. Author and storyteller, Angeles Arrien says that, when people become devouring, it's really out of fear of not *being* enough.

Like many behaviors in Western culture, devouring is an inevitable consequence of disowning the feminine principle. Where the feminine principle is not honored, women fall under the spell of the hag's insatiable appetites, and men who have no relationship with their inner feminine become voraciously greedy and predatory. Hindu mythology reveres the goddess, Kali, who symbolizes both desire and devouring — the Great Mother and the hag. Cultures that honor a dark goddess know that if all aspects of the feminine are not valued, the aspects that are disowned cast their spells and take charge of peoples' lives. In our culture women aspire only to be "good mothers" and, when they do not live up to their own — or someone else's — concept of the good mother, they feel shame and usually try even harder. Yet in many cultures, images and deities of imperfect mothers are deemed as necessary in the larger scheme of human experience as the nurturing, unconditionally loving mother. An eighth-century Hindu drama sings praises to Shiva in his eternal dance with Kali:

> *Crazy is my Father, crazy my Mother,*
> *And I, their son, am crazy too!*
> *Shyama (the dark one) is my Mother's name.*
> *My Father strikes his cheeks and makes a hollow*
>   *sound:*
> *Ba-ba-boom! Ba-ba-boom!*
> *And my Mother, drunk and reeling,*
> *Falls across my Father's body!*
> *Shyama's streaming tresses hang in vast disorder;*
> *Bees are swarming numberless*
> *About her crimson Lotus Feet.*
> *Listen, as She dances, how Her anklets ring!"*

In many fairytales, a husband or father "hands over" a young maiden or daughter to an ominous creature. Men make bargains with hags and demons that affect females for the rest of their lives. While there is something deeply disturbing about the willingness of Rapunzel's father to bargain with the hag, the bargain is much more complex than the simplistic, feminist criticism that the father is promising the hag his future child because he considers the child his property to do with as he wishes. We must not lose sight of the fact that his life is on the line as well.

Men are often blamed for starting wars. While they are the ones who initiate and carry out warfare, it is inaccurate to conclude that warfare is inherently part of the masculine psyche, as some feminists do. As in the Rapunzel story, men often do their "dirty deed" at the behest of the collective or another individual. In a culture in which women participate as feverishly as men in "consumerism," it is crucial that we distinguish patriarchy from masculinity. As Marion Woodman writes, "Women can be worse patriarchs than men."

Men are frequently "demonized" by feminists as the originators of power and control. Throughout time, however, the hag or some other symbol of the dark feminine has appeared in a variety of forms in art, music, literature, drama and ritual. Almost every culture on earth has a dark feminine figure in its mythology, except for America. We have "Miss Liberty" who "stands beside the golden door," but where is the hag, the crone, the witch, the devouring feminine?

At the beginning of the Gulf War, Saddam Hussein referred to the war as "The Mother Of All Battles." Thomas Moore notes in *The Care Of The Soul* that the word gun was derived from a Scandinavian woman, Gunnhilda, whose name means "war."[3] Curiously, whenever predominantly male soldiers march into harm's way, Kali and her companion, Durga, goddess of war, are chuckling wildly over humankind's denial of the dark feminine.

Marion Woodman has been criticized as anti-woman because of her insistence that the feminine shadow be owned. Yet she continues to courageously assert that, "The old petrifying mother is like a great lizard lounging in the depths of the unconscious. She wants nothing to change. If the feisty ego attempts to accomplish anything, one flash of her tongue disposes of the childish rebel. Her consort, the rigid authoritarian father, passes the laws that maintain her

---

[3] Thomas Moore, *The Care of the Soul: A Guide for Cultivating Depth and Sacredness in Everyday Life* (NY: Harper Collins, 1992), p.134.

inertia. Together they rule with an iron fist in a velvet glove. Mother becomes Mother Church, Mother Welfare State, Mother University, the beloved Alma Mater, defended by Father who becomes Father Hierarchy, Father Law, Father Status Quo."[4]

European invasion of North America and its inevitable legacy, Manifest Destiny, possibly the most glaring example of uncontrolled desire in modern history, planted American culture firmly in the garden of the hag. Beneath the "lamp beside the golden door" that welcomes the world's tired and poor, is a dark red ocean containing the blood of native peoples, animals and ecosystems decimated so that desire might be fulfilled. Yet America has never confronted its own feminine shadow — Big Bertha, Enola Gay and Memphis Belle. Military planes, tanks and aircraft carriers are invariably referred to as "she" or "her." During World War Two, thousands of women, including my own mother, worked in munitions factories as the newly-formed Women's Army Corps boasted its slogan: "The woman behind the man behind the gun."

So back in the garden of the hag in our story is a very frightened man who has surreptitiously dropped down over the wall to fulfill his wife's desire and prevent her from dying. Should he have confronted the hag and risked being killed, leaving his wife a widow and his child fatherless? Should he have refused to promise the hag that she could have the child she demanded?

Myths and fairytales arise from, and evoke, the unconscious. They are not products of the logical, rational, conscious mind. Thus, to judge what people "should" or "should not" do in a fairytale is to project ego onto soul. In the domain of soul, people do what they do, and the consequences are usually mixed. In this fairytale, a child is con-

---

[4] Marion Woodman, *The Ravaged Bridegroom: Masculinity in Women* (Toronto: Inner City Books, 1990), pp.17-18.

ceived, but she spends her childhood imprisoned in a tower. Eventually she wins her freedom, but at a terrible price. In the realm of the hag, there is no Plan A or Plan B. "Order" and "chaos" become equally meaningless terms. It is easy to evaluate what Rapunzel's parents, the prince and Rapunzel herself might have done differently. It is a much more difficult task to allow each character in the story, especially the hag, to speak to our own personal wounding and the human condition itself.

This is a story about desire. Had the father not secured the rampion, a child would not have been conceived. Rapunzel IS the parents' desire come to life and then lost because the desire to preserve one's own life is usually greater than the desire to hold on to another life.

But what about the hag's desire? Why does she want an infant which she will eventually imprison in a tower and come to visit every day?

What is it about the innocent, young feminine that the hag wishes to capture and hold?

Many of us have grown up in families in which a devouring mother blatantly or subtly held us captive. The feminist perspective of such scenarios is that women become devouring mothers because they are oppressed on many levels. While this is certainly true, the situation involves many more complex dynamics than women's oppression.

At this point I feel it necessary to relate a personal experience. When I was six years old, my parents separated for a time, partly because they weren't getting along and partly because I was very ill, and it became necessary for my mother to take me to another climate in order to improve my health. One day at school we were told that we would be seeing a movie about Rapunzel. I was completely mesmerized by the movie and asked to see it again. After I saw the movie, I could think of nothing but Rapunzel. I had dreams about Rapunzel and became thoroughly obsessed with the fairytale.

As an adult, when I became fascinated with archetypal psychology, I quickly understood why I was so captivated by the story of Rapunzel. Rapunzel's story was my own. As an only child in the household of an emotionally absent father, I was psychically imprisoned by a violent and emotionally troubled mother. In many ways I lived in a tower and was prevented from relating to virtually everyone except my mother. The effects of my relationship with my mother had profoundly damaging and devastating consequences in my adult life.

After devoting many years and enormous resources to working through the relationship with my mother, it is becoming increasingly possible to empathize with my mother in terms of why she felt it necessary to capture and hold me. I now understand that my mother, like many individuals both female and male throughout time, was under the spell of the dark feminine archetype.

The dark feminine, in both women and men, desires to capture, possess, confine, devour and feed off anything vital, alive, luscious and innocent — qualities so unlike itself. I have worked with many women over the years who felt devoured by their fathers — men under the spell of the negative anima who emotionally, sexually and spiritually consume their young.

The hag in our story may be a teacher of lessons, but she is nevertheless a horrifying force. Like the hag, my mother had the capacity for growing fecund gardens, yet she rarely experienced her aliveness without consuming the vitality of the vulnerable around her. Hags in the psyche are inherently lonely, depleted, bitter and vindictive. Like the dark masculine energies with which they are so closely connected, they present a terrifying exterior, but are in fact deeply empty and alone.

In a television interview with Jeffrey Dahmer before his death, he clearly explained that his obsession with killing, mutilating and cannibalizing other human beings was an attempt to keep them close to him and make sure they would never leave.

Whenever desire is fulfilled and something new is born, we can count on the hag showing up on that very day, walking into our house, claiming the new energy for herself and walking away with it — or at least trying to. As in the Inuit story of "Skeleton Woman," so brilliantly told and interpreted by Clarissa Pinkola Estés, the dark feminine pursues relentlessly and will not be assuaged until we become willing to give her a warm fire, reach out and touch her dried, tangled bones and lovingly put them back in place.

In the Hopi Indian culture of Northern Arizona, a purification ceremony — called Powamu, or the Bean Dance — takes place throughout the month of February. The purification rites of this ceremony are intended to cleanse the hearts of the people and prepare them and the earth for planting corn in the spring. Most of the activities of Bean Dance occur during a particular weekend, but one aspect of the ceremony transpires over the course of the month. A female ogre, named Soyoko, visits each home in the village to demand accountability from every man, woman and child for their shortcomings or wrongdoing over the past year. In more recent times, Soyoko's ominous visits have been more focused on the misdeeds of children than adults.

Soyoko is an awesomely ugly hag, dressed in black, who carries a staff in one hand and a knife or saw in the other. She is surrounded by an entourage of male ogres who are called mudheads because of the masks that cover their heads and cause their heads to look like brown balls of mud. Soyoko wears a basket on her back. The basket is for carrying naughty children to the enormous fire that she and the other ogres build very early on the morning of her last visit to each home in the village. A typical last visit from Soyoko may go something like this:

Soyoko and the other ogres walk from the fire they have built on the edge of the mesa to one of the houses. As they walk, they exude hideous growls and moans. One can almost hear torment and death in their ghastly sounds. Soyoko knocks on the door. An adult member of the household, usually the father, sprinkles the threshold with cornmeal and asks Soyoko "To what do we owe the honor of your visit?"

Soyoko then reminds the family that she had visited them once or twice before, and that when she did so, she asked that the male members of the household go hunting and bring her a rabbit or several field mice on a stick. She has also asked that the female members of the house grind a certain amount of roasted sweet corn called *totse*. During this last visit, she may confront any family member, but especially the children about their bad behavior and threaten to put them in her basket and take them to the fire if they don't shape up. Often the threats become aggressive to the point where some of the ogres may grab a child and threaten to take him or her away. The parents are prepared, however, having secured an enormous amount of food, the only thing that ever satisfies Soyoko. They offer corn, slabs of ribs, vegetables, loaves of bread and other pastries and beg that Soyoko be appeased and not eat their children.

As each item of food is offered, some of the ogres take it to the *kiva* (an underground ceremonial chamber where all ritual begins and ends), and by the end of the day, a huge cache of food accumulates. After enough food has been offered to satisfy Soyoko, she departs, but often not until all the male children in the household have been doused with a bucket of water and stern warnings have been given about the consequences of continued misbehavior. As Soyoko leaves, the family breathes a collective sigh of relief that the ogres have come and gone until next year.

The culmination of the Soyoko ritual takes place in the late afternoon as residents of the village and some tourists gather in the plaza near the kiva to which Soyoko has retreated. Soyoko and the mudheads emerge from the kiva and come down into the plaza. Also emerging from the kiva are ceremonial dancers, perhaps twenty in number, who form two parallel lines. Every other dancer is dressed as a woman, and the other dancers are dressed as men, but all dancers are in fact, male. The mudheads line up between the dancers and the kiva.

For about ten minutes, the dancers sing and dance while Soyoko and the ogres witness them. Then gradually, one mudhead or two begins moving away from their line and making sexual advances toward the "female" dancers. Each time they do so, Soyoko, hits them over the head with her staff and sends them back to their place in line. The obscenities exacerbate. More and more mudheads break away and begin lying on their backs looking up the dresses of the female dancers, then fondling, groping and simulating copulation with them. Eventually, the ogres become out of control, and Soyoko is overwhelmed with their incorrigibility. Gradually, Soyoko herself is seduced into the debacle and begins dancing as sensually and erotically as the mudheads. It is as if Soyoko is discovering her body and her sensuality for the first time. Ultimately, the mudheads overpower Soyoko, tear off a top layer of her clothing, and Soyoko runs out of the plaza, and the ceremony ends. Then at the end of the day, all the food collected and stored in the kiva is redistributed throughout the village.

Witnessing the Soyoko ceremony was a powerful experience for me. I was keenly aware that the entire village had spent the day in fear of her. I had felt the fear as I walked through the village trying to avoid her entourage, occasionally being spotted and growled at by ogres, all the while my Hopi friends warning me, "Be careful that Soyoko doesn't get you. Sometimes the ogres hold outsiders hostage in the kiva until their friends bring enough food to get them released, and we just gave all our food to Soyoko!" As I watched the antics of Soyoko and the mudheads in the plaza, I witnessed an example of the transformation of the hag. By feeding Soyoko and giving her the attention she demanded, her vulnerability was revealed, and she became as human as the people she had threatened all day in the village. Soyoko succumbed to her own imperfection. She was transformed into a sensuous, carnal, human female. Soyoko would come back again the following February and terrify the village once more with her ominous, devouring darkness, but on the other side of that darkness, what we might call her "bright" shadow, is a softer vulnerability.

 I stood dumfounded as Soyoko, the dancers and the residents of the village emptied the plaza. "Is this all there is to it?" I muttered to one of my Hopi friends.

 "Yes," she said, "Now come on up to the house and eat with us!"

CHAPTER 3

Under the Spell of the Hag

For until the demonic powers of the dark goddess are claimed, there is no strength in the woman to grow from daughter to an adult who can stand against the patriarchy in its inhuman form.
  — Sylvia Brinton Perera, *Descent To The Goddess*

Why did the hag take Rapunzel to live with her in the forest? Why did the hag live in the forest part of the time and in the garden behind the house of Rapunzel's parents the rest of the time?

The forest has historically been a symbol of the domain of the Great Mother. In the forest, vegetative life thrives and grows wildly — free of any cultivation or control. In the domain of the archetypal feminine, there is abundance and vitality, as was evident in the hag's garden. A forest is one of the easiest places to survive and thrive, in contrast to deserts, oceans or mountain tops. In the forest there are all manner of resources for staying alive — green plants, berries, bark from trees which can be made into soap and healing salves. However, the forest can be very dark because the sun's light is obscured. In the territory of the hag, the sunlight of the positive masculine is virtually nonexistent, obscured by an imbalance of the feminine. In the dark forest which so frequently occurs in fairytales and usually symbolizes the unconscious — demons, monsters and witches dwell.

Nevertheless, residing in the dark forest with the hag, Rapunzel grows. This is significant because the territory of the dark feminine does not necessarily inhibit development, but the development is offset by the absence of a positive masculine presence. As a result of the absence of a positive masculine presence, Rapunzel becomes a passive participant in her own entrapment.

One of the most haunting questions in this story is: How did Rapunzel and the witch get up into the tower in the first place? The tower had no door. The story is very clear that Rapunzel was taken there at the time of puberty or early adolescence. How is it that she consented to go up into the tower with the witch? If she got up by herself, couldn't she have come down by herself? What power did the hag have over her to make her resign herself to imprisonment?

If young women are not adequately fathered, they succumb to all manners of imprisonment. The men's mythopoetic movement has raised the consciousness of many men to the consequences of inadequate fathering. In a world where mothers have carried most of the blame for inept parenting, the men's movement has finally brought the responsibility of the father into higher focus than ever before in Western culture. However, women are equally wounded, in my opinion, by the lack of positive fathering.

The young feminine in the presence of the mother complex or negative mother archetype colludes in its confinement. It is content to stay removed from the ground, incarcerated in towers of lofty ideals or high-minded spiritual principles that have nothing to do with the real world. In the tower, the young feminine remains out of the body, imprisoned, untried, imagining itself to be one of the birds in the trees and unable to recognize or appreciate the positive masculine when it finally manifests.

When the body of the girl gives way to the body of a woman, the dark feminine is sure to take a young lady deeper into the forest. The unconscious holds much suffering for the young feminine possessed by the hag. For young females in this culture, the deeper parts of the forest may lead to levels of denial and dissociation from the body that result in unwanted pregnancies, multiple abortions and babies having babies. It may mean imprisonment in the towers of addiction, prostitution, or gangs — or more "acceptable" prisons such as anorexia or bulimia, marriages, children and careers that a young woman really wouldn't choose to have if she weren't under the spell of the hag.

The young feminine is an aspect of the psyche present in all human beings — males as well as females. However, it is virtually impossible for boys in our culture to be perceived as men unless they disown and despise the feminine — in themselves and in the world. Being called a wimp is a fate worse than death, and sanctioning or participating in violence against women is not only accepted but expected. As young males form "Spur Posses" and routinely address females as "bitches," they not only deteriorate into rapists and tyrants, but disavow their own emotional life and any connection with soul.

In indigenous cultures, males cannot be initiated into manhood without encountering the hag directly through transformative ritual. While it is true that indigenous initiation rituals for young males are conducted primarily by older men, it is also true that such rituals involve confrontations with hags, witches, ogres or dark feminine forces. Initiation for tribal males is a process of being taken into the underworld in some way by male elders, but it also includes the paradoxical experience of encountering the feminine in a way that facilitates a young male's separation from his mother and insures full entry into manhood. In indigenous cultures this does not mean disavowing either one's mother or the feminine. Curiously, dangerous ritual encounters by the initiate with the feminine, reinforce rather than negate the value of the feminine principle. One of the many hopeful aspects of the men's movement, I believe, is the emphasis placed by Robert Bly, Michael Meade and others on men coming to know and struggle with their inner feminine.

Feminist critics of the men's movement often characterize its emphasis on initiation and separation from the mother as misogynist. They argue that women are socialized to form relationships while men are socialized not to be in relationship, therefore, men do not need to learn more about separating, especially from women. Such a grave misperception of initiation does not grasp its archetypal significance and only literalizes it. It also assumes that female values such as connection, relatedness and commitment are superior to male values like separateness, competition and freedom.

For several millennia, myths and fairystories have been showing us that separation from both parents, regardless of our gender, is deeply embedded in the human psyche. But Rapunzel cannot separate from the hag. There is no strong, nurturing male presence to provide a dynamic alternative to the suffocating tyranny of the devouring feminine, and under the spell of the hag, it is not possible to come down from the tower Rapunzel probably consented to climb and enter. When the prince finally comes and wants to take her away, she welcomes the prospect but sabotages her freedom by disclosing her relationship with him to the hag.

What is the spell Rapunzel is under? In this story, the hag symbolizes both the archetypal dark feminine, as well as the mother complex. Robert Johnson, speaking of the positive archetypal feminine says that it "is the bounty of nature, which gives us our life and all that we need for that life and which is anyone's legacy by the fact of being alive." Conversely, the negative feminine is stingy, withholding and conditional. The mother complex, a synergy of the mother archetype and one's personal, human mother, is usually a toxic force in the psyche. Whether an individual is female or male, and whether one has experienced separation from one's personal mother or not, the mother complex is a force that must be reckoned with, if one is to become a whole person.

When Rapunzel has come of age, the hag "lays down the law" instructing Rapunzel how it will be from now on. "This hair that has grown so finely from your head which is such a long and thick growth of hair that it reaches far, far behind you, I shall show you how to braid it, and after we have made the two braids from it, I shall show you how to throw it out the window so that it can drop all the way to the ground. You will live here in this tower, and I shall come and visit you every day. When I come I shall call out your name, and only when you hear that name will you throw down your braids, and then I shall climb up the tower and visit you here in the tower and bring you the things you need, for only I know what you need."

In many myths and in most indigenous cultures, hair symbolizes instinctual life force energy. Hair suggests not only life force but a particular kind of life force that is connected with an individual's primal, animal, wild, instinctual nature. The key element of the instincts is freedom. Instinct does not like to be fettered or impeded, yet this is exactly what happens to Rapunzel. Her life force is not only taken captive by the hag, but in a very rigid, stultifying manner.

In this interaction between Rapunzel and the hag, there is a glimmer of intimacy with which most individuals struggling with a negative mother complex can identify. Abuse is often accompanied by genuine human affection between the abuser and the abused. I have yet to meet any child of toxic parenting who experienced their relationship with the parent as unequivocally negative. The hag compliments Rapunzel on her beautiful hair, but while the beauty does not go unrecognized, the beauty is totally in service of the hag and her needs. What is more, the hag teaches Rapunzel how to submit her life force, her beauty and her feminine power to the hag. "After *we* have made the two braids...," the hag says, emphasizing that Rapunzel is being forced to collude in meeting the hag's needs.

The recovery movement over the last decade has poignantly informed us of the devastating consequences of abusive parenting, underscoring the fact that toxic parenting always involves some aspect of collusion between parent and child. The word *collusion* means "the sharing of an illusion." Both parent and child "share" the illusion that healthy parenting is taking place and that the abusive acts are, in fact, the way that parents are "supposed" to treat their children.

In physical and sexual abuse, a child's body is literally invaded and captured by an adult for the gratification of the adult's needs. In more subtle forms of toxic parenting, an adult "climbs up and down" the life force energy of a child at the behest of the adult. As I have worked with individuals over the years, I have heard infinite horror stories of physical and sexual assault on children, and in some cases, the literal status of a child's hair has become part of the abuse. In some abusive families, cutting the hair is a threat to a parent who interprets the action as an affront or personal attack on the parent or the family system. In other families, not keeping the hair short is unacceptable.

One of the most shattering scenes for me in the movie, *Mommy Dearest* was the point at which the inebriated, hysterical Joan Crawford took large scissors and began hacking off the hair of her daughter, Christina. I believe that one reason I was so captivated by the Rapunzel story at the age of six had to do with my own mother's insistence that I keep my hair short so that it would not be "messy." Only after I left home did I feel the freedom to wear my hair as long as I wanted. Perhaps this is why I have no words to explain the anguish I have felt in hearing stories about white settlers invading Native American tribes and cutting off their long hair in the Europeans' pathetic attempts to "civilize" the natives.

The mother complex develops out of unspoken, unconscious "deals" made between a mother and child, and the result in the internal world of the grown child is that she/he is still in the tower of the mother, existing energetically under spells cast decades ago. Similarly, a man's anima or inner feminine can cast a spell on his children for life, creating uncanny emotional incarceration. The braids are woven, the life force energy is twisted and intertwined by the fingers of the dark feminine. Unless they are made conscious, complexes come and go as they wish, casting more spells and endlessly exploiting the young feminine, in a woman or in a man. They call us out by name and usurp our instinctual energy in order to gain access to our innocence and vulnerability.

In a culture where children are stolen, battered and abused on every level imaginable — by members of both genders — the story of Rapunzel brings up a particularly distressing issue for anyone engaged in honest exploration of the feminine shadow: the abuse of children by female perpetrators. Elizabeth Herron and Aaron Kipnis in *Gender War, Gender Peace: The Quest For Love And Justice Between Women And Men,* note that, according to the 1992 *Statistical Abstracts of the United States,* women are the primary batterers of children and that case studies indicate that women commit about one third of the sexual abuse of boys and a significant number of girls.[5] Energetically, when a child is kidnapped, battered, molested or neglected, the feminine shadow is at work. The nurturing feminine protects, cherishes and nourishes; the negative feminine devours. A chilling poem about a battering mother, written

---

[5] *Statistical Abstract of the United States: The National Data Book* (1992), 112th edition, U.S. Department of Commerce, Bureau of the Census, SA, p.83.

by a twenty-four year-old Native American woman offers a glimpse of the devouring feminine in action:

NOT A MOTHER'S LOVE

Your terror was your insanity
Your love was false, but you
thought it was pure.
False love, sick lies, numerous manipulations,
Unwarranted abuse.
The beatings...only because
you had to vent your anger...
toward yourself, your life,
your own personal torture.
Why?
Why hate so much? Why punish,
why hurt, why abuse?
You can't say...
But the insanity speaks for you...
Only through you.
Your torment,
Your pain.
What grief, what sorrow,
Your ruined life.
You can't love. You can't understand,
Or even comprehend.
You only know pain, misery, despair
and hatred.
You blame to stay alive, you hate to
fuel the blame. And in the end...hurt all.
Wise up!!
This is not a mother's love.

— Wende Williams

The Rapunzel fairytale challenges the feminist notion that it is primarily masculine energy which perpetrates violence and assault in the world. I believe that one reason many feminists label certain myths and fairytales misogynist is that they deny, or do not grasp, the symbolic significance of them. The Rapunzel story is replete with symbols of the feminine shadow and the mother complex. It is the story of an older female victimizing a younger female. This fairytale, as well as feminine images from a variety of cultures, such as Snapping Vagina in Navaho mythology, Medusa of ancient Greece, Ereshkigal of the Sumerian Inanna myth, the Germanic Goddess, Hel and, of course, Kali, offer profound and palpable nuances of the feminine shadow.

Carl Jung noted that at least eighty percent of the human shadow is pure gold. In the shadow — the parts of self that we disown, dwells a treasure trove of healing and creative energy. If we view each aspect of the Rapunzel story as an element of the psyche, we notice that the story ends with a reunion of the feminine and masculine principles that had been previously estranged. Each character's interactions with the hag suggest what does and does not work in relating to the feminine shadow. A young woman whose name essentially means desire experiences the fulfillment of her desire and enters maturity as a result of her lifelong intimate relationship with the dark feminine. A young man who can only see the innocent young feminine is tricked and blinded by the dark feminine, forced to wander in search of his lost love and eventually reunited with her. In the aftermath of being tormented by the hag, he forgot about being a prince and followed only the desire of his heart: to hear again the sweet sound of Rapunzel's voice. *Without encountering the hag, the feminine and masculine principles cannot be integrated.*

When women can struggle to develop a relationship with their feminine shadow, they are invariably empowered. When men dare to explore the negative and positive aspects of the anima, the courage to be vulnerable evolves, along with intention to protect and serve the vulnerability of all beings. Northern California author and soul-centered psychotherapist, Francis Weller, emphasizes that the darkness wants us to ask it what it wants from us. If we can actively, consciously engage with the darkness, we are transformed from victims into vital, autonomous human beings.

When human beings disown the feminine shadow, they inevitably project it onto others. Thus, the man in denial of his inner hag accuses the women in his life of never being satisfied and always wanting more. Similarly, the woman who disowns her feminine shadow often finds herself in the role of what Elizabeth Herron describes as the Princess/Victim. Like the enabler in relation to the alcoholic, the Princess/Victim waits for all those "nasty, brutal, patriarchal, inherently inferior" men to change so that she can finally experience gender equity and live in a just world. The Princess/Victim, though she may deny it, feels helpless and waits for males, whom she experiences as victimizers, to either leave the planet or somehow be shamed into transformation.

Curiously, the hag, who obviously despises men and maleness, is as treacherous and vicious as any man could be. In fact, *a femininity that disowns men and maleness cannot help but resemble the very aspects of maleness that it so passionately abhors.* My own experience with women who hold contempt for men is that in some aspect of their lives, they are extraordinarily patriarchal.

Failure to make a distinction between actual males and a patriarchal system invites projection of one's feminine shadow onto masculinity as the enemy. Indigenous traditions honor the paradoxes of humanity and divinity, understanding that deities and spirit forces, as well as people, hold aspects of both darkness and light. European-American culture dichotomizes good and evil, which encourages a tendency to identify one gender as "good" and the other as "evil." Identifying the danger in this tendency, Elizabeth Herron notes that: "The degree to which any group denies its own shadow is inevitably equal to the need it has to project the blame for all its sorrows onto others. If we fail to attend to our shadow, we breed denial about our own capacity for abuse. Denial about the potential for abuse of power is dangerous to any group."[6]

To cope with the uncanny isolation of being imprisoned in a tower with no access to anyone but the hag, Rapunzel looks out over the forest and sees the birds in the branches of trees. She begins singing with them as if she is one of them. The birds are her only companions during countless hours spent alone in the tower. One can feel not only the dissociation and delusion Rapunzel is experiencing, but a seduction into a disembodied spirit world against which she has virtually no defense. Birds in fairytales are frequently symbolic of spiritualization. Jung associated them with supernatural aid and flights of fancy.

Rapunzel's emotional escape into the trees brings to our attention the crucial difference between spirit and soul. Soul is much more connected with the feminine principle than spirit. Soul lives in the earth, in the moist, wet and dark places, whereas spirit lives in the trees and the sky and is more associated with the masculine principle. Indigenous traditions integrate spirit and soul, unlike modern cultures which have not only separated soul and spirit, but have clearly disowned soul in favor of "rising to the top."

Francis Weller speaks of the Heroic Fantasy of our culture in which everything and everyone is supposed to ascend, transcend, and get to the top, as soon as possible. The Heroic Fantasy values perfectionism, dissociation from the body, power, control and the intellect. Soulful states of messiness, connection with the body, vulnerability and loss of control attended by deep feelings that cannot be quanti-

---

[6] Aaron Kipnis & Elizabeth Herron, *Gender War, Gender Peace: The Quest for Love and Justice Between Women and Men* (NY: William Morrow, 1994), p.151.

fied or analyzed are all anathema to the Heroic Fantasy — a fantasy which *is* the quintessence of techno-corporarchy.

The dark feminine and the dark masculine are almost always joined in dubious partnership, not only in the inner world but in the external world as well. Rapunzel is imprisoned by the hag and in the process is forced to split off into the archetypal male world of disembodied spirit. When the dark feminine takes action, it almost always functions in a masculine mode or in collusion with it, to destroy an individual's connection with soul which contains aspects of both the positive masculine principle and the positive feminine principle. In the psyche, the mother complex usually operates in collusion with the animus of the personal mother which a woman has internalized. Thus Rapunzel has been captured not only by the dark feminine, but by the negative masculine as well. The undeveloped, naive Rapunzel, mesmerized by the masculine world of spirit, is not totally disconnected from soul, however. She is able to sing — perhaps her only connection with soul — and thereby bring to herself what she needed, the prince.

Until very recently the women's movement has been resistant to, or possibly incapable of, perceiving the ways in which it has subtly incorporated the negative masculine principle from which it has fought to extricate itself. In more recent years, the women's movement has entered a phase which author Peg Jordan describes as "feminism's third wave," also referred to as the women's spirituality movement. Deeply embedded within feminine spirituality is a dynamic connection to the earth and the body. It includes what is sometimes called "eco-feminism" and archetypal images of the Goddess. Of this third wave of feminism, Jordan notes in her 1992 article in *Magical Blend Magazine:*

> *As it enters its next phase of maturity, the women's movement is no longer an isolated we-versus-them mindset of victimhood and blame. Like its counter-*

part, the men's mythopoetic movement, this latest chapter of feminism insists on a deeper introspection, a diligent soul-searching aspect. It requires that a woman disentangle from the battle, stop waging war, and tell the truth about her own internalized patriarch, the very entity that she swore was outside herself and swore to eradicate.[7]

No female figure in the Rapunzel story offers an image of an integrated woman. All are acting out the particular spell that each is under, split off from the positive masculine principle. That Rapunzel is able to survive in the desert at the end of the story suggests that she was on the way to becoming a mature woman. In order to even have an opportunity to become such, it was necessary to leave the tower of the hag.

I believe that for the past thirty years, women have been endeavoring to leave not only the prisons of patriarchy, but also the towers of their *internal* hags and patriarchs. Peg Jordan suggests that in all these years, what needed liberating was not just women, but the feminine principle — within men as well as within women. Both feminine spirituality and the men's mythopoetic movement have tapped into archetypal energy which is guiding many women and men in their quest for love and justice with each other by laying the foundation for a paradigm of partnership.

How does a woman break the spell of the hag and leave the imprisonment of her feminine shadow? How does she extricate herself from the dark feminine within which is as lethal as any external patriarchy?

How does a man break the spell of his negative feminine self and remain intact? To do so means risking the loss of control, security, relationships, and possibly one's very life. Such a dilemma brings to mind a dream I had some years

---

[7] Peg Jordan, "The Third Wave of Feminism," *Magical Blend Magazine* (January, 1992), p.53.

ago in the throes of my inner work with my own mother complex:

I dream that I am in the house of a very ugly, dirty, psychotic old woman. She has neurotic dog that she smothers with attention. She lets the dog defecate on her kitchen counter then cleans it up and then wipes her mouth with the cloth. I have come to her house for the purpose of repairing, remodeling and restoring it. The house is damaged beyond repair, and there is no hope for it at all. It needs to be completely destroyed and rebuilt or it needs much more help than I am capable of providing. I never really converse with the old woman, I just watch her, feeling thoroughly disgusted and appalled at her crazy, bizarre appearance and behavior. I have been sent to do an impossible task that I cannot do without help or which perhaps cannot be done without destroying the house.

It is not possible to break the hag's spell by oneself. Assistance, both human and divine, is necessary. Just as Rapunzel must surely have come to believe that she could not survive without the hag, the feminine shadow convinces us that there is no life beyond her prison. If we are fortunate, a prince in the psyche, whose father may be the king of our inner world, responds to our song of despair and delusion.

CHAPTER 4
Leaving the Mother's House

> *The devouring ogre of our patriarchal age is the Great Mother gone crazy, going to eat her children. It is she (and the unacknowledged Feminine in a man) who prowls the silence.*
> — Mary Hugh Scott, *The Passion of Being Woman*

It is a day like any other day. Rapunzel is alone in the tower. She is a young woman. She has never been outside the forest nor spoken with anyone besides the hag. She is bored. She sits at the window of the tower looking out into the bird-filled branches and imagines herself to be one of the winged creatures. She sings, perhaps with a wistful longing in her voice. She has no way of knowing the power and effect of her voice because she knows no one but the hag. Rapunzel's voice has never really been heard. If the hag heard it, we can only imagine that she would be impervious to such sweetness and at best, experience it as another silly, sentimental aspect of the young feminine. Or on the other hand, the hag may have grown fond of Rapunzel's voice and delighted in the fact that the voice was yet another asset of the "prize" she held captive in her tower. In any event, Rapunzel had not sufficiently heard her own voice. If she had, she might have felt overwhelmed with the inconsistency of the power of her voice and being incarcerated in a tower.

Yet this day is *not* like any other because on this day, a young man of royalty is riding through the forest, gazing upward through the branches into the sky. Suddenly he is smitten by the sound of the most beautiful voice he has ever heard. He determines that the voice is coming from a tower and searches in vain for a door to the tower. There is no door. At this point, he could have dismissed the whole thing, gotten back on his horse, ridden away and forgotten about the events of that day. However, something in the voice was so compelling, so intriguing, so mystifying that he had to return the next day.

That the young man was riding through the forest in this manner seems significant. He is not focused on a quest or a particular destination. The horse is not galloping with great speed nor is the prince driven with intention. He "happened" to be passing through the forest. One can sense an innocence and lack of maturity about him, as well as an openness to whatever he might encounter in the forest. He is willing to follow the voice and allow himself to be moved by it. What is more, he is willing to return the next day to find out more about the voice and its origin.

Like many females in the modern world, Rapunzel is unaware of the power of her voice. Marion Woodman says that "Women in particular, have lost their voices. That's true both metaphorically and literally. The voice tends to come from the throat because we're afraid to breathe deeper. We're afraid to hit the pain."

A part of herself that Rapunzel imagines to be merely a way of passing time is, in fact, a potent asset that draws to her a relationship that will create upheaval and change her life forever. Unfortunately, the power of Rapunzel's voice is a frequently-overlooked detail in this story.

Earlier in the story, we noted that imprisonment in the tower with only the companionship of the hag did not deter Rapunzel's physical development. Nor did it completely stifle her connection with soul. The story specifically emphasizes the mysterious sweetness in her voice that the prince finds mesmerizing and irresistible. Some feminists, asserting that men run the world, argue that despite the social changes engendered by the women's movement, women really have little power. If power is defined exclusively in terms of affirmative action and gender equity, there is little doubt that men still hold more political and economic power. Yet as Elizabeth Herron points out: "Women's arenas of power are often different from men's... Women have incredible power to create and sustain the relationships that make up the fabric of our culture. We have tremendous social, emotional and intuitive powers — plus enormous sexual power, which we have used throughout time to manipulate the world and achieve our desired goals... These different arenas of power do not limit us or deny us access to men's traditional domains, but simply establish us as intrinsically potent beings in our own rights."[8]

Unfortunately, because of gender-role programming, many women have not become fully conscious of the power they hold in a variety of aspects of their lives. Many women, symbolically speaking, are imprisoned in internal towers of the negative feminine and their destructive animus. They are either resigned to these towers or are endeavoring to change the external world around them in the hope that achieving external power will ameliorate the internal experience of imprisonment.

The prince is symbolic of the animus. As a woman develops, so does her animus, evolving through childhood interactions with both parents. Her relationship with her father, her interactions with her mother's animus and the seductions of her culture all influence animus development. Rapunzel had virtually no options for the development of the animus. She was isolated from men and from the world.

Without consciousness of her animus, a woman cannot integrate masculine qualities into her personality. Instead,

---

[8] Kipnis & Herron, op. cit., p.146.

she becomes "possessed" by them and may increasingly introject the qualities of the patriarchy she is at odds with. In the process of feeling her hatred of male domination, she risks falling into the trap of hating all men because without a relationship with the animus, she is unable to distinguish between individual males and a patriarchal system. Or, as we noted in the last chapter, a woman may also become stuck in waiting for men to become "good guys" which is another form of animus possession and a powerful, insidious distraction of patriarchy. Naturally, as long as a woman sits and waits for men to change, she does not have to develop a relationship with her animus.

As in the Greek myth of Medusa, Rapunzel is "chained" to the dark feminine, just as Andromeda was chained to Medusa's rock. In the Greek myth, Perseus, another animus figure, killed Medusa and liberated Andromeda. In many myths and fairytales one sees that a woman cannot fully separate from either her mother or father without the support of her masculine self. Of this Marion Woodman writes:

> ...*the woman has to be separated from the mother, and for that to happen she has to surrender to the masculine principle — externally or internally. Either the external man carries her off sexually or she identifies with her inner man; in either case she is in danger of animus possession.*[9]

Echoing the Demeter-Persephone myth, this part of the Rapunzel fairytale emphasizes that in order for the young feminine to develop into mature womanhood, although it might prefer to stay with the mother, it must be carried off into the underworld and be symbolically penetrated and impregnated by the creative masculine. For an individual woman, the old "Demeter System" must give way to the

---

[9] Marion Woodman,"Tending the Shadow," Lecture Series with Robert Bly, San Francisco, CA, October, 1991.

new "Persephone System" in which the young feminine in the psyche is ravished by the creative masculine, that is, the positive animus. In other words, the mother complex must "die" so that a woman can come into full relationship with her creative masculine self.

Similarly, a man must struggle with his mother complex before he can experience the wholeness of his masculine self. Furthermore, in order for a man to join with a woman in mature partnership, he must be able to see his partner for the woman she is, instead of seeing his mother's face on his beloved. Thus when Robert Bly, Robert Johnson and other mythopoetic voices of the masculine soul speak of "killing the mother," their intention is not misogynist nor are they speaking of literally killing anything. "Killing the mother" is an aspect of individuation which any human being undertakes in confronting the mother complex. No part of the psyche, including the mother complex can be made extinct, but complexes can be transformed and their energy utilized for healing and creativity. Only then can any individual become a whole person.

When the prince appears in the story, Rapunzel, although not consciously aware of it, is ready to leave the hag's tower. The timing is important. The prince does not arrive when Rapunzel is a child. Nor does he arrive the first time when the hag is present. He arrives when Rapunzel is an adolescent — an increasingly isolated, delusional and probably depressed adolescent at that, and at a time when the negative feminine is physically out of the picture.

It is important to note that although the prince is an animus symbol, he is not fully grounded in the masculine at this point in his life. He has not yet encountered the negative feminine. Even if he is the son of a king, he is innocent and puerile — callow and untried. His innocence allows him to follow his desire, and as we have already noticed, desire always wakes up the hag. Nevertheless, the prince possessed a certain groundedness and stealth which enabled him to see the hag before she saw him. The story reveals all too clearly, however, the price one pays for attempting to trick the hag. Often we believe that we are getting away with something behind her back, but eventually, we are found out, and all hell breaks loose.

Jungian analyst, Polly Young-Eisendrath in *Hags and Heroes* speaks of the negative mother complex as "related to the idea of devaluing or excising the feminine from one's identity and activity." The hag in a man, says Young-Eisendrath, "...can be constellated as a man's anima state when he feels the threat of a real or imagined bully in himself or in the environment."[10] When one genuinely ponders these words, one begins to see the enormous implications for the culture and for the planet with respect to the negative mother complex and the role of the hag in the individual and collective psyche.

When individuals, females as well as males, are unconsciously defending against the feminine in themselves through warding off their own mother complex and projecting it onto women or men in their environment, the result can only be a cultural and collective attempt to "excise the feminine from one's identity and activity." Another way of saying this is that our culture and our world appear to be defending against a planetary negative mother complex which manifests by way of men going to war against men and men controlling most of the world's wealth and men decimating ecosystems. In reaction to this, many feminists define masculinity as the culprit while men's rights advocates clamor for equal acknowledgment of men's oppression. Meanwhile, the hag stands in the shadows shrieking and raging, her two or three broken teeth hanging in the black cavern of her omnivorous mouth. What havoc will

---

[10] Polly Young-Eisendrath, *Hags and Heroes: A Feminist Approach to Jungian Psychotherapy With Couples* (Toronto: Inner City Books, 1984), p.82.

she have to wreak next on humankind in her relentless insistence on being seen? What amount of devastation is required for men *and* women to face the feminine shadow in themselves and in the world?

Several thousand years ago human beings lived, for the most part, in a matriarchy in which the Great Goddess was the supreme being and the mother of all life. Many devotees of feminine spirituality unequivocally evaluate that time in history as superior to any other. Arguing for the dissolution of patriarchy, they extol the virtues of returning to "the rule of the goddess" as humankind's last hope for survival. Ironically, their fervor is inconsistent with the feminine principle itself. The feminine principle is above all the principle of wholeness. It asks to be seen in its totality, from the voluptuous breasts of the Great Mother to the grotesque horrors of the enraged hag. The feminine principle is not served by juxtaposing a "benevolent" matriarchy or "Good Mother Earth" with a "diabolical" patriarchy — a dichotomy which further polarizes the feminine and masculine and submerges humankind into increasingly insidious quagmires of self-destruction.

An excerpt from the writings of Theodore De Banville entitled *The Goddess* captures the awesome energetic purview of the feminine:

She had opened an immense hole in the soft ground, which she quickly digs up with her skeleton fingers, and bending her ribs and inclining her white smooth skull, she heaps together in the abyss old men and youths, women and children, cold, pale, and stiff, whose (eye)lids she silently closes. "Ah," sighs the dreamer, who sadly and with heavy heart sees her accomplish her work, "accursed, accursed be thou, destroyer of beings, detestable and cruel Death, and mayest thou be dominated and desolated by the ever-renewed floods of mortal life!" The grave-digger has arisen. She turns her face; she is now made of pink and charming flesh; her friendly brow is crowned with rosy corals. She bears in her arms fair naked children, who laugh to the sky, and she says softly to the dreamer, while gazing at him with eyes full of joy: "I am she who accomplishes without cease and without end the transformation of all. Beneath my fingers the flowers that have become cinders bloom once more, and I am both She whom thou namest Death, and She whom thou namest Life!"

The feminine shadow wants to be seen and heard. She wants her powers of death to be as fully honored as her powers of life. She wants her uterus to be valued not only as a womb, but also as a tomb. She pleads with all human beings, regardless of gender, to come down from their ethereal towers of sanitized, heroic perfectionism and sit with her in the dark, muddy, messy, terrifying caverns of death and dismemberment. In order to even entertain such a possibility, women and men must make a commitment to join *with* each other in facing the hag. Endless cacophonies of indictments across the gender gap and pedantic diatribes about rights and political correctness only postpone the urgent necessity of coming to terms with the hag and fuel her fires of indignation over humankind's unwillingness to acknowledge her.

So there in the forest, the prince watches and waits. He is not completely unconscious. He is paying attention. And yet he chooses to move into the territory of the hag in order to satisfy the longing Rapunzel's song has created within him. The moment the prince decided to go to the base of the tower and call out Rapunzel's name, he entered the hag's domain.

When we recall the interaction between Rapunzel's father and the hag in the garden, we realize just how long she is willing to wait before she strikes back. Can we really assume that she wasn't watching the tower all along? Isn't it more likely that she was observing the entire love affair from afar, waiting for the exact slip of the tongue Rapunzel demonstrated? Rapunzel is totally unaware of anyone outside herself but the hag. Nothing has prepared her for the appearance of this young man in her tower. This is not unlike women and men in the throes of mid-life upheaval with whom I have worked. As they reflect on their lives, they notice times when a relationship, or a job or something in their life provided an alternative to being chained to the rock of a mother or father complex, or some other force to which they were bound. In pondering those experiences, they realize that they were so unconscious and so imprisoned in a particular tower that they could not recognize the alternative as such. They were frightened by it or perhaps dismissed it as foolishness.

Rapunzel was fortunate given that the prince had found her when she was unable to find him. Lost in her dreamy spirit world of looking out into the branches, she never bothered to look down at the earth, except when the hag called out her name. If she had, she might have seen the prince walking around below her window. Furthermore, Rapunzel is doubly fortunate in that unlike most of us in the modern world, she had nowhere else to go. She could not escape the impact of this earth-shaking event.

The prince needed to mimic the hag in order to get Rapunzel's attention, and this detail should not be overlooked. A woman under the spell of her mother complex may not be able to see or feel a man who is unlike her mother in his intention — a man who hears and honors her voice and who wishes to offer her a choice about which realm she wants to live in. In relationships between women and men, women transport into the relationship not only their unfinished business with their fathers, but with their mothers as well. Very often a woman re-creates and plays out her negative mother complex with her male partner who bears an uncanny resemblance with her mother on a variety of levels. Likewise, in the inner world, a woman under the spell of the mother complex cannot recognize or consciously engage with her positive animus. The terror Rapunzel felt at the first sight of the masculine should not be minimized. We live in a culture that demeans the positive masculine as much as it devalues the feminine principle. In a world of what Marion Woodman calls unmothered mothers and unfathered fathers, nothing prepares most women for any kind of conscious relationship with their animus. Most of our mothers have no conscious relationship with their animus and are therefore living out the most negative aspects of their masculine selves. Most of our fathers have no grounding in positive masculinity, and our culture offers women a "choice" about masculinity that is not a choice. Essentially it says, "accept patriarchy and co-exist with it [in which case a woman can never develop a conscious relationship with her animus], or retaliate against patriarchy by shaming and blaming men in an attempt to empower yourself in the world." A woman who perceives masculinity as the root of all evil cannot tolerate the possibility of claiming any part of herself as male. She dare not see herself as anything other than a "strong woman." Therefore, it seems to me that most women in our culture are not unlike Rapunzel in the degree of fear and ignorance they hold in relation to their animus. When the negative feminine is all a woman has ever known, it is overwhelming, if not impossible, to really see the positive masculine — within oneself or in an actual man.

Without initiation rituals that honor manhood and womanhood as sacred, women and men, and people in same-sex relationships for that matter, are not prepared to genuinely see each other. Not only has Rapunzel never seen a man before, but the prince at first sees only the light side of the feminine — the beautiful, enchanting, erotic, sensual, innocent young maiden with an irresistible song. For Rapunzel and the prince to genuinely see each other, formidable adjustments will have to be made in their vision. Each will need to endure their own solitary, grinding, inner initiation. Both will be forced to descend to a world beneath the elevated, airy plane of an idyllic romantic fantasy.

Recently I watched a talk show in which men were relating their experiences of being present while their wives were giving birth. Several men were moved to tears as they told of allowing themselves to be touched by witnessing such a profound, life-changing event. Still other men expressed the disgust, repulsion and anger that surfaced for them in the birth experience. One man commented: "I grew up on a farm, and I can handle animal blood, but human blood makes me sick." Still other men confessed that they lost interest in their wives sexually after the women had given birth. They stated that their revulsion in witnessing the birth experience impeded their desire to make love with their wives.

In a culture of diet industries, tummy-tucks, face lifts and epidemic proportions of anorexia and bulimia, women and men will go to uncanny lengths not to see or touch the domain of the hag with the dirt under her fingernails, the matted hair, the empty eye socket, the wrinkled skin and the cavernous mouth with its two or three rotten, broken teeth. Where there is moistness and wetness, blood, excrement and bodily fluids, the hag is there waiting to be seen, and if she is not, she will surely have to create another messy situation, trying once more to get our attention.

For some period of time, Rapunzel is able to hold her connection with the hag alongside the connection with her new love. We can well imagine the swelling tension in her body and soul as she endeavors to hold such glaring opposites. The Terrible Mother is her companion during the day, her beloved prince her consort in the night. Delicious as her new love may be, it is a momentary ripple in the ocean of her lifelong possession by the hag. Treacherous and terrifying as she is, the hag is the only human connection Rapunzel has ever known — the only one with whom she has spoken, broken bread or wandered the forest — the only one who has called her name until the prince came into her life.

Each time Rapunzel moves from contact with the hag to contact with the prince, the mother complex and her masculine self become further polarized. The tension mounts. Her body pulsates with delectable anticipation as the prince calls out her name and ascends the tower one more time to shower her with passionate kisses. Her heart plummets when the prince again climbs down the wall and she must not only long for him throughout the day but struggle, in the presence of the hag, to hold inside herself the most exquisite emotions she has ever known. How does one entertain and pass time with a hag when one's soul and body are about to explode with sensations which, if verbalized, would send the old woman into a fit of murderous rage?

A modern woman may revel in her creativity and positive masculine talents — she may delight in her ability to articulate the concepts of her profession, she may prize her savvy and gutsiness, her triumphs along the corporate ladder may be multifarious, she may be the envy as well as the enemy of her colleagues — she may truly be superwoman. Yet under the spell of a negative mother complex she cannot maintain a vital connection with her positive animus, nor with actual males in her life who challenge the spell the mother has cast on her. She must constantly do battle with herself in order not to become a hag. Within a woman who is not grounded in the depths of her feminine soul, an unholy marriage between her mother complex and the negative animus occurs. Sometimes she will be suffocating and devouring; at other times she can match any man around her in drivenness, self-judgment and criticism of others.

A woman under the spell of the inner hag either does not have her own voice or is completely detached from the power of the voice she has. Leaving her mother's tower seems like an interesting idea, yet there is always an excuse for not doing so. She is not conscious enough to speak up clearly and say, "I've had it! This is enough. I will find a way down from this tower." Denial and rationalizations flow from her lips: How would I get out of the tower if I don't use my own braids? I'd love to go, but I certainly cannot use my own life force to secure my freedom. Other people are depending on my life force to climb up and down the walls of my prison.

Eventually an option or two may occur to the woman incarcerated in the mother complex. (Fake braids! What an ingenious concept!) Her animus may bring any number of alternatives to her attention, but just about the time she is actually on the verge of departing from the influence of the complex, she will literally or metaphorically "give herself away." She will regress to the little girl status of malleable putty in the hands of the negative mother. She will betray herself and people around her.

Under the influence of the spells cast upon women and men by any number of complexes, people — especially women — give themselves away by acting passive-aggressively, rather than assertively and with intention. While it is true that women have been socialized to be passive-aggressive, that is, to passively defend themselves through manipulation, vindictiveness, or other hostile behaviors, it is also true that at some point in the development of the feminine self, it becomes necessary to take a stand on behalf of the truth of one's soul, claiming and speaking one's voice with intention. Proscriptions against voicing one's truth may be as severe as the hag's threats of violence, or they may be more subtle. A woman once shared with me a childhood incident with her mother in a restaurant. She recalled that when she discharged energetic, childlike sounds with her young voice, her mother became tense and said, "Please! You're being too loud. Lower your voice. It carries." Of course, children need to be educated in civilized social interaction, however, this woman's experience is all too familiar to most women in this culture.

And so it happened that the same voice that drew the prince to her in the first place, the voice that said to him, "Please do come to see me," the voice that made excuses for why Rapunzel could not leave the tower — that voice now betrays both Rapunzel and her beloved. Rapunzel's life is about to change forever. Childhood is over. Passivity is over. She is about to incur the full force of the hag's wrath.

There is always a price to pay for leaving the domain of the hag. And for every woman or man who attempts to extricate themselves from the mother complex, there is a terrible price to pay. In this story, uncontrolled rage spews forth. Rapunzel is brutally shamed and reminded that this tower belongs to the hag and her alone, and certainly, nothing masculine is welcome. "Who do you think you are?" the hag screams. Rapunzel's beauty, a source of both envy and contempt for the hag, is chastised.

From this point, the rest of the story is one of descent. It is time for the young feminine to come down to earth away from the cool shade of the lush forest and into the scorching desert heat. The silken ropes, her access to a new life with the prince, are destroyed. Rapunzel's hair, symbolic of her life force, her instinctual energy, is cut off. And with vehement fury the hag demonstrates her ultimate philosophy of devourment: You belong to me alone. Either you stay here in this tower and be my exclusive possession, or you will be cast out into the desert and left with no one.

Both women and men in the modern world exist in a pre-exile Rapunzel state of not understanding the immensity of the hag. We do not comprehend that the Terrible Mother, who is the shadow side of the Good Mother Earth, has us imprisoned in individual and collective towers of unconsciousness. This Great Mother is, as Theodore De Banville writes, the Mother of Life and the Mother of Death. In many fairytales, as in this one, a hag and a beautiful, innocent woman are juxtaposed. They are, in fact, the same woman. The Great Mother is the psyche, the soul, the Mother of the Muses — the music of life. She is, in the words of Thomas Moore, "The font of all that we are." And at the same time, she is a malevolent, annihilating hag whose ominous force proliferates with each moment of humankind's denial of her existence.

Michael Meade tells a story of returning home from an anti-nuclear protest where people spoke repeatedly of "our poor mother earth." He remembers pondering this phrase while driving on the freeway and then realizing that if the Great Mother were to merely shrug her shoulder, the entire freeway system of the West Coast could be devastated in a few seconds.

Without a consciousness which embraces the totality of the Great Mother, women disown the Terrible aspect of her and as a result remain Rapunzels who despite decades of social and political "consciousness raising," are held captive in towers of the negative feminine, struggling not to become hags themselves. Without awareness of the distinction between the Great Mother and individual women, a man shrinks into a terrified little boy who experiences his wife as a hag who has the power to tear him to pieces. He might even become a hag himself, by slapping his wife and turning the dinner table upside down because the mashed potatoes are lumpy.

The only way out of the hag's tower, whether the tower of the mother complex in the inner world, or the tower of ecological disaster in the external world, is to consciously engage with her. It may be necessary to "give ourselves away" any number of times before we have enough awareness to struggle with her. Invariably, however, we will have to descend, no matter how stubbornly, to the unkind, dusty, steaming, barren, deserts of earth-borne embodiment. In the territory of the Great Mother's defeat, there is a different kind of fertility — the possibility of birthing and reclaiming the beloved parts of soul that have been torn away from us by complexes and culture.

The Great Mother, like many archetypes and complexes of the psyche, is a mixture of complicated energies that want to be seen and do not want to be seen at the same time. Like the hag in this story, she may disappear during the night and reveal herself only in the day (or vice-versa). She may play tricks with us and thwart any attempts to know her, yet of one thing we can be certain: This formidable giantess will do whatever is necessary to command the respect of individuals and all of humanity.

CHAPTER 5

In Exile

> *The whole truth is not merely about recounting the issues, with countervailing male and female victimization statistics. It is also about directly and personally communicating the feelings and real human experiences behind the political and social issues.*
> — Elizabeth Herron and Aaron Kipnis,
> *Gender War, Gender Peace: The Quest For Love and Justice Between Women and Men*

In a 1994 episode of television's *Northern Exposure,* which takes place in the fictitious town of Cicely, Alaska, disc jockey, Chris, receives a letter from his high school flame, Meredith, who announces that she is on her way to visit him. Chris is ecstatic and begins obsessing about the upcoming reunion with Meredith who he remembers as a veritable goddess — Botticelli's Venus, to be specific. But when Meredith arrives in Cicely, she is no longer the voluptuous blonde "babe" that Chris remembers. She is now a scientist traveling in a pickup truck with a camper shell, wearing a baseball cap and outfitted in full L.L. Bean attire.

Chris is astonished, beside himself with disbelief that a woman who had been so breathlessly beautiful could look so ordinary — so mediocre in her physical appearance. During the course of their brief visit, Chris is unable to get past the dramatic change in Meredith's persona. While she is making every attempt possible to connect with him emotionally, Chris is pre-occupied with her "disappointing" appearance and hears virtually nothing she says. She opens her heart to him and speaks freely of her values and aspirations, but Chris is distracted by the fact that Meredith no longer plucks her eyebrows.

Chris arranges to accompany Meredith on one of her scientific water-sampling expeditions. When he knocks on the door of her camper, a blonde woman, dressed as Meredith had been dressed, opens the door. Her hair is wildly disheveled, and her crooked nose and bulging eyes are accompanied by a conspicuous, dark wart on her chin. Chris is flabbergasted. Suddenly the high-school, heart-throb Venus has become, in Chris' words, a hag. In desperation, he visits the town's only doctor, Joel Fleishman, who assures Chris that his eyesight is intact, and Chris remains devoid of any logical explanation for his bizarre experience with Meredith.

Eventually, Chris stumbles onto a passage from Jung on the subject of projection, seeing what we need to see in other human beings — particularly those of the opposite gender — as a result of the wounds we carry from the past. The lights go on, and Chris gets it. In a moment of astonishing clarity, he realizes that he has been projecting a fantasy onto Meredith which she has not and cannot become. With great remorse, he returns to her camper, uttering his profuse apologies through the door. In a few moments the door opens, and a gorgeous blonde woman who more closely resembles the Meredith Chris remembers from high school emerges from the camper, tenderly kisses him goodbye and drives away. *That* Meredith was not the puerile young woman who used to boogie with Chris at Springsteen concerts, nor was she a hag. She was a lovely woman whose beauty and grace had ripened into a commanding presence. What was momentous for Chris was not that he could not rekindle the flame with Meredith, but that he was able to genuinely recognize and own his projections. Ultimately, he announces on the radio in one of his typically soul-baring monologues: "I said goodbye to someone today, and I don't even know who she was."

Something like the vignette featuring Chris and Meredith occurs incessantly in relationships between men and women. Archetypes, complexes and destructive animus and anima impediments are projected onto the beloved in frantic attempts to placate the terrorism of inner demons. Men and women for years and for lifetimes project and carry each other's distorted definitions of human love. Fortunately for Chris, as for the prince in the Rapunzel story, after his encounter with a hag-like woman, something shifted.

Back at the tower in the fairytale, the seething hag returns to lie in wait for the prince, invested not only in ostracizing Rapunzel for her "disloyalty," but maliciously determined to trick and destroy the prince. Why *is* the hag so enraged? Is it simply a matter of losing the young feminine to a strange male admirer? Is she incensed because Rapunzel and the prince have been carrying on right under her nose and in her territory at that? As we noted earlier, it is likely that she was watching from afar the whole time. So what drove the hag to vindictive determination to entrap and destroy the prince?

At this point in the story, we are again confronted with the titanic power of the feminine — the hag's unrelenting insistence that anyone who toys with people and things in her domain must come to terms with her. In the modern world it is increasingly clear that human kind is not allowed to disturb the Great Mother's intricate ecosystems without forfeiting a horrible price. As Laurie Garrett reminds us in her chilling investigative work on *The Coming Plague,* even if the ozone layer can be salvaged for another decade or so, it is only a matter of time until virulent infections more pernicious than HIV will ravage enormous portions of humanity. Never mind rampant nuclear stockpiles being garnered by terrorist politicians who consider it their divine duty to vaporize every last vestige of Western civilization. The clock is ticking, the experts declare, for the shrinking potency of antibiotics. Already, certain bacterial infections are demonstrating total immunity to those "invincible" drugs whose names end with *illin* and *mycin*. Western medicine is about to come full circle — returning to a time when the common cold and a minor ear infection become incurable or could require surgery in order to be contained.

In 1994 astronomers informed us that a black hole at least two billion times the size of the sun, which they called "the mother of all black holes," had been discovered. It is said to be "devouring stars like a ravenous beast," eating up entire galaxies like a cosmic vacuum cleaner. A *Newsweek* article[11] reports the alarming increase of environmental, toxic estrogens known as xenoestrogens which are found in DDT and a plethora of plastic products. The link between xenoestrogens and dramatic decreases in sperm counts in both humans and animals, along with large numbers of male alligators being born in Florida's Lake Apopka with penises one-quarter the normal size and testosterone levels so low that they are probably sterile is ironically becoming labeled "the feminization" of the ecosystem. Estrogen is the only human hormone which, in its chemical composition, contains a phenol (toxic) ring around one of its molecules. What is more, not only women make estrogen: so do men, but at a much lower rate. Some endocrinologists have speculated that increased estrogen in the environment (together with the estrogen our bodies already produce) is creating epidemic proportions of breast and prostate cancers. In the United States, a woman dies of breast cancer every eleven minutes, and a man dies of prostate cancer every fourteen. It would seem that despite other inequities, women and

---

[11] "The Estogen Complex," *Newsweek*, (March 21, 1994), p.76.

men are almost equally at risk as the toxic feminine ravages our eco- and immune systems.

If we are paying attention, we might read this as another example of the Great Mother's unwillingness to tolerate being ignored. Whether on earth or in the heavens, she will not endure intrusion into her domain without presenting her bill. Wherever there is a desire of any kind — the desire to ravish a rain forest for timber, the desire to thrust phallic pipes into the earth to extract oil, the desire of a woman to bear a child or the desire between two human beings who passionately love each other — in every moment of desire of any kind, the hag is activated. She may appear out of nowhere as she did to Rapunzel's father, demanding explanation, or she may lie in wait in the very places that hold what we cherish most.

We should not fail to notice the particular manner which the hag uses to entrap the prince. She could have lain in wait for him at the base of the tower and attacked him when he looked up at the window and called Rapunzel's name. Likewise, she could have cut the braids while he was halfway up the tower. That she chose this precise method of entrapment is not incidental. It seems to me that this detail underscores the reality that the hag insists not only on being seen, but wishes to be seen in the very space where a beautiful woman dwells.

Like Meredith in the *Northern Exposure* episode, the feminine is multi-dimensional. As Edward Whitmont writes in *Return Of The Goddess,* "She may play and dance as Artemis, allure as Aphrodite, domesticate as Vesta, or be maternal as Demeter." Wherever the innocent, beautiful, irresistible young feminine appears, a treacherous, devouring hag lurks in the shadow of the young feminine. Therefore, a man must know that when he gives his heart to a woman, he has consented, consciously or unconsciously, to encounter the hag. She may at first blend into the woodwork of the psyche, shooting invisible but palpable barbs into the relationship between a woman and a man, or she may lie in wait, holding out for the perfect moment when a man has opened his heart, fallen madly in love with a magnificent woman and becomes vulnerable enough to trust the access she has offered him.

In telling the story of the Holy Grail, Robert Johnson emphasizes that it took Parsifal twenty years to ask the right question: "Whom does the Grail serve?" Johnson asks: "What is this mute prohibition which keeps Parsifal from asking the question which would give him citizenship in the Grail castle...?" The answer, Johnson says, lies in Parsifal's inability to take off the homespun garment made for him by his mother: that is to say, his mother complex. Johnson offers one definition of the mother complex: "That inborn tendency in every man to look backward and be caught in an infantile wish for the security of mother and infancy."[12]

All relationships are affected by the mother complex. In *Men and the Water of Life,* Michael Meade devotes an entire chapter called "Moving the Mother," to the need for men to attend to the incompleteness of the mother in their consciousness. He notes that, in the male psyche, the mother complex, a man's inner feminine (anima) and the Great Mother of the world all meet. Throughout his life these feminine energies interplay in a man's interior life to create what Meade calls "spells" or wishes, demands, broken emotions and fantasies. Consequently, Meade maintains that "What we make of 'mother' as woman, as Great Mother, and as web of relationships will determine what we make of women, the world, and the intricacies of our hearts."[13]

---

[12] Robert A. Johnson, *Lying With the Heavenly Woman* (San Francisco: Harper, 1994) pp.18-32.

[13] Michael Meade, *Men and the Water of Life: Initiation and the Tempering of Men* (San Francisco: Harper, 1993), p.129.

If a man unconscious is of, and does not attend to, his mother complex, his wounded feminine self, and the Great Mother within himself, he will most assuredly be besieged by her in the world as was the prince by the hag. This happens most frequently in a man's relationships with women. Projections, both light and dark, will laser from his mother complex and lacerated anima toward the women in his life. The hag will lie in wait, attack him, claw his face with her broken fingernails and drive him out of the idyllic tower of unconsciousness he happens to be climbing at the moment.

As Michael Gurian puts it in *Mothers, Sons and Lovers,* a mature man must confront the shadow feminine:

Mythology is very wise about this. The Stone Boy must confront the hag in the teepee. The frightened husband must confront the leopard woman in the African tale of the same name. Perseus must confront the Medusa. Without that particular confrontation (confrontation that can last months or years in real time), the Warrior within the man will live in fear of the devouring Feminine. He will become intimate with a mate but not know what masculine boundaries should be, ultimately withholding affection and punishing the woman, in myriad ways of silence, abuse and distance, for moving across those unnamed boundaries.[14]

Rapunzel is taken down from the tower; the prince jumps. In descending to earth, both an actual man, and a woman's negative animus, must tumble to defeat as deception is pierced with brambles of excruciating reality. The old vision must be destroyed. The extent of one's blindness must be understood, and without knowing the outcome, the defeated masculine, in both a man and a woman, must wan-

---

[14] Michael Gurian, *Mothers, Sons and Lovers: How A Man's Relationship With His Mother Affects the Rest of His Life* (Boston: Shambala, 1994), pp.224-225.

der in the blackness of uncertainty and profound loneliness until it can fully rejoin and cherish the feminine.

In the modern world, one of the most encouraging indications of the defeat of negative masculine consciousness is being expressed by the men's mythopoetic movement. Although the media has endeavored to trivialize the men's movement and virtually declare it dead, thousands of men's groups and gatherings of men occur every week throughout the Western world. The extent to which mainstream media and the feminist press have roasted the men's movement, confirms, in my opinion, the scope of the threat which men gathering together to address their personal and collective wounding represents to the *status quo.*

For women to claim their power in the early days of the women's movement, men had to be confronted and often shut out so that women could take the space required for their struggle. Just as Rapunzel made her descent to earth before the prince, women began to wake up to their oppression years before men did. Within the past decade, however, men have begun acknowledging that the same techno-corporarchy which some women claim gives men all the power, is in fact sucking *their* souls dry. In their extraordinary and comprehensive book *Dancing in the Flames,* Marion Woodman and Elinor Dickson emphasize that "While violence against women and children has become symptomatic of the present state of our culture, and has recently received much attention, the real problem often goes unrecognized. At the root of this social malady is a pervasive feeling of male impotence, a psychic impotence that most men are loath to confront, let alone confess. Such feelings of inadequacy or impotence are either buried or acted out as aggression or rage."[15]

---

[15] Marion Woodman and Elinor Dickson, *Dancing in the Flames: The Dark Goddess In the Transformation of Human Consciousness* (Boston: Shambala, 1996), p.93.

The Rapunzel fairytale is often perceived as a woman's story, yet Rapunzel lives in the male psyche as well. Mothers and fathers in our culture frequently desire a male child more than they desire a female child, however, more often than not, the young feminine of the male child is "handed over" to the hag. In the absence of an integrated, dynamic masculine presence in a young boy's life, his gentleness, sensitivity and tenderness are mangled by the wounded anima of the men around him and the destructive animus of his mother. He learns wisely to disown his feminine self in order to survive. Like Rapunzel, his hair is cut off — his vital, instinctual life force energy is severed because it is perceived as too feminine or too unconventional or just *too much*. However, as long as he adheres to the cultural programming that turns him into a Marlboro Man, he is essentially a prisoner in the hag's tower. Like Rapunzel, a man in mid-life may be fortunate enough to be exiled from the tower when he begins questioning whether the first half of his life is how he wants the second half to be. Another part of himself, a positive masculine presence whose father is a king, may be trying to contact him, but in order to join with that aspect of the psyche, he must encounter the Great Mother, his mother complex and his negative anima. Frequently in mid-life, men experience what it is like to be Rapunzel, all alone in a soul-less desert of defeat and despair, as well as what it is like to be the prince — lost and wandering without vision or direction in search of the feminine self which most men are forced to disown very early in life.

In mythology throughout the world, the archetypal feminine is personified in the three aspects of the maiden, the mother and the crone. All three aspects are present in the Rapunzel fairytale. Although the archetypal masculine occurs in a variety of forms in mythology, the three which appear in the Rapunzel story are the father, the prince and the king. Up to this point in the story, little has been said about the king. Who is this king whose son has fallen in love with the young maiden, Rapunzel? Clarissa Pinkola Estés, in her interpretation of the "Handless Maiden" fairytale, notes that the king of the psyche represents a treasure-trove of knowledge in the underworld. He holds the ability to take inner knowing out into the world and put it into practice without apology. He "rules" the process of death, rebirth and coming to consciousness. In a woman's psyche, Estés says, the king represents the transformation of ruling attitudes and laws.[16] Frequently the king appears in mythology as a symbol of a higher law than the established order. Thus the king is that part of the psyche in both men and women that offers an inner authority or a viable alternative to the patriarchal mode of being in the world.

Obviously the prince is not only the son of a king, but probably also the son of a queen. Out in the desert, Rapunzel has no one with her, and she knows only what she has learned from the hag. The prince, on the other hand, carries with him a royal ancestry — the transformative aspects of the positive archetypal masculine, as well as his connection with the queen who in mythology represents the nourishing aspects of the Great Mother. In reuniting with the prince, Rapunzel, and any woman who develops conscious relationship with her creative animus, gains access to the king and queen of the psyche.

Until a man has encountered the hag, the devouring feminine within himself, he cannot complete his journey toward mature manhood, nor can he tolerate the eruptions of the hag from his female partner which are certain to arise in intimate relationships. Furthermore, a man who has not developed a conscious relationship with his own anima continually seeks maiden lovers and frequently is incapable

---

[16] Clarissa Pinkola Estés, *Women Who Run With the Wolves* (NY: Ballantine Books, 1992), p.419.

of relating to a mature, grounded, empowered woman. The process which Michael Gurian calls "rescuing the beloved feminine within a man" occurs only after confrontation with some aspect of the dark feminine, and like the escape and blinding of the prince, the rescue often does not look heroic or gallant.

Likewise, until a woman has faced her witch-bitch-hag self and come down to earth from the suffocating domains of the Terrible Mother's house and her own mother complex, she will remain disconnected from her creativity and life force energy or worse yet, she may become an "imitation man" living out her animus-possession in an equal opportunity patriarchy. Without this crucial inner work, women and men remain polarized from each other and from themselves.

The Rapunzel story is relevant to the war between the sexes in the modern world, for it seems that most women and men feel very much as Rapunzel and the prince did during the years of their estrangement. Typically, both women *and* men experience, but cannot make sense of, the various aspects of Rapunzel and the prince within themselves. Tragically, the toll this takes on relationships between men and women is horrific. Even more egregious is the price we pay as a species hurling toward extinction as a result of destructive masculine and feminine values that sanction the pervasive, implacable poisoning of the planet.

Author Mary Hugh Scott in *The Passion of Being Woman* asserts that gender wars and the fate of humankind are inextricably connected. Of this she says:

The central disease that infects all of civilization is the diabolical split between the sexes... When the whole culture sees and values both the Masculine and the Feminine as the necessary and different parts of one whole, then society can be transformed so that men and women can come together, drawn by the natural affinity between the sexes, which easily bal-

ances the two aspects of being human. When the sexes stop warring, so will the rest of the world.[17]

Like Rapunzel, many women sit alone in the desert feeling battered, betrayed and sorrowful about lost years or decades of giving the best parts of themselves away to husbands, lovers and children at the expense of their hopes, dreams and creativity. Many men are wandering in search of their lost feminine self, defeated, having lost their vision and their control, defending against dropping into horrible despair. The war between the sexes, so essential for the sustenance of patriarchal culture, has created untold anguish for every man and woman on earth.

Anthropologist Margaret Mead maintained that, when one gender suffers, the other gender suffers, too. Women and men carry enormous pain in their souls and bodies from gender wars they did not ask to be born into and which they have fought, consciously or unconsciously, all of their lives. In attending countless gatherings of women and men during the past few years in which both genders freely and honestly speak their pain to each other, I have come to believe that the place in which we are authentically equal as men and women is in our pain. I have experienced without exception that when both genders can speak and hear each other's pain, women and men move into another realm and quality of communication. Hearts open. The truth is told and heard. Differences, necessary as they are, become smaller. In such an environment, men and women frequently join in a partnership far more profound and viable than any structures produced by enforced quotas, sexual harassment training or politically correct language.

It may well be that it is only in our *shared* pain that we truly find gender equity. For Rapunzel and the prince, it

---

[17] Mary Hugh Scott, *The Passion of Being Woman: A Love Story From the Past for the Twenty-First Century* (Aspen, CO: MacMurray & Beck Communications, 1991), pp.269-70.

was only through their individual suffering and the determination to find each other through it, tha joyous reunion was made possible. Conscious struggle with the feminine shadow engenders not only the marriage of masculine and feminine within a woman or a man, but facilitates the transformation of the very nature of relationship itself. If we are willing to dance on the edge of the hag's fire, we may be fortunate enough to reclaim the beloved feminine in ourselves and in the world and bathe in her healing waters and luscious fonts of creative ecstasy.

CHAPTER 6

The Reunion

Love — stronger than death and harder than hell —
— Meister Eckhart

In fairytales, behavior and events are timeless. It is impossible to know how long Rapunzel remained alone in the desert, nor is it possible to know how long the prince wandered blindly. We do know that by the time Rapunzel and the prince found each other, the prince had lost all hope.

We can only imagine Rapunzel's life after being cast out of the tower, carrying the prince's child. In mythology the desert — sometimes referred to as "the wilderness" — is not a place of fertility, nor is it conducive to giving birth. Few climates could pose more challenges for a pregnant woman. The desert is a hostile environment where survival is an incessantly grueling dilemma. Biblical prophets and ascetics often went to the desert in fasting and prayer — a situation lending itself much more to blazing revelatory visions than the dreamy, cozy comfort of pre-natal existence. The desert is, symbolically speaking, a much more masculine than feminine environment.

Hence the story reminds us again that the feminine gives birth not only as a result of penetration by the masculine, but in close proximity to it. Separated from the shady forest, Rapunzel dwells in the domain of masculine, solar energy and not only survives, but gives birth. Obviously, her throat does not become so dry that she cannot sing — indicating that she still has her own voice, and it still has the power to draw the prince to her. As a child, Rapunzel grew strong and graceful, and now as a pregnant woman in the desert, she continues to develop. The feminine principle endures.

In the barren, arid, wilderness, we imagine the primal, instinctual, animal aspect of Rapunzel guiding her to water, shade and the hidden treasures of lush nutrients that deserts hold if one knows where to look for them. Unlike the state of incarceration in the tower, the desert forces Rapunzel to explore, for her life and the life of her child depend on it. In other words, she had to learn the masculine mode of functioning in the world. She had to learn about doing as well as being.

The story implies that Rapunzel is not a long distance from the forest because the prince "coming out of the forest into a barren land," began to hear her song. Perhaps there was even the opportunity to return to the shelter of the forest, yet she remained in the desert. Could Rapunzel have actually chosen to stay in the wilderness? Could she have come to believe that her inner world was even more important than her external world? Could it be that because Rapunzel was transformed by the desert, she cherished the very place that had pushed her to the limits of her strength and endurance?

The feminine principle needs desert places to develop balanced integration with the masculine. Total immersion in feminine energy may feel safe and comforting, but without the balancing influence of the masculine, the shadow feminine, within an individual woman and in the external world, will manifest as the helpless Princess/Victim or the besieging hag. The "wilderness" for a woman might take the form of a serious illness, a divorce, the loss of a child, flailing about in the throes of an addictive process, menopause, aging, even physical death. The desert places offer an opportunity for initiation which in all cases involves at the very least, a symbolic death.

In her poignant and personal book, *The Alchemy of Illness,* Kat Duff describes illness as an initiation rite in which "one is chopped or torn to pieces by monstrous spirits who then strip the flesh from the bones." She emphasizes that illness serves to compensate for one-sidedness and offers the possibility of re-establishing equilibrium. Thus if there is an imbalance of feminine or masculine energy in any situation, the psyche and often the body, quite naturally moves toward homeostatic realignment. For Rapunzel in the desert, and for the prince wandering blindly, initiation was taking place. And, says Duff, "In the long dark night that is the fulcrum of any true experience of initiation, one cannot be assured of return; one must be still, and wait without hope."[18]

Rapunzel and the prince both had to die. In mythology, killing or death is a signal that some kind of integration is occurring. For Rapunzel, compliance and naiveté had to be killed. Obedience to, and dependence on, the negative mother needed to die. Illusions about her ability to survive the blistering desert and keep her unborn child alive were destroyed. Gone were the days of placid dissociations fed by the boredom of sitting comfortably at the window of the hag's tower. Eventually in the desert Rapunzel must surely have realized how little she had settled for. Like the prince, Rapunzel's vision was in need of transformation. She had seen such a small part of the world and, in the tower, remained essentially disembodied. Initiations always bring us "down to earth" which in mythology symbolizes becoming more present in the physical body. Frequently, modern women, like the mythological Persephone, are grabbed by the ankle, symbolically speaking, and abducted to the underworld through illness, eating disorders, chemical dependency, menopause, insomnia, attended by whatever pierc-

---

[18] Kat Duff, *The Alchemy of Illness* (NY: Pantheon Books, 1993), p.97.

ing screams the body must discharge to compel a woman to finally take up residence in her physical being.

In a culture which ostensibly values political correctness, men and women frequently engage in competition for the "worst" victim status. A polarizing patriarchy seduces us into comparing our wounds. Therefore, in making sense of the Rapunzel story, it may be tempting to wonder whether it is worse to be a pregnant woman alone in the desert with absolutely no survival skills, or to be a blind prince, wandering alone in the dark for a period of years. The answer is: Both predicaments are equally horrible.

The prince in the Rapunzel story is reminiscent of Parsifal in the Grail Legend. In his youth, Parsifal blunders into the Grail Castle, ill-prepared to ask the question which would have healed the fisher king. As Robert Johnson reminds us, Parsifal did this because he had not yet shed the homespun garment of his mother complex. Like the prince in the Rapunzel fairytale, Parsifal wandered about for twenty years before he asked the right question. The moment that Parsifal asked the right question, the fisher king was healed.

Like the prince wandering blindly and like Parsifal, twentieth-century men are confronted with the fisher king wound in mid-life. Robert Johnson refers to this wound as "the mislocation of the meaning of life." He also describes the fisher king wound as a man's disconnection from his feeling function. To ask the right question, Johnson says, a man must differentiate between his personal mother, his mother complex, the mother archetype, his anima, his female companion (spouse or lover) and the feminine aspect of the divine which Jung called The Wise Old Woman.[19]

Making these distinctions is an enormous task, even if one has 20/20 vision. But when a man is blind, as was the prince, when a man has been catapulted out of his favorite

---

[19] Robert Johnson, op. cit., pp.17-67.

heroic tower by the terrifying rage of some treacherous hag, when he has fallen to earth and lost his vision, how can he sort out these six aspects of the feminine? Like Parsifal, says Johnson, he must necessarily *wander*. We should not take this word for granted. It is enormously significant. Wandering is the antithesis of what patriarchy teaches men, or women for that matter, about being a competent, responsible adult. Wandering is essentially a feminine activity, diametrically opposed to the shadow masculine values of power and control. Only by losing patriarchal vision, only by wandering in the dark without it, can anyone, male or female, reclaim the feminine within and without. What is more, a necessary aspect of wandering is a willingness to follow, rather than try to fix, one's wounds.

Whether it be Persephone casually and unconsciously picking flowers in a garden from which she is snatched into the underworld by Pluto, or Rapunzel or the prince, initiation happens whether we are open to it or not. As a Latin proverb goes, "He who goes willingly the fates will lead; he who does not go willingly, the fates will drag." The door to the initiatory process is opened only through defeat.

Since twentieth-century women, aspiring toward gender equity, have been forced to adopt patriarchal methods to win their freedom, the defeat of an animus-possessed woman and the defeat of a man can look very similar, especially in mid-life. This "coming down to earth" and following the wounds, this ability to endure the merciless heat of a sizzling desert when one is "with child," is the path of initiation which enables one to reclaim the inner masculine and feminine selves. The prince in a woman, as well as a man, must lose his former vision and wander in the void of not knowing so that he can truly cherish the feminine principle. Rapunzel in a man, as well as a woman, must endure the scorching heat of the alchemical fires of initiation where something is trying to be born — where gold is trying to emerge from baser metals.

In the external world, it is also the initiatory process which allows women and men to unpretentiously join with each other to co-create new inner and outer worlds. The feminine is always found in the dark, and the feminine principle is the principle of relatedness. *Without encountering the hag, without going into the dark, without the transformation of a maiden into a wise woman, without conscious suffering, men and women cannot join as allies in the struggle for survival in which the species and the planet is engaged at this eleventh hour of the twentieth century.*

Unfortunately, not only are the majority of men in our culture unwilling to come to terms with the feminine shadow in themselves and in the world, but so are many women. In the evolution of any movement for human dignity and against oppression, there comes a time for introspection and an honest look at how the oppressed have internalized the values and methods of the oppressor. Some feminists, including Catherine MacKinnon, Susan Faludi, and Gloria Steinem, claim to support women's owning the ways in which they have internalized patriarchy, yet they remain entrenched in what another feminist, Naomi Wolf, calls "victim feminism." Victim feminism holds that patriarchy is the same as "male hegemony" or a "sex/gender system" in which men work to keep women cowering in submission. Some feminists claim that men ultimately seek to turn all women into "Stepford Wives" or, as Margaret Atwood suggests in *The Handmaid's Tale*, the hidden agenda of the male hegemony is to transform women into female servants or personal attendants for the entire male gender.

As is often the case with liberation movements, revolutions in attitudes and behavior burst forth in spite of centuries of suppression, crying out to be embraced and understood by an archaic, stultifying hierarchy of power and control. In the early days of the women's movement in America, it was essential to target male domination and sexism in all of the institutions of the culture, as well as in the attitudes and beliefs of both genders. However, if the principles of equality and women's empowerment are not grounded in soul, in the feminine principle, and if the feminine shadow is not owned in the culture and in an individual woman, inevitably and invariably, the quest for expression of positive feminine values becomes yet another arena for the unholy marriage of the shadow feminine and the destructive animus.

Shadow feminism, as I prefer to name it, now exudes a plethora of qualities which bear a frightening resemblance to the negative masculine principle. One hears a righteous arrogance, as mentioned in an earlier chapter, regarding the female gender. Female values and methods are perceived as "superior," while the male mode of feeling and expression are derided as "inferior." Understandably, when one has been deeply wounded by aggressive, invasive masculine energy or the absence of a positive masculine presence in one's childhood, and when one grows up in a culture where the positive masculine is disowned as much as the feminine principle, it is difficult to open oneself to the possibility that constructive, worthwhile masculinity even exists. However, outside of the fertile garden of symbolic imagination, apart from soul, the quest for equity subtly and seductively deteriorates into an arid, austere polarization that harms women as well as men.

One of the most popular themes in current gender-polarizing feminism is that of *transformationism.* This is essentially a belief in the superiority of women's ways of knowing. Christina Hoff Sommers, philosophy professor at Clark University in Boston, writes in her book, *Who Stole Feminism: How Women Have Betrayed Women,* that this belief allows women to segregate themselves in their own culture and increases divisiveness along gender lines. What is more, Sommers points out, this doctrine ironically allows insecure men to patronize women once more, denouncing them as the irrational sex that thinks with its heart and not its head.

When the shadow of anything is at work, we can be certain that soul will be betrayed by skewed definitions and profaned themes. The very word *transformation* is a case in point. The process of transformation has to do with the changing of the essential nature of someone or something — the caterpillar-to-butterfly metamorphosis that necessarily involves death, decomposition and rebirth and that reverberates throughout body, mind and spirit. The negative masculine's forte is its ability to usurp some aspect of the feminine, such as transformation, gut its internal organs and strip bare its complex accouterments, setting it down coldly, firmly and rigidly in cerebral academic parlance in the name of "women's ways of knowing." Furthermore, the negative masculine cannot allow that both women and men have different and unique ways of knowing. It cannot tolerate the possibility that both kinds of knowing can exist side by side, complement each other and offer balance when a surplus of one or the other develops. No, the negative masculine must be superior, and usually with a great deal of righteous arrogance.

Yet another aspect of shadow feminism is its lack of soul. The absence of humor, wit and beauty is palpable in its heady denouncements of the "sex/gender system." In fact, gender-polarizing feminism attacks many forms of art and advocates in the words of Catherine MacKinnon, an ability to "see through art and create the uncompromised women's visual vocabulary."

Unable to distinguish any differences between misogyny and lightheartedness, the new feminism leaves one cold with its barren lack of humor and its incessant suspicion that every joke, every nude painting or sculpture of the female body is a subtle form of sexism worming its way into our patriarchally-programmed consciousness. In the name of honoring the feminine, the negative masculine has turned many of these women into what Christina Sommers calls "gender wardens," policing, patrolling and surveilling the culture for any and all manifestations of misogyny.

In the middle of writing this chapter I happened to tune in to a local television news broadcast. The lead story featured a ghastly report of a young mother who, two weeks earlier, had intentionally dropped her fourteen month-old male infant into a pan of scalding water. The child suffered severe burns for which he received no treatment and then died. Several months earlier, a woman in the San Francisco Bay area grabbed her toddler foster son in a fit of rage, shoved a garden hose down his throat to punish him for crying, and when his crying did not cease, she tore off his pants, forced the garden hose into his anus and severely lacerated his colon. The toddler died within two days.

Rock-abye-baby on the tree top,
When the wind blows the cradle will rock,
When the bough breaks the cradle will fall,
And down will come baby, cradle and all.

"It is no accident," says Jane Goldberg in *The Dark Side of Love,* "that this lullaby is, as are many others and nursery rhymes as well, a death threat wrapped in melodic refrain. In fact, it contains the only two stimuli...feared by infants: a loud noise and loss of support. Such are the complexities, contradictions, ambiguities, and subtleties of mother love." Goldberg emphasizes that the real task of motherhood is to dispel "the dark shadows at the heart of motherhood with the light of conscious awareness."[20]

When I hear stories of women abusing children, I am not only horrified on behalf of innocent, helpless children who are victims of such atrocities, but I am also deeply shaken by the capacity among all human beings for committing

---

[20] Jane G. Goldberg, *The Dark Side of Love* (NY: Tarcher/Putnam, 1993), p.131.

evil, heinous acts of violence. In the early days of my involvement with feminist politics, I usually filtered stories of child abuse by females through my feminist analysis. Of course, I deduced, women are burdened with almost total responsibility for child care, and when the burden becomes too heavy, they snap. After all, women are an oppressed class — a victimized minority. Were it not for the oppression women have received from men, according to my worldview at that time, they would never commit violent acts.

Today, at the age of fifty, I reflect back on my own childhood in which I was abused on many levels by females; I witness the culture around me which is now the most violent society in the history of the human race. As I do my own "shadow work" and recognize my own capacity for violence and aggression, I have come to the painful and humbling awareness that women do not behave violently merely because they have been oppressed by men. The hag lurks in the shadows of every woman's inner world, and if a woman does not pay sufficient attention to her, and if a woman lacks sufficient ego strength and psychic defense structures, the hag will inevitably erupt. A woman almost never grabs an Uzi, walks into a public place and sprays strangers with bullets. Typically, the hag overwhelms a woman in the secluded drudgery of her home where children scream and fuss, always wanting something, triggering an avalanche of terror and rage in defense against being devoured by their needs. Or perhaps the hag is being projected onto a woman by her emotionally and physically violent husband or boyfriend. Unaware of her own hag, groomed from an abusive childhood to unconsciously gravitate toward and remain in abusive relationships, and caught in the web of her partner's devouring anima, she sees no other options than to kill or be killed.

Even more frightening is the reality that women, as well as men, are becoming more violent. In the California county in which I reside, arrests of female spouses for battering male partners increased fifty-percent between 1992 and 1993. Arrests of males battering females increased by only eighteen percent. An increase in female violence seems to be occurring in a number of areas in the U.S. The CBS television news program *Sixty Minutes* recently featured a story about Paxton Quigley, author of *Armed and Female,* a woman who, a decade ago, crusaded ardently for gun control. Today, Ms. Quigley is teaching women how to arm themselves and develop impeccable marksmanship skills. Sarah Brady, co-author of the Brady Bill, challenges Quigley's position that having a gun makes a woman safer. A woman may feel safer with a gun, says Brady, but she isn't.

I cannot help but imagine that standing on the edge of a firing range full of women clad with noise protectors and plastic goggles blasting bullets into the center of a target is the hag, holding her sides with laughter. Women, as well as men, are now doing her dirty work, and once again, no one sees the hag, who wants to be seen, yet does not want to be seen, at the core of the volcano of violence spewing across the nation.

In a world where aggression, violence, betrayal and exploitation are epidemic among both genders, we need to stop kidding ourselves: In both the feminine and masculine shadows resides the potential to do unfathomable harm to ourselves, other human beings and the earth. There are also evil aspects to the goddess. Jungian analyst Ginette Paris, author of *Pagan Meditations* and *The Sacrament of Abortion,* writes of the goddess Artemis, who had a reputation for making bloody sacrifices.

Regarding the dark nature goddesses, Paris explains:

> *Nature Goddesses are sometimes linked to a bucolic sentimentality, the belief in innate goodness championed by nineteenth-century romanticism and seen*

> *today in the resurgence of interest in forgotten Goddesses. But there is more than one type of nature Goddess... The image of an ancient pre-patriarchal matriarchy, snug as grandmother's house, does not jibe with the dark side of Artemis, symbolized by a crescent moon. Nor does it jibe with another lunar Goddess, Hecate the terrible, who is the dark side of the moon, symbol of sorcery and magic. Both Artemis and Hecate, who is always clothed in black, have a harsh edge to them that rules out pastoral romanticism and balances out the generous side of the nourishing Goddesses. There is no such thing as a good Goddess and a less good one. Each is an aspect of reality, and in every religion that recognizes a maternal deity fostering life there's a complementary figure standing for death, ending, rupture. Mother nature is both the giver of life and the taker of life, for there is no life without death. It is therefore appropriate to correct the too sweet and tender view of predominantly matriarchal religions by remembering the fearsome aspect to women's fully developed powers.*[21]

Woodman and Dickson in *Dancing In the Flames,* remind us that from the perspective of psyche or soul, the words "positive" and "negative" really do not apply to the Goddess, that is, the divine feminine. Yet it is essential for our conscious minds and egos to distinguish between the dark and light aspects of the feminine archetype. Likewise, it is necessary to make distinctions between the dark and light sides of actual human beings because both women and men have extraordinary capacities for experiencing and behaving from both aspects. "The Goddess," according to Woodman and Dickson, "symbolizes the energy we need to

---

[21] Ginette Paris, *The Sacrement of Abortion* (Dallas: Spring Publications, 1992), pp.33-34.

become whole, to proceed toward consciousness." This is so for both women and men.

And where do we find Her? She is most accessible to us in the Kali/Soyoko elements of our own personal psyches — those energies in us that would devour, dismember, ravage, engulf, possess and annihilate. She resides in our addictions, our depressions, our rages, our passive-aggressive denial systems, our despair. The "politically correct" lids we tighten around the pressure cookers of our unconscious, hag-possessed souls as individuals and as a culture is yet another pretext of techno-corporarchy to persuade us that we have made the hag extinct.

Ultimately, shadow feminism serves the very patriarchy it purports to "transform." Books about "shadow work" and gender reconciliation do not become bestsellers. Patriarchy thrives on perpetuating gender wars, from the nuclear family to the White House. A system that relies on gender wars for its existence does not take kindly to a "partnership Presidency" such as the one Bill and Hillary Clinton have created. The bumper sticker, "Impeach Clinton — And Her Husband Too", is not some anomaly theme unique to a reactionary, blue-collar subculture. It lies, in my opinion, at the heart of the well-orchestrated, vicious attacks on the Clintons issuing from individuals and groups profoundly threatened by equal partnership between women and men.

Ironically, the new feminism which fails to distinguish between a patriarchal system, the masculine principle and individual males, not only perpetuates gender wars, but in the final analysis, does not serve to empower women. While it is true that many women truly are victims of male violence, sexism and an economic system that still discriminates against them, it is also true that just as a developing human being does not truly become an adult until that person can be accountable for his/her flaws, individual women and the female gender cannot empower themselves unless they are willing to confront the shadow feminine, alongside all of the lovely, glorious, awesome, mysterious wonders of the positive feminine. In fact, *to disown the feminine shadow and project one's suffering onto the male gender invariably demeans women.* Expounding on this irony, Christina Sommers writes:

> *That is the corrosive paradox of gender feminism's misandrist (male-bashing) stance: no group of women can wage war on men without at the same time denigrating the women who respect those men. It is just not possible to incriminate men without implying that large numbers of women are fools or worse... Misandry moves on to misogyny.*[22]

Just as men need to make the distinctions Robert Johnson speaks of regarding the masculine principle, women need to distinguish between their personal fathers, their father complex, the father archetype, the animus, the individual males in their lives and the masculine aspects of the divine. To make these distinctions, a woman must develop a relationship with the hags, witches and ogres of the feminine psyche. If she can do so, she may also be able to bridge the gap between the feminine and masculine within herself, as well as the gender gap in the external world.

Slowly, yet increasingly, some women and men are following their hearts in search of gender reconciliation in an attempt to form equal partnerships where both genders can build a universal human culture. An essential aspect of this endeavor is the willingness of women and men to be accountable for their part in the gender wars — an openness to owning how both women and men have harmed each other, their own gender and themselves. In so doing, men and women necessarily listen to each other's pain. Only in the telling and hearing of each other's pain do we recognize how remarkably similar we really are.

---

[22] Christina Hoff Sommers, *Who Stole Feminism: How Women Have Betrayed Women* (NY: Simon & Shuster, 1994), p.256.

A few years ago, I wrote a tribute to men in my life who were engaged in "men's work" with the following poem entitled *"Family Reunion":*

FAMILY REUNION

*Where are you my beloved brother
With the drum in your hand,
Dancing around the fire of the sacred Masculine,
All hairy and sweaty and delirious with delight in
 newly-discovered embodiment?
Your drumbeat pierces my heart, and my chest
Begins heaving with sobs because I feel your pain
 AND your joy.*

*Did you say you're grieving the loss of your father?
So am I.
Did you say he was like some faded necktie hanging
 silently
in a dark hallway closet where the door is only
 opened
when company comes?
Did you say you felt suffocated by your mother's
 loneliness
and sometimes felt more like her husband than your
 father did?
So did I.
Did you say you're nauseous from swallowing a
 lifetime of fear
you dare not be seen with?
Did I hear you say that you were hired by your
 family and every woman you've ever loved to be
 responsible for every thing and every one?*

*Oh, my brother, it seems that we grew up in the
 same family but never saw each other until now.*

I can't dance with you because it's your dance —

It belongs to you and all your brothers.
But I can watch from over here in the firelight.
I can weep and laugh and growl outside but
  alongside your celebration.

You see, I was there the first time they told you not
  to cry.

The violent rage of frightening grownups who
  "gave me something to cry about" sent tremors
  through my small, frail body as it did yours.

Like yours, my mind tried to make sense of senseless
  values and souls as bland as Midwestern diets all
  offered up and sanctified in Jesus' name.
Your first wet dream and my first menstruation —
Sacred solutions of puberty —
Miraculous manhood and womanhood —
Disallowed, dirty, disgusting, disowned,
  disgraceful —
"Nice girls don't!"
"Real men always do."

Somehow, my brother, I was even with you in that
  rice paddy
that day you were toking on the finest shit from
the Golden Triangle and that VC booby trap blew
  your hand off —
The same hand that changed the oil on your '57
  Chevy,
The hand that used to catch your son's fly balls at
  Little League Practice
The hand that caressed your woman's soft breasts.
I lived in a war zone years before you ever went to
  Nam.
And I was with you all those years after when you
  sat and stared At Jack Daniels in your silent,

*powder keg bitterness and all you could do was
drink and curse and fu——ck feeling anything.*
I can't tell you how I knew your despair, but I did.

Maybe it's because I knew the ghost that was my father.
Maybe some part of my father that isn't dead yet knows me.

I see myself in your eyes, my brother, and I recognize that dance you're doing.
It's like the one I do around my feminine fire, and someday,
When the time is right, let's build a third fire —
Not the Masculine fire or the Feminine fire,
But the fire of both.
And let's dance and talk about old times and all the places
we've been together and how we've been with each other all along
and where we might want to go together, now that we know for sure
That you're my brother, and
I'm your sister.

Perseverance through horrendous suffering enabled Rapunzel and the prince to be re-united. Only through the sharing of each other's pain can a woman and man, or the masculine and feminine aspects within an individual, be joined. This heart connection between the feminine and masculine must be watered with tears. Of this Aeschylus wrote: "He who learns must suffer. And even in our sleep, pain that cannot forget falls drop by drop upon the heart, and in our own despair, against our will, becomes wisdom to us by the awful grace of God."

CHAPTER 7
The Tears of the Feminine

If the right funeral is going on, no one can go to war.
— Proverb of the African Meru Tribe

On a beautiful Indian Summer day in late October, 1993, I received a phone call from a close friend who informed me that a lump had been discovered in her breast and that she was going to have a biopsy. Fear surged through my own body since my grandmother had died from breast cancer, and I therefore, with vigilance regarding my own health, had gotten regular mammograms since the age of forty. My breasts are highly fibrocystic, and for some time, radiologists had been observing one area of my right breast which could have been a suspicious mass or merely fatty tissue. However, I was overdue for my mammogram and had been procrastinating for a couple of months. My friend's situation shook me, and I decided that I really must get around to making the appointment. A few evenings later, while undressing, I began examining my breasts and felt a strange mass on my left breast. More fear surged through my body because twenty-five years prior, I had a lump in that breast which turned out to be benign. That night my procrastination ended, and a new chapter in my life began.

A few days later I sat in the examination room of my radiologist's office. He entered the room with two mammography films in his hands. Placing them in front of the reading lights, he pointed to a suspicious area of the upper right quadrant of my right breast. "As you know," he said, "We have been watching this spot for some time, and it hadn't changed. Now it has, and I strongly suggest you have a biopsy." He also reassured me that the mass I felt in my left breast was merely fatty tissue.

This is certainly a curious development, I thought. I don't get it. I have dramatically cut back on my intake of chocolate and caffeine, both of which, certain studies conclude, contribute to the development of breast lumps. I'm healthy as a horse otherwise. What's going on? Then it occurred to me that like the lump twenty-five years ago, this one was probably benign too. This happens all the time to women with fibrocystic breasts like mine, I reasoned.

Two days later, I sat in the radiology department of a local hospital where another friend worked as a technologist. She and several other techs reviewed my films at my request for the benefit of my having additional opinions. My friend's eyes widened, her facial muscles tightening. She pointed to the so-called stellite configuration in an area of the breast known in medical parlance as "the forbidden zone." Turning to face me directly and looking into my eyes, she softly but firmly said, "It doesn't look good."

I felt as if the wind had been knocked out of me, but I soon regained my composure when I remembered that my friend isn't a doctor and hadn't been trained to read films like radiologists are. I was angry with her and the other techs who concurred with her opinion, and I vowed not to worry about this until I had the biopsy. However, two days later during the pre-biopsy appointment with my surgeon, he reiterated my friend's assessment almost verbatim. In that moment, I knew that the worst was probably true and that I was being asked to enter another initiation.

In the recovery room moments after the biopsy, I sipped apple juice as my friend, the radiological technologist, stood beside my bed resting her hand on my upper arm. She had just entered the room a moment or two ahead of my surgeon. I knew they had been talking, and I knew the news was bad. My doctor, a brilliant, kind, middle-aged, Asian-American man, gently put his hand on my foot, looked into my eyes and tenderly said, "Carolyn, it *was* malignant." He said that the lump was very small, had been detected early and that I had many options. In an instant, a parade of ancestors who had succumbed to cancer flashed before my eyes. Grotesque, horrific scenes of suffering relatives praying for mercy on their deathbeds consumed my mind and body as my surgeon dispensed cautious optimism. I had already firmly decided that if the lump were malignant, I would do nothing less than have a mastectomy. My surgeon reemphasized the many options I had and that I had plenty of time to explore them.

In a few moments my surgeon left, leaving me and my friend alone in silence. I stared into space as warm tears rolled slowly down my cheeks. I'm going to die, I thought. This is the beginning of death. It may be a literal death. I may actually die. My life, however short or long it may be, will never be the same again.

Within the next month, test results produced very good news. I decided to have the lump removed and receive radiation therapy thereafter, instead of having a mastectomy. The lump was removed, and there was no cancer in the lymph nodes. The size of the lump and its receptivity to estrogen and progesterone were clearly in my favor. DNA testing revealed that the tumor was growing very slowly. After doing more research in one month than I had done in my entire undergraduate and graduate studies, I reluctantly began radiation treatments, knowing that this too was a risky process with many possible side-effects.

My surgeon referred me to two medical oncologists, both of whom suggested that I take the so-called preventive drug, Tamoxifen. This low-grade chemotherapy medication performs a "search and destroy" mission in the body, supposedly annihilating any renegade cancer cells and blocking estrogen in the body which is believed to feed breast cancer cells. After researching its side-effects and conferring with some women who had taken it, I chose not to take Tamoxifen. My decision was unorthodox and earned me the label of "non-compliant patient" among the team of physicians with whom I continue to work in my after care.

I received third-degree burns in radiation therapy and experienced some energy depletion. Since radiation of the breast sometimes secondarily affects rib bones, I have two rib fractures which cause some discomfort, but continue to heal. I also have four tattoo markings on my breast which are necessary for proper measurements prior to radiation treatments. I was given the option of having removable markings which are actually more difficult for the radiation therapist to see than the tattoo. However, I asked for the permanent markings because I wanted a reminder — four blue dots on my chest that will never let me forget this particular initiation.

Today I am in excellent health. Recent mammograms indicate no recurrence of cancer, and I have made profound changes in diet, exercise and the establishment of my priorities — all of which serve to keep me conscious. I no longer take anything or anyone in my life for granted. Each moment, each experience has meaning, has something to teach me if I am paying attention.

The friend who called me about the lump in her breast shortly before mine was discovered was a former house mate from the early years of my residency in Northern California. I know that we were probably part of a cancer cluster. At that time we shared a house with our friend, the X-ray technologist, all three of us living with several cats and dogs. Since fleas are an enormous problem in Northern California, we chose to have the house regularly treated for pests. Although the pesticide company insisted that the treatment was harmless, both my former house mate and I have had cancer, and two of our cats died of cancer as well within the past two years. Coincidence? Perhaps.

One of the most momentous revelations in my healing crisis was the mammogram itself. Shortly after the biopsy, I took the film to my therapist's office and asked that we look at it together. It seemed important to me somehow, to have her join me in viewing the image of the mass inside my body which had the potential to kill me. I had noticed, prior to this therapy session, that the lump itself configured in shape and shadow to form what resembled the face of the devil. I asked my therapist if she could see the "face." She did see what I saw but also saw something I hadn't seen. Right beside the face was also the outline of a configuration of tissue resembling a tiny fetus curled up next to it. I was dumfounded when I observed the two forms side by side. Here in my own body was the juxtaposition of birth and death, light and darkness.

My personal cancer crisis produced not only a transformation within me but also caused me to ponder the whole issue of cancer in the context of our culture, and especially the epidemic proportions of breast cancer among women. Research continues to suggest a strong correlation between breast cancer and exposure to pesticides. Nationwide, one in eight women is stricken with breast cancer, but in Marin County, California and in Sonoma County, its next door neighbor in which I reside, the statistics are one in seven women. In fact, Santa Rosa, my hometown, has been dubiously nicknamed "Mastectomy Town" by local surgeons. I cannot help but wonder what effect the close proximity of vineyards, heavily sprayed with pesticides by the wine industry, has on the health of women in the North San Francisco Bay Area. Nor can any thinking person deny the formidable proportions of environmental toxification and epidemic incidences of all forms of cancer and virulent infections around the world.

Early in my series of radiation treatments, I was moved to write a poem which addresses both the personal and collective aspects of a life-threatening, degenerative illness. One morning, as I climbed onto the cold radiation therapy table under the monstrous linear accelerator which disperses a variety of radioactive rays into the body, I reflected on my experience in that moment and what it had to do with the faces I saw in the malignant lump which had been removed from my breast. I include the poem here:

THE FACES OF CANCER

Good Morning, linear accelerator —
Technomonster on which my precious,
    round breast is silhouetted
So that every cancer cell in it can be killed.
How is it that the radiation that kills
Can also cure?
How is it that my lifetime of linear thinking,
Which probably set off the renegade cells
    in the first place,
Has come down to six weeks of blistering my breast,
Compliments of Mr. Linear Accelerator?
"Be careful now," I caution myself,
"You're coming dangerously close to
blaming yourself for your illness."
Blaming myself is part of what got me here.
In the waiting room, I see the other part:
Disfigured women and men reading magazines
Around a coffee pot and doughnuts
The oncology staff has so generously provided.
My tech, reeking with cigarette smoke
Draws lines on my body as if she were designing
    a new stealth bomber.
No one calls me Dr. Baker here.
No one cares.

*I am a cancer patient, Breast #3,552
Meaning that cancer doesn't care, and
  cancer is very patient.*

*I'm one of the "lucky ones," they say,
For today I don't have to lose my breast or
  my hair or my eyesight or my sex life.
Today I just sit here being no one special
In a waiting room full of other people who
  aren't' lucky.
We all know where cancer has attacked each of us
By which parts of our bodies are clothed or
  gowned.
I'm wearing a gown over sweatpants.
I may as well be wearing a sign that says:
  "Breast Cancer."
That man over there has his shirt on but no pants:
  "Prostate Cancer."
In this room, no one cares about Bosnia
Because we're in Oncology Herzegovina.
In this room, no one is black or white
But truly, tragically gray.
(Am I the only one with rosy cheeks?)
In this room no one cares about gender equity
  or political correctness.
It's about my breast and your prostate.
It's about the air we breathe and the toxins we eat
And the dying planet we all inhabit.
Welcome to the Medical-Industrial Complex —
America's number-one "growth" industry.*

*My therapist and I stare into the mammogram
We hold up to the light bulb.
I say, "See the lump. It has a devil's face in it."
She says, "Yes, I see. But do you see the other
  face?"
"What other face?" I ask,*

*And sure enough, right alongside the devil's face
Are the face and body of an unborn fetus.
Every opposite of my existence has converged
    in this ordeal
Called "recovering from cancer" —
Life/death; Feminine/Masculine; Toxic/Organic;
    Linear/Circular; Knowing/Not Knowing.
Birth and death congealed in my breast.
I count my blessings with my grams of fat.
I slosh my tinctures and teas,
Take my vitamins and my walks,
Say my prayers, meditate and record my dreams,
Not knowing, despite anything I do,
When birth and death might congeal again
In some other part of my body.*

*The questions before me each morning
    when I awake is:
What will I do with the faces today?
How will I live the vitality that is bursting
    through my veins
And at the same time give audience to the
    demon that travels alongside it and
    wants me dead?
Never again can I look at the face of one,
    without seeing the other,
And that's all there is to do, for now.*

Writing this poem allowed me a place to express my rage, fear, despair and grief regarding the initiation I was trying to endure as consciously as possible. Contained within the word *intention* is the word *tension*. The poem allowed me to state my *intention* to hold the *tension* of the opposites in body and soul — the face of demonic annihilation alongside the face of rebirth and transformation.

While the word *initiate* means "to begin," an initiation is not only a new beginning, but always an ending. Since both are aspects of time, *timing* in initiation is crucial. In speaking about initiation, Michael Meade emphasizes that the feminine principle is the pivotal aspect of any initiatory experience. One aspect of the feminine in mythology is the Three Horai, a trio similar to the Three Graces or the Three Sirens. The Horai are "goddesses of the correct moment." When the Horai are not present, the goddesses of revenge such as Hera, show up. When one undergoes an initiation, the entire psyche is remade, and the goddess of the correct moment offers herself.

The reunion of Rapunzel and the prince took place at exactly the right moment. The story says that after Rapunzel saw the prince, she picked up her child she had given birth to in the desert. The inner marriage, the union of the feminine and masculine within oneself and in the world, cannot take place before the right moment, and before the union can occur, that which one has created or given birth to, must be picked up, embraced and held.

For me, having breast cancer was one of the most profound initiations of my life. It had to occur when it did, not before or later. The breast tissue which eventually became a malignant tumor had been there for some time. In fact, as I mentioned earlier, the radiologist had been watching it to see if it might change. Even a year or two earlier in my life, I had not completed enough inner work to contain such a crisis. What is more, had the cancer been discovered even a month or two later, the outcome could have been much different.

Fortunately, I was able to undergo my ordeal with breast cancer within a context and with intention, consciously holding the experience in my heart as an initiation. Moreover, as a result of many years of inner work, I knew that all people have potentially initiatory experiences all the time. The issue is not *whether* we have initiatory experiences but the *context* and the *intention* of an experience.

Malidoma Somé, West African teacher of ritual, says that "When initiation happens out of context, it become more painful and more lethal than an initiation that happens within a framework that is supervised by the wisdom of the ancients."[23] Thankfully, I am able to say that almost as soon as I learned that I had breast cancer, I began to see the initiatory experience as more important than the outcome, yes, even more important than living or dying. I knew that I had to give the experience a context, treat it as an initiation and somehow find a way to have it "supervised by the wisdom of the ancients."

In this culture, it behooves every individual who desires conscious initiation to both intentionally create initiatory ritual and to allow every life crisis to become an initiatory experience by attending to it as if it were a gift from the gods and goddesses. Among indigenous peoples, initiation is a process whereby the imprinting of parents upon a child is transformed, and only through such a process, is it possible for a child to become an adult. In the modern world of techno-corporarchy devoid of ritual, we are imprinted, or perhaps more accurately, bombarded not only with the influence of parents and other caretakers, but with the entire culture itself. Indigenous traditions generally hold that until the psyche is substantially remade from within through a variety of initiations, an individual cannot develop into a mature adult but merely becomes a larger child.

In his book, *Sibling Society,* Robert Bly notes that "With no effective rituals of initiation, and no real way to know when our slow progress toward adulthood has reached its goal, young men in our culture go around in circles." Bly speaks not only to the plight of uninitiated men in the society, but to the plight of women as well, emphasizing that because of our disconnection with initiation rituals, we

---

[23] Jerry Snider interview with Malidoma Somé, "Of Water and the Spirit," *Magical Blend Magazine* (Winter, 1994), p.20.

are "losing our ability to mature." Initiation benefits not only the young woman or man who experiences it, but the community in general. Indigenous cultures know that to omit initiation in a society is to ordain its youth with a mission to obliterate, rather than preserve that society. Thus we should not be surprised, says Bly, that we are creating what Freud called "the pure culture of the death instinct."[24]

Initiations are always dangerous. Whether one is engaged in a tribal initiation ritual or battling cancer, there are no guarantees that one will come out on the other side alive and intact. One cannot know in advance if one will encounter the wrath of Hera or the blessings of the Horai. It is not uncommon in tribal initiations for people to die or go mad. For this reason, the context of the initiation and the ritual container provided for it are crucial.

In my situation, giving the initiation a context and an intention meant informing myself as thoroughly as possible about my condition and my options. While this may seem like nothing more than good common sense, I was appalled during my healing crisis to discover how many people with all kinds of cancer do not do their homework and allow other people to take charge of their experience. Furthermore, I needed to find my bottom line. I needed to imagine all the possible scenarios a woman can face in having breast cancer and weigh the many factors to discover my limits. Was I willing to undergo chemotherapy, lose all my hair and spend a good portion of my day vomiting or in bed? Was I willing to take Tamoxifen for five years or even for the rest of my life — a drug manufactured by one of the world's leading producers of pesticides — which, for many women, exacerbates menopausal symptoms, increases insomnia and depression, sometimes permanently destroys libido and occasionally adversely affects one's eyesight? In

---

[24] Robert Bly, *The Sibling Society,* (Reading, MA: Addison-Wesley, 1996), pp.42-44.

short, I needed to face the possibility that the most aggressive treatments might fail, and I might endure excruciating pain and ultimately die.

Creating ritual was one of the most important aspects of putting my initiation in a context. During those weeks after the biopsy and before surgery, I was inundated with support from my friends, both female and male. Many of the men in my life rallied to my side and expressed their outrage over the number of women in their lives who were confronting breast cancer. Some of them became more conscious of their own bodies and became more vigilant regarding their risk of prostate cancer. Nevertheless, when it was time to create ritual space in preparation for my surgery, it was to my women friends that I turned for support.

I invited several powerful women friends to join me in a circle of drumming, chanting, poetry and truth-telling in my home a few days before the surgery. As we sat in a circle around an altar to which each woman brought a talisman, we spoke our fears, rage, sorrow and hope with respect to being women on planet earth at this time in human history. In ritual space, I allowed myself to receive the love, wisdom and strength of my sisters whose energy and empowerment I took with me into the operating room.

On the day of my surgery, I sat in prayer before my altar and called upon the ancestors I knew by name who had succumbed to cancer. But I called even farther back into time for my ancient ancestors from beyond memory, time and space and asked them to uphold me as I walked into the fires of initiation.

My surgeon, who likes to have music playing in the operating room, invited me to bring a tape or CD of my choice. As I slid off the gurney and onto the operating table, I handed the nurse one of my dearest possessions: The soundtrack from the television series *How The West Was Lost* with music by Carlos Nakai and Peter Kater, playfully reminding my surgeon that the "serenade for surgery" was *How The **West** Was Lost,* not *How The **Breast** Was Lost.*

In a few seconds, with Native American flute sounds lingering in the background, I saw myself riding on a long stretch of road between Second and First Mesas on the Hopi Reservation. I looked up and saw on my left, Walpi, "Mother Of The Mesas," the oldest continually-inhabited village in the United States. I slipped into unconsciousness feeling the presence of the Great Mother and my ancient ancestors. Yet in the same moment I was aware that I was lying on this particular table at this particular time having this particular surgery because the Terrible, Devouring Mother had manifested in my body and was asking for my undivided attention.

As I continue to sit with the reality of my mortality and the possibility that cancer could manifest again in some part of my body, I reflect on the presence of the hag in my body and in the body of women and men in this culture. I associate the presence of cancer with the hag because of the devouring, rampion-like nature of the disease. Eastern medicine associates cancer and other degenerative diseases with a surplus of feminine, yin energy and prescribes the most yang or masculine substances for its prevention and treatment. As I noted in Chapter 5, certain kinds of cancer are being linked with the proliferation of environmental estrogens and the "feminization of the ecosystems."

Following the suggestions of Kat Duff, Thomas Moore and Marion Woodman, I have dialoged extensively with the "faces" in the breast lump. I have asked them why they appeared in my breast and what they want from me. They have repeatedly informed me that they want me to be able to hold the tension of the opposites of life and death, as well as good and evil, in one body, for therein lies my rebirth and transformation. The faces, manifesting in the breast, the ultimate symbol of female nurturing, remind me that the feminine shadow contains both the power to take my life and to transform it without a literal death. The faces have revealed their presence in my body in order to remind me that I cannot afford to project the feminine shadow of the inner world onto "the patriarchy," individual males, females, or anyone or anything outside myself.

The faces offer me an opportunity to willingly move deeper into the shadow feminine within myself, allow the symbolic deaths that need to occur and open myself to whatever wants to be born. The faces have taught me that although I want very much to live a long and healthy life, my literal, physical longevity is less important than my quest for wholeness and transformation. Nevertheless, my hope is that it is possible for me to experience both transformation *and* a long life.

If I, or anyone, is to be transformed through an initiatory experience, tears are mandatory. In mythology, tears are necessary for cleansing and consciousness to unfold. Just as the prince regained his sight when Rapunzel's tears fell upon his eyes, conscious vision can only be restored through the feminine function of grieving. Illness and other crises often move one into myriad configurations of sorrow. Only through conscious mourning can any initiation become a rebirth. Childhood wounds must be grieved. What may feel like wasted years of the first half of life, whether or not they really were wasted, must be grieved. Lost relationships, lost opportunities, lost time, lost lives come screaming and wailing upon the heart's door in mid-life. Whether the sorrow manifests as a malignant lump in the breast or depression or bitterness or loss of creativity, loss of memory, loss of sexuality, it asks to be consciously, thoroughly and respectfully grieved.

Indigenous peoples know that grief is an integral part of human existence. Moreover, the vast network of community and ritual space inherent in their traditions provide the containment and support necessary for conscious mourning. Michael Meade states that to be a modern man or woman means to be out of ritual, without community and inundated with loss.

In the fleeting hours of the late twentieth century, earthlings are being confronted with more loss each day than at any time in recorded human history. From morning until night and while we sleep, people, species and huge segments of the ecosystems are dying in unprecedented proportions. To be alive at the end of this decade, this century and this millennium, is to be perpetually engaged in a planetary funeral. The only appropriate or healing response at any funeral is grief. Even as scientists warn us that if we do not radically alter our behavior, our species may be extinct in two decades, even as some well-meaning crusaders devote their entire lives to saving the planet, it seems to me that the most authentic, immediate and potentially transformative response to the massive funeral in which we live is individual and collective mourning. If we do not mourn, does it really matter what we *do*?

When asked about "saving the planet," Malidoma Somé replies:

Instead of trying to save the planet, we need to stop and listen to the message the earth is trying to tell us. To hear that message you have to shift hierarchies from one that talks about saving the planet to one that is willing to listen.[25]

Only through grieving can Rapunzel and the prince — the masculine and feminine within the psyche and the world — be reunited. Only the tears of the feminine can wash the blindness from our eyes and restore clear vision. Only conscious mourning can integrate the Terrible Mother and the Nurturing Mother. Perhaps if we can mourn sufficiently, the devouring feminine will not have to annihilate life on planet earth as we know it. Only by opening to the fright-

---

[25] Malidoma Somé interview, "Of Water and the Spirit," op. cit., p.22.

ening presence of the treacherous hag within ourselves and within the world and being willing to engage in the wrenching grief her wounding evokes, can women and men, parents and children, nations, tribes, families and all human beings authentically, empathically and courageously join with, rather than, destroy one another. The way of the feminine is not above or beyond or around or in spite of its shadow, but *through* it.

I am reminded of D.H. Lawrence's poem, *Song of the Man Who Has Come Through:*

Not I, not I but the wind that blows through me!
A fine wind is blowing the new direction of Time.
If only I let it bear me, carry me, if only it carry me!
If only I am sensitive, subtle, oh, delicate, a winged
  gift!
If only, most lovely of all, I yield myself and am
  borrowed
By the fine, fine wind that takes its course through
  the chaos of the world
Like a fine, an exquisite chisel, a wedge-blade
  inserted;
If only I am keen and hard like the sheer tip of a
  wedge
Driven by invisible blows,
The rock will split, we shall come at the wonder, we
  shall find the Hesperides.
Oh, for the wonder that bubbles into my soul,
I would be a good fountain, a good well-head,
Would blur no whisper, spoil no expression.
What is the knocking?
What is the knocking at the door in the night?
It is somebody wants to do us harm?
No, no, it is the three strange angels.
Admit them, admit them.

The way *out* is *through* the mourning, the surrender to the "three strange angels," which remind us of the three Horai or the goddesses of the correct moment who wish *not* to harm us, but to transform us. If human beings were grieving consciously, they would not be destroying themselves, each other and the earth. The feminine shadow will continue her upheaval until we make ourselves extinct or until we painstakingly mourn our losses. But since we have spent most of our lives in this culture denying our losses and defending against sorrow, how do we learn to mourn?

According to Robert Bly, one of the tragic realities of our "sibling society," is that "we are the first culture in history that has 'colonized' itself." Increasingly it appears that we must adopt the *indigenous* attitude and that regardless of our ethnic origins, we must "un-colonize" ourselves.

One definition of *indigenous* is "not adaptable." In one sense, indigenous people are extremely adaptable, otherwise they could not have survived for thousands of years. On another level, they are not adaptable at all in that their essence, like the essence of all human beings, is intrinsic and innate. Given that the interior spiritual self of humans is intrinsic and innate, it is appropriate to say that all humans are "indigenous." No matter how any of us is colonized or forced to become someone or something we are not, nothing can erase the indigenous, interior self.

Perhaps the most fundamental aspect of the indigenous attitude is the experience of paying attention to, and living from, the heart. Poet and corporate consultant, David Whyte, speaks of the urgency of paying attention to the world as we find it — allowing ourselves to stay connected with the natural world and to be moved by it. If we lose sight of the "agonizing beauties of the natural world," Whyte says, we will resort to lifestyles of power and control over people and things to fill the vacuum in the heart. The key word in Whyte's admonition is "agonizing," for paying attention to the natural world and the desires of one's heart *is* a distressing experience. Desire, as we have already noted, always wakes up the hag — the complexes, archetypes and inner demons that we keep at bay by retaining a little or a lot of distance between the conscious mind and the heart. "Living from the heart" does not mean living in a continual state of bliss. Quite the contrary. It means opening to sorrow and grief as another aspect of being fully human and fully alive.

If one can become open to the natural world and allow oneself, for better or worse to be moved by it, one begins to feel and experience what is most important to oneself. Despite well-intended attempts to teach values in public schools and ceaseless moralizing by the religious right, human beings who have been "colonized" by the ravages of childhood wounding and cultural soul murder cannot develop humane values without empathy, and empathy originates in the heart. Empathy is the conscious awareness of another human being's capacity for every kind of injury based on one's own experience of vulnerability. If one feels one's own heart, then one can feel not only the vulnerability of fellow human beings and other endangered species, but one can then move more fully into compassion which literally means "the sharing of passion."

Some people believe that if they feel compassion, they must launch a crusade to change the external situation. One day while writing this chapter I took a break to watch the Whitewater Hearings on CNN. While European-American males argued self-righteously about the extent of "the betrayal of the American people," a silent statistic flowed across the lower portion of the screen saying: "Eighteen thousand Rwandans now dead." Later the same day, a San Francisco Bay Area physician left her private practice to fly to Rwanda to help save lives. This dramatic example of compassion followed by action is only one kind of authentic response to human suffering. While taking concrete action is essential in a disaster of such staggering proportions, it is equally important to attend to what Michael Meade calls "the interior ecology."[26]

In the interior ecosystem we unearth the parts of the psyche that have been starved, dispossessed, contaminated and colonized. In the interior ecosystem we also find the threads of ritual and mourning that reach back to ancient ancestors from whom various forms of colonization have estranged us. If we can grieve the staggering losses of our internal colonization, we have access to the raw material of the shadow feminine and the shadow masculine — the inner "colonizers," as well as the indigenous self. Then, if we can stand by the ritual fire and mourn Rwanda, the Gulf War, Vietnam, Bosnia, the hourly destruction of rain forests and animal species or any of the massive natural disasters which the hag belches forth from moment to moment, we may be able to engage in the "right funeral" and facilitate transformation in both the internal and external ecosystems. Only from that place can we then act with grace in the "correct moment" to make a difference in the world.

The tears of the feminine are very different from the political correctness of the feminist agenda. Twenty to thirty years ago the women's movement was a powerful force of consciousness-raising and transformation in American culture. At that time feminism stood for independence, self-reliance, personal responsibility and the inherent equality of all people. Today, however, political feminism has become a dysfunctional ideology as steeped in patriarchal attitudes and methods as was the Reagan Administration's posturing against the Soviet Union, indulging in caustic rhetoric which labeled the Soviet bloc an "evil empire" that needed to be brought to its knees.

The majority of American women feel alienated from political feminism and find little in it with which to iden-

---

[26] "Thresholds of Change," January, 1994 lecture series by Michael Meade at Marin Headlands, California.

tify. Because it has not confronted its own shadow, feminism is now exhibiting many of the characteristics which it associates with "the patriarchy," such as shaming, blaming, manipulating and attempting to control men in order to feel empowered in relationship to them.

I believe that the women's movement has failed women for two reasons. First, it continues to struggle unilaterally for the concerns of women. It insists on blaming men for women's suffering and from that defended posture, cannot imagine the possibility or value of dialog between the genders. Some feminists are willing to communicate with men who adhere to the feminist agenda and who believe that the way to change other men is to shame them into politically correct behavior. But heaven help the man who speaks openly about how the culture wounds and oppresses men as well as women! And heaven help the woman who questions the feminist agenda! She will immediately be labeled a "backlasher."

Such polarization is much like a basic premise of McCarthyism in America during the Cold War: that is, "You can't talk to the Russians." It was permissible in those days to dialog with exchange students or defectors, but few people had any faith in peace talks because everyone "knew" that Communists were incapable of telling the truth. Furthermore, anyone who insisted that the Soviet people are human beings too, risked the accusation of being a "communist sympathizer." Nevertheless, we discovered in the eighties, through the tenacious efforts of Mikhail Gorbachev and others who kept dialoging, that once you begin dialoging with your "enemy," he or she soon ceases to be your enemy.

The second reason for the failure of the women's movement is its unwillingness to become consciously reflective of its own shadow. As long as men are the "enemy," there is no point in dialoging with them. Gender-polarizing feminists cannot afford to hear about the ugly realities of many men's lives and intractably persist in perpetuating the illusion that men have all the power and privilege because hearing men's pain is intolerable and thoroughly incongruent with the feminist ideology.

In the early years of the women's movement, women quite naturally and necessarily developed solidarity with each other around their oppression by males. In those days, sisterhood was relatively easy to feel and deepen. However, in gatherings of women in the nineties I have noticed that the kind of bonding and "instant connection" so many of us felt profoundly with each other in the sixties and seventies is virtually non-existent. The sense I make of this is that one factor which contributed to women's solidarity two and three decades ago was our mutual need to demonize men. In gatherings of women where the demonization of men is still a primary aspect of the agenda, connections between women seem easier than in contexts where women are simply trying to connect with each other *without* scapegoating males. It is as if, somehow, we needed our identities as "victims" to feel solidarity with our sisters. When the victim posture is shifted, however, and we become more self-reflective, we are left alone with each other and the shadow feminine within ourselves.

I believe that political feminism's recalcitrant insistence on struggling unilaterally with gender issues, its commitment to demonizing maleness, its failure to distinguish "patriarchal" from male and its knee-jerk response to any form of self-reflection as "victim blame," has rendered it not only an ineffectual instrument for social change, but also yet another toxic element of the oppressive system it purports to oppose.

For over fifty years, both the Soviet Union and the United States were able to postpone facing the shadow in their own societies by projecting it onto "the enemy." Since the Cold War has ended, both societies are in decay and disarray. The Cold War turned hot has come home to

America's inner cities where uninitiated young men and women are in the process of incinerating the remains of a dying culture. If political feminism could open itself to dialoging with men, both the "feminized" and the "unfeminized," what is left of the women's movement would no doubt begin experiencing profound upheaval. Deep pain and anger would have to be felt. The simplistic world view of the oppression of morally "superior" women by morally "inferior" misogynist males as the basis of all human suffering would be shattered. Gender McCarthyism might then give way to Gender Glasnost.

An inevitable consequence of such an opening would be the confrontation of the feminist world view with its own shadow. In facing her shadow, a woman begins to ask disturbing questions of herself such as: "What part of me has been taught to be submissive? Why do I need to keep blaming men for my unwillingness to speak my truth? How do I collude in my oppression? How do I sometimes lose my power in the presence of men? What is my part in my inability to break the Glass Ceiling? Where is the violent place inside me that I keep disowning and projecting onto men instead?"

Psychologist Judith Sherven speaks of the "power of victimization." She points out that we do not have an acceptable language for describing the power of victimization because any attempts to do so are labeled as blaming the victim. Nevertheless, after millennia of male domination and thirty years of the women's movement, women are still not speaking up, and often, when we assume we are not going to get what we speak up for, we shame or blame men instead of taking a stand in our own behalf. In the feminine shadow, there is tremendous power in shaming people, and since shame has been one of the few recourses of the disenfranchised female gender, it comes so naturally to us that most of us are not even aware when we are doing it.[27]

Each time a violent crime against women dominates the media, a tidal wave of attention focuses on the issue of "male violence against women." Yet we hear little of the soul violence women can and do inflict on men through manipulation, shaming, verbal abuse, passive-aggressive behaviors and the unspoken rage many women feel when they find out that they have not married the prince of their childhood fantasies. If and when we begin looking at the soul violence of women against men, we will also be forced to look at the multi-generational lineage of "unmothered mothers," as Marion Woodman names them, who have not known how to take care of themselves in a relationship with a man, do not speak up for themselves in relating to men and pass on to their daughters a legacy of passive-aggressive behaviors and sexist attitudes toward men.

It is true that women have been trained in powerlessness, but how long will we continue to disown the shadow feminine within ourselves by endlessly reiterating that fact? Char Tosi, a Midwest therapist and founder of *The Woman Within,* speaks incisively of women's "lack" of power:

I think women see men as having power, I don't think they understand what woman power is. I believe that women often function from a place of not being enough, not good enough, a place of insecurity and low self-esteem. They replace that insecurity with false power, with wanting to have power over men. One of the most effective ways I have seen women using to gain power over men is by shaming men,

---

[27] Judith Sherven, interviewed by Jack Kammer in *Goodwill Toward Men: Women Talk Candidly About the Balance of Power Between the Sexes* (NY: St. Martins Press, 1994) pp.13-22.

using their tongue to put men down, to shame their sexuality, to shame their success.[28]

Until women can fully own their feminine shadow, they cannot experience the fullness of their creativity. In *Woman Within* workshops, facilitators structure exercises in which women can access their destructive energy and express it through movement, facial expressions and voice. Participants experience their destructive energy and feel its power, but they also experience a phenomenal freeing up of their creative energy.

Though facing one's shadow is not a prerequisite for creativity, when the shadow *is* faced, creativity flows more freely and often surprises us with a vibrant fecundity — a lushness from which we are invariably exiled to the extent that we attempt to exile the shadow. Equally true is the reality that creativity is an aspect of our desire, and therefore, awakens the shadow feminine. Thus we both "need" the shadow for the enhancement of creativity, and at the same time, are guaranteed an encounter with it at some juncture on the creative path.

Shadow work opens the heart and establishes the heart, rather than the mind, as the seat of inspiration. In fact, the word *inspire* originates from the Latin word *inspirare* meaning "to breathe into." Thus when we enter the territory of the shadow, we become more embodied, more ensouled and more whole so that more of us is available for the creative process.

Several years ago, I found mythology virtually intolerable, nor was I able to write poetry of any kind. My writing style, although clear, incisive and almost laser-like, lacked depth, texture, color and passion. It was boring — even to me. As a result of exploring dark places in the psyche through active imagination, dream work, and most importantly, grieving, I began experiencing the imaginal world

---

[28] Char Tosi, ibid., p.79.

for the first time. I found it all the more alluring and intriguing as I began experiencing the resonance of certain images with my own body. I discovered that authentic movement and other expressive arts, entered into for their own sake and not because they would "get me somewhere," circumvented my resistance to the archetypal, mythopoetic world. Thus I began experiencing an intensifying hunger for poetry and stories. Soon I was writing poetry, telling stories and gorging myself with myths. Secondary in significance only to my grief was the presence of ritual in my life. Grief and ritual embrace and support each other in the psyche and for me, transform the horrors of the shadow into creative juices previously unavailable to me.

The tears of the feminine offer no guarantees, but they do offer the possibility of transformation — the restoration of vision and an opportunity to return to the forgotten royalty of the queen or king that each of us truly is. Rapunzel and the prince retired to the castle with their children. Surely they had learned too much to try to live "happily ever after." The tears of the feminine pronounce the end of knowing in a linear, rational, techno-corporarchal fashion and the beginning of the journey toward becoming a fully alive, creative, vital, passionate human being in connection with and service to the community.

Emily Dickinson wrote courageously of this death of cerebral knowing in her poem, *I Felt A Funeral, In My Brain:*

> *I felt a funeral, in my Brain,*
> *And Mourners to and fro*
> *Kept treading — treading — till it seemed*
> *That Sense was breaking through*
>
> *And when they all were seated,*
> *A Service, like a Drum —*
> *Kept beating — beating — till I thought*
> *My mind was going numb —*

*And then I heard them lift a Box
And creak across my Soul
With those same Boots of Lead, again,
Then Space — began to toll.*

*As all the Heavens were a Bell,
And Being, but an Ear,
And I, and Silence, some strange Race
Wrecked, solitary, here —*

*And then a Plank in Reason, broke,
And I dropped down, and down —
And hit a World, at every plunge,
And Finished knowing — then —*

When the "right funeral" is taking place and the tears of the feminine are being shed, we stop making war on ourselves, each other and the earth. The feminine is honored and no longer needs to devour and destroy in order to be seen. As in the Rapunzel fairytale, masculine and feminine are joined, offspring are generated and the soul returns to its royal home where the formerly disowned feminine and the undeveloped masculine may now dwell as king and queen.

This is not a permanent state of "happily ever after," but more like being present moment to moment for all the initiations that earthly life among one's fellow creatures offers. Coming home is a lifelong process, and no matter how many times the opportunity for homecoming occurs, the tears of the feminine cool the fires of personal and planetary holocaust. Only the right funeral and sufficient grieving provides enough moisture for a wounded woman or man, and that to which they have given birth, to swim back to the royal home from which we have all originated.

CHAPTER 8

Breaking the Spell

> *One of the secrets of breaking the spell is to go further into it.*
> — Michael Meade, *Men and the Water of Life*

Myths and fairytales are timeless because of their ability to arouse numinous energies in the soul which have been obscured by the merciless anxieties and upheavals of modern life. I see this confirmed each time I work with women and men in workshops where a story forms the basis of our exploration for a day or a weekend. One facet of working with fairytales which makes them extraordinarily powerful is the utilization of the story to evoke images in the psyche. I have noticed that people in groups working with these images, using certain structures, frequently experience profound healing, as well as protracted shifts in their vitality and creativity.

Of paramount importance in working with story images is the awareness that each detail in the story represents a part of the psyche. Thus in workshops where people explore the Rapunzel fairytale, we notice first of all the parts in the story that "leap out and grab us." For example, one woman says that when she heard about Rapunzel's mother standing at the window craving the rampion, she felt her entire body tingling as she caught a glimpse of her mother's insatiable devouring energy. A man begins weeping when the hag says, "I will come here and visit you every day and bring you the things you need because only I know what you need." That particular statement stirred deep grief in his chest as he recalled feeling trapped as an only child in the tower of his parents' lifeless marriage.

I encourage people not only to write about the images in a journal but, more importantly, to draw them. Frequently, people protest that they "can't draw," yet when time, space and permission are given to let the psyche express itself through crayons, pastels or pens, almost invariably astounding images come forth.

Along with drawing images, we sit with specific questions such as: What was my mother's unquenchable desire that caused her in some way to give me to the hag? What was my father's part in that? How has the hag manifested in my own life? How have I (whether one is female or male) been imprisoned by the dark feminine? How have I participated in that imprisonment? For men I sometimes ask the question: How has the dark feminine kept you from your positive masculine self? And for women I ask: How has imprisonment by the dark feminine kept you from your positive feminine self? Still other questions arise such as: How have I incorporated the hag and become like her? How have I expressed the devouring feminine in my life?

By working with such questions, participants have the opportunity to notice the ways in which they have lived or experienced all of the characters in the story. Frequently even objects and places such as the rampion, the tower, the wall, the braids, the brambles, the forest, the desert and the castle evoke as much energy as the characters of the story.

A particularly compelling, sometimes disturbing, but almost always healing aspect of working with the Rapunzel fairytale in workshops is each person's discovery of the hag within. After images are drawn and discussed with a partner — and later with the group — people move into a quiet, meditative space and begin an inner dialog with their images of the hag. After ample time to complete the process, as people return from their inner dialog and check in with the group, it is not uncommon to hear feedback such as "This is the first time I have ever looked so closely at my shadow self." Or: "All my life I've been trying to push her away because I thought she would hurt me if I didn't, but when I just listened to her, I realized that all she wants is my attention." Or as one woman speaks with tears of joy: "I feel like a thousand pounds have been lifted off my shoulders." Quite often people experience encouragement and even excitement about the possibility of developing a relationship with this newly-discovered part of themselves.

I have noticed that without exception, when people consciously dialog with the dark feminine in themselves, they experience an unprecedented sense of empowerment. One woman shares that, "The Dark Goddess has enabled me to claim my darkness and to have the strength to let the doors of my underworld be opened instead of my trying to desperately keep them slammed shut — the doors of grief that I had to store in by body virtually since my conception. I feel like my inner self has been handed a sword which enables me to cut through the illusions and through relationships that have not served me. In this way, the sword fiercely protects me."

LAURA

A woman named Laura tells the story of her own encounter with the dark feminine. Laura had been working on developing her voice — both in the context of speaking and writing, to express her political convictions with respect to social justice. Throughout her adult life she felt fearful and inadequate verbalizing her beliefs about anything. Nevertheless, at one point she wrote a letter to a local politician expressing her sentiments. No sooner had she sent the letter than she began feeling self-doubt and remorse. That night, she had the following dream:

> *A very sinister woman is stealing my car battery. I feel great dread upon seeing her, for she is truly evil. Then I feel hands around my neck and I am being strangled.*

She took the dream to her therapist who sat quietly with Laura as she explored the image of the sinister woman. She soon realized that the sinister woman in the dream, "stealing her juice," was like the hag who kept Rapunzel locked in the tower. Laura's body was filled with terror as she stayed with the frightening dream image. Continuing to breathe and following the sinister woman, Laura realized that this dark feminine energy was trying to possess her because she had not been paying attention to it, indeed, did not even realize that it existed in her psyche. Almost the moment Laura recognized this part of herself, something shifted in her body. She felt relief. She spent time each day for about a week, dialoging with the sinister woman, as well as writing about her in a journal. Although Laura continues to be fearful at times, she says that "After working like this with the dream, I felt renewed strength in my ability to trust the source of my political writing, and I am no longer burdened with self-doubt."

Not all people work with story images in the same way. Some people prefer to work with the images more internally by way of dreams or inner dialog, while others need to experience the images externally as the energies of the story's characters manifest in their lives.

JAMES

James is a poet and writer who grew up with a moody father and a mother who never uttered a harsh word and behaved as the ideal, nurturing female whom James experienced as "bestowing" on him the blessing of the "ideal son." He entered adult relationships with women, expecting to find a woman who, like his mother, would be as kind-hearted and adoring as his mother. Instead, James found himself in numerous relationships with women whom he experienced as nagging and critical. In fact, says James, "I think that all men unconsciously believe that every woman they love will sooner or later turn into a hag." Like so many men in our culture, he came to believe that he had only two choices in relating to women: He must either avoid commitment entirely, or if he chose commitment, he must find a way to avoid intimacy. Otherwise, he would be devoured by the dark feminine.

After two divorces, as he was entering mid-life, James joined a men's group. While he continued to date women, he began relying on those male friends who were engaged in men's work for his primary source of nurturing. The affirmation and support from other men empowered him. For the first time in his life, James felt validated as a man and realized that he no longer needed to look to women to substantiate his maleness. As he established his own gender ground, he discovered a different motivation for relating to women. Whereas in the past he had developed relationships with women to be adored and affirmed as a man — which actually prevented him from seeing these women as whole persons — James now related to women much more from a place of empowerment and much less from need.

Standing on firmer gender ground, James decided that instead of fleeing, either physically or emotionally or both, when his female partner became critical, he would stay present and work with the criticism. Earlier in his life, James, like the prince in the Rapunzel story, climbed over a variety of windowsills in numerous towers, expecting to meet a beautiful, adoring princess, but instead, was dumfounded by the presence of a treacherous hag. Repeatedly, he jumped from each tower and landed in the brambles of pain and confusion, being blinded for a time until he could regain some vision and make another attempt to discover another "princess" in another tower.

Today James is in a relationship with a woman who does not adore him, but does honor and respect him. When he feels the presence of the hag in himself or in the relationship, he is determined not to flee but to remain and work with his fear alongside his partner, rather than separating from her.

James also notes that his willingness to struggle with the dark feminine has enhanced his creativity. "Whereas I used to go after a project and try to make it happen, I now open up and surrender and see what wants to happen through me. I feel poetic rather than feeling like I'm writing poetry. I've noticed that it's only when I become receptive to the feminine in whatever form she shows up, that full creativity is possible."

HANK

Hank is approaching fifty and has been a psychotherapist for several years. He prefers to describe his experience as "learning to dance with the hag." Like James, he spent a number of years fleeing from women, but as a result of his upbringing and his training as a therapist, he learned to "appear" present and available in relationships, even while he was creating distance. "I needed to do men's work and secure the affirmation of my masculinity from men, instead of expecting my female partners to do that for me."

Hank says that in his dance with the hag, it is important for him to be able to say 'no' in order that he might be able to genuinely say 'yes.' In other words, when he becomes aware of his wife's needs, he must assert his own needs, and not merely surrender to hers. Likewise, if he does not respect her needs, then her moods come back at him, and he feels paralyzed.

Hank expects to be dancing with the hag for the rest of his life. He has not "overcome her," nor does he wish to do so because he knows she has much to teach him. However, using an analogy from chemistry in which certain atoms combine with other atoms in varying proportions, Hank notes that these days "my valences are balanced." This means that at this time in his life, Hank's emotional chemistry is no longer imbalanced in a frenzied effort to defend against the dark feminine in his marriage, or in himself.

Taking his relationship with the feminine even farther than in his own marriage, Hank sees himself in partnership not only with his wife, but with the earth. Reflecting on his many years of men's work which increasingly included his work with the feminine in himself and in the world, Hank redefined for himself the meaning of the word *husband* — an Old English word which means not only a man joined to a woman, but someone who is a steward, a manager and who uses resources wisely. Today, Hank is "husbanding" not only in relation to his wife, but as an environmental activist who challenges men to join him in husbanding the earth. He passionately believes that as long as men are in fear of and reaction to the dark feminine, they must try to control and possess it. Their attempts to defend against the hag in themselves, in women and in the world, says Hank, cause men to act out their violence upon women and children and incessantly assault the environment.

VALERIE

After several months of working with a number of fairy-tales — including Rapunzel — Valerie, a thirty-five year-old woman with two small children experienced a profound encounter with her feminine shadow. Valerie had grown up with a physically abusive mother and a father who abused her sexually. As the unexpected, youngest child of a troubled, alcoholic mother, Valerie received the brunt of her mother's bitterness and rage. She had only partial hearing in one of her ears as a result of being brutally beaten by her mother and entered adult life feeling scapegoated and targeted by everyone in her life.

Parenting was especially difficult for Valerie as she constantly struggled to contain the rage that was triggered by the neediness of her two year-old daughter. She had been in therapy many years before I met her and clearly understood the darkness of her own inner hag. Not surprisingly, she identified with both the hag and the princess at different times in her life.

In her therapy and in our workshops, she had begun to develop a conscious relationship with her animus — her masculine self. For Valerie, her positive animus often appeared in dreams as a strikingly handsome and benevolent Native American medicine man.

One night Valerie was awakened with a terrifying nightmare and could not go back to sleep. She remembered little of the dream except that she had been chased to the edge of a cliff by a frightening feminine force. She chose to utilize this quiet time in the middle of the night, while her children were asleep, to work with what she called her "deadly predator," using a technique which Carl Jung called *active imagination*.

For many weeks she had been drawing images of her dark feminine predator and now took them out of a large brown envelope where she kept them. She sat with each one for awhile then put them aside as she turned out the light and sat up comfortably in her bed. She mentally took herself to a safe place and imagined herself in a large space capsule which was encased in thick, unbreakable Plexiglas. The capsule was her "control room" which could be seen out of and into, yet remained impenetrable. She imagined that the capsule also had a sound system which enabled her to hear and be heard by anyone outside the capsule. She allowed herself to feel the safety of this imaginary environment, as well as the safety of her actual environment — the comfort and quiet of her home, the support of her therapist, her friends, the validation she had received in our workshops, as well as her spiritual practice.

Having settled herself in the "capsule" and with a potent sense of safety, Valerie opened her awareness to the dark feminine presence that had pursued her in the dream and threatened to erupt in her relationship with her children for as long as she had been a mother. She also invited her "medicine man animus" to sit beside her as she began the process of dialoging with the predator. Soon she noticed what seemed to be a swamp-like, primal creature outside the window of her capsule. She immediately associated it with the creatures in the "Alien" movie series and suddenly found herself identifying with the role played by Sigourney Weaver. As the wet, slimy, horrifying being battered the window of her capsule, attempting to shatter her boundaries and devour her, Valerie continued to breathe and stand her ground. Courageously she mentally shouted, "What do you want from me? Why are you here?"

"I want to destroy you forever," came the reply.

"Why do you want to destroy me?" Valerie asked. "I'm a nobody."

"I want your vitality, your juice, your aliveness," the creature answered.

"Why do you need my aliveness? Don't you have enough of your own?"

"No!" screeched the subterranean monster. "I'm ugly and slimy and filled with rage and pain. But you are beautiful and alive and people listen to you. No one listens to me."

Continuing to breathe, Valerie felt something she had never experienced. She felt empathy for this part of herself — in fact, she felt some sadness and compassion for this demonic force. For the first time in her life she was paying attention to it and feeling something about it besides horror and dread. Nevertheless, she knew she must stand her ground and remain firm with the predator.

Feeling the empowering presence of her animus beside her, she firmly said, "I will not allow you to feed off me and destroy me, but I will listen to you. I don't want to get rid of you anymore, but I won't let you hurt me."

Gradually the battering on the window of Valerie's capsule subsided as she continued to ask the predator to tell her about its pain and rage. Her breathing slowed and became deeper. Her heart stopped pounding and she stopped sweating. No sooner had she noticed these changes in her body than she began growing drowsy, wanting to sleep. She thanked "the alien" for speaking to her and said that she wanted to have a conversation with it some other time. In a few minutes, she was sound asleep and woke up the next morning feeling refreshed.

Valerie had many more conversations with the predator after this one. But in her words, "This experience moved the tectonic plates in my psyche." Over time she became much more patient with her children as she gradually felt more empathy with them. She continued to draw images of the predator, the features of which softened and appeared more human in the months following her first dialog with it. In recent years she has taken painting, pottery and movement classes and learned to play the piano — something she had wanted to do as a child but dared not ask for.

Valerie says she still struggles with low levels of rage. She realizes the depth of the scars from her upbringing, but is delighted to be able to say that she has a life, and questions whether she could have had a life, had she continued to deny her feminine shadow.

Of one thing she is certain: The energy she expended most of her life to keep her "deadly predator" at bay, is now being utilized to craft a life that is truly hers.

Valerie does not attribute the transformation of her life to any one experience of actively imagining the dark feminine in her psyche. Yet, in the context of the diverse forms of healing and support which she had created in her world, her dialog with the deadly predator became a momentous catalyst.

Everyone who breaks the spell of the dark feminine does so in her or his own way. How we do this or where it takes us matters less than our willingness to go into the spell, rather than away from it.

"Now I become myself," writes the poet, May Sarton:

"Now there is time and Time is young.
O, in this single hour I live
All of myself and do not move
I, the pursued, who madly ran,
Stand still, stand still, and stop the sun!"

CHAPTER 9
Coming Home

This is our meditation practice as women, calling back the dead and dismembered aspects of ourselves, calling back the dead and dismembered aspects of life itself... The Creation Mother is always also the Death Mother and vice versa. Because of this dual nature, or double-tasking, the great work before us is to learn to understand what around us and what within us must live, and what must die. Our work is to apprehend the timing of both; to allow what must die to die, and what must live to live.
— Clarissa Pinkola Estés,
Women Who Run With The Wolves

Everyone returns home sometime.   — Rumi

A 1994 headline in a San Francisco Bay Area newspaper "Last-Resort Treatment Punches Holes In The Heart," proclaimed yet another technological feat in Western medicine which punctures the human heart to allow blood to enter capillary muscles and tissues that have been starved by blocked arteries. I was compelled to save the article which seemed to reach in and grab my own heart as I pondered the extent to which modern human beings have literally closed down the heart while techno-corporarchy refines "blasting the heart" to an art form. The story is a metaphor for the tragic dilemma of twenty-first century humanity: How can we re-open our hearts to life, to soul and to our fellow creatures when the heart-murdering forces of the modern world, which cause us to close the heart in the first place, continue to besiege our frail humanity?

Indigenous people living in or on the fringes of European-American civilization tell us that the human race is in a coming home process. But what does this mean? Where is home, and how do we get there? Almost every indigenous tradition reminds us that home is in the heart, but if the heart is closed, how can we open it from within rather than resorting to methods of force and domination?

Contained in fairytales, myths, songs, stories and poems are elements of the indigenous attitude which serve to open the heart and carry us to a new sense of home in the middle of the modern world. On the journey home, this attitude is both a requirement and an outcome. *Indigenous* means "intrinsic" or "innate." It also means "not adaptable."[29]

Another way of seeing the indigenous attitude is to recognize that, no matter how "colonized" or "conquered" one is, a part of the psyche remains that can never be adapted — a part that is indigenous, and this aspect of ourselves is "home." Some part of every human being knows where "home" is, and that is the place which moved millions of people to tears as they fell in love with "E.T." as he innocently, resolutely attempted to "phone home."

Regardless of how non-indigenous our heritage may be, all of us are descendants of indigenous people. The current fascination by non-indigenous people with the ways and traditions of indigenous cultures is indicative, in my opinion, of modern humanity's attraction to the many archetypal energies from which we have become estranged. It is as if we remember our tribal existence and language. Indeed, our indigenous heritage must be present in some part of the psyche or we could not recognize and appreciate it in

---

[29] "Thresholds of Change," January, 1994 lecture by Michael Meade at Marin Headlands, California.

indigenous people. Although we cannot return to the past, we long for and resonate with the songs, stories and drumbeats which call up ancient memories that are far deeper than colonization by a mechanistic world can penetrate.

Indigenous traditions speak of "the ancestors" — energies much larger and older than our deceased grandfathers or grandmothers. They tell us that through stories, drums, singing and dreaming, we can pluck the fibers that reach back to the ancient ones in the spirit world. Some people believe that the key to our survival as a species lies in our ability to connect with these fibers and call forth the assistance of our ancient allies in the ancestral world — a world sometimes referred to as the "other world," the "under world" and the "inner world."

In indigenous traditions it is the elders who are most connected with the ancestral world and can freely summon assistance from that other world. Michael Meade suggests the following four qualities of an elder[30]:

First is *the elder's access to inner resources.* Another way of thinking about this is to notice that the extent to which modern humanity has lost connection with inner resources is the extent to which we have become "colonizers" — dependent on acquiring and controlling the resources of others. Indigenous people have been raised from the cradle to know and utilize their inner resources. How then do modern people, so out of touch with inner resources, reconnect with them?

The Rapunzel fairytale reveals not only the price that humans pay for not being conscious of the shadow, but the necessity of building the ground of one's own gender to wholly relate with the other gender. Cultivating gender ground invariably unearths the shadow, and, as we explore both the feminine and masculine shadow, we begin to develop the domain of our gender which facilitates coming

---

[30] Ibid.

to terms with all of the internal forces depicted in the story: The mother of Rapunzel who desired the rampion; the father who bargained away his child; the hag; the young feminine; the prince and his probable father, the king. As we build firmer gender ground, we refine inner resources which imbue us with the capacity to become elders.

The second quality of the elder is his or her *sense of an inner authority that is larger than external authority*. This is not to suggest that a sense of inner authority entitles one to flagrantly disobey external authority in the name of internal principles. However, one's sense of inner authority is related to a third quality of the elder: courage. The English word *courage* has its origins in the German, French and Greek words for *heart*. The courage of the elder is the courage of having one's heart present and speaking the truth from one's heart rather than defending theories or concepts of the mind.

One example of this kind of courage took place prior to the California State elections of 1994. In that election a majority of California voters affirmed Proposition 187, a referendum which would deny governmental services to illegal immigrants. Even before the election, many health care providers spoke out against the proposition indicating that they would not deny services to undocumented individuals nor would they inform immigration authorities that such individuals had attempted to obtain these services. Hundreds of physicians, nurses and other medical personnel throughout the state went on record to voice their intention to break the law if Proposition 187 were passed. One nurse stated on television that she would go to jail rather than deny services to sick people — a stunning example of speaking the truth of one's heart from an inner authority which one reveres more than the external authority of legalized cruelty.

A fourth quality of an elder is his or her *capacity for survival*. This means not only the ability to live through myriad challenges to one's existence, but the ability to maintain one's indigenous self by finding and touching the fibers that reach back to the ancestors. Connection with the inner indigenous self allows us to survive by living within prescribed limits which originate in the other world. Centuries of alienation from the other-inner-underworld have engendered the colonial mind which has no limits and constantly seeks to expand outward into the territory of other beings in order to survive.

Indigenous people know that real change only occurs when something dies. In the other-inner-underworld, we invariably encounter the hag. The Mother of Life and of Death reminds us of what the indigenous self already knows: *To survive it is essential to realize that everything and everyone is in the process of dying and that it is important to consciously participate in the dying.* In the Rapunzel fairytale, the puerile, colluding young feminine had to die and become exiled in order to give birth and reunite with her beloved. The undeveloped prince who attempted to disown and trick the devouring hag, had to be blinded by her and wander helplessly in darkness in order to join with a mature woman and the child he and she had conceived. Neither Rapunzel nor the prince literally died, but to be sure, very large parts of them did. We live, ironically, in a culture that frantically and heroically disavows death and, in so doing, is decompensating into flagrant collective annihilation. *Paradoxically, it is the acceptance of death as a part of life, whether the death be literal or symbolic, that enriches our lives and enhances our capacity for survival.*

Yet another aspect of survival is *the re-making of language*. The language of modernity is the language of colonization. English is a restricted, stilted language which developed among Europe's shipbuilding and merchant population. It is a masculine language in the sense that its emphasis is on "getting things done." Consequently, the English language does not contain the embellishments or nuances of indigenous languages. Nevertheless, the English language is rooted in the indigenous world, and, if we can play with it poetically, we can eventually "uncolonize" it. For example, as noted earlier, the word *intention* holds within it the word *tension*. As we come to understand that intention is achieved by holding the tension of opposites — as we reflect upon and live our language in a different way — as we sing songs, tell stories and hold poetry in our hearts, we are able to pluck a few fibers that connect us with the ancestors and our indigenous origins.

A fundamental facet of coming home to the indigenous self is ritual. Like all other archetypes, ritual is in our bones. The question is not whether we practice ritual or not, but how?

Do we desire to continue practicing unconscious rituals such as going to the mall, watching Monday night football and perpetually putting unholy substances to which we are addicted into our bodies, or are we committed to practicing sacred rituals in a conscious manner?

In *Ritual, Power, Healing and Community*, Malidoma Somé emphasizes that sacred ritual requires a purpose or an intention. Like the experience of initiation, people engage in ritual all the time. Just as the difference between a sacred initiation and a profane one is intention, the difference between a sacred and a profane ritual has to do with purpose.

I am reminded of a ritual created by a group of women I facilitated during a weekend workshop, the theme of which was "Coming Home." One woman brought her two month-old, female infant knowing that ritual would be an integral part of the weekend and having a sense that it might focus on herself and her child. As we sat in a circle reflecting on what kind of ritual we would like to create, and after calling in the ancestors, the women unhesitatingly chose to create such a ritual. Several intentions for the ritual were verbalized: The blessing of mother and child; the honoring of motherhood in a culture that inadequately supports mothering; the healing of all of our mother wounds; the honoring of the archetypal Mother in every woman; the death of parts of self that need to die and the birth of aspects of the psyche that struggle to come forth in each of us.

The process of creating the ritual was as important, if not more important than the ritual itself. We kept the focus on our bodies and emotions — creating ritual from the heart and not the head. As the facilitator, my role was not to take an active part in devising the ritual but rather to witness the process, hold the energetic container and offer input where necessary regarding practicalities such as time or other physical constraints. As the women listened to their bodies and allowed physical sensations and emotions to come to consciousness, they brainstormed the possibilities, wrote them down, and offered everyone an opportunity to speak and be heard. Gradually, but almost effortlessly, the ritual began to unfold according to what felt true for each of woman.

The setting of the ritual, was a large, sprawling retreat house in the rolling hills of Northern California on eight acres of land bordered by a dense forest. Most of our sessions were conducted in a spacious view of forest and open fields.

During the hours of planning, there was a great deal of clear, focused intention, as well as holding the tension of uncertainty about the outcome. As the plans for the ritual unfolded, we sat in awe of what seemed to be manifesting through us as we called on the help of the spirit world and surrendered to the mysteries. As part of the planning, we allowed space for the shadow aspects of mothering to be acknowledged. Some of the women spoke of times in their experiences of mothering when they were not as assertive as they would have liked to be or when thoughts or images of harming their children came to consciousness amid the stress of insufficient support for their mothering.

As we pondered the opportunity before us, we noted that while we wanted to focus on the birth of a new life and the honoring of motherhood, we also wanted to acknowledge birth's opposite, death. The group decided to honor the death and rebirth process by asking each person to bring with her to the ritual two pieces of paper. On one would be a short statement about some part of herself which was in the process of dying. This piece would be thrown into the fire. On the other piece would be a sentence or two about some part of herself that was trying to be born which would be placed in a special basket on the altar. Upon entering, each woman would have the opportunity to have her face marked with lines of ash, an ancient symbol of death, as well as having petals of dried flowers placed upon her head.

The next morning as the ritual began, mother and child sat on the floor in the middle of the room. Each woman entered the room separately receiving her ashes and flower petals then taking her place in a circle around the mother and infant. The group began chanting an African song which calls in the ancestors of the spirit world, and every woman in the group began weeping as the melody moved us to places of grief, longing, and sorrow. At the end of a very long chant, each woman in the circle spoke words of blessing to the mother and her lovely infant.

As planned the day before, we walked outside together in silence on a crisp autumn morning. Fallen leaves crackled under our feet as we moved down a hill and to the edge of a forest where a very large redwood seemed to preside over the rest of the trees, providing the perfect location for the burial of the pieces of paper on the altar which held our affirmations of rebirth. Wrenching sobs and wailing pierced the silent, chilly air as we all stood weeping under the massive "mother" of all of the surrounding trees. Then one by one, we each dug up a shovel full of dirt, depositing the pieces of paper in the earth with blessings, tears and prayers that the earth might receive and nurture the parts of us that were waiting to be born.

For a few moments in time, every possible aspect of the feminine was present and palpable for each woman. Each woman's story of unwantedness, abuse, neglect and lack of cherishing by a personal mother was felt in the body of each woman in the group. The loneliness and lack of support in mothering experienced by our own mothers and all of the women in the group who were mothers, resonated in each of our bellies. We had created more than a ritual. We had managed to unite each woman's personal history with timeless, colossal forces beyond the sphere of any of our individual lives.

Sitting together again in the meeting room a few minutes later, each woman verbalized what the ritual meant for her, and without exception, each woman felt that we had tapped into the other world and the formidable archetypal energies of the Great Mother. Several women expressed relief in that participation in this ritual which honored both mothering and the new infant, facilitated the healing of their sense of unwantedness in relation to their families of origin. Every woman in the room who was a mother felt deeply moved by such a profound honoring of motherhood which none of the women present had ever experienced before.

The long-term effects of a ritual such as the one this group created will take months and years to process. Nevertheless, the women who took part in it continue to speak of the power and healing the creative process of this particular ritual manifested in their lives. They also insist that opening to the feminine shadow and the Terrible Mother with all of the grief, sorrow and despair which attend those underworld forces, allowed them to heal another piece of their own mother wound as well as the wounding many of them experienced as they became mothers.

Less than one month after the ritual described above, the nation was horrified by news from a rural South Carolina town that a young mother named Susan Smith had confessed to murdering her two young children. The following week, a picture of the assailant mother emblazoned the cover of *Time Magazine* accompanied by the headline: "How Could She!"

In a culture where the demonic aspects of the devouring feminine are split off and polarized from its nurturing and protective aspects, the horror of such a tragedy which took place, ironically, in a little town named Union, bears yet another witness to the ugly reality that the mother archetype has the capacity to create and to destroy. Behind the persona of an apparently innocent young mother who tearfully pled with her sons' fictitious kidnapper to return her children to her, lived Kali in a culture which continues, even in the face of such chilling violence, to disown her.

Coming home is possible only when we have the courage to face the evil and darkness within the psyche and find a way to dialog with it, not only for the purpose of preventing its revolting eruptions in our lives, but to harness its healing and creative power in the quest for personal and planetary transformation. Dialog with the darkness can take place in ritual, in therapy, through art, working with dreams, telling stories, singing songs, writing and speaking poetry — wherever we are willing to risk encountering the myriad energies that dwell in the world of the imagination. Yet we cannot enter that world with a closed heart because we imagine from our hearts rather than our heads. Thus we return to the challenge of holding opposites: Endeavoring to maintain an open heart while hazarding the unknown, frightening possibilities of destruction inherent in the darkness.

Coming home requires participation in death, for only in death can anything or anyone be truly reborn. To come home, we must be willing to create the right "funerals" in our lives and in our communities and shed as many tears as it takes until the losses and deaths are sufficiently grieved.

If we desire a homecoming, we must be willing to struggle with both our individual and cultural complexes, realizing that the transformational process is never finished and that the completion of one initiation is organically linked to the beginning of another. The words of a poignant poem, entitled *Lunch*, written by a friend, Donna Smith, capture the dance between the forces of life and the forces of death:

> *Life and death, the unlikely,*
> *But perfectly suited couple*
> *Lunching at the next table,*
> *Were enamored in their*
> *Favorite conversation*
>
> *As to who suffers more pain*
> *Or more joy. I watched*
> *As death fingered*
> *The iris blue vase, quaint*
> *On the table edge; its single*
> *Full bloom being slowly*
> *Orbited this way and that.*
> *Life leaned closer to appreciate*
> *Any smell, looking pleased,*
> *But making a point of its cut*
> *Nature. "Flowers are nice,"*
> *Death said, adding, "Tomorrow*
> *It will be mine." Life, equally*
> *Possessive, reached over*
> *As if dismissing a slight,*
> *And brushed the perfect petals,*
> *Then straight into death's*
> *Certainty, smiled:*
> *"Until tomorrow then."*

One way home is the path of building our own gender ground, as well as grappling with ways to reconcile with the other gender through conflict, dialog and patient commitment to discovering how we are alike as well as different. For women, this means a willingness to consciously, courageously confront our darkness at the same time we insist that men confront theirs. "Women are not merely kind and sweet, victims of a sexual rapaciousness we want no part of," writes Erica Jong. "Nor," she continues, "are we defanged, declawed, neutered creatures. In the name of a false feminism, we have been asked to pretend to be."[31] Thus, the ways in which we have betrayed ourselves and each other as women must be mourned.

For men, the way home is fraught with facing the terror of the dark feminine and the dark masculine in themselves. It requires a willingness to risk being blinded by the hag and having to wander in the darkness of "not knowing" for as long as it takes to reclaim the desires of a man's heart so that he can come home to the castle of kingship that loves, honors and protects women, children and the earth.

To find his way home, a man must have the courage to encounter the most horrifying fears the hag evokes for him — fear of suffocation and devourment by the feminine, fear of emasculation, fear of defeat and dismemberment, however real or imagined. Only when a man can confront the hag within himself, instead of projecting her onto the women around him, can he come home to grounded, embodied, integrated masculinity.

The way home demands the development of the animus and the anima. It forces women and men to encounter both Rapunzel and the prince in the psyche. It necessitates confrontation with the insatiable mother who craves the rampion as well as with the faltering father who is willing to bargain the future of his child. And above all, the way home requires numerous encounters with the hag.

There is no "happily ever after," and hags never die. Physics has shown that energy can be transformed, but cannot be made to disappear. Complexes cannot be destroyed,

---

[31] Erica Jong, *Fear of Fifty* (NY: Harper Collins, 1994), p.290.

but they can lose much of their autonomy and power in the psyche. Human beings can change, permanently and profoundly, yet scars remain. Evidences of former struggles stay with us, but if we are faithful to the calling of our hearts homeward, it may be possible not to annihilate the weapons which nearly destroyed us, but one day experience them as irreparably damaged "souvenirs" of our commitment to becoming whole — as this dream with which I was gifted a few years ago suggests:

> *I dream that I am in my mother's house and I see a very frightening pair of her shears which are meant for my destruction. They are slightly damaged but are still instruments of death. I steal them, running out of the house and down the street through many yards and past many buildings. I am terrified that I will be found out. But I am on a mission to put these shears in a place where she will never find them. I look for trash containers and places where they will never be discovered by her. As the dream ends, I don't remember getting rid of them, but what I do remember is that they have become broken and damaged while I still have them.*

Coming home does not happen automatically or without effort. Whether we are women or men, coming home requires consciousness of the vastness and complexity of the feminine shadow and a willingness to struggle with it. Within the feminine shadow dwells the raw material of magnificent creativity and extraordinary transformation. Engaging with the dark feminine offers no cure, no exemption from suffering, nor does it come with any guarantees. Some individuals, nevertheless, have found it worth the pain and perils inherent in the process as Octavio Paz writes in his poem, *After:*

*After I cut off the arms of those who reached out to
  me,
And after I boarded up all the windows and the
  doors,
And after I built my house on a knoll inaccessible to
  flattery and fear,
And after I filled my pit with poisonous water,
And after I forgot my name and name of my
  birthplace
and the name of my race,
And after I hurled monosyllables of scorn and
pocketfuls of silence at my loves
And after I judged myself and sentenced myself to
perpetual waiting and perpetual loneliness,
I heard, on the stones of my dungeon of syllogisms,
The sweet, tender, humid, sensitive sound
of the onset of spring and the return of spirit.*

Epilogue

As this book goes to press more than thirty years after the birth of the women's movement in this country, numerous books and periodicals are beginning to address the wholeness of the feminine psyche, including its dark side. There is new fascination with the Goddess — the Black Madonna, the Wild Woman — unprecedented in the modern world, and many women and men are meeting Her in their dreams, in mid-life crises, in illness and in the innumerable initiations with which the psyche presents all of us on the threshold of a new millennium.

A significant number of men involved with what I have referred to here as the "mythopoetic men's movement" in the eighties and early nineties are no longer part of a movement, *per se,* but are making a difference by taking the inner healing experienced in men's work into the world. An article in *The Christian Science Monitor* notes that while men are in turmoil about their roles in society, many men from the so-called men's movement are reaching out in their communities and in their relationships with women in struggle for social change and environmental restoration.[32] The same men, scoffed at by the media a few years ago for hugging trees and beating drums, are now toiling to end male violence and become responsible stewards of the earth.

Women, particularly as we enter the initiatory ground of our menopausal years, are discovering that the dark femi-

---

[32] "A Second Wave of Ethusiasm for Brotherhood," *Christian Science Monitor,* 16 April 1996, front page.

nine to which we were oblivious in our younger, idyllic years during the sexual revolution, is alive and well in our bodies and screams for our attention through hormonal shifts, chronic fatigue, cancer and compromised immune systems. We sense that in our aging, thinning bones, we carry the memory of witch burnings and five thousand years of patriarchal denunciation of the feminine principle.

Nearly as many books on gender and relationships between women and men abound as books on the Goddess. Gender awareness and sexual harassment trainings flourish in the workplace. Yet as women continue to gain equality and as women and men seem to interface more than at any time since the Industrial Revolution, we all continue to exist under an oppressive paradigm — call it patriarchy, techno-corporarchy, modernity — which at its core abhors the dark feminine, yet at the same time is utterly possessed by her. Only a society in severe decline could tolerate the expenditure of millions of dollars to investigate the alleged transgressions of Hillary Clinton and at the same time fail to become outraged by the fact that the National Rifle Association now has a *female* president.

During the final weeks before the publication of this book, I had a personal experience which I am compelled to mention here. Upon returning home one evening I was approached by my next-door neighbor, a man in his late thirties who told me that earlier that evening, he had witnessed two adolescent boys vandalizing my car while it was parked in front of my house. He tried to run after them but remembered that one never knows these days which teenagers are carrying guns and which aren't, so he called the police. A few days later, after my car was repaired, it was again parked for a brief time on the street. Another neighbor from across the street overheard two adolescent boys walking past my car and commenting, "Isn't that the car we fucked up the other night?"

This experience brought home to me in a very personal manner, the epidemic proportions of meaningless, random, senseless, violence and destructiveness being inflicted upon our "sibling society" by enraged adolescent males. I felt fortunate that neither my body nor my home had been harmed, *and* I began to reflect on what this incident might be trying to sat to me.

Criminologists are now telling us that adolescent crime is increasing so exponentially that ten years from now, we will look back at 1996 as "the good ole days." Men who work closely in mentoring relationships with young inner city males — men such as Michael Meade, Malidoma Somé and Orland Bishop repeatedly remind us that if these young males are not initiated into the sacred rites of manhood, they will unequivocally incinerate the entire culture.

So far, gender feminism has opposed all attempts to initiate young men, erroneously equating it with the profane rituals of fraternity hazing. Groups of men gathering together to grieve the trauma of war, the loss of their fathers or to initiate young men have been perceived by gender feminists as inherently part of a backlash against women. I find this frightening in the face of the surging violence of young males which has the potential to overturn three decades of advances made for women. Women need to support the mentoring process. We need to rethink political feminism's opposition to all-male high schools and colleges. In the face of the escalating fire storms of young male violence, we need to ask ourselves if supporting the well-intentioned aspirations of promising young women like Shannon Faulkner to enroll in all-male institutions is the most skillful application of our efforts to alleviate anarchy and the burgeoning bloodbaths in our city *and* suburban streets.

I hasten to add that I do not support taking away resources from young women, but rather I call upon gender feminists to consider that girls joining gangs and the teen pregnancy — "babies-having-babies" — phenomenon are not only an inevitable consequence of the patriarchal oppression of females but are inextricably connected with the suffering of young men and the absence of positive masculine presence in the lives of both boys and girls. In adolescence as in adulthood, when one gender suffers, so does the other.

No work in the world is more imperative, than the work of female and male elders reaching out to mentor young women and men. Being an elder has little to do with age and much more to do with how much we have uncolonized ourselves and to what extent we are living our lives from an inner attitude of indigenousness. In order to accomplish this, we must confront the dark feminine within ourselves and within our culture. We must comprehend that a twelve year-old girl having a baby whom she believes will finally be the person who never abandons her and the fourteen year-old boy doing a "drive-by," are manifestations of the same hag we have been busy disowning, both individually and collectively, since we inherited Hiroshima from the previous generation.

Women and men must now examine their own hearts and determine the extent to which we are willing to take our place in the paradigm that threatens to annihilate all of us — and our planet. In this book I have offered some insights about how individuals and the cultural paradigm might be transformed. The most urgent work any of us can do, in my opinion is the work of acknowledging the dark Goddess in ourselves and in the culture, consciously engaging with Her, thereby allowing Her, in all of Her exquisite beauty *and* formidability to infuse us with Her wondrous creativity and bring forth the rebirth of our bodies, our relationships and our ecosystems.

— Santa Rosa, California 1996

Glossary of Terms

Anima: The unconscious feminine aspect of a man's personality. The anima is often revealed in dreams by images such as a hag, a seductress, a queen or other feminine images. The anima influences how a man relates to others and also affects his emotional life. If he becomes unconsciously "possessed" by his anima, he may seem moody, effeminate or overly sensitive. If a man represses his anima, he may act it out through behaviors associated with the violent or chaotic aspects of the feminine archetype. The wounding of a man's anima prevents him from appreciating and expressing the full range of his emotions.

Animus: The unconscious masculine side of a woman's personality. Whereas the anima in a man influences his relatedness, the animus is the aspect of a woman that thinks, reasons, and achieves in the world. The animus influences a woman's ability to focus her attention on her creativity and what she needs to accomplish, as well as her ability to have her own voice and speak her truth. If a woman is unconsciously "possessed" by her animus, she may become rigid, opinionated, controlling, argumentative. The wounding of a woman's animus prevents her from developing and maintaining her boundaries.

Archetypes: Universal themes or motifs found in religions, dreams, myths and fairytales throughout the world regardless of cultural differences. Carl Gustav Jung believed that archetypes reside in the personal unconscious of each individual as well as in the collective unconscious of humanity. Common archetypal themes are those such as the mother, father, savior, scapegoat, hero, heroine, divine child, and wounded healer.

Complex: An internalized and "charged" configuration of psychic energy associated with childhood experiences and archetypal energies. For example, Jung held that the Mother archetype resides in the unconscious of every individual. A *mother complex* is a particular configuration of psychic energy which evolves as a result of the distillation of the mother archetype with one's experiences of a personal mother. It is often referred to as the "introjected" mother. Complexes contain both positive and negative attributes.

Ego: The part of the personality identified as "me." It is the gatekeeper of the conscious mind which serves to contain feelings, images and impulses of the unconscious mind. While the ego is only a very small part of the human psyche, its role as gatekeeper is essential in protecting the personality from becoming overwhelmed by the contents of the unconscious. Like an orchestra conductor, the ego regulates which parts of the psyche, both conscious and unconscious, will be "heard" at any given time.

Feminine Principle: An archetypal energy in the psyche that exists prior to and supersedes socialization in a culture. The feminine functions in the psyches of both female and male individuals. In mythology, art, dreams and fairytales, the Feminine is characterized by relatedness, sensitivity, creativity, nurturing, chaos, and organic process rather than linear productivity. The Feminine contains both light and dark attributes.[33]

---

[33] From the perspective of the psyche, "light" and "dark" are meaningless. In the psyche, the energies of archetypes and complexes are whole. It is the conscious mind and the human feeling function that categorize these energies into "light" and "dark" or "positive" and "negative."

Masculine Principle: An archetypal energy in the psyche that exists prior to and supersedes socialization in a culture. The masculine function exists in the psyches of both male and female individuals. In mythology, art, dreams and fairytales, the Masculine is characterized by achievement, thinking, rationality, generativity, order, focus, intention, protection, assertiveness and empowerment. The Masculine contains both light and dark attributes.

Shadow: Any part of the psyche which is disowned or perceived as "not me." It is unconscious and contains traits which the ego rejects or ignores. The shadow is not always dark. It holds any disowned aspects of the self which an individual may have unconsciously rejected at an earlier time in order to survive. It is possible to reclaim many aspects of the shadow and thereby increase psychic energy.

Soul: The animating, feeling, expressive, imaginative aspect of humanity and the world, as distinct from the intellect. Sometimes used synonymously with the *psyche*. The soul or psyche is both individual and collective, conscious and unconscious. The soul pertains to matters of the heart and is the essence of our human-ness in both its light and dark aspects.

Techno-Corporarchy: A term coined by author Sam Keen and used extensively in his book *Fire In The Belly*. Keen replaces the term "patriarchy" with "techno-corporarchy" to convey the reality that both women and men in Western civilization are wounded by a system of power and control which Keen calls "the war, work and gender-role ethic," originating from the values of technological superiority and corporate hierarchy.

About the Author

Carolyn Baker is a consultant, educator and storyteller living in Northern California. She holds a B.A. in history and an M.S. and Ph.D. in Health and Human Services. She is the Director of Fourth World Institute which offers education and healing processes in eco-psychology, gender reconciliation, cross-cultural awareness, environmental interdependence, transitioning from old to new paradigms, ritual, and sacred space. She is an acclaimed workshop facilitator and has written and taught for many years from an archetypal, transpersonal perspective on the Dark Feminine.

Carolyn Baker may be contacted at:

P.O. Box 15185
Santa Rosa, CA 95402
U.S.A.

or via electronic mail (email) at:

CBaker1996@aol.com

TO[...]
FAINTING
KEEP REPEATING,
IT'S ONLY A MOVIE
..ONLY A MOVIE
..ONLY A MOVIE
..ONLY A MOVIE
..ONLY A MOVIE
..ONLY A MOVIE

Wes Craven's Last House On The Left:
The Making of a Cult Classic

First edition published October 1997
This revised edition published June 2000

FAB Press, PO Box 178, Guildford, Surrey, GU3 2YU, England, U.K.
(email: info@fabpress.com)

Text copyright © 2000 David A. Szulkin

Designed by Harvey Fenton
Typesetting and Layout by Harvey Fenton and David Flint
Printed and bound in Great Britain by The Cromwell Press Ltd.Trowbridge, Wiltshire.

This Volume copyright © FAB Press 2000
World Rights Reserved.
No part of this book may be reproduced or transmitted in any form or by any means, electronic or mechanical, including photocopying, recording, or by any information storage and retrieval system, without the prior written permission of the Publisher.

Illustrations from the collections of David A. Szulkin and Roy Frumkes.
All on-set photographs are used by courtesy of Wes Craven.

Back cover photograph:
Sadism incarnate. The killers loom over Mari as Krug prepares to inscribe his name in her flesh.

A CIP catalogue record for this book is available from the British Library

ISBN 1 903254 01 9

About the Author

David Szulkin is a freelance writer based in Los Angeles. He holds a degree in film from New York University, and has been a contributor to Fangoria magazine since 1989. He served as a script reader for Miramax Films and Laurel Entertainment, and has gone on to work as a video editor, grant writer and publicist for movies and television. Mr. Szulkin was honored as an invited guest speaker at the Harvard Film Archive in 1999, and is currently writing his second book.

Author's Acknowledgements

The author would like to thank Wes Craven for his generous cooperation and assistance.

Thank to the following for their invaluable contributions to this book:

Marshall Anker, Steve Chapin, Sean Cunningham, Steve Dwork, Lucy Grantham, Yvonne Hannemann, David Hess, Jim Hubbard, Martin Kove, Fred Lincoln, George Mansour, Steve Miner, Sandra Peabody, Jeramie Rain, Marc Sheffler, Richard Towers and David Whitten.

Additional thanks: Cerise at Wes Craven Films, David Beach, Russell Bello, Robert Bonica, Grant Dodds, Art Ettinger, Greg Herger, George Maranville, Ross Markonish, Jared Mazzaschi, Phil Palmieri, Gerald Peary, Rich Pontius, Steve Puchalski, Jon Putnam, John Quackenbush, Joel Shepard, Rick Sullivan, Evan Torchin, and Robert Valenzi.

Special thanks to Harvey Fenton and Roy Frumkes for their help in making it happen.

Publisher's Acknowledgements

Deborah Bacci, Bill Bennett, Francis Brewster, Paul J. Brown, Nigel Burrell, Mitch Davis, David Flint, Julian Grainger, Graf Haufen, David Kerekes, Jean-Paul Lacmant, Marc Morris, Tom Skulan, Claire Thompson and everyone else involved in the production, promotion and distribution of the first edition of this book.

Wes Craven's
LAST HOUSE ON THE LEFT
The Making of a Cult Classic

David A. Szulkin

A FAB PRESS PUBLICATION

CONTENTS

To Avoid Fainting, Keep Repeating:
It's Only A Movie... Only A Movie... Only A Movie 7

Planning The Sex Crime Of The Century 23

Babes In The Woods:
A Crash Course In Guerilla Film Making 45

Cutting, Slashing, Slicing And Dicing 101

Krug Plays A Mean Guitar:
The Musical Score 118

The Launching Of A Thousand Lunches 127

Now You See It, Now You Don't:
In Search Of The Uncensored 160

Rip-Offs And Rehashes 171

Last Thoughts On The House 188

Appendix I:
Selected Filmographies 192

Appendix II:
The Shooting Schedule 208

Appendix III:
The Ballad 210

Appendix IV:
Props and Equipment list for Night of Vengeance shoot 212

Index 213

Last House on the Left: Credits

Note: Credits vary according to which print of the film is viewed. All information shown in italics is not shown on screen in any version, and is presented here for reference purposes only.

"The events you are about to witness are true. Names and locations have been changed to protect those individuals still living."

Sean Cunningham Films Ltd. presents

THE LAST HOUSE ON THE LEFT
(U.S. release under this title on 23 August 1972*)

© 1972 The Night Co. all rights reserved

director of cinematography Victor Hurwitz
original music by David Alexander Hess
(and Steve Chapin (uncredited))
produced by Sean S. Cunningham
written & directed by Wes Craven

Sandra Cassell *(Mari Collingwood)*
Lucy Grantham *(Phyllis Stone)*
David A. Hess *(Krug Stillo)*
Fred Lincoln *(Fred "Weasel" Padowski)*
Jeramie Rain *(Sadie)*
Marc Sheffler *(Junior Stillo)*
Gaylord St. James *(Dr. John Collingwood)*
Cynthia Carr *(Mrs. Estelle Collingwood)*
Ada Washington *(Ada - driver of chicken truck)*
Marshall Anker *(sheriff)*
Martin Kove *(deputy)*
Ray Edwards *(mail man)*
[uncredited]: Jonathan Craven (kid with balloon)

film editor Wes Craven. assistant editor Stephen Miner.
costume design Susan E. Cunningham. assistant director Yvonne Hanneman.
associate producer Katherine D'Amato. sound Jim Hubbard. gaffer Dick Donovan.
production assistant Steve Miner. production assistant Steve Dwork.
wardrobe & make-up Anne Paul. special effects Troy Roberts.
mix R.S.I. sound mixer Gary Leibman. opticals & blow-up The Optical House.
title design David Miner. unit production manager Larry Beinhart.
color by Movielab.

On all versions except Canadian, British, Dutch and Japanese video releases:
a film from Lobster Enterprises.
Sean S. Cunningham Films Ltd.

alternate / test-marketing titles:
KRUG & COMPANY
*(July 1972 theatrical release title; played for one week under this title;
also shown once in the UK under this title)*
SEX CRIME OF THE CENTURY
*(original title of the script;
played briefly under this title in upstate New York, summer 1972)*
THE MEN'S ROOM
(very briefly shown under this title in upstate New York, summer 1972)
NIGHT OF VENGEANCE
(shooting title)

* **Note:** Although the onscreen credits name the film **THE** LAST HOUSE ON THE LEFT, most press material and advertising is missing the article. Since all of those involved in making the film refer to it as 'LAST HOUSE ON THE LEFT' or simply 'LAST HOUSE', this is how the film will be referred to herein.

Chapter 1

To Avoid Fainting, Keep Repeating:
It's Only A Movie... Only A Movie... Only A Movie...

"When Sean Cunningham and I made Last House on the Left, our attitude was that we were going to do this tiny little film for a company in Boston, and it was only going to be shown in two or three theaters up there. Nobody was ever going to see it, and nobody was ever going to know that we did it. So we essentially said, 'Let's be as bad boys as we can. We're going to show things that people have never seen before on a movie screen, we'll pull out all the stops, and just do whatever the hell we want.' And by doing this, we were basically going to teach ourselves how to make a feature film."
- director Wes Craven

"Last House on the Left was a singular anomaly... the strangest film I've ever worked on, and at the same time, the most realistic one."
- actor David Hess

On October 2, 1971, in the town of Westport, Connecticut, a small film crew led by writer/director Wes Craven and producer Sean Cunningham began shooting a low-budget exploitation movie called *Night of Vengeance*. No one could have guessed that the two struggling, inexperienced filmmakers were on the verge of a defining moment in their careers, or that *Night of Vengeance* would become the controversial horror classic *Last House on the Left*.

Loosely based on Ingmar Bergman's *The Virgin Spring*, *Last House on the Left* was released in 1972 and marked Craven's directorial debut. The film tells the sordid tale of two hippie girls abducted, raped, and butchered by a fugitive 'family' of four degenerates. When they unwittingly seek refuge at the home of one of their victims, the killers meet with the bizarre, gruesome revenge of the murdered girl's parents. The movie's audaciously violent and perverse sensibility, along with its twisted humor and home-made, underground style, made it an instant cult hit, despised by many critics and celebrated by its fans. Craven has characterized *Last House* as "anti-social," "a howl of anger and pain," "a real thing of rage," "a protest film," and "the primal scream of my cinema."

Love it or loathe it, *Last House* was undeniably a landmark in the evolution of modern horror, predating Tobe Hooper's *The Texas Chainsaw Massacre* even in the use of a chainsaw as a murder weapon. Radically departing from the comic-book escapism of monster movies, *Last House* delved into the disturbing milieu of human depravity and murderous sexual sadism. While schlock director Herschell Gordon Lewis invented the "splatter movie" in the 1960s (his 1969 film *The Wizard of Gore* also featured a chainsaw sequence), *Last House* launched splatter into the '70s with a gritty realism far more unsettling than the patently ludicrous, campy theatrics of the Lewis gut-churners. Crude and confrontational, *Last House* hit a raw nerve

THE EVENTS YOU ARE ABOUT TO WITNESS ARE TRUE. NAMES AND LOCATIONS HAVE BEEN CHANGED TO PROTECT THOSE INDIVIDUALS STILL LIVING

It's Only A Movie...

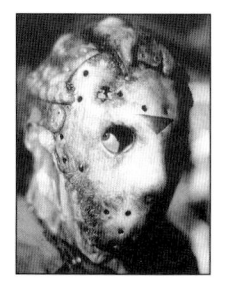

(right)
Freddy Krueger of Wes Craven's *A Nightmare on Elm Street* was named after Krug, one of the villains in *Last House on the Left*.

(above)
Friday the 13th's Jason owes his existence to *Last House* producer Sean Cunningham.

seldom touched before or since; in its warped reflection of the peace-and-love era, it is truly the Altamont of horror films.

In retrospect, *Last House on the Left* is all the more groundbreaking in that it paved the way for the influential latter-day efforts of its director and producer. Were it not for *Last House*, Wes Craven might never have had the inclination or the opportunity to make *The Hills Have Eyes* (1977), *A Nightmare on Elm Street* (1984), or the phenomenally successful *Scream* (1996). Likewise, Sean Cunningham deliberately harkened back to the shock-horror aesthetic of *Last House* when he conceived the idea for the original *Friday the 13th* (1980). Thus, *Last House* indirectly stands as grand-daddy to all the bastard sons of Freddy and Jason who stalked the silver screen during the 1980s. With *Scream* and its sequels, Craven has come full circle, simultaneously parodying and perpetuating the genre he indirectly helped to create with his first film.

LAST HOUSE ON THE LEFT

Of course, beyond the obvious blood-and-guts, *Last House on the Left* bears no resemblance to the '80s slice 'n' dice pictures exemplified by *Friday the 13th* or the self-referential slasher-*chic* of *Scream* and its recent imitators. Cunningham succinctly delineated the difference between the brutality of *Last House* and the gory campfire story of *Friday the 13th* in a 1980 interview: "If you examine it, *Last House on the Left* has a sort of cynical edge to it. It seems to say, 'You want horror? Well, here's *real* horror.' *Friday the 13th*, on the other hand, is a roller-coaster ride, a funhouse sort of thing."[1]

"I don't think *Last House* was really the progenitor of those [slasher] movies," Craven says. "The violence in *Friday the 13th* was bizarre, but it wasn't real; it was goofy. I was more interested in psychological underpinnings and irony... and I think Sean discovered that he was much more interested in being entertaining rather than assaultive. *Last House* didn't allow you to have fun at all."

Craven and Cunningham are the first to admit that *Last House* was the roughly-hewn product of amateurs who were, in Cunningham's words, "out there inventing the wheel." Yet the movie packs a powerful impact both in spite of and, at times, *because* of its very lack of polish and professionalism. The film's Super 16mm newsreel-style cinematography brought an unsettling immediacy to its woodsy scenes of torture and terror; a slick Hollywood production could hardly have evoked the same aura of menace. Of course, the grainy film stock and shaky, hand-held camera were mostly a matter of necessity; the quasi-documentary style was the only one the filmmakers knew, and the only method feasible on a shoestring budget. Similarly, the energy of the film's cast of unknowns contributed greatly to its unnerving quality; the presence of big name stars would undoubtedly have made the picture less convincing.

Despite its technical flaws, *Last House* shows that even as a beginner, Wes Craven had a knack for capturing an audience through stories which play on basic human fears. The director attributes this strength to his background as an academic and a lifelong passion for literature and mythology. Indeed, *Last House* owes its basic narrative to an ancient legend, and the process of adapting this story awakened Craven to his own talent for creating modern tales of terror.

David Hess poses with a machete during a break in filming. This rare behind-the-scenes shot was originally published in *Video Viewer And Monthly TV Movie Guide*, Vol.2, number 8, Feb. 1983.

It's Only A Movie...

A shot from the opening scene of Ingmar Bergman's *The Virgin Spring*. Bergman's Oscar-winning film inspired the storyline of *Last House on the Left*.

The Story

The relationship between *Last House on the Left* and Ingmar Bergman's 1960 Academy Award winner *The Virgin Spring* has been alternately denied and over-emphasized by various critics. The credits of *Last House* include no mention of the source material, and the film begins instead with a phony documentary-style disclaimer that "The events you are about to witness are true. Names have been changed to protect those individuals still living." Craven himself confirms that he used the basic structure of Bergman's film as a dramatic template without expecting anyone to notice the resemblance.

The Virgin Spring was inspired by a medieval legend known in fourteenth century Sweden as *Tore's Daughter in Vange*. In Bergman's brooding film, Karin (Birgitta Petterson), the pampered, virginal daughter of farmer Tore (Max von Sydow) is sent by her mother Mareta (Birgitta Valberg) on a pilgrimage to the village church. Despite her mother's objections, Karin asks to be accompanied on the journey by her wild, adopted sister Ingeri (Gunnel Lindblom), a pagan servant girl who is pregnant with an illegitimate child.

While traveling through the forest, Karin is separated from Ingeri and subsequently waylaid by a trio of roving herdsmen. The nameless clan of vagabond brothers consists of a dissolute leader (Axel Duberg), his mute henchman (Tor Isedal), and a small boy (Ove Porath). After a brief seduction, during which Karin naively succumbs to the strangers' flattery, the encounter turns hostile. The two men rape and murder the innocent girl, while the boy only watches the crime in horror. Hidden in the nearby brush, Ingeri also witnesses the incident, but does nothing to prevent it.

It's Only A Movie...

By a quirk of fate, the goatherds later appear at Tore's doorstep seeking shelter. Tore welcomes them into his home and offers them dinner. During the meal, the youngest of the guests recognizes a prayer as one recited by Karin, and becomes nauseous with guilt. He is haunted by the crime and the image of the dead girl. The murderers later betray themselves when their leader attempts to sell Mareta a distinctive item of Karin's clothing. Mareta alerts Tore to her suspicions, and the truth about Karin's fate is confirmed by the remorseful Ingeri, who has returned to the farm. Tore plots revenge on the killers, and at dawn, he slaughters them in a violent rage. The vengeful patriarch even breaks the twelve year old boy's neck by hurling him against a wall, afterwards sobbing, "God have mercy on me for what I have done!"

Tore, Mareta, and Ingeri then go with a party of servants to retrieve Karin's body from the woods. Upon finding the slain girl, they are consumed by despair. Tore cries out to God: "You see it and you allow it. The innocent child's death and my revenge, you allowed it! I don't understand you!" Searching for meaning in the tragedy and seeking to atone for his murderous deeds, Tore vows to build a church at the site of his daughter's death. These pleas for divine forgiveness are answered when a magical spring bursts forth from the ground beneath Karin's body.

In *Last House on the Left,* Craven ingeniously adapted this simple, compelling story to 1970s America, embellishing the events with an ample dose of shock value and filtering the tale through an irreverent counter-culture sensibility. Where *The Virgin Spring* resolved in a somber, holy rebirth, *Last House* left nothing sacred and offered no hope of redemption.

Last House on the Left begins in the rural Connecticut home of a middle-class American family, the Collingwoods. We meet Mari Collingwood, a beautiful, naive flower child one day shy of sweet seventeen, and her parents: John, a doctor (Gaylord St. James) and wife Estelle (Cynthia Carr). Mari's parents warn her about the "bad neighborhood" where she and her friend, the rebellious Phyllis Stone (Lucy Grantham), are going to attend a concert by a violent rock group called Bloodlust. Although Mari's parents argue with her over typical generation-gap issues of the day, John reveals his soft spot for his daughter with an early birthday present: a necklace with a peace symbol pendant.

Driving to the concert, the girls tune into a radio broadcast detailing the prison escape of two dangerous criminals. This leads to the introduction of the movie's villains. The lead baddie, Krug Stillo (David Hess) is a domineering, violent brute whose past crimes include "the 1966 triple-slaying of a priest and two nuns"; his sidekick, Fred "Weasel" Padowski (Fred Lincoln) is a cold-blooded psychopath noted for "child molesting, Peeping Tom-ism and assault with a deadly weapon." The cons are traveling with two accomplices: Krug's junkie son Junior (Marc Sheffler) and Krug's "animal-like" bi-sexual mistress Sadie (Jeramie Rain). Although the criminals are planning to leave the state, Sadie complicates their agenda by refusing to sexually gratify Krug and Weasel until they bring her "a coupla chicks" to satisfy her craving for "equal representation."

Arriving in the seedy East Village neighborhood where the concert is to be held, Mari and Phyllis walk around looking to "score on some good grass." They approach the loitering Junior, who lures them

It's Only A Movie...

The worst is yet to come for Mari and Phyllis...

back to the criminals' hideout with a promise of an ounce of Colombian pot. By doing this, Junior hopes to please his 'family' and obtain a heroin fix from his father, who controls him through his drug habit. Realizing too late that they have walked into a trap, the two girls are taken hostage by the gang. While Mari looks on in terror, Phyllis is beaten and raped. Even as this grim turn of events unfolds, Mari's parents busy themselves preparing a birthday celebration for their daughter.

The following morning, the villains force the girls into the trunk of their getaway car and drive out of the city, ostensibly heading for Canada. Meanwhile, concerned over Mari's absence, Mr. and Mrs. Collingwood call in the local sheriff (Marshall Anker). The redneck cop and his dim-witted deputy (Martin Kove) prove to be of little help, complacently munching on Mari's birthday cake and mouthing useless platitudes.

By happenstance, the criminals' car breaks down directly across the street from the Collingwood residence. Unaware of the bizarre coincidence, the criminals take the captive girls into the nearby woods, aiming to "have a little fun" while they are stranded in the remote area. As she is dragged away, Mari's eyes widen in shock when she spots the mailbox marking the entrance to her home.

Leaving the Collingwood house, the two bungling cops pass right by the criminals' abandoned car. The lawmen decide not to investigate the suspicious vehicle; the sheriff proclaims, 'We've got more important things to do... that ain't gonna find us Mari Collingwood.'

In the isolated, idyllic forest, the criminals subject the two girls to a harrowing ordeal of sexual torture and humiliation. Junior does not participate in the cruelty, and begs Krug to stop when the proceedings turn violent. When Krug leaves the scene, Phyllis decides to make a run for it, distracting the villains and allowing Mari to go for help. While

It's Only A Movie...

Phyllis is stabbed in the back by Weasel after her escape attempt is thwarted in an isolated graveyard.

Sadie and Weasel chase Phyllis through the woods, Mari convinces Junior to help her escape, promising him a fix from her father's medical supply. As a token of friendship, Mari gives Junior her peace-symbol necklace.

At police headquarters, the sheriff and his deputy hear a radio bulletin describing the killers' car. Recalling the sight of the abandoned car near the Collingwood home, the cops roar off to save the day. Unfortunately, the police cruiser runs out of gas and the two buffoons spend the remainder of the film futilely attempting to hitch a ride in a number of broadly comic scenes.

Eluding her pursuers, Phyllis makes her way to an old cemetery on the edge of the highway. Just as she is about to escape to freedom, Phyllis runs into a machete-wielding Krug. At the same moment, Sadie and Weasel emerge from the woods behind her. The horrified girl realizes she is doomed, as the three killers close in on her. Weasel knifes Phyllis in the small of the back, then kicks the fallen girl repeatedly as his companions look on in predatory satisfaction. Phyllis crawls off into the woods, but Sadie, Krug and Weasel easily catch up with her. The three sadists savagely stab Phyllis to death, stopping only when she is finally disemboweled.

As they attempt to flee across the street to the Collingwood house, Mari and Junior run into the blood-spattered trio of maniacs by the edge of a pond. Cornered by the murderers, Mari fearfully asks if Phyllis managed to escape. Weasel silently answers her by dropping Phyllis' severed hand on the ground. Krug throws himself upon Mari, carving his name into her chest with a switchblade and brutally raping her. In the aftermath of the rape, the criminals finally realize the horror of their own actions, appearing guilty and disgusted by what they have done. In a trance, Mari wades into the pond, whereupon Krug grimly takes a gun from Weasel and shoots the defenseless, dazed girl.

LAST HOUSE ON THE LEFT

After changing clothes, the killers show up on the Collingwoods' doorstep (with the withdrawal-wracked Junior in tow) looking to call a mechanic. Since the Collingwoods' phone is broken (a contrivance established earlier in the film) and the house is "in the middle of nowhere," the killers accept the parents' hospitality. Although the killers attempt to masquerade as plumbers and insurance salesmen, the Collingwoods sense something unsettling about their guests.

The criminals are the first to realize that they have unwittingly entered the home of their victim when they see a photo of Mari; the parents' suspicions are subsequently aroused when Estelle notices Mari's peace-symbol necklace dangling around Junior's neck. Finding bloody clothes in the killers' suitcase, and overhearing an incriminating conversation between Junior and Krug, Estelle realizes the full truth of the situation. The Collingwoods find Mari by the edge of the pond, but are too late to save their daughter's life. Bringing Mari's body with them, they return home to take vengeance on the murderers.

Estelle lures the lecherous Weasel out of the house by seducing him, while John searches for weapons and booby-traps the house to prevent the other three from escaping.

Tying Weasel's hands behind his back on a pretext of kinky sex, Estelle takes a most painful revenge on the villain by biting off his member during fellatio. Weasel's screams awaken Krug and Sadie, who find John standing over them with a shotgun. However, neither the shotgun nor the elaborate traps are a match for Krug, and a fight follows in which Krug gains the upper hand, taunting and pummeling the doctor.

Suddenly, a shot rings out and Krug whirls around to find Junior shakily pointing a pistol at him and threatening to kill him. Unfazed by the attempt, Krug orders his snivelling son to kill himself instead. Buckling under to his father's bullying commands ("Blow your brains out!") Junior puts the gun in his own mouth and pulls the trigger.

As Junior crumples to the floor, Krug realizes that Dr. Collingwood has sneaked off amid the confusion. The vengeful doctor then emerges from the basement of the house, wielding a roaring buzzsaw. While Krug attempts to fend off the chainsaw attack, Sadie manages to make it out the front door, where she runs into Estelle. A struggle between the two women ensues, during which Sadie accidentally falls into a swimming pool in the Collingwoods' yard.

The sheriff and his deputy finally arrive on the scene, but are too late to intervene. In a frenzy of carnage, John beheads Krug with the chainsaw, while Estelle simultaneously slashes Sadie's throat. In the wake of the slaughter, Mr. and Mrs. Collingwood are left bloodied and dazed, exhausted and seemingly debased by their own violence.

The Meaning Behind the Mayhem

Both Craven and Cunningham have asserted that the excessive bloodshed and brutality in *Last House on the Left* were meant as a backhanded protest against violence and its sanitized portrayal in movies and television. Cynics argue that the movie exploits the very violence it purports to decry, and that the filmmakers' defense of *Last House* is merely an excuse for wallowing in gore and degradation. A close examination of the film and the way in which it came about reveals that both opposing arguments hold some truth.

It's Only A Movie...

True, *Last House* was first and foremost an exploitation flick; such was the nature of the assignment handed to Craven by the film's financiers. Yet both intentionally and unconsciously, the director also set out to explore what he calls "the darkness beneath the surface of apparent goodness," a theme he traces back to personal conflicts with his own religious upbringing. At the same time, Craven notes, the mayhem of *Last House* embodied the social and artistic upheaval of the '60s and early '70s.

"*Last House* was very much a product of its era," Craven says. "It was a time when all the rules were out the window, when everybody was trying to break the hold of censorship. The Vietnam war was going on, and the most powerful footage that we saw was in the actual documentary films of the war. There was a great amount of feeling that, 'The worst of it is being censored, so let's try to get our hands on what's *really* going on over there.' There was also very much a spirit going around that, 'It's time we showed things the way they really are.' In *Last House*, we set out to show violence the way we thought it really was, and to show the dark underbelly of the Hollywood genre film. We consciously took all the B movie conventions and stood them on their heads... so that just when you thought the shot would cut away, it didn't. Someone gets stabbed, but then they get back up and start crawling... death becomes much more protracted and sexual. That was all a breaking of convention."

Junior (Marc Sheffler) and Krug (David Hess).

"*Last House* did not play by the rules that had been established for handling violence, where the people who did violence were always bad, and if a good guy did it to the bad guy, it was very clean and quick," Craven continues. "That was the sort of attitude that America had gone into Vietnam with... that *they* were the bad guys and we'd go in like *Gunsmoke*, face 'em down, and bang, they'd be dead. The fact of the matter was that the war involved horrendous killings piled upon killings."

The Vietnam era saw the appearance of many movies which displayed an unprecedented level of graphic violence. Stanley Kubrick's *A Clockwork Orange* and Sam Peckinpah's *Straw Dogs* were both controversial hits in 1971 and dealt with violent themes similar to those explored in *Last House*. In a year-end survey of the movie industry, *Variety* named 1972 the year "Rated V for Violence"[2]. In the original script for *Last House*, off-handed dialogue mentions that both Krug and Weasel were former soldiers. In one scene, Krug informs Mari, "...You'll have plenty of time to feel the pain... Weasel was a specialist at that back in Vietnam. He got so good at it that they transferred him out of the combat zone." Another early draft of Craven's screenplay has the oafish sheriff admiring Mr. Collingwood's stamp collection and remarking that his son sends him "pretty postcards from Vietnam."

In addition to its oblique anti-war commentary, *Last House* captures the ugly underbelly of flower-power, which was in its death throes at the time the film was released. At the outset of the film, Estelle Collingwood remarks to her daughter, "I think it's crazy... all that blood and violence. I thought you were supposed to be the Love Generation..." Mari and Phyllis wonder "what it would be like to make it with Bloodlust..." and subsequently learn the answer to that question all too well. The fate of the girls makes for a grisly, cynical commentary on the demise of the hippie dream, as does the scene of Junior Stillo sliding down a wall with his brains blown out and a peace-symbol dangling around his neck. As the refrain of movie's theme song repeatedly reminds us, "The Road Leads to Nowhere."

As pop culture, *Last House on the Left* may be considered the celluloid counterpart of rock bands like Alice Cooper, Blue Cheer, and Black Sabbath, who stumbled onto the nascent style of heavy metal in the late '60s and were scorned by critics of the day for their pioneering efforts. As Craven did with *Last House*, these musicians tapped into an aggressive form of entertainment which bluntly addressed the turmoil, anger, and drugged-out disillusionment that seeped through the cracks in hippie idealism. Songs like Cooper's "Dead Babies" and Sabbath's "War Pigs" could never be called subtle or profound, but like *Last House on the Left*, they remain potent and evocative emblems of their era. And just as contemporary rock groups cannot truly recapture the primitive, wild sound of their forefathers, so do most modern horror pictures lack the gut punch that *Last House on the Left* delivers in its best moments. Even Craven himself, whose directorial skills have since developed light years beyond the crude level of *Last House*, has rarely duplicated the simple, savage impact of his debut.

"I would never make a movie that raw again," Craven candidly remarks. "Not that I regret making it... but I think if you spend too long working in that area, you brutalize your soul. Even *The Hills Have Eyes* was a stretch for me. You start to wonder how much can you protest violence when you're making a living from it. When you're making a film like that for a year, or a year and a half, it's not an easy place to live." Ironically, Craven says he nearly turned down the offer to direct Kevin Williamson's *Scream* screenplay because its opening sequence (which includes a disembowelment) reminded him of *Last House*.

Not that *Last House* is entirely as grim as its reputation would imply. In direct contrast to its cynicism, the movie is marked by an odd kind of innocence that reflects the young, hungry enthusiasm of its cast and crew. Amidst the carnage, the movie displays a cavalier humor which clearly shows that Craven and company were having fun with the material. "There was a very serious side to it, and at the same time, we also had this sense that we were doing this outrageous cinematic prank on a culture that we felt was reeling out of control in Vietnam," Craven says. "We were all very anti-Establishment at that time in our lives -

It's Only A Movie...

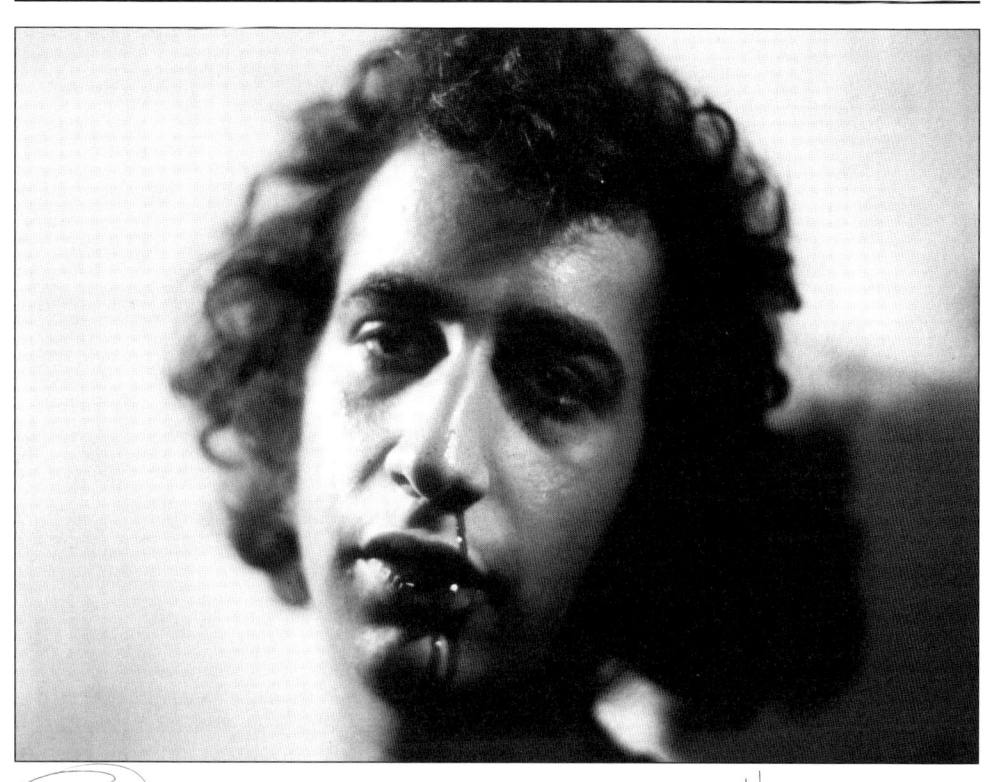

Junior's suicide: a classic image of '70s burnout.

Catch-22 was, I suppose, one of my most influential novels at that time, which I had read in college. With *Last House*, we were trying to be shocking, and at the same time we were looking at horror in a way that was darkly comedic."

Like all of Craven's genre films, *Last House* liberally displays the director's sense of humor. Comic dialogue broadly lampoons Freud, women's lib, the generation gap, hippies, straights, cops and B-movie clichés; the movie's low-brow subplot involving two inept policemen seems more suited to a Laurel and Hardy short than a horror film. While Krug and his outlaw clan reminded many viewers of the Manson Family, Craven says that these characters were actually exaggerated spoofs of gangster-movie archetypes. Vignettes which feature Krug and his gang kibitzing and tossing off one-liners seem to portray the group as outlaw anti-heroes a la *Bonnie and Clyde*. In this respect, *Last House* anticipates the discomforting black humor of John McNaughton's *Henry: Portrait of a Serial Killer* (1990) and Oliver Stone's *Natural Born Killers* (1994).

In depicting the deviant killers, Craven deliberately violated traditional notions of the black-hearted movie villain. One of the film's most revealing moments is a pivotal scene in which the gang shows visible signs of guilt and shame. The killers even show concern for each other in their own twisted way; in a particularly morbid moment after Phyllis is captured and stabbed, Krug asks Weasel 'Feel better now?' Regardless of the characters' repugnant actions, Craven reminds us that they are, after all, only human. In the shooting script for the film, Krug says to Mr. Collingwood: "..Aw, listen, Doc, I'm just tellin' you what I know you're thinkin'... You an' me, we got the same kinda thoughts - it's just that I do 'em, too, and you don't."

LAST HOUSE ON THE LEFT

It's Only A Movie...

Krug and company attempt to crudely integrate themselves into polite society.

Throughout the movie, Craven plays on the notion of identity. 'You gotta change your head around... become someone else altogether...' Sadie tells Junior early on in the movie. Although the gang tries to literally and figuratively get "out of the state," they, too, are led down the road to nowhere. "The idea of changing identity is something that has always fascinated me, especially with characters in genre films," Craven remarks. "I felt that it was poignant, that it somehow gave the characters a human dimension."

"*Last House on the Left* went against the grain of typical movies by taking characters that just kept on going down and down and down, until they were utterly despicable... and then staying with them beyond that and getting to *know* them..." Craven remarks. "In the later part of the movie, the audience sees that the killers can be embarrassed or uneasy about the way they hold a fork at the dinner table with people who they think are from a higher class. That sort of reversal made the movie very unsettling to audiences; I think that was part of the reason why so many people were enraged by it."

In effecting the reversal of the good and evil families, the film undergoes a shift in tone. The initial progression of the story is frighteningly believable; by contrast, the Collingwoods' vengeance is outlandishly contrived. For all its dementia, the third act of *Last House on the Left* is almost mock-Hollywood in its construction; the build-up and release of the various traps, Dr. Collingwood's triumphant entrance with the chainsaw, and the gnashing shock of Weasel's castration all essentially function as crowd-pleasers. These manipulative tactics are ultimately used to a subversive end when the film abruptly concludes on a note of bleakness. After making the revenge enjoyable and darkly comic, Craven denies his audience the comfort of basking in satisfaction, instead provoking them to question their own pleasure in the violence.

LAST HOUSE ON THE LEFT

The themes and narrative devices with which Craven first experimented in *Last House on the Left* have frequently recurred in his work as screenwriter and director. Freddy Krueger, the razor-fingered dream demon of *A Nightmare on Elm Street*, was in many ways a mythologized version of the scum-of-the-earth killers in *Last House*. (The name 'Krueger' was, after all, an homage to 'Krug'.[3]) Craven originally envisioned Krueger as a hellish, supernatural incarnation of the All-American child molester - tellingly, the first *Elm Street* film has Freddy stalking the subconscious minds of teenagers whose parents murdered him in an act of vigilante justice.

Most significantly, *Last House* introduced Craven's signature use of the family and home as a setting for nightmarish conflict. The horrors in Craven's most personal movies (*Last House*, *The Hills Have Eyes*, *A Nightmare on Elm Street*, *The People Under the Stairs*) often unfold in a deceptively normal American family environment where violence and repression collide.

Craven has said that his own upbringing influenced the family motif in his work. In an *Los Angeles Times* interview, he commented on his experiences growing up in a Fundamentalist household: "We weren't allowed to do much of anything - drink, smoke, play cards, have sex, or go to the movies. I was the quirky kid who read books all the time, painted, and read poetry. You wouldn't exactly call me a rebel, because I had a very strong religious streak, but there was zero dialogue between us. We couldn't talk about anything."[4] The original screenplay for *Last House on the Left* began with the following quote from (of all people) Yoko Ono: "Violence is just one of those feelings that come when you're unable to communicate. Art is communication."

"The family is central to my own life, and I think it's central to our culture," Craven says. "Wrenching changes have happened in the modern reality of our families and in our perception of them. In television and movies, we've gone from the *Dobie Gillis* and *Life with Father* versions of the family to *Married With Children* at best... and, at worst, *River's Edge*. Over time, I began to be aware that I was making one film after another going back to the family theme... and that the films I did which were not strictly based in a family situation, like *Deadly Friend* or *Swamp Thing*, didn't have the feeling of core Wes Craven films. I try to stay close to the family in my films, because I find that's where some of our most powerful, primitive emotions are buried."

In particular, Craven's second film, *The Hills Have Eyes* (1977) was a return to the thematic territory of *Last House*, playing on the parallels between "good" and "evil" families. Craven recalls that *Hills* came about when producer Peter Locke asked him to do "another *Last House*." In keeping with the family dynamic, the original title of *The Hills Have Eyes* was *Blood Relations*. According to records at the American Film Institute, another working title for the picture was *The Family Who Woke Up Screaming*. While *Hills*' story of a middle-class "white-bread" family under siege by a clan of desert-dwelling cannibals was inspired by research Craven had done on the infamous Sawney Bean crime family[5], the film was also an expansion on ideas the director had toyed with in its predecessor.

"Without realizing it, while I was writing *Last House* I got into the idea of mirroring one side to the other," the director explains. "That is, likening the Collingwoods to Krug's family, where essentially Sadie was the wife, Junior was the son, and Weasel was the dark uncle, the dark

It's Only A Movie...

EXCLUSIVE BRONX SHOWING
DON'T LOOK IN THE BASEMENT
&
LAST HOUSE ON THE LEFT
Midnight Shows Fri. & Sat. only
Dale THEATRE
231ST STREET & BROADWAY
548-1252

This newspaper advertisement, dated 28 January 1980, serves to illustrate the lengthy theatrical run enjoyed by *Last House on the Left* in the USA.

side-kick if you like. Once Krug and his family were in the parents' house, I started to like them. I felt badly that they realized they could never aspire to that sort of [bourgeois] life, that they had their own squabbles between them, and they couldn't quite get the blood off them... they didn't know how to put a tie on and things like that. At the same time, I liked the idea that these very straight parents could become absolutely lethal and conniving, that the father could go completely over the top and pick up a chainsaw and cut somebody's head off."

"I used the theme in a more conscious way with *The Hills Have Eyes*, where I constructed these two families as mirrors of each other," Craven continues. "I found it a very interesting way to look at ourselves, as a nation and as people, to think of ourselves as having the capacity not only for great good but for great evil. It creates a more rounded point of view than the type of thinking that dictates, 'Well, I'm an American, so I can do no wrong,' or 'I'm a law-abiding citizen, therefore I could never kill anybody or do anything violent.' One way or another, we're all capable of anything."

In keeping with this idea, both *Last House* and *The Hills Have Eyes* end with a frozen image of the respectable parent transformed into a blood-spattered homicidal maniac. Craven carried his vision of the strait-laced, God-fearing parents as potential killers to the furthest extreme in his underrated *The People Under the Stairs* (1991). In that film, characters named Man (Everett McGill) and Woman (Wendy Robie) hold a group of children prisoner in a labyrinthine house of horrors. The aberrant behavior of the Bible-quoting Man and Woman plays like *Leave It to Beaver* gone haywire; at one point, the crazed Man rampages through the house with a shotgun while clad in leather bondage gear!

Perhaps above all, *Last House on the Left* remains a remarkable example of determined novices managing to craft a successful feature film from extremely limited resources. Like the early efforts of George A. Romero (*Night of the Living Dead*), John Carpenter (*Assault on Precinct 13*), Tobe Hooper (*The Texas Chain Saw Massacre*), David Cronenberg (*Shivers*) and Sam Raimi (*The Evil Dead*), *Last House* was crafted by a feisty, daring group of independents who used the horror genre to buck the odds of the movie industry. *Last House* also was a triumph of movie marketing; its popularity was fueled by the use of the advertising slogan, "To Avoid Fainting, Keep Repeating: It's Only A Movie," which became one of the most effective and oft-imitated promotional tags in exploitation history.

While *Last House* never brought in the box office gross of a horror blockbuster like *The Exorcist* or *Halloween*, it proved to be one of the longest-running pictures on the market during the '70s, and even into the mid-1980s, especially on the drive-in circuit. "In today's numbers, the gross of *Last House* was never very high," Sean Cunningham comments. "Those were the days when you could get 150 prints of a movie and play it off city by city… there was no national advertising involved. I think the film did about three or four million dollars in rentals. Bear in mind that our original cash budget on the film was only about $45,000, and by the time we blew the film up to 35mm, we still had considerably less than $100,000 in it." According to one source, *Last House* had grossed in excess of $18 million by the time of a 1982 re-release designed to cash in on the *Friday the 13th* slasher craze.

Despite its financial success, *Last House* was an unsightly albatross around the necks of its creators for many years. Craven admits its hampered the progress of his career for several years, and Cunningham says it branded him as a purveyor of "puke-in-a-bucket" for nearly a decade. However, in the long run, the movie paid off in ways that the film makers never could have predicted. "Over the years, I had been identified with the success of *Last House*, although I had been trying to do more conventional movies, comedies and dramas," Cunningham explains. "I didn't like the stamp of 'disgusting low-budget producer' which had been following me around as a result of *Last House on the Left*. But, after doing a couple of children's movies, I was trying to figure out what to do in order to keep the lights on! I decided to take out an ad in *Variety* announcing *Friday the 13th*, 'The most terrifying film ever made, from the producer of Last House on the Left…' I had no script for *Friday the 13th* at that point; I was just trading

The Texas Chain Saw Massacre, one of several highly influential low-budget horror movies which changed the face of the genre during the 1970s.

It's Only A Movie...

Krug and his gang torture Mari and Phyllis (off camera).

on the notoriety of *Last House*. I had no idea that I was going to start a minor industry, with eight or nine sequels. It was a case of doing the right thing for the wrong reasons."

Widely censored and universally vilified by critics (with notable exceptions including Roger Ebert and James Schamus, a film scholar and producer whose credits include *The Ice Storm*) *Last House on the Left* occupies a singularly infamous niche in its genre. To this day, the film is banned outright in Britain and Australia, and despite a number of official and bootleg video releases in circulation, a definitive 'uncut' *Last House on the Left* has yet to surface.

Yes, as the advertisements proclaimed, it's only a movie. But on many levels - as cult phenomenon, as early '70s outrage, as proto-splatter movie, and finally as an unparalleled example of low-budget lunacy - *Last House on the Left* deserves a closer look than it has been afforded by film historians.

Notes

1 *Fangoria*, Vol.1, No.6, p.16. June 1980
2 The phrase "Rated V for Violence" was actually coined by ad-men at Hallmark Releasing, the company which financed and distributed *Last House on the Left*. (see Chapter VI)
3 Craven recalls that 'Krug' (rhymes with 'crude') was a bastardized version of 'Krupp,' the name of a German arms manufacturer who supplied munitions to the Nazis.
4 Patrick Goldstein, "Flying High With a Sultan of Slash," *Los Angeles Times*, July 9, 1985
5 Sawney Bean was the leader of a murderous, inbred clan of bandits who lurked in caves off the coast of Scotland during the fifteenth century.

Chapter 2

Planning The Sex Crime Of The Century

The events that led to the making of *Last House on the Left* began in an office building located at 56 West 45th Street in midtown Manhattan. The site was a center of activity in New York's film industry, housing a variety of production companies, editing facilities and motion picture laboratories. It was here that Wes Craven and Sean Cunningham first crossed paths at the dawn of the Seventies.

At the time, neither of the two aspiring film makers had any particular proclivity for the blood-drenched horror movies that would play such a crucial role in their professional lives. It was a unique set of circumstances that prompted the monstrous birth of *Last House on the Left* and fatefully steered Craven and Cunningham into the horror genre.

Craven (born in Cleveland, Ohio on August 2, 1939) grew up in a working-class Baptist family of which he was the only member to attend college. Raised under strict religious rules, he enrolled in 1959 at Wheaton College, a Christian school in Illinois that boasted evangelist Billy Graham as its most famous alumnus. Majoring in literature and psychology, Craven began to develop his creative talents even as he questioned the rigid Fundamentalist doctrine espoused by the school and his family. He wrote for and briefly edited a campus journal called *Coda*, which was condemned by the school when some of Craven's short stories overstepped the bounds of religious propriety.

"I had a long history of wanting to be a writer, and I wrote prose and poetry throughout college," Craven says. "I had other artistic inclinations as well... I drew cartoons all through college, and also had a lot of musical ability; I played guitar a lot... So there were a lot of talents floating around, but nothing really to do with photography or cinema whatsoever."

One of Craven's earliest moviegoing experiences occurred during his senior year of college, when he snuck off to see *To Kill A Mockingbird* (1962), an act which he says could have resulted in his expulsion. He nonetheless continued to indulge his interest in cinema, cultivating an appreciation for foreign films by Fellini, Bunuel, Truffaut and Ingmar Bergman.

Wes Craven during his college days.

After earning his B.A. from Wheaton in 1963, Craven entered an intensive graduate program at Johns Hopkins University in Baltimore, Maryland, where he wrote an unpublished novel. In 1964, he completed his masters' degree in writing and philosophy and married Bonnie Broecker, with whom he had two children, Jonathan and Jessica. Craven spent the next few years as a teacher, starting out at Westminster College in New Wilmington, Pennsylvania. "It was a Presbyterian school, out in Amish country," Craven says. "There were a lot of young teachers there who didn't yet have doctorates or tenure, a lot of artists and people who wanted to be writers, so it was a very interesting group of nomadic intellectuals."

Following a year at Westminster, Craven accepted a position as a humanities professor at Clarkson College, an engineering school in Potsdam, New York. At Clarkson, Craven first discovered his interest in filmmaking by working with a group of students on a 16mm short called *The Searchers*. "I had bought a 16mm camera as a novelty, not really knowing why," Craven recounts. "Some students found out about it, and they came to me asking if I would start a campus film club with them, which we did. *The Searchers* was just a silly thing, sort of a *Mission: Impossible* type of story. It was about forty-five minutes long, and technically very primitive. We made it on reversal stock, so there was no negative; we just showed the print. We ran a quarter-inch tape along with the film that had the soundtrack on it. We'd adjust the tape speed with a rheostat; if the sound got ahead of the picture, we'd slow it down a little bit. The movie was quite successful on campus, and it was a heady experience for me."

One of Craven's good friends at Clarkson was Steve Chapin, a musician and electrical engineering major who attended the school from 1964-1969. "Wes and I had become really close while I was attending Clarkson College," Chapin recalls. "Wes was a guitar player, and I'm a bass/guitar/recorder player, and we used to hang out a lot, playing music and doing the hippie thing. He was also a disc jockey at the campus radio station... He used to do the late night rock show [which Craven called "Seasons of Love"] from eleven to one in the morning, and occasionally he brought my band in to jam. We used to smoke a lot of grass, which was kind of wild because he was the professor and we were students. It would have been bad for all of us if we got caught!"

As Craven's interest in moviemaking grew, he became disillusioned with academia. "By the end of that semester, I was told by my department chairman that I needed to start seriously working towards a PhD. I polled the people I knew who had PhDs, and I found they were all miserable! I decided instead to quit my job, and go to New York City to try to learn more about film. So, during my summer vacation [1968], I went into places like Leacock-Pennebaker, who I believe were making

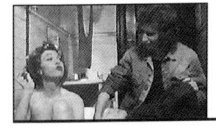

Monterey Pop at the time. Norman Mailer was in there screening some of his films, like *Beyond the Law*, some of those very late-60's/early-70's attempts at American auteur movies."

Craven's friendship with Steve Chapin proved to be an important factor in the former academic's entry into the film business. "After I had graduated and Wes left the teaching profession, he and his family lived for a while in Brooklyn Heights, in the same building where my mother lived," Chapin says. "Peter Locke [producer of Craven's *The Hills Have Eyes*][1] also lived there for a while. So we used to see Wes around a lot… since my brother Harry was dabbling in the film business, and my uncle was Ricky Leacock of Leacock-Pennebaker, there were connections between my family and Wes' career as a film maker."[2]

Although Craven's introduction to New York's film world was an inspiring one, it did not lead to any work. "At the end of the summer, I went back and taught a year of high school [in Potsdam]. Steve Chapin told me that he had a brother Harry who was a film editor in New York. Steve said that if I wanted to, I could look up his brother, and Harry would talk to me about possibly giving me a job, and if not, he could teach me something about film. So at the end of the second summer [1969], when I realized I was not going to get another job [teaching college] for the next semester, and that I would have to go back and teach high school, I finally looked up Harry Chapin."

During the late '60s, Harry Chapin was making industrial films (for IBM among others) and editing television commercials and documentaries. Chapin also made some of his own movies; one of these, a collaboration with Jim Jacobs entitled *Legendary Champions*, won the Academy Award for Best Documentary in 1969 and was honored at the New York and Atlanta film festivals. Soon afterwards, Chapin went on to fame as the singer/songwriter of such folk-rock hits as "Taxi" (1972) and "Cat's In the Cradle" (1974).[3]

With the help of Harry Chapin, Craven began making his first inroads towards a career in film making. "Harry Chapin taught me the basics of film making, this would be in 1969, and I managed to get a job in the place where he was renting editing space," Craven explains. "This post-production house [Roland Condon Film Management] had fired their messenger, and so I took the place of a seventeen year-old messenger. I had a wife and two kids, and we moved the whole show down to New York City. I worked my way up very quickly, demonstrating that I was capable of a lot more than messenger work. I began writing treatments with Harry, and doing some rough cutting with him. We made a couple of industrials for Time-Life together. I was also being trained as a post-production supervisor, so I was taught a great deal about quality-control of a print, [color] timing, lab work, and the whole editing process."

Although he was gaining invaluable experience through his contact with the New York film scene, these were tough times for Craven. By the early '70s, he was divorced and living in poverty on New York's Lower East Side. At one point during this period, he drove a cab to make ends meet. Although Craven frequently felt discouraged, he remained undeterred in his desire to learn the craft of moviemaking.

"I was around a lot of documentary film making because this place was supervising the post-production of documentaries for Time-Life," Craven continues. "There were some very interesting people making them… one person was Michael Wadleigh, who was making at the time a very obscure documentary on a music festival that turned out to be *Woodstock*. So I was just around that whole scene, picking up whatever I could learn. I was synching up dailies at night for various films, taking odd jobs, and that's how I first met Sean Cunningham."

Sean S. Cunningham (born December 31, 1941, New York) got into the film business in 1970 after working as a stage manager on and off-Broadway. Where Craven is soft-spoken and introspective, Cunningham comes across as brash, sardonic, and businesslike; the producer's comments about the early days of his career are frequently punctuated with good-natured laughter. When asked how he launched his career in film, Cunningham replies, "You don't have to pass a bar exam to become a movie producer... You just have to buy some stationery!"

In a 1971 interview for the *Boston Herald-Traveler*, Cunningham recounted the story of how he got into the theatrical world: "I went to Franklin and Marshall College in Lancaster, Pennsylvania, where I intended to start my career as a doctor. I became interested in the theater there, and spent all my time at it. I also realized I had wanted to become a doctor for all the wrong reasons, that I wanted the status, and that I wasn't really equipped to deal with a scientific discipline, but more with a creative discipline.

"I thoroughly enjoyed my enormous involvement in theater in college, and didn't enjoy at all the scientific discipline of memorization of material. I went to grad school for film and drama [at Stanford], and decided I didn't want to act anymore, but wanted to direct. Next, I got one of those lucky breaks, in a way. A friend of mine was involved at Lincoln Center, and called me and asked if I wanted a job. I had great visions of being tapped as a leading man, and found the job was as a dresser. I befriended the stage manager, and really learned the craft. I then toured as stage manager with *The Merry Widow,* and to make a long story short, I was hired at the Mineola Playhouse on Long Island to produce the Plumstead Players revivals of *The Front Page* and *Our Town.*"

Both of these productions were successful, but Cunningham commented at the time, "Theater is an anachronism - it doesn't last. Film is a lasting creative statement." More to the point, in a 1992 interview with the author, he reflected, "I had raised some money for theatrical projects, and that didn't seem like a very good financial investment... I figured maybe I could raise some money for movies, and figure out how to make them as I went along. It seemed like fun, so that's what I tried to do."

To this end, Cunningham rented a one-room office in the West Forty Fifth Street building in early 1970 under the imprint of Sean S. Cunningham Films/ Lobster Enterprises. He also had a separate space next door to the small production office in which he set up some editing equipment. "We were trying to do anything to keep the lights on, essentially," he says. "We had purchased some Steenbeck editing equipment, along with some sound transfer equipment, and as a result we could effectively do post-production. We would go out and shoot little hand-held commercials, or testimonials, that kind of stuff. It was very informal; we were just trying to figure it all out."

Cunningham's office became a meeting place for various editors, technicians and producers, including most of the crew who would lend their energies to the making of *Last House on the Left*. "Having an office was really impressive at the time, because hardly anyone in New York besides the Maysles [brothers] and Leacock-Pennebaker had offices," says Yvonne Hannemann, who worked on *Last House on the Left* as Craven's assistant director. "Everyone was always trouping in and out of Sean's office, borrowing things and making phone calls."

Steve Dwork, who worked as a production assistant and still photographer on *Last House on the Left*, says that he became involved with the movie through "…sheer physical proximity. I was working with a friend of mine on a film for Planned Parenthood, and we were renting editing space at Lobster Enterprises. It was a small office, with three or four relatively small rooms and a central entryway, so everybody sort of overheard everything that was going on all around. At some point I was asked by Sean and Wes whether I was interested in helping the cause of getting this film done, and I said, 'Sure, why not? Sounds cool.'".

Wes and Sean get 'Together'

Craven and Cunningham first collaborated on a movie appropriately called *Together*. A softcore pseudo-documentary purporting to explore the swinging practices at an Esalen-like retreat run by a sex therapist named "Doctor Curry", *Together* was Cunningham's second feature as both director and producer. Cunningham's first feature, which also presented itself as a sex education picture, was a primitive nudie called *The Art of Marriage*[4].

Together was shot and edited in a patchwork manner. The film apparently began production under the title *Kama Sutra* in May of 1970; shooting continued through July, when funds ran out. Filming resumed in September, and continued sporadically through December. Craven became involved with *Together* when Cunningham hired him to synchronize dailies for the film. As the project moved towards completion, Craven's role expanded to that of "associate producer."

Cunningham's partner at the time, Roger Murphy, was the film's cinematographer and editor. The cast included the young and beautiful Marilyn Chambers, prior to her fame as the "Ivory Snow Girl" and star of the Mitchell Brothers' *Behind the Green Door*. The film was scored by studio musician Manny Vardi, who played on the *Last House* soundtrack, and narrated by one "Jan Peter Welt."

At the time of *Together*'s Boston premiere at the prestigious Saxon theater (which normally presented Hollywood fare such as *Around the World in 80 Days* and *Ben Hur*) Cunningham commented: "…I knew I wanted to make a positive statement about sexual roles, and the essentiality of breaking down people's hang-ups and shame toward their bodies, but I had no idea that the *Together* now being shown would be the film I would be make. I sold shares to many people, and started to make the film… we made most of it around Westport, Connecticut and with very few professional actors. We made the first rough cut last December [1970], and the film just didn't work, so we re-

Craven and Cunningham collaborated on *Together*, a pseudo-documentary about sex released in 1971. Copy in the above ad resembles a line of dialogue from *Last House on the Left*. ("If God had meant women to go around with their busts exposed, Mari Collingwood, He wouldn't have given us clothes!")

shot footage, and re-cut, and finally it came out, after a total of five cuts, exactly as we wanted it to, which is the film now playing... to capacity audiences, I might add."

It was during the lengthy period of cutting, re-cutting and re-shooting *Together* that Craven began working for Cunningham extensively. Craven explains, "*Together* had already been shot, and Sean hired me to synchronize the dailies from a three or four-day reshoot of additional material they had done. After that was synched up, they asked me to come aboard as assistant editor. The film turned out to be a tremendous learning experience. Roger was my mentor; he was an irascible, brilliant, very highly skilled photographer and cinematographer... He also really understood editing. They were literally making up this documentary out of whole cloth. But Roger and Sean had many partings of the ways, so what happened was that, I would say, about six months into this, Roger left for the first time. And Sean was left with me knowing more about the film than anybody else except for himself. So I would take my crack at editing it, and about a week later, Roger would come back, and he and Sean would make up, and Roger would tear apart everything I did. But he'd say, 'Oh, we'll keep this one little section, it looks pretty good, and here's how this could work...' I'd watch this very hard, fast school of cutting something and having it undone by somebody who was better than me... and I really learned the basics of editing. Between Harry Chapin and Roger Murphy, I learned in very quick time, from the point of view of two very bright men, how to cut material."

Ultimately, Craven's work on *Together* was not confined to the editing room. "We went off and shot two days in Puerto Rico[5] and they actually allowed me to direct a couple of sequences," he continues. "I also took sound, and did some additional writing, so I had my hands in the nooks and crannies of that film. And just before the final sound mix, Roger and Sean parted ways for the last time. Sean and I got that film ready for mix under horrendous conditions of no money and no sleep for practically two weeks. We stayed up all hours just working through the night... and we bonded. We really became war buddies at the end of that process."

In attempting to secure a distribution deal for the finished picture, Cunningham initially met with rejection. Determined to recoup his investment, the producer took the film to a Boston-based company called Esquire Theaters of America. This move would prove to be instrumental in the making of *Last House on the Left*.

Esquire owned and operated a chain of movie theaters in New England and upstate New York, including mainstream urban venues, shopping-mall multiplexes, rural drive-ins and porno houses. In its heyday, the company controlled over a hundred screens, and dealt with film distributors all over the United States. Esquire expanded its operations at the dawn of the '70s to include distribution under the banner of Hallmark Releasing Corporation, and *Together* became Hallmark's first release. The main partners in Eaquire/Hallmark were Philip Scuderi, Steve Minasian, and Robert Barsamian. At the time of *Together* and *Last House*, the company maintained two offices, one in Boston and the other in the back of a drive-in theater in North Wilbraham, Massachusetts.

"Actually, I helped make the original distribution deal for *Together*," recalls George Mansour, who worked for Esquire/Hallmark as a theater booker during the '70s. "Sean had made the movie on his own... he was in New York and wanted to show us the film. He knew we were a chain that was willing to play lots of exploitation movies. He barely had enough money to come to Boston, but he flew up and we watched the movie in a little cinema we owned that was located across from our offices, near Boston Garden. To the best I can recall, we paid Sean about $10,000 for *Together*, and we took over the picture."

Together arrived at a time when hardcore porno was in the process of breaking out of the peep-shows and into the lucrative arena of big-screen exhibition. The less explicit sex films like *Together* were soon to be rendered obsolete by the headline splash of early '70s hardcore landmarks like *Deep Throat* and *The Devil in Miss Jones*. It was the dawn of so-called "porno chic," when curious middle-class couples began lining up at adult theaters to see what all the fuss was about. Since *Together* was more daring than the nudist-camp sexploitation pictures that preceded it, but not as harsh and coarse as the new breed of hardcore pictures, it found a certain niche among upscale, suburban couples and curiosity seekers who would have blanched at going to see a film like *Deep Throat*.

In *Together*, Cunningham supplied the target audience, which he called "the Reader's Digest crowd," with a gentle, romantic alternative to peep-show product. The photography and cast were aesthetically pleasing, and the movie was geared to a "couples" sensibility. Hallmark stressed this angle in booking and marketing the picture. Where the majority of '60s and '70s skin flicks played exclusively in urban art cinemas, drive ins, or "grindhouses," Hallmark deliberately booked *Together* into high-profile mainstream theaters and suburban shopping mall multiplexes. Free screenings of the movie were held for local clergy, police and civic groups in order to avoid the legal hassles which often surrounded sex films at the time. These free screenings also helped generate that most-valued commodity in motion picture promotion: word of mouth. The movie was aggressively advertised with radio spots and strategically-placed fliers at shopping centers; the ad copy called it "the beginning of communication, and the end of ignorance!".

The "world premiere" of *Together* took place on August 8, 1971 at a multiplex in Providence, Rhode Island called the Four Seasons. "The Four Seasons was the premiere moviehouse in Providence at the time," Mansour notes. "It was a real classy theater, where we'd normally play movies like *Chinatown* or *The Godfather*... it was not a porno house."

**LOOK FOR YOURSELF!
JUDGE FOR YOURSELF!**

SEE **MARILYN CHAMBERS**

IVORY SNOW'S 99 44/100% PURE GIRL OR PORNO QUEEN!

in the movie that thrust her into the public eye!

(Must Be 17 Yrs.)

Together

the ORIGINAL, UNCUT (X) RATED VERSION!

SUN. MAT. 2:00   DAILY 7:30 & 9:00

DOLLAR NIGHTS!
MON. & TUES. ADMISSION $1.00

A 1973 re-release of *Together* capitalized on the notoriety of Marilyn Chambers, who appeared in the film prior to her emergence as an adult film star.

The movie immediately began to rake in the long green, mostly due to the buzz generated by its promo campaign. "WHAT CAN YOUR CHILDREN SHOW YOU ABOUT LOVE?" one ad pointedly asked. "LOOK FOR YOURSELF! JUDGE FOR YOURSELF!" Some print ads used only the image of a smiling, healthy young lass; others featured a photo of a long-haired couple groping each others' posteriors. But central to all the film's promotion (and its success) was the ad copy, written mostly in the form of (bogus) quotes from sample audience members.

The juxtaposition of glowing raves with prudish negative comments engendered just the right amount of controversy and curiosity. Where one "uninhibited" moviegoer would gush "I thought it was terrific - it stressed the importance of feeling!", the other side would rage, "It's terrible that they show movies like this - I can't believe it!" More to the point, one disgruntled customer griped: "It's a big come-on! Not what it pretends to be!"

"The interesting thing about *Together* was the review that appeared in the *Providence Journal*," Mansour says. "Newspaper reviews were unusual for X-rated movies at the time. We had held the movie over for a second week because it was doing so well, and we wanted to use the *Journal* review as part of the advertising. The paper refused to take our ad, saying that it was not something that they would run in their paper! First we tried to excerpt their review, and when they refused to do that, I said, 'OK, we'll print the entire column, word for word.' And they still said, 'No, we won't take that sort of trash in our newspaper.' I said, 'What do you mean? You wrote it! You published it!' They said, 'Running that review was an editorial decision; we're the advertising department, and we have different standards.'"

Newspaper reviews aside, Hallmark's promotional pitch paid off in a big way. *Together*'s regional success convinced American International Pictures that the film was worth releasing nationwide. AIP, which had previously shunned any involvement with X-rated movies, subsequently entered into an agreement with Hallmark in which AIP served as the smaller company's national distributor. Both companies saw great profit from the arrangement.

Despite the film's wide exposure during its original release, *Together* is unavailable on videocassette and considered at present to be a lost piece of history. *Variety* reviewed *Together* in December of 1971, commenting, "This is another of those pornos which poses as a serious study of sex in order to justify prurient peeking… [it] starts from the premise that everybody's been doing the wrong things, so let's all watch it done right… [the cast is] turned loose in the woods at some out-of-the-way retreat where you can be free and natural… aside from the touching and talking, however, the good-looking group never does anything else…" The *Variety* reviewer concluded his analysis with the observation, "There are hints that *Together* is actually three films edited into one."

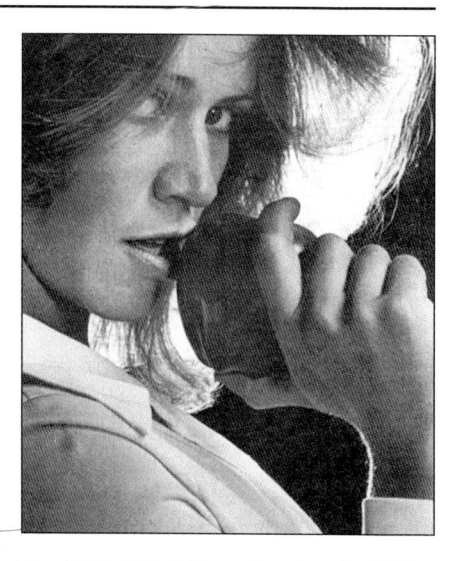

The "touching and talking" included scenes where the young, naked cast played ring-around-the-rosy and recited explicit names for their genitalia. "*Together* was essentially based on a lot of the sensitivity and human-awareness books that were coming out at the time," Craven says. "There was a lot of paraphrasing from a writer named Rollo May... Sean's father [John Cunningham] actually played the doctor; we called him 'Roland Curry'. There were a lot of puns like that in the movie. Sean's brothers and sisters did a bunch of talking-head interviews in it... Marilyn Chambers was known as Marilyn Briggs back then; one of Sean's brothers knew her. Although there was some nudity, it was really very 'proper'... but Sean was very canny in that he played it up as being controversial and showed to the Catholic Church and the PTA. I think it cost $70,000 to make, and grossed something like 7 million dollars."

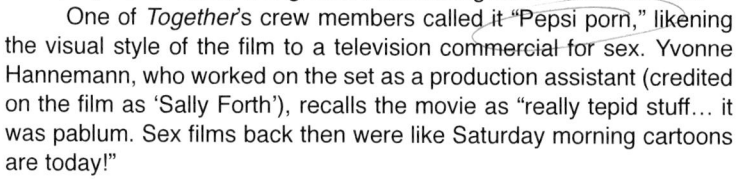

Together star Marilyn Chambers.

One of *Together*'s crew members called it "Pepsi porn," likening the visual style of the film to a television commercial for sex. Yvonne Hannemann, who worked on the set as a production assistant (credited on the film as 'Sally Forth'), recalls the movie as "really tepid stuff... it was pablum. Sex films back then were like Saturday morning cartoons are today!"

Unrated at the time of its initial release, *Together* was issued in two different versions, one of which was slightly edited down to avoid the hassles with police and bluenoses which surrounded many screenings of X-rated fare at the time. The differences between the versions were minimal, however, and the film was later rated R by the MPAA (see Chapter VII). George Mansour remembers one of the racier scenes, which he says contributed to the film's popularity. "There was a scene where a girl, I think it was Marilyn Chambers, takes a yellow flower and uses it to caress this large, flaccid black penis... and as she's caressing it, it gradually becomes erect. That was the big scene, the one unusual thing in the film... Hallmark's rationale for the success of *Together* was the fact that there was a vast audience who had never seen an erect black penis!"

By early February, 1972, *Together* had cleared $1,066,971 at the box office and occupied the #2 spot on Variety's 50 top-grossing films chart, right behind the latest James Bond picture, *Diamonds are Forever*. The movie ran for thirty-one weeks in 1972 at New York's Rialto theater, and even as late as 1974 was still flickering on the screens of Boston area movie houses. But well before *Together* showed its long-term "legs" at the box office, the wheels were in motion for the next Cunningham/Craven venture: *Last House on the Left*.

Wes Craven recounts the initial spark for the project as an informal offer: "The people at Hallmark approached Sean with the idea of doing a very violent, scary movie. Sean came to me and said, 'Look, if you want to write this film, I'll let you direct it'... Sean had a Steenbeck editing table set up in his office, so he said, 'You can cut the film right here, and we'll become partners in it.' It was an extraordinary offer, and I, of course, took him up on it immediately."

SEX CRIME OF THE CENTURY

Produced by Sean S. Cunningham
Written and Directed by Wes Craven
Original Score by David A. Hess
Distributed by Hallmark Releasing Corp.

Starring David Hess, Jeramie Rain, Fred Lincoln,
Marc Sheffler, Sandra Cassell, Lucy Grantham

"It was almost instant," Cunningham says of the deal. "I imagine that we raised the money to do *Last House* over the summer, just a few months before we started shooting... It was one of those things that, when you start out, seems so easy and obvious. Everybody had made a lot of money on that little *Together* movie, so the natural enough thing for the distributors to do was to ask us, 'Well, you wanna do something else?' And Wes and I said, 'Uh, yeah! We'll make a regular movie where people talk!' *(laughs)* So Hallmark put up the initial money for us to do *Last House*."

"Hallmark made a great deal of money from *Together*, and I know Sean felt at one point that he had been ripped off on the deal," Mansour recalls. "But, of course, a lot of that money would not have been possible if not for the fact that we had access to a lot of moviehouses, and that we devised a good ad campaign. So perhaps it was as a reward, or as a kind of compensation for the fact that Sean was not paid as much money as he should have been paid for *Together*, that we financed *Last House on the Left*. Hallmark's financing the production of a movie was an unusual situation, because most of the films that that the company released were acquisitions - they were usually very low-budget European movies on which we'd indiscriminately change the titles."

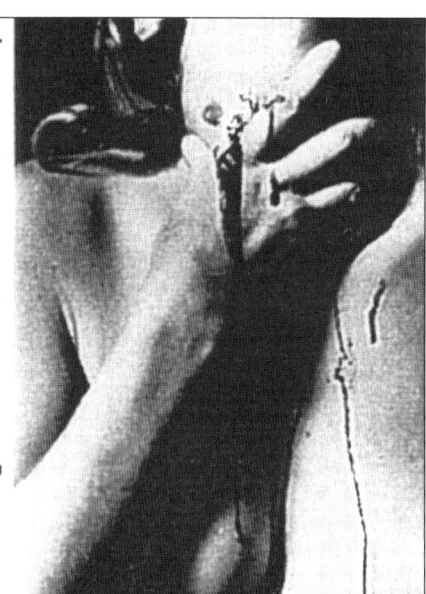

Hallmark's backing gave the film makers an advantage many independent movie producers do not possess: the guarantee that the movie would be released in theaters. Most low-budget mavericks are faced with the daunting task of convincing backers to pour money into a potentially shaky investment, and *then* having to shop the finished product to a distributor and pray to see a decent return. Here, by contrast, the backers, distributors, and exhibitors were essentially the same group of people.

With Hallmark's offer on the table, the partners wasted no time in filling the bill. The writing, casting, financing and overall planning of the production that would eventually evolve into *Last House on the Left* were all accomplished over a period of approximately two months, from early August to late September of 1971. In this formative stage, the project was known as *Sex Crime of the Century*, a title which would be dropped, reinstated, and dropped again before the film was officially released.

To this day, Cunningham maintains that the inspiration for the violent sensibility of *Last House* came from a heady discussion about the role of violence in movies. He recalls this fateful conversation which helped shape the idea for Wes Craven's script: "My recollection is that Wes and I came out of the '60s as sort of 'flower children'… that's not quite the right phrase, but we were both graduates of that peace-and-love generation. And one day we were watching a Clint Eastwood movie, I don't remember which one, but it was like *The Good, the Bad and the Ugly* or one of the Sergio Leone movies. We noticed that there were something like five hundred and twelve dead bodies in the movie, but the nature of the violence was like, 'Bang! Bang! You're Dead!'… but you're not really dead. That led to a conversation about how if you ever saw a movie in which it looked like you *really* killed one person, that it would be a real mind-fuck… it would be really disturbing. We thought it might be worth doing as a way to turn violence around on itself, to make people re-evaluate that which they call entertainment. 'You want to watch a movie where people are dying? Watch *this*!'"

The gang closes in on the defenseless Mari. "You want to watch a movie where people are dying? Watch this!" When Craven and Cunningham were planning Last House on the Left, one of their aims was to show the harsh, brutal reality of interpersonal violence.

Regardless of this lofty rationale, there's simply no getting around the fact that *Last House* was conceived as a down-and-dirty exploitation flick; for the time, this was nothing unusual. The newfound freedom of the late '60s to show previously-taboo aspects of sex and violence on screen made the early 1970s one of the most prolific eras in exploitation history. Like many upstart film makers of their generation, Craven and Cunningham found in the '70s exploitation boom an excellent opportunity to learn feature film production.

"We were not conventional film makers," Cunningham remarks. "In fact, you could say that we were not film makers at all, but were just trying to become film makers. We were just off on the fringe, knocking on the door and trying to find a way in. So, bearing that in mind, what we thought at that point was: 'What can we do that people will pay money to go see?' And I think, at some level, the answer to that question is 'CIRCUS.' You know, with *Last House*, we were just doing this strange magic-show, this gronky old *thing* that *maybe* people would pay money to see… and if people did go to see it, and if we actually got to make another movie, wouldn't that be fun? Making that movie was sort of like being 'naughty', like somebody left a camera in our car and we were trying to figure out what to do with it! *(laughs)* That was the kind of attitude we had, like, 'God, can we get away with this?! This'd be kinda fun!' It wasn't until much later that we started to take the film much more seriously."

With the violence theme in mind, Craven quickly came up with a framework for the film by borrowing the plotline from Ingmar Bergman's *The Virgin Spring* (*Jungfrukällen*, 1960). "I had seen *The Virgin Spring* about a year before I wrote *Last House*, and I loved the turnaround of the story," Craven says. "I thought it made for an incredible modern fable, as well as an ancient one. But it wasn't as if I sat down and went scene for scene… the Bergman movie stuck in my mind, and that was about the extent of it. I just liked the idea of the girl going off on the

Martin Kove as the deputy.

pilgrimage and meeting the shepherds who rape and kill her, the shepherds hiding the crime, and then, by a quirk, running into the parents who, in the middle of the night, discern what the connection is and set about killing these people in a very ruthless and evil way."

"I wrote the script in a very short time," Craven says, recalling that the earliest version of the screenplay was written during a long weekend at a friend's house on Long Island. "I think it was completely done in about two weeks. The people at Hallmark were knocked out by what I wrote; the original budget for the movie was going to be $50,000, but they gave us an additional $40,000[6] after they'd read the script."

Sex Crime of the Century was Craven's first attempt at screenwriting and comprised sixty single-spaced typewritten pages. In this bare-bones treatment, Craven took sex and sadism to unspeakable extremes. Craven first realized that he had written something controversial when he sent his script off to be mimeographed. "I went to pick up the copies of the script, but they kept getting delayed because all of the secretaries had been passing it around. They couldn't believe it!"

Indeed, Craven's first draft makes the finished film look like Disney material. For example, one scene featured Krug and Weasel engaging in necrophilia with Phyllis' mutilated corpse; the sequence of Mari's rape and defilement was also rougher and more prolonged. Other incidental sex scenes included Mari masturbating in the shower at the opening of the film and fantasy sequences of Mari and Phyllis getting it on with the rock group Bloodlust.

For Craven, writing such an ultraviolent and sexually explicit screenplay was certainly a departure from his Fundamentalist upbringing; according to the director, it was something of a rebellious gesture. "That was a period of my life when I was completely breaking away from all of that background," he comments. "I'd recently been divorced, and I was living in New York in this kind of communal housing… it was a very alternate kind of lifestyle, and at the same time, obviously society itself was going through enormous changes... so we were very much underground in feeling. When I wrote *Last House*, Sean's instructions to me were to pull out all the stops, pull all the skeletons out of the closet and do the most scarifying film imaginable... so I started out writing a film that was even more extreme than what we ended up shooting. There were elements of what was almost pornography to it. It was conceived as the be-all and end-all of outrageous films."

Craven wryly offered another reminiscence about his *Last House* script in a 1998 interview: "When I first went out to Hollywood, I had a friend named Phil DeGuerre who was helping me to find an agent. Phil asked me for a writing sample, so I sent him the screenplay for *Last House on the Left*. He called me back and said, 'I'm going to keep this as a souvenir, because no one would ever believe that you wrote something like this. But my advice is, don't ever show this to anybody again, or you'll never get hired in this town!' So I put in a drawer and haven't looked at it for years." Craven's inscription on a copy of the script given to a friend's son reads: *"Wait until you're 21 to read this - and then burn it!"*

Money and marketing were undoubtedly the motivating factors behind the pornographic origins of *Last House*. At the time the project was conceived, X-rated films were on the cusp of their emergence as an immensely profitable genre; the combination of sex and gore was a kink that sexploitation merchants had flirted with since the advent of hardcore fare. Features such as *Widow Blue* (aka *Sex Psycho*, 1971) and *Hard Gore* (1973) pandered to the worst of both worlds and, understandably, met with little success. As the project developed, the partners recognized that Craven's scenario was strong enough to play effectively without relying on gratuitous sex. "Before we started shooting, we realized the story was so good that we didn't want to go in that direction," Craven says. "I think that decision was very much to the credit of the film itself, and to the credit of the actors."

"At one time, we were talking about having a whole bunch of sex in the picture," Cunningham admits. "Although we were thinking of that initially, we wound up saying to ourselves, 'It's just not a good idea, if we're going to try to tell a story.' Rather than just being an excuse to have a bunch of people running around having sex, the movie became a reason to try to tell a story. And the sex became less necessary as the story evolved." Financial and practical considerations also undoubtedly played a part in the decision to eliminate the sex scenes.

Cunningham helped with the rewriting of the script during pre-production, crossing out superfluous dialogue and scenes which were simply unfeasible from a financial standpoint. A second draft of *Sex Crime* shows a lot of penciled comments from the producer like, "Doubt it!" and "I don't think this helps." The story's denouement in which the Collingwoods take revenge on the killers changed substantially both in pre-production and later during the shoot. In one early draft, Dr. Collingwood changes into a karate outfit and attempts to kung-fu Krug to death! Although the chainsaw scene is present in the first draft manuscript, Wes Craven relates that he had an earlier idea for the climactic fight.

There's an interesting story behind that chainsaw scene, because I had written it as a scalpel fight," Craven says. "The character was a doctor, and I thought it would be very interesting to have a doctor who would know every little vulnerable point in the body, and could make these insidious little cuts that would leave somebody bleeding to death. We noticed that there was some movie out that had a bunch of guys fighting with chainsaws… I remember seeing the poster on Times Square, it was kind of a cheap low-budget action film. So Sean said, 'Fuck the scalpel, let's get a chainsaw going!'"

By September 17, 1971, the screenplay had been rewritten two more times and bore the title *Night of Vengeance*. Though most of the 'blue' scenes had been tamed down or excised entirely during the various rewrites, *Night of Venegance* was still far from tame. Thus, Cunningham's response to the question of how the two partners went about casting *Last House*: "Who'd do it?!"

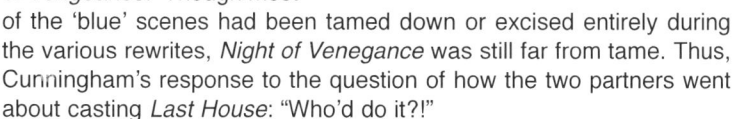

The producer goes on to explain that "…it was a non-union film, and we didn't have a formal casting call. This was New York in 1971; it was a very different world, it wasn't at all like it is now. Today, you'd send out a script, and use a casting agent, and actors would be interviewed and re-interviewed. But just to do that process alone would have eaten up 25% of our budget!"

Fred Lincoln (a.k.a. Fred Perna)**,** a veteran of the X-rated film industry who was one of the first actors hired for the film, recalls the original script for *Last House* with an incredulous chuckle. When asked how the film evolved towards a more straightforward shock-horror approach, Lincoln replies, "Well, we kind of talked even before we shot the movie that it [an X-rated *Last House*] really couldn't be done. I read the script, and it was absolutely the most disgusting thing I'd ever seen… I mean, it was *really* hideous. Sean realized somewhere in there that it couldn't be pulled off."

Lincoln was probably the most experienced actor in the cast of *Last House*; he had been a stunt man on *The French Connection* (1971), and appeared in numerous TV commercials, off-Broadway plays, and sexploitation films. One of Lincoln's early appearances was in 1971's *Fleshpots of 42nd Street*, directed by Staten Island filmmaker Andy (*Bloodthirsty Butchers*) Milligan. Lincoln also claims to have worked with Otto Preminger.

"One of the first things we did in casting was look around for big and scary people to play Krug," Wes Craven says. One of the actors who responded to the Krug casting call was Brooklyn-born Martin Kove, who had previously appeared in *Little Murders* (1971) and James Ivory's cult item *Savages* (1971). "I believe I was sent down to audition by my agent at the time, a guy named Red Adams," Kove says. "They initially wanted me to play Krug, and I just didn't want to do the part. I didn't want to play such a beast, and I didn't want to do the things that

"Let's get a chainsaw going!" Dr. Collingwood becomes the aggressor at the climax of *Last House on the Left*.

Planning The Sex Crime Of The Century

Krug desperately attempts to ward off Dr. Collingwood's chainsaw attack.

he did in the movie. Portraying that kind of a killer was too dark for me. I was more interested in doing the comic relief, so I asked to read for the part of the deputy." The film makers agreed to cast Kove as the deputy, leaving the Krug role unfilled.

As fate would have it, Kove knew another actor who was interested in breaking into film. David Hess tells the story of his last-minute audition with his typical dramatic flair. "My sister and Marty Kove were living together at the time," Hess begins. "I was totally enmeshed in my music at the time; I was writing music, and I'd just finished doing two albums. I was wiped out, and I didn't want to hear from music anymore. I'd just gotten off Broadway, I'd done five months in "Dark of the Moon" at a little grungy theater… I was doing too much! Marty calls me up, and he says, 'Listen, you gotta come down here for this audition… you're so right for this role.' I said, 'I don't know what you're talking about, Marty, but fill me in.' He says, 'Well, look… just meet me at my apartment.'

"So, I went over to their apartment. And Marty's got these sweaters laid out on the living room couch. And he starts piling sweaters on me, one after another… and this is September in New York, one of the hottest days of that year's Indian summer. He was putting the sweaters on me because he wanted to beef me up, since the role of Krug called for this big guy. Now, I'm not small… I'm six foot one, and I weighed about two hundred pounds at the time. And Marty pushes me into this old beat-up station wagon that he was sharing with my sister, and we start driving down Fifth Avenue. At this point, he still hasn't told me what this appointment is about. And at Forty-Seventh and Fifth, he drops me off and says, 'It's up the street… here's the address, I want you to audition for a film.' By this time I'm livid; we've been stopping and starting in traffic, it's hot, I'm caked with sweat

LAST HOUSE ON THE LEFT

underneath all these sweaters. I'd just come back from a work-out, and this is not my idea of fun. Marty says, 'You're late, you'd better run.'

"I run up the street, and I'm thinking, 'Why am I doing this to myself?' I go upstairs, and I come bursting into this office. And I scream at the top of my lungs, 'LISTEN, I'M HERE FOR A FUCKIN' AUDITION, NOW WHO THE FUCK DO I GOTTA SEE?...' I mean, I'm swearing like a madman. The secretary is looking around, and these two guys, Wes and Sean, come out from the inner office. Their eyes are wide as saucers… they think I'm gonna kill 'em! They made me sit down in the office, and ten minutes later I went in and read from the script. I also mentioned that I was a songwriter and musician, and gave them a tape of my music. Fifteen minutes later I had the role of Krug."

"When David Hess came in, he was full of energy, and I thought he had a really striking face," Wes Craven says. "David also offered to do all the music for the film, which was a big plus! Although he wasn't as big as the Krug we'd envisioned, he had a very photogenic face, and a lot of intelligence, so we decided to go with him. The rest of the cast was an amalgam of people who were simply willing to do it. It was conceived as very bloody, and a lot of the lines were very earthy, to the point of being obscene. I believe the only solicitation of more conventional people was for the parents. If I'm not mistaken, both of the parents were played by local New York soap opera regulars.[7] I believe the mother [Manhattan-based actress Eleanor Shaw, credited onscreen as 'Cynthia Carr'] was a soap opera person. She had a very interesting contract; one of the paragraphs in it was 'The producers guarantee that I will not be asked to perform fellatio on any of the cast members.'"

The role of Dr. John Collingwood went to actor Richard Towers, who was working as a talent agent when he saw a casting notice for the film in a local show biz tabloid. "When I auditioned for Sean Cunningham and Wes Craven, it was originally supposed to be a porno film, and that's the script I read," Towers relates. "A couple of weeks later, I heard from them that I had gotten the role, but that they had changed the script and it wasn't going to be a porno film but a 'cult' film or whatever you want to call it. I was working for Lloyd Greenfield at that time, who was the manager of Tom Jones and Englebert Humperdinck, and I was also a member of the Screen Actors' Guild. This wasn't a SAG picture, so I was concerned with the fact that maybe I would have a problem with the Guild. So I thought, 'Well, maybe I should change my name.' I went to Lloyd Greenfield and I told him what had happened, and he said, 'That's great! We'll change your name.' I asked, 'What will we call me, Lloyd?' And he said, 'Well, let's see… How's about Gaylord St. James?' And that's the way it ended up on screen."

Towers passed word of the auditions on to one of his clients, a struggling twenty-one year-old actor named Marc Sheffler, who ended up playing the part of Junior Stillo. "Basically, the entertainment business is all I ever really wanted to do," Sheffler says. "I began when I was young, doing little parts in plays in school, clowning around, and then when I got older I studied at the Pittsburgh Playhouse. I went from there to New York City, and did stand-up comedy, and hung out… and got this job in this very strange movie. *Last House on the Left* was my first film appearance." Sheffler recalls that his audition required him to read the nightmare scene where Junior sobs, 'I'm sorry! I'm sorry!' After leaving the audition, Sheffler returned to Towers' office, where he

Planning The Sex Crime Of The Century

The infamous "piss your pants" scene.

found a message already awaiting him: he'd won the part. "I remember them asking me, 'What the hell did you *do*?'," Sheffler laughs.

"The audition for *Last House* was a normal process," Fred Lincoln comments. "I had auditioned for Sean on a different film that he had done [possibly *Together*] and I didn't get the part, so he called me for this one. I went in to read, and then I came back again on a call-back. The second time, I brought Jeramie Rain with me. I had suggested her for the part of the girl."

Rain, who attended Michigan State University, had moved to New York City approximately a year before she was cast in *Last House on the Left*. She laughs when asked to explain the connection which brought her into the picture. "Fred Lincoln worked for my answering service at the time; he was a guy who answered the phones! Fred got me the audition, and when I read the script for the first time, it had me cutting a girl's breasts off and eating them! I was so horrified at this, but Sean and Wes said, 'Oh, don't worry, that'll be taken out. Don't pay any attention to that stuff.' Thank God, they did take all of that out... but everything else in the script basically stayed the same. I didn't like it, but when you're living below the poverty level in New York City and someone offers you a paying gig, you take the part. There was no preparation for any of this. They paid me six hundred dollars for my work on *Last House*... that's what a great businesswoman I was at the time! I used the money to buy myself a dog, a little Doberman puppy. That was the only good thing that came out of it."

Although Craven says that the Manson family murder case was not an influence on the film, the Sadie character evokes both the murderous actions and the well-known nickname of Manson Family member Susan Atkins. Ironically enough, Rain was actually portraying Atkins in a bizarre off-Broadway play at the same time that she appeared as Sadie in *Last House*. "I was doing the Susan Atkins part in that play, *22 Years: A Rockumentary*, at Café LaMama [a Greenwich

LAST HOUSE ON THE LEFT

Wes Craven (centre) poses with cast and crew members on location.

Village avant-garde theater] for a year before I was in *Last House*, and continued while we were shooting the movie," Rain says. "I was killing Sharon Tate every night!" The Manson case inspired numerous exploitation flicks of the day; one blatant retelling of the story, *Sweet Savior* (1972, aka *The Love-Thrill Murders*) starred Troy Donahue as a murderous Manson-like "messiah." Other low-budget shockers were less literal; a Manson-esque hippie cult became rabid zombies in David Durston's *I Drink Your Blood* (1971), and AIP's *Deathmaster* (1972) featured a commune of hippie vampires led by bloodsucking, long-haired guru Robert (*Count Yorga, Vampire*) Quarry.

Although the original script described Mari Collingwood as a blonde, it was dark-haired, pretty Sandra Peabody (or Sandra Cassell, as she is credited on the film) who ultimately signed on for the role. The actress, then twenty-two, had responded to a casting notice in the New York trade publication *Backstage*, and was returning from a cross-country road trip when the film makers called on her to audition. "I had gone out to see what the wild West was like, and I was heading back towards New York," Peabody recalls. "I had a few days to go, when I got a message from my answering service regarding that film. I called Sean Cunningham's office and set up a day to meet them... they originally wanted me to read for the part of Phyllis. Then, when they met me, they changed their minds and decided to cast me as Mari. They told me that the script would be changed, because it was pretty wild, and I didn't want to do it the way it was originally written. Even before I came in, there had been a change in the kind of auditioning that they were doing. I know they were talking to some other actors about doing it as an X-rated movie, and by the time I came in, they had decided to do it just as a violent film, without all the sex. I don't know if it was because of money, or because they'd simply gotten the OK from the backers, but they promised that all of that [porn] was totally out... and they did take it out."[8]

Lucy Grantham and Sandra Cassell.

Peabody's co-star Lucy Grantham says she does not recall the specific circumstances of how she came to be involved with the film. Grantham grew up in Great Neck, Long Island, and attended the University of Wisconsin, where she majored in theater. Shortly after graduating, she returned to New York and somehow ended up auditioning for *Last House*. "At the time that I was cast in *Last House on the Left*, I was not really giving my full effort to acting," Grantham says in retrospect. "I was partying a lot, and working a couple of other jobs, and not really being as diligent about acting as a lot of other girls were at that stage. I wasn't answering every ad, or going to every open call, and I was never a member of the Screen Actors' Guild. The audition for *Last House* was very informal."

"I remember thinking when I first read the script that it was very graphic, and being a little embarrassed about some of the details of some of the scenes I was going to be involved in, and even the ones I wasn't involved in," Grantham adds. "It was a little raunchy, a little sketchy. But on the other hand, when I met and got to know Wes and Sean, I recognized that they were real quality people, so that allayed any fears I had that this was going to be some kind of a low-grade thing. I could see from meeting them that they were bright and intelligent, and I immediately recognized that they were ambitious… I had no idea - and I'm not sure that *anybody* did - that this was breaking ground. I wish I had been prescient enough to know that."

"Sandra Peabody and I were so different," Grantham reflects. "Sandra was this sweet, rather naïve 'good girl,' and I was much more rebellious in my personality, much more of a risk-taker, much more 'out there.' She was more ladylike and shy than I was. I could really whoop it up with the guys, and I always liked to, and I'm still like that; my personality is very fun and outgoing. Sandra and I were really going in two very different directions, both in the script and outside of the script, so there was no sense of competition between the two of us. In fact, Sandra was very much like the character she played in the movie, and so was I. I imagine that Wes recognized these qualities in us when he cast us in the film; I'd like to think that he did, anyway."

The casual nature of the casting process for *Sex Crime* is well illustrated by Marshall Anker, who played the part of the sheriff.

"Believe it or not, I was introduced to Wes Craven in a marcobiotic restaurant called the Paradox, on 7th Street between 2nd and 3rd Avenue in the East Village," Anker relates. "My friend Perry Gewirtz, who is also an actor, had met Wes there previously. Wes was just sitting there eating. They got to talking, and Wes mentioned that he was doing a movie, for which he'd written the script. Perry asked him whether I might be good for the part of the sheriff. Craven said, 'Why not?...'

"I came down to the restaurant, and Wes asked me, 'Would you do it for X dollars a day?' 'OK, yeah.' It was very casual; there wasn't even a handshake, he just said something like, 'I'll call you next week.'" Anker continues. "Then they brought me in to the offices of Sean Cunningham and actually auditioned me with the script. I think they asked me for some kind of accent, so that's when I came up with the sheriff's persona, based on a custodian I used to know at Brooklyn College who was a big, strong guy but had a high voice, like he was basically repressed and holding in his temper. I think the audition took place about a month before we shot the film. That original script was much worse than what you saw on screen, more obscene, but I liked my scenes. Somewhere along the line, I heard that Wes Craven had a degree in philosophy, and I'm looking at this script, saying to myself, *'A man with a masters' degree in philosophy wrote **this**?!'* It was weird, and at first I thought there was something a little bit spooky about this guy. However, I later heard that there were these backers from Boston who had *told* Wes and Sean something like, 'We'll put in eighty thousand, or a hundred thousand, but we want the most violent script you could write.' So I think he [Craven] deliberately wrote it that way, because that was the offer: you write a violent script, and we'll back it."

Of the project as a whole, Sean Cunningham remarks, "It was just one of those things where somebody says, 'Hey, I've got an idea... let's make a movie!... you write, I'll produce, you direct, and I'll make sandwiches, and I'll take sound!'; it was very primitive, student-level film making. It was like doing a high school play, or community theater, where everybody works around the clock for no other reason than to do the play."

Yvonne Hannemann remarks, "I remember that a few weeks before the shoot there was some last-minute fund-raising going on. Bear in mind, in those days, things were different. Everything is so much more expensive now that there are all sorts of other considerations that go into making a movie. But in those days, people would just sort of cluster together and say, 'Oh, we're gonna make this film.'" Legend has it that Cunningham's 'last-minute fund-raising' continued during the shoot. Wes Craven tells the story that Cunningham used to come up with the money to pay the director's salary by playing poker on the Amtrak commuter train from New York to Westport!

When asked how much of *Last House* was planned out during pre-production, Craven replies "Precious little. I didn't know how to plan a film. I didn't know how to shoot a master shot, I didn't understand the concept of coverage, and I didn't know a great deal about film direction. The only experience I'd had in cutting film was basically documentary experience. I didn't use storyboards at all for *Last House*; I used them in *The Hills Have Eyes*, which I completely storyboarded myself. I literally did not know any of the rules or techniques of film... we simply went out to make a movie without knowing how to do it."

Planning The Sex Crime Of The Century

Notes

1 As a novice film editor, Craven worked on several of Locke's movies during the '70s, including *You've Got To Walk it Like You Talk It* (1971) and the X-rated *It Happened in Hollywood* (1973).

2 The ties between Craven and the Chapin family persist to this day; Steve's older brother Tom Chapin married Craven's ex-wife Bonnie and is the stepfather of Craven's children.

3 After a prolific career as a musician and social activist, Harry Chapin died tragically in a car crash in July, 1981. "Harry's songwriting was very cinematic in its form," Steve Chapin reflects. "Many of his songs revolved around storytelling." One of Chapin's last hits was a follow-up to "Taxi" called "Sequel".

4 *The Art of Marriage* was recently unearthed and released by Something Weird Video. Cunningham's name is not on the movie's credits (the movie is billed as a presentation of "the Nevada Institute for Family Studies") but the year, title and content of SWV's release all match up with the director's description of the film in an interview with author Maitland MacDonagh. Hosted and narrated by one "Howard J. Brubaker," the film features a hippie couple going through the paces of various sexual positions while the deadpan narrator explains the action a la Masters and Johnson.

5 The Puerto Rico shoot took place sometime during the winter of 1970/71 and involved an epilogue for the film. "We wanted to shoot sunny, romantic stuff, and we couldn't do it in the middle of the winter in New York," Cunningham explains.

6 Cunningham says that at the time of production, *Last House* was budgeted at $45,000, and that "at the end of the day, we had considerably less than $100,000 in it, including post-production costs." Whatever the exact figures, all involved with the film concur with Cunningham's description of the budget as "laughable."

7 In point of fact, Richard ("Gaylord St. James") Towers was known mainly as a stage actor and talent agent at the time. His only soap credit was a CBS series called *The Doctors and the Nurses*, which aired during the '60s. "Tell Wes I'm sorry, but I didn't really do many soaps," he laughs. "Maybe I should have!"

8 David Hess confirms Peabody's account of the casting process. "They [Cunningham and Craven] had been talking to this package of other actors about doing it as an X-rated film, but they [the actors] didn't want to do it for the money that was being offered. Wes and Sean never really wanted to do it as a porno film, so when that fell through, they saw it as a window of opportunity for them... that they could change this from a porno into a slasher movie, which was what they had in mind to begin with."

Marshall Anker ("The Sheriff") in a New York coffee shop in 1997.

(photo by David Szulkin)

Babes In The Woods:
A Crash Course In Guerilla Film Making

"The fact is that if any of us knew what we were doing, we never would have gotten the picture made... because we would have said 'This is impossible!'"
- **Sean Cunningham**

The shooting of *Last House on the Left* (under its working title, *Night of Vengeance*) began on October 2, 1971 and lasted approximately four weeks, with some additional makeup days carrying over to the first week of November. Like most low-budget productions, it was an arduous and often chaotic experience, characterized by long hours, hard work, and low-to-nonexistent pay. Pressed for time and strapped for cash, the filmmakers quickly discovered that making a feature film was a much more exhausting endeavor than they had anticipated. Despite the demanding nature of the project and its often gruesome subject matter, most of the cast recall having a good time on the set.

"It was a wild and crazy shoot," Craven laughs. "Everybody worked their asses off doing that film... it was a very difficult movie to make, because we were dealing with an extremely tight budget and attempting to do a very ambitious film in such a short period of time. *Last House* introduced me to the fact that you don't sleep for five weeks when you're shooting a film. But it was also a lot of fun, especially shooting the outdoor scenes, with all that running around, falling, and screaming... it was great."

Most of the film was shot around Cunningham's house in Westport, Connecticut, aside from a few urban scenes lensed in Manhattan. The film makers found many of the locations during the shoot by simply tramping around the woods. "This little house that Sean was renting at the time happened to be situated on the ruins of an old fish hatchery," Craven explains. "The area had a large variety of lakes, ponds, and streams. We shot there a great deal, because almost everywhere we turned, there was a very different-looking locale. Within, I would say, a three hundred foot radius of Sean's house we found the lake where the mother bit off Weasel's cock, the woods where Lucy's character was killed, the old graveyard, and other locations... it was an extraordinarily rich little area. Then we filmed around Sean's mother's house; that location gave us the swimming pool, the interior of the parents' bedroom, and things like that. We also jumped the fence into a state park and reservoir area for shooting a lot of the deeper woods scenes, like the one down by the waterfall. We did all of this shooting without permits... it was very much guerrilla film making."

"We hardly looked like a film crew," Cunningham laughs. "We were, literally, kids running around with a camera. We didn't run into any problems with the locals; although everything we were doing was without permits, we weren't stopping traffic and throwing bodies in the street. We'd park the car by the side of the road, run into the woods and hope the game warden didn't catch us. We used my mom's house [in the nearby town of Weston, Connecticut] as a kind of backlot, and also shot a lot of stuff in the woods behind this house where my wife and I were living in a garage apartment."

"We set off to make the film using the skills that we knew, which were based on a cinema verite, hand-held camera style," Craven says. "That's why we got a documentary film maker, Vic Hurwitz, to be the cameraman. He had his own camera, which was a converted Auricon, carried on the shoulder, like all the Time-Life documentary guys used. It was a very small crew... I wouldn't be surprised if it was no more than seven or eight people."

In addition to cinematographer Hurwitz, the core of the technical crew included Jim Hubbard (sound man), Yvonne Hannemann (assistant director/script supervisor), Katherine D'Amato (associate producer), Larry Beinhart (unit production manager), Troy Roberts (special effects) and several production assistants, including still photographer Steve Dwork and future director Steve Miner, whose most recent credits include *Halloween: H20* (1998) and *Lake Placid* (1999).

Wes Craven and assistant director Yvonne Hannemann on location during the *Last House on the Left* shoot.

Miner became involved with the production soon after the shooting had begun. "I was a ski bum in Colorado, and I had decided that I wanted to get into the film business. I grew up in Westport, and I knew that there were a number of industrial and educational film makers there. So I moved back home to Connecticut in hopes of finding some work. I heard that somebody in town was shooting a movie, and it turned out to be Sean Cunningham. I didn't know Sean at the time, but I had grown up with his younger brothers. So I asked Sean to give me a job, and he did... at something like fifteen dollars a week! I was a gofer, but I ended up doing a little bit of everything because nobody knew anything. I held the boom mike, I carried lights, I took script notes, did assistant camera work, took the cast and crew to get lunch... I'd do anything that was needed. I remember a lot of twenty hour days, trying to finish up and get out of a given location. We didn't have strip boards [the industry standard for organizing the elements of a film shoot] so we would be going through the script, crossing out pages, wondering, 'Did we shoot this part yet?'"

Victor Hurwitz died shortly after the release of *Last House* at the age of 41, when he was run over by a truck while riding his bicycle through Manhattan on July 5, 1973. One of the few crew members who knew the cameraman well was sound man Jim Hubbard, who had worked with Hurwitz as a freelance team on various documentary and industrial film shoots for several years prior to the shooting of *Last House*.

"Vic Hurwitz was a particular kind of cameraman, in that he liked to create and fix things," Hubbard says. "He was a very secretive man; I never did see the inside of his apartment, even though I knew him quite well. And the other people I knew who knew Vic all said the same thing… He never let anybody inside his apartment. But he was always very kind; at the time when I first started doing sound for him, I had almost no equipment, and he outfitted me with all kinds of microphones and things that he'd fixed at no charge. One day, Vic announced that he had built a Super 16mm camera. He used the body of an Auricon, and I remember him saying that the most difficult part of the job was finding a lens that would accommodate Super 16. He went through something like a hundred lenses; the only lenses that would fit were television camera lenses. When he finally got it right, he put an ad in *Variety* that said 'CAMERAMAN WITH SUPER 16 CAMERA AVAILABLE TO SHOOT FEATURES.' Sean Cunningham called him, and Vic called me saying, 'Would you be interested in going out on a low-budget feature film?' That's how it got started. I can remember times during that period of shooting *Last House* when a roll of film would come back from the lab with a little scratch in it, and Vic would stay up all night working on his camera, fixing the pressure plate. Then he'd get a half-hour's sleep, and I'd pick him up in the morning to go to Connecticut and shoot. It was, at times, rather exhausting."

"The cameraman [Hurwitz] was one of the better people on the set," Sandra Cassell recalls. "That guy was great. He told me, 'Have something else in your life besides acting, because it's a terrible business.' He was a real fatherly kind of guy to me. He died a few years after *Last House* on his bicycle… it was really horrible and tragic."

The Super 16mm format, which had just been introduced at the time of *Last House*, recorded a (roughly 40%) larger image than a standard 16mm camera could capture. The configuration of the Super 16 frame lent itself well to the blow-up to widescreen 35mm; the format was also more portable and less expensive than 35mm. "*Last House* was a pioneer in its use of the Super 16mm format," Hubbard says. "After the first week of shooting, they took some of the 16mm footage of the river and the creek and enlarged it to 35mm. They took that and intercut it with some film that had been originally shot in 35mm as a comparison. I remember being very impressed with how well the image held up to the test. I recall Sean talking to Vic about a week to ten days into the shoot, saying that he was very pleased with the rushes, and that the footage really looked much more professional than he had expected… that this could actually be a good, solid low-budget production. I think he realized that he could be a little more pretentious with it, that a better film was going to come out of it than just exploitation."

"We set about making the film by staging scenes, beginning to end, and filming them from three or four different angles, figuring that we'd cut it together just like a documentary," Wes Craven says. "We decided to use hand-held camera for all of the action sequences, and a tripod for anything with a dialogue scene. That was the essential style of the film… to try to capture a very reality-based situation. I was very impressed by some of the footage that we saw coming out of Vietnam; that seemed to have a lot more immediacy and truth to it than anything else I was aware of, so that was the style that I adopted. We also used three different film stocks, both for financial reasons - because we had access to them and they were cheap to buy - and also for stylistic reasons. We went down in graininess or up in graininess depending on whether the content of a scene was light or dark."

Craven's simple strategy for directing the film did not account for the many external obstacles the production would encounter. "One of the things about *Last House* was that, on the one hand, we were playing grown-up with real financing, and advertising in *Backstage,* and trying to do it the proper way, but on the other hand, no one had done any of these tricks before," says Yvonne Hannemann. "It took much, much more than anyone ever expected."

The division of responsibilities on the set was anything but compartmentalized. "I was the producer of record," Sean Cunningham says, "…but I was also doing other things wherever I could. If I had to help do sound, or run and get a location, or go off and get dinner for the crew, I'd do it."

Of his collaboration with Cunningham during the shoot, Craven remarks, "It was very much an equal partnership. A great deal of the time, I slept in Sean's living room on a pull-out couch and I had breakfast with him and his family every morning. We used Sean's cars, his house, his mother's house; Sean's wife, Susan, made the costumes for the movie… *Last House* was very much a family-made movie."

"Sean Cunningham was really the mover and the driver, the guy who was arranging the shooting schedule and keeping it all together," Jim Hubbard asserts. "It's been my experience that there always has to be one real 'honcho' on every film shoot, and Sean was really the strongman for *Last House on the Left*. Wes did a fairly good job of directing the film, but he wasn't always that sure of himself. There were a few times when, for one reason or another, Wes wasn't there or needed some help, and Sean took over. I believe the end of the chain-saw scene was one of those times that Sean stepped in to help direct, and he was much more forceful and authoritative about it than Wes."

Cunningham admits that he directed some scenes in *Last House* "after a fashion," but is quick to add that "…Wes was the director, and I don't want to take any credit away from him." As Hubbard notes, Cunningham's occasional handling of the directorial reins was markedly different from Craven's laid-back, *laissez-faire* approach. "I don't think Sean spoke in a quiet tone of voice until we had the wrap party at his house," laughs David Hess.

"My vision of Wes throughout the making of *Last House* is of a very quiet, almost beatific person," Hannemann recalls. "He was very mellow and wise. I think Wes' strongest point was being able to accept suggestions and to rewrite as he went along. Wes had a lot of little 'meaningful/artistic' shots that he really wanted to work in, but he often didn't have time to do them. He always wanted it to be sort of arty, and I guess the movie did have a wry commentary to it… I think Wes saw where the movie was going, and if it was not necessarily where he wanted it to go, he saw how to make it work. He was really adapting to all of it very well and very quickly."

Babes In The Woods

Wes Craven directs actress Lucy Grantham (Phyllis) during the chase sequence.

"Wes was so young, he was like a hippie," Sandra Cassell laughs. "I lived down in the Village back then, and to me, Wes was just another hip, cool dude. He was very natural and real… I don't think he ever had an ego. When we were actually shooting I remember him being very controlled, and I think he had set in his mind what he wanted to do - it wasn't like he was fumbling. Although he was easygoing, he made clear-cut decisions. But although Wes was laid-back, the atmosphere on the set was not really relaxed, what with all the characters running around, and the fact that we didn't have a lot of time."

As the production progressed, Craven continually revamped the script to fit the shooting schedule and the locations. Some of the movie's most memorable scenes were the product of these last minute revisions. Weasel's "home dentistry" nightmare, Phyllis' agonizing crawl through the old cemetery, the killers' remorseful reactions to the defilement of Mari, Junior's gun-in-mouth suicide, and Sadie's splashy demise in the family swimming pool are all examples of scenes wholly or partially improvised during the shoot.

"The script evolved in fits and starts," David Hess explains. "It was basically a repertory piece, in that there was an unpredictable chemistry between the actors, especially the bad guys. Because of the nature of the people involved, their youth, their naiveté, their incredible energy, the film evolved into this repertory kind of thing where a lot of what was done was really extemporaneous and off-the-cuff. There was a lot of improvisation, and Wes was smart enough to let the camera run."

LAST HOUSE ON THE LEFT

"The most important thing in making a film like *Last House* is to allow the movie to *happen*," Hess adds. "I think one of the biggest problems in the film industry today is that it's become so compartmentalized and specialized. Today's film industry doesn't allow for the organic flow of a movie like *Last House*. People are too afraid about their money and their investments, and they stultify all of the creativity. I remember Lee Marvin once telling me, 'David, stop being inventive… hit your marks, say your lines, and exit…*that's* being creative.'[1] That's good advice in some situations, but I think that there's a lot of spontaneity missing from the film industry in general."

Fred Lincoln offers a more practical reason for the impromptu changes in the script: "A lot of the film was improvised, mainly because we couldn't *do* some of the script we had to begin with! So a lot of the stuff in *Last House* just came about [at the moment] when we did it. It was really a fun thing… except, for some reason, Sandra was afraid. Sometimes, she was scared to death… In fact, she left the production after one or two days, and we had to talk her into coming back!"

When asked if she was upset during the shoot, Sandra Cassell replies, "I was upset because I'm an emotional person, and I reacted to what was going on as if it were real. I had a really hard time with some of the scenes, because I had come out of American Playhouse, where it was all about preparation, and everything had to be real. I ended up doing a horrible job in the film. I was very upset, and I felt like I should have channeled that, but I couldn't… I was a young actress and I was still learning to balance any emotions I had from outside of the film into my scene work."

"Sandra was a real neophyte, and she often needed to be encouraged or consoled by Wes," Steve Dwork recalls. "Wes was kind of the Good Guy for her, and she was somewhat terrified by Sean, who was the big Producer. During some of the more demanding scenes in the woods, Wes spent a good deal of time with her, basically telling her, 'This is for God and country; you've got to do this.'"

"I remember once we were riding on the train from New York to Westport, and somebody from the movie said to me, 'Sandra, you look like a cow that's just been slaughtered!',", the lead actress recalls. "I said, 'Well, that's because I don't really know how the script is going to be changed.' The thought of a lot of these scenes upset me, and a lot of the time, I wasn't quite sure what was going to be done until we actually did it. I was convinced that however a scene was shot, that it would be OK, because I trusted Wes and Sean. They promised me, 'It's all changing…' - and a lot of it did. Scenes were written in while we were working; there was one time that we went to an ice cream place, and I was trying to pick out different ice creams, and Wes said, 'Oh, we're going to have a scene like that in the movie!' because of the way I was doing that.[2] It was really spontaneous… Of course, that was the Seventies. One of the characters was a method actor, so he was trying to live his part… He'd come after us with a knife at night, trying to freak us out. This was the guy with the dark curly hair [David Hess] - he tried to play his role on and off the set. It was like, 'Lock your doors and windows at night, you don't want him to come get you!' I was scared; I thought this guy had really been a killer at some time in his past!" In contrast to the lead actress's recollection, Marshall Anker remarks, "David Hess was really a congenial guy. I find it hard to believe that anybody thought he was really like his character." Likewise, Fred

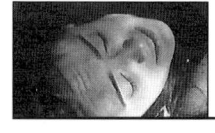

Lincoln comments, "David is a nice guy; he was into his role, but nobody ever got hurt. We were just having fun."

"I have terrific memories of the crew and the cast, and the kind of relationship that we developed in the course of shooting the film," Lucy Grantham reflects. "I remember it being very beautiful in the area of Connecticut where we shot. I have not had occasion to be up there since, but I remember it being very pastoral and quiet. We were living, for the most part, in Sean's house, which was an unusual situation that brought us all very close. There was a lot of partying and a lot of fun. I remember the whole project being part of something else, which was kind of a 'happening' involving this particular group of people that had come together, were working together, living together on a temporary basis, and just partying! The experience had a gestalt to it; it wasn't just making a movie. There was a sense of family, almost like being on a commune, and maybe even a sense that we were thumbing our noses at the world by doing our own thing. "

When asked how much rehearsal time was allotted for the cast, Yvonne Hannemann responds, "Almost none! It was very interesting, because the actors really got into their characters, and they *stayed* in those characters for a few weeks! They really lived and breathed those roles… The girls sort of huddled together, and David Hess was really fearsome. David truly *was* this menacing character throughout the shoot. I had the frightening task of waking David up in the morning to go and shoot… and having to move the cast along, and rehearse them as much as we could. Looking back on the shoot, it's all a jumble of jumping into the car, hurrying off to the next location, the actors hating their lines, refusing to say them, and waiting to talk to Wes about changing the dialogue. The girls were always afraid, and they would be cowering even during lunch! Of course, those lunches were always very memorable, because Sean used to go out and get Kentucky Fried Chicken every day. Since I was a vegetarian, all I ate was Oreo cookies and coleslaw! Sean had this belief that if people just had something to nibble on, they would be kept happy. Since the primary goal was to

Spanish poster
Although the ad copy refers to Mari, the photo on this poster is of Phyllis... This error has been duplicated from the original U.S. poster of the same design, shown on page 4.

The cast and crew of Last House on the Left prepare to shoot; Wes Craven is at far right, back to camera.

keep the budget down at all costs, they were continually giving us junk food. That diet really brought us all down to the lowest common denominator."

"There was nobody there [on the set] to say, 'You can't do that!,'" so we ended up doing a whole bunch of things that normally wouldn't be done," Cunningham admits. "I mean, how many times can you feed people Kentucky Fried Chicken… *straight* ?!"

"I acted in another film right after *Last House*, and I remember being impressed because they actually tried to *direct* me," Jeramie Rain laughs. "They told me when I was doing too much shtick with my face, and actually talked to me about what it meant to be on film; on *Last House*, there was *nothing*. I just ran around and that Sadie character came out. I'm not saying that what I did was great; I simply *did* it."

Richard Towers offers a similar recollection: "Actually, I think Wes was just in it to get it done. Not to say anything disparaging about him, but I don't think we got into a lot of character development. Everybody just did what they did… I thought my performance was all right. There was nothing great that I had to do, except for the scenes with David where we had the fight at the end with the buzzsaw. He beat the hell out of me, but that's okay, because I cut his head off!"

"All of the actors were really *into* the film," Marshall Anker says. "We were all getting a lift back to the city one time… I think Martin Kove was driving. Jeramie Rain asked me what I thought of the script. I said I liked my scenes. She said, 'What about the rest of the script?' I said, 'No comment.' And she said, 'What do you mean, no comment? Come on, make a comment, what about the scenes that don't involve you?' I said they were V-I-L-E, vile… Jeramie didn't like that. You see, when actors and actresses get involved in a making a movie, they're so gung-ho about it, especially when they're young and just starting out. They convince themselves that it's a great script, and they're all hopped up about it. And I gave her [Rain] an argument. I said, 'What the hell do you think this is, Shakespeare? You think this is iambic pentameter?!' I was sarcastic, and she didn't like that, because she really believed in what she was doing. I said, 'You better interject some comedy in there, ad lib some funny lines'… she said, 'I have a funny line!' and told me that line about how every time she sees the Grand Canyon she crosses her legs."

Of his approach to the role of Weasel, Fred Lincoln explains, "It wasn't hard for me to draw on hostility. I used to be like Weasel in real life; I grew up on the streets of New York [in Hell's Kitchen]. The '70s really changed my outlook on life; I became a non-hostile person."

"Fred made a good psychopath," Steve Dwork remarks. "I honestly didn't know how much of his performance was acting,". "Not that I dealt with Fred all that much off the set, but either he got into the role prior to appearing and didn't leave it until departing, or he wasn't playing a role at all. I don't remember him *not* acting like that character… Looking back on it, he reminds me of a young James Woods."

"Fred was a lot of fun. He was very wild," Lucy Grantham says. "He was unconventional, and very much of a rebel… He was a very funny, smart guy."

"The whole unit sort of fell into groups," Hannemann says. "The two actors playing the parents just drove in for the day to their parts, and left when they were done. They seemed more professional than the others… They had already been acting, and they had much more of a presence about them."

"I remember the parents coming in with their plastic garment bags slung over their shoulders; they really reminded me of soap opera actors. They had that look," Steve Dwork remarks. "They were the least involved in the film out of any of the cast members."

"I only stayed out in Connecticut two times," Richard Towers confirms. "One time, Eleanor Shaw and I shared a room at the house, and I think another time I stayed in a motel. The rest of the time, Eleanor Shaw and I commuted in the morning from Manhattan to Westport… it was an easy forty-five minute drive. At that time, Wes was a very young director; as I remember him, he was very thin, and he had long, scraggly hair… nothing like he looks today! Anyway, I was young, we went up there, and we did what we had to do. I think there was hardly any re-shooting of any of the scenes, because they wanted to do it as quickly as possible. But my remembrance of the whole thing is very good… we had a ball! I think I only met Sean Cunningham once or twice; he was a nice man, very pleasant, but that's the only relationship I had with Sean. There was one scene towards the end of the picture, where they needed a body lying on the couch, face-down… and they didn't have a body! So I said to Wes, 'Why don't we let my wife do it?" And he says, 'Great! Bring her up tomorrow, and she can be the body on the couch!' So, my wife was actually in the movie, which was kind of fun."

Of the crew and cast's reaction to the film's violence, Steve Dwork comments, "None of us were particularly fazed by it. Nobody was politically correct about it… It was like, 'We're here, we're doing this film, some of it's a bit yucky, but it's not the first time this has been done.' There was nothing under- or over-whelming about it. Even with some of the sexual scenes, I don't think anybody on the set was really put off, except Sandra, who was involved in doing it. She was not into any of that, professionally or otherwise, which was an understandable reaction on her part… I mean, if I was being stripped naked and slashed about with fifteen strangers standing around watching, I don't think I would deal with it too well!"

"In general, there was a certain camaraderie among the cast and crew," Dwork adds. "There *had* to be a camaraderie, because at that low-budget level, it's the only way you can get something done. We would get up at the crack of dawn and work a good sixteen hour day. When you're trying to make a film for close to no money, everything starts out as a snafu and you've got to try to work your way out of it. Trying to make the film work and look professional was a difficult task, but I think they [Craven and Cunningham] did a pretty good job of it. It's interesting that even at that point in time, with my lack of technical knowledge, I could see that Wes was something special. Not that I knew Wes was going to make it big or anything, but I recall thinking to myself, 'This guy's cool; he's got a good handle on things.' Sean definitely took a great interest in Wes and saw in him someone who was going places. Sean was a wheeler-dealer, making things happen and somehow managing to pull this whole thing off, which was impressive; he was good at pep-talks. You would see Sean saying to people, 'Someday, something might come back to you from this film,' and everybody believing him."

"I was on the outs with the whole group," Jeramie Rain says. "I didn't like to stay in Connecticut, so I drove back and forth from New York every day. I really didn't hang out with the crew or anybody else; I got in my little car at the end of each day and took off. The rest of the cast mostly stayed at Sean's mother's house."

"I don't think Sean's mother quite realized what was going on," Hannemann laughs. "There must have been fifteen people staying in her house, including the key actors. I imagine her saying 'How nice of you to have some of your little friends over, Sean…' and then being confronted with David Hess sitting there with that menacing look!"

The cast also stayed at a motel called the Pequot Motor Inn when not holed up at the Cunningham residence. "David Hess, Marty Kove and I were quite mischievous during the shoot," Marc Sheffler says. "We did a lot of clowning around. David and I became instant friends; sometimes you meet people, and there's some kind of personality connection that makes up for not having known these people your entire life. David and I have that connection, and we're still close friends to this day."

"We had a lot of fun," Kove agrees. "There were never any negative trips at all during the shoot. We did a lot of laughing, and had a lot of good times."

* * * * * * * * * *

The following pages feature analyses of selected scenes from *Last House on the Left*, accompanied where appropriate by commentary from the cast and crew. The scenes are organized roughly in the chronolgy of the film's storyline. Appendix II shows the shooting schedule as it was planned prior to production, as well as some sparse notes from the diary of sound man Jim Hubbard which show how the planned schedule changed as the shoot progressed.

* * * * * * * * * *

At Home with the Collingwoods

The movie opens with a placid, deceptively innocent montage establishing the bucolic forest location where much of the story unfolds. We then see a postman drive up to the Collingwoods' mailbox, where he is greeted by the family dog. Sorting through a stack of birthday cards addressed to Mari, the rustic character announces: "Looks like Mari's getting cards from half the civilized world; you'd think she's the only kid to reach the age of seventeen. 'Course, she is about the prettiest piece I've ever seen." Following this low-brow Greek chorus, the credits appear over a scene of Mari taking a shower and examining herself in a mirror while her mother gripes at her from offscreen.

The mailman was played by New York actor Ray Lovering, who is identifed in the film's end credits by the pseudonym 'Ray Edwards.' In an early draft of the screenplay, the mailbox prop was supposed to bear the legend: 'JOHN COLLINGWOOD, M.D.' with handwriting underneath reading 'MARI COLLINGWOOD, V.D.' The venereal innuendo was replaced in the film by a simple heart-with-arrow symbol. Likewise, the shower scene was toned down from its more salacious presentation in the script.

The next scene, set in the Collingwoods' living room, quickly establishes the main characters with an almost sitcom-like tone of banality. The complacent Mr .Collingwood puts down his paper and sighs, "Same old stuff, murder and mayhem. What's for dinner?" Addressing Mari, Mrs. Collingwood clucks, "I think it's crazy… all that blood and violence! I thought you were supposed to be the Love Generation!" Here, Craven introduces a key plot device: Mari's peace symbol necklace, a birthday present from Daddy ("Maybe it'll bring you luck!") which later betrays the killers.

The bickering between the Collingwoods, emblematic of the '60s generation gap, hints at Craven's core theme of the dysfunctional family. Early drafts of this scene made the parents decidedly less sympathetic, with the mother portrayed as a frigid, cynical alcoholic and the father coming off like a lecher. Phyllis, frowned upon by Mrs. Collingwood as a bad influence, jokes about her own homelife: "My parents are in the iron and steel business… my mother irons, and my father steals!"

The living room scenes (the opening dialogue between Mari and her parents, the scene of Phyllis meeting Mari's parents) were among the first to be shot. Craven's notes from the shoot show many scribbled diagrams which seem to indicate that he was unsure of exactly how to film the expository dialogue.

Richard Towers: "I remember that one great close-up of me, where I say something like, '*Tits?!* What's with this *tits* business?' I always thought that was kind of funny."

Mr. Collingwood's description of Bloodlust as a group "who dismember live chickens during their act" corresponds to the notorious real-life incident in which shock-rocker Alice Cooper threw a live chicken out into a crowd during a 1970 concert appearance; the bird was torn to pieces by the rowdy audience. A cover version of Cooper's song "No More Mr. Nice Guy" appears in Wes Craven's *Shocker* and provided the advertising slogan for that film.

Babes in the Woods

Before setting off to attend the much-anticipated Bloodlust concert, Mari and Phyllis enjoy an idyllic interlude in the forest. The two girls share a bottle of wine which Phyllis has hidden in a stream, and later wander by a waterfall. Mari reveals her thoughts on her budding sexuality ("I feel like a woman for the first time in my life.") A brief dialogue between the two girls follows in which Mari wonders "what it would be like to make it with Bloodlust."

In Craven's script, the interaction between the girls took place in Mari's car; the scene was adapted to the wooded setting during the shoot. A lengthy monologue in which Phyllis describes her relationship with her estranged father was dropped from the scene, along with an exchange in which Phyllis offers Mari "blood-red" downers ("they'll make you smooth as butter!"). Much of the girls' dialogue as it is heard in the film does not appear in the script and seems to have been improvised by the actresses. These scenes served as a means of creating audience sympathy for the two girls, making the later events of the film all the more horrifying.

The dialogue about "what it would be like to make it with Bloodlust" was originally scripted as a framing device for two sequences visually depicting the girls' sexual fantasies. The extravagant fantasy sequences, one violent and orgiastic, the other tender and ethereal, were never shot; the screenplay called for "dope-crazed musician-priests," "priapic guitar necks" and "wobbling testicles of drums."

Driving Down the Road to Nowhere

The footage of Mari and Phyllis driving to the concert in the Collingwood station wagon (in reality, Cunningham's car) was one of the earliest scenes shot for the movie. By one crew member's account, the sequence was filmed without sound to test the quality of the Super 16mm camera equipment. "I believe that footage of the girls driving into New York was done before the movie went into production, as a test," Jim Hubbard notes. "I remember Vic telling me that he'd been up there in Connecticut to do this test shoot with Sean, and it must have been that scene, because we never shot that during the production." In the script, the girls were to drive the green Cadillac which was ultimately used as the villain's getaway car.

The 1966 Triple-Slaying of a Priest and Two Nuns

As the girls drive to the concert, they hear a radio broadcast giving a description of the of the criminals and recounting the prison escape of Krug and Weasel. The radio announcer's narration leads into a montage in which we meet the members of the Krug Stillo gang for the first time. Junior is introduced first as he waits outside a liquor store for his father in a drugged-out slouch. Krug emerges from the store, and as father and son walk down the street, they pass a small boy holding a balloon. In a comical illustration of his ruthlessness, Krug casually pops the little kid's balloon with his cigar. This humorous vignette may

Babes In The Woods

Mari and Phyllis drinking wine by a waterfall. The scene was filmed in a reservoir not far from producer Sean Cunningham's home in Connecticut.

have been Craven's nod to Hitchcock's *Strangers on a Train*, in which the psychopath Bruno (Robert Walker) maliciously breaks a youngster's balloon with the end of a cigarette. The first draft of Craven's screenplay included dialogue between the Collingwoods which mentioned Hitchcock's *Psycho*.

The child with the balloon was actually played by Craven's seven year-old son Jonathan, who has grown up to work with his father on projects like the *Nightmare Café* television series and *(Wes Craven Presents) Mind Ripper* (aka *Hills Have Eyes III: The Outpost*). The radio announcement of the "daring daylight escape of the convicted murderers, dope pushers and rapists" evinces Craven's black humor, spoofing the hard-boiled crime genre with lines like "Krug Stillo is serving a life sentence for the 1966 triple slaying of a priest and two nuns." A margin note in the shooting script indicates that Craven considered shooting the mock-noir scene in black-and-white.

The original script elaborated on the background of the killers in an even more outrageous manner; Krug's crimes included "the single-handed rape of an entire dormitory full of mentally retarded girls," while his accomplice Weasel was charged with "pig-fucking"! The radio announcer's description of Sadie kicking a German Shepherd to death at the scene of the prison escape plays on the notion of the "kick-the-dog scene," a time-honored dramatic device designed to make the audience hate (and root against) an evil character.

The Hideout

The interior scenes of the criminals' sleazy apartment hideout were shot in a building on West 87th Street. The apartment was so small that, according to one crew member, "we could barely fit the actors in there, let alone all the lights and equipment."

LAST HOUSE ON THE LEFT

Krug: Junior, get your ass out on the street and pick up a couple of girls -- good-looking ones. I don't care how you do it, but you damn fucking well better not come back until you've got 'em -- and make it fast.

[handwritten: UP: I. -- I CAN'T GET NO GIRLS TO COME WITH ME --]

Junior: ~~Pop, I...I don't want~~ KRUG!... look, I need a fix, not this sort of _____

Krug: You get! (He makes a motion as if to go after Junior, and the young man quickly goes out. As the door to the flat slams behind Junior, we cut to a car door just as it slams also. Zoom back to reveal Phylis Stone and Mari Collinwood, locking up the great Green Cadillac on a dingy sidestreet on New York's Lower East Side.

Phylis: Now, ~~the~~ first thing we got to do is score on some ~~really good~~ grass -- ~~that way we can get wrecked during the concert, and have a little present, too, for after, when we go back to meet them.~~

Mari: Golly, it's an awful neighborhood. My mother was sort of right!

Phylis: Shit, it aint awful, it's just funky, that's all. Now keep your eyes open for someone who ~~looks like he~~ might be ~~doing a little~~ dealing.

The two are walking quickly along the sidewalk, and the shot pans with them from the side. Just a moment after Phylis says her last line, we see Junior drift by in the shot.

Phylis sees him and as their eyes meet, she pauses and goes back. Junior appears miserable and turned on at the same time, as if he can't bear to talk to anyone his own age, and yet, here are two girls, and they are actually coming up to talk to him.

Phylis: (conspiratorily): Hey man, you wouldn't know where we could score on an ounce of good grass do you?

Junior: (TORN) Uh, no.

In one scene set in the apartment's tiny bathroom, Sadie soaks in the tub drinking a beer while Junior raps to her about his dream of being a frog on a lilypad. As Junior croaks 'Ribbit! Ribbit!', Sadie prankishly pulls him down into the bathwater.

Marc Sheffler: "I actually wrote the bit with the frog. It was something that I had in my little bag of comedy tricks. I talked to Wes about it and he said, 'Well, let's shoot it and see how it is, and if I like it, we'll use it.' Wes was quite a good director in that sense… He doesn't thumbnail actors. If something evolved out of the progression of a scene that was dramatically better than what was on the page, Wes was always willing to go for it."

Jeramie Rain: "When I was in the bathtub and they wanted me to do that song, 'Singin' in the Rain,' I had never heard the song before. So they had some grip give me this dreadful, way off-key rendition of it, and I just parroted that in one take - and that's what they ended up leaving in the movie." The insistence on using 'Singin' in the Rain' may have been a tip of the hat to the song's appearance in Stanley Kubrick's *A Clockwork Orange*, which had just been released to great notoriety at the time of shooting.[3]

Jeramie Rain has a further recollection about shooting the apartment scenes: "They used to make me take off my favorite ring whenever I was called upon to do a scene," the actress recounts. "When we were shooting in that apartment, I gave the ring to somebody on the set to hold until we were done. After I was done with my scene, I went up to the person and asked for my ring. The person denied ever having it, and I never saw it again. The ring had belonged to my grandmother, and it was worth a lot more than what I got paid for acting in the movie."

opposite:
Page from the second draft of the *Sex Crime of the Century* script, showing the 'scoring' scene together with Wes Craven's hand-written amendments.

An extra ounce of Good Stuff

According to Jim Hubbard, the scene in which Mari and Phyllis make their ill-conceived attempt to buy grass from Junior was shot on 21st Street between Second Avenue and Third Avenue. The location was close to New York City's police academy, a fact Hubbard recalls because the presence of police radios caused interference with his sound equipment and a delay in filming. In the finished film, police sirens can be heard in the background of the scene.

The scene in which Mari and Phyllis are taken hostage in the apartment and harassed by Krug, Weasel, and Sadie is one of the scarier portions of the film. The realistic acting, hand-held camera and claustrophobic space all work to great effect, as does the ironic cross-cutting between the criminals encircling the girls and Mari's parents baking her a surprise birthday cake.

Lucy Grantham: "That was one of my favorite scenes in the movie… I felt more comfortable with that kind of high drama than I did with some of the other dialogue scenes. I could have done a thousand takes of that… I just got into this zone!"

The dialogue between Phyllis and Weasel during this sequence features a nice moment of foreshadowing which originated as a magic-marker scrawl in the margin of Craven's shooting script. After Phyllis spits in Weasel's face, Weasel raises his knife and says, "Do that again and you're dead." Later in the film, the wounded Phyllis spits a mouthful of blood in Weasel's face, and the killer makes good on his threat.

Krug and Junior outside the gang's getaway car, just before they drive off with Mari and Phyllis stashed in the trunk.

The fire escape caper

Early the next morning, Krug and his gang throw their two bound and gagged captives into the trunk of the Cadillac convertible and drive out of the city. This business occurs in full view of a number of passing cars which cruise by in the background.

David Hess: "I sprained my ankle going down that fire escape. We were shooting in a condemned place... The scene was shot in downtown New York, not too far from the Fulton fish market. The fire escape itself was weakened in many places, so it was really rickety and dangerous. When I think about the stuff I did, it's unbelievable! I could have been killed... but one didn't think about that."

Sandra Cassell: "One serious scene was where that guy put me over his shoulder, ran down a couple of flights of stairs and threw me into a car. Those guys were kind of mean to me when they did that... especially that method actor [Hess] who was *trying* to be mean all of the time."

Jim Hubbard: "I teach pre-production classes, in which I discuss preparations for getting a film off the ground as inexpensively and well-planned as possible. I often use that fire escape scene as a perfect example of poor planning. What happened was that Sean and Wes went out looking for the location, and they found a perfect alley, right down near the Holland Tunnel, just north of Canal Street. It was a very forbidding, dark alley between two buildings. They went out on a Sunday afternoon, and they found it, and they said 'That's it! Perfect!' They told everybody to meet down there Monday morning. Everybody met there at eight o'clock A.M., and the alley was full of cars parked bumper to bumper because it was a working day. So the whole cast and crew had

Babes In The Woods

Krug and Sadie enjoy each others' company as the gang cruises down the highway.

to sit on their asses while Sean and Wes went out and hastily looked for a make-up location. They eventually found one, but to do that one scene of the gang going down the fire escape took from eight in the morning till two in the afternoon, because of all the time wasted. That was supposed to be a very dark, dramatic scene, but it just turned out to be straightforward and ordinary... the scene was open, with a lot of light. It was supposed to be very sinister and frightening, but they just couldn't do it."

Cruisin' with Krug

Like the fire escape sequence, the scene of the gang driving down the highway in the convertible plays as an oddly light, humorous moment in the film. Backed by the upbeat, *Bonnie and Clyde*-like "Baddies Theme," the killers are having a lark even as they drive toward an unspeakable series of events. With Junior at the wheel, Sadie 'rides' Krug in the back seat (an act which elicits a groan of embarrassment from actress Jeramie Rain). Looking on, the pesky Weasel distracts them with a running commentary which betrays the movie's original title: "I wonder what the meanest, foulest, rottenest, woodsiest sex crime ever was? Hey, Krug, what do you think the *sex crime of the century* was?"

Though muffled sound quality obscures much of the ensuing dialogue, the discussion involves the Boston Strangler (Krug admires him) and 'Sigmund Frood.' who Sadie insists is the world's foremost sex criminal for creating the idea of a 'puh-haylus.' Craven had written a much longer, bawdier Freudian spiel for Sadie, culminating in the assertion that "Freud screwed up sex for the entire Western world, and

LAST HOUSE ON THE LEFT

if that isn't the sex crime of the century, I don't know what is!" Jump-cuts in the sequence may have resulted from the trimming of some off-color dialogue.

Jim Hubbard: "It took me at least three hours to rig that car for sound. I was in the car as they were shooting, down on the floor behind the front seat. I had microphones rigged up on the visor; I couldn't put any microphones on the actors because they were rustling around too much. Part of the time, the camera crew was following the car in another vehicle. The rest of the time, Vic Hurwitz was sitting on the passenger side door of the Cadillac… with his feet on the car seat and his ass hanging out over the road!"

Jeramie Rain: "I can tell you a funny story about that car. Once, when we were in between takes, I was resting on the hood of that convertible, with my head leaning over and my arms down. Somebody went by and thought that there had been a terrible car accident. They reported it, and all these cops came… it was a mess!"

Off to a rough start

The criminals' plan to escape with their captives into Canada goes awry when the convertible breaks down "in the middle of nowhere." When Junior fails to fix the car, Krug decides to "have a little fun" with the helpless girls. Just as the killers drag the girls into the adjacent woods, Mari spots the mailbox marking the driveway of her parents' home.

Wes Craven: "I remember the first day of shooting, we shot the scene where they stop at the driveway and pull the girls out of the trunk. We put this mailbox up in somebody's driveway, and we were about three hours into filming when they came home and said 'What the hell are you doing in our driveway?' They threw us off their property. We lost all of that footage and I think we eventually ended up [shooting the scene] at Sean's driveway."

Sean Cunningham: "I remember the first day of principal photography… we all piled into my two cars; I had a little Dodge Dart and a station wagon. We loaded up all the equipment, it was all tied to the top of the cars, and we drove for about an hour out to this wooded area where we were going to shoot. Everybody was standing around, and they unpacked the camera, and we discovered that we'd literally forgotten to bring the film. There was a conversation along the lines of, 'I thought *you* brought the film!' 'No, I thought *you* brought it!' Ah, well…"

"Piss your pants!"

Even as John and Estelle express their mounting concern over Mari's absence to the sheriff and his deputy, the criminals take Mari and Phyllis deep into the woods opposite the Collingwood property. In the seclusion of the forest, Krug, Weasel and Sadie force the two captive girls to perform a series of humiliating sado-sexual acts for the gang's amusement.

Lighting a cigar, Krug initiates the mean-spirited circus of perversion by ordering Phyllis to urinate in her pants (!). When Phyllis refuses to cooperate ("you sick mother!"), Krug orders Weasel to slice Mari with

Babes In The Woods

Junior unsuccessfully tries to convince his father to stop the madness.

Babes In The Woods

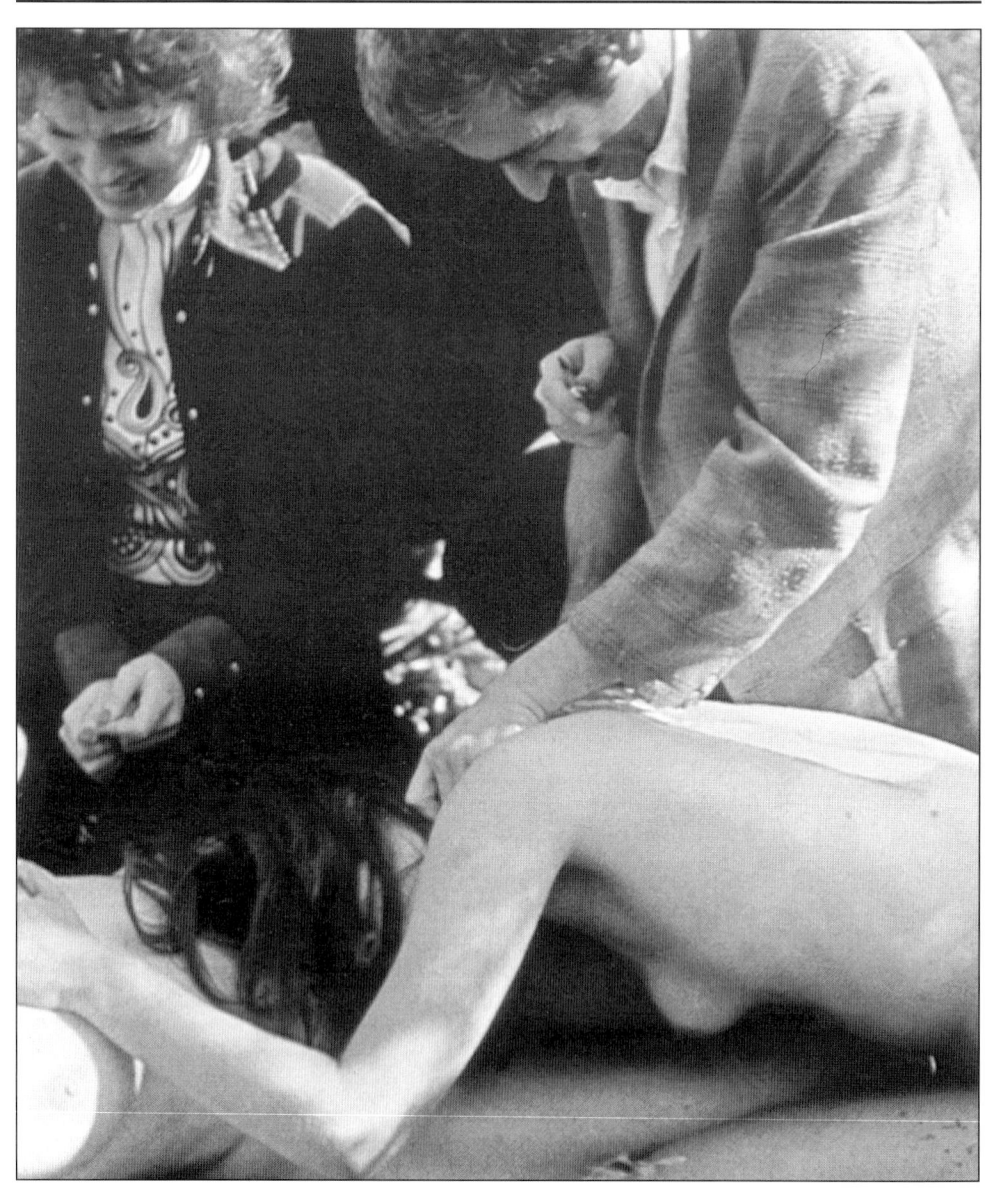

Sadie and Weasel torment the naked, helpless girls.

his knife, whereupon Phyllis complies with the perverse demand. His sadistic appetites whetted by this display, Krug then demands that Phyllis strip off her pants. Egged on by Weasel and Sadie, who cackle with glee throughout the scene, Krug forces the two girls to beat each other for the group's amusement ("Hit her in the stomach with all your might...")

With that, Junior (who has been looking on with consternation throughout the proceedings) finally reaches the limits of his tolerance and yells: "Stoppit! You're gonna kill someone if you're not careful..." In a portion of the sequence cut from most prints of the movie, Junior tries to sidetrack Krug from his violent inclinations by suggesting that the two girls "make it with each other." Krug, Sadie, and Weasel take to this idea all too well, forcing the girls to strip and awkwardly make love.

LAST HOUSE ON THE LEFT

Britain was the first country in the world to be graced with a video release of Last House On The Left. Replay (a division of *VPD*) placed this advertisement in the British video trade press.

(source: Video The Magazine issue 1, June 1982)

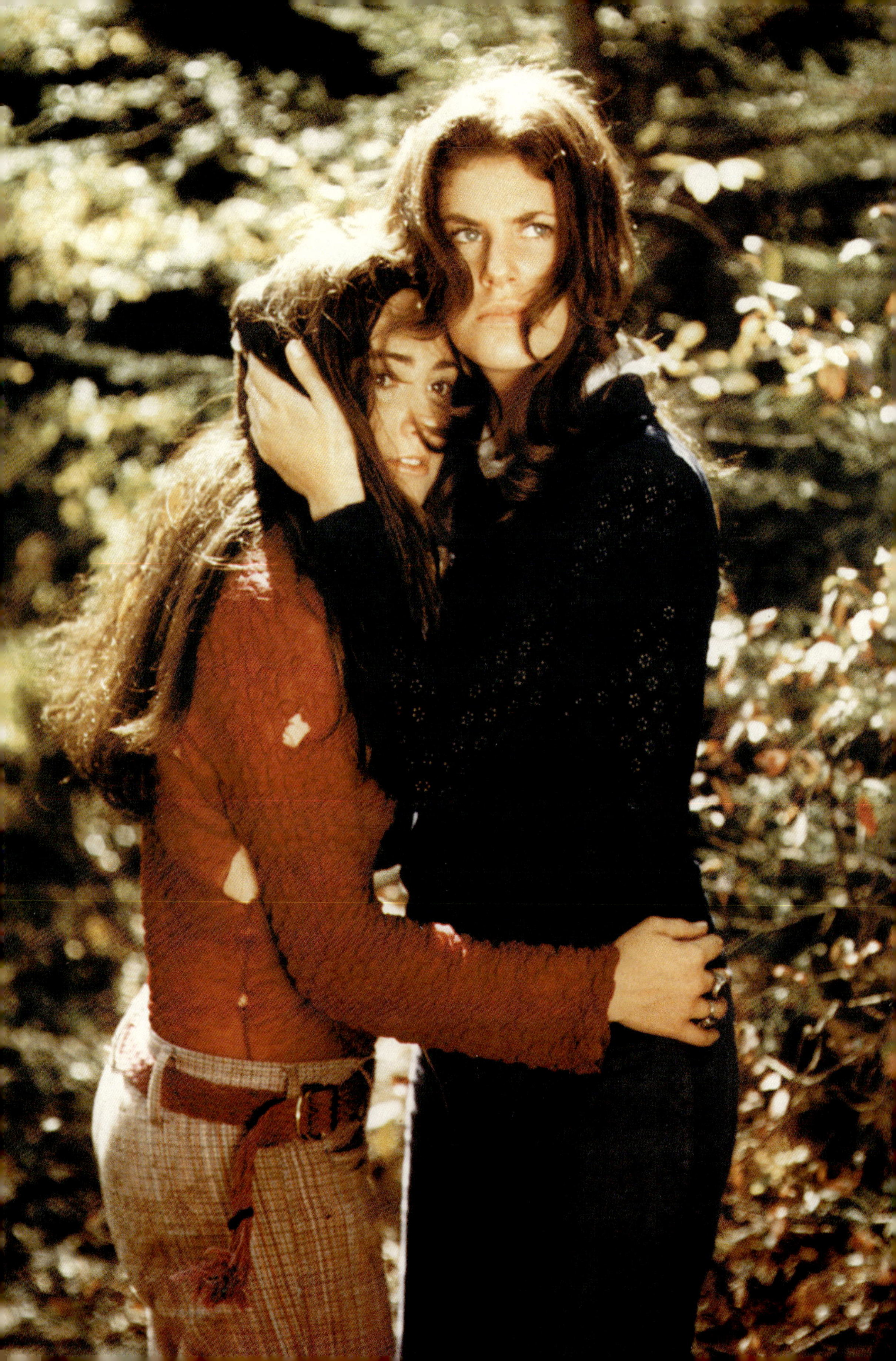

above: The killers relax in Mari's bed

below: Krug takes Weasel's gun in order to shoot Mari

right:
Krug lowers Phyllis' lifeless body to the ground as Sadie points towards the mortal wounds in her abdomen.

below:
Mari is shot by Krug. This image is only seen during the sequence representing Junior's nightmare, near the end of the film.

left:
The weak-willed Junior blows his own brains out after his father turns on him during the climactic showdown with the Collingwoods.

below:
Phyllis makes a run for it, but she is quickly caught in a graveyard and stabbed in the back by Weasel. She flinches in agony as Krug and Sadie swagger towards her.

above and below: **The blood-drenched gang finally kills Mari.**

above: Poster to promote a 1999 Harvard University revival screening.

left: Marc Sheffler smiles as a makeup man displays the bloody appliance.

below: Lucy Grantham is covered in stage blood during the filming of her death scene.

Italian poster (courtesy Greg Herger)

Babes In The Woods

One of the film's most infamous scenes.

This stark and ugly sequence is arguably the most disturbing portion of the entire movie. The sickos' snickering commentary from the sidelines ("You wanna pair'a those pants, Weasel?"; "This is really a riot, man, I dig it!"; "Sock it to her, baby!" etc.) was all unscripted. The obviously improvised dialogue, coupled with shaky, documentary-like camerawork and a lack of music through most of the scene, makes the sequence especially creepy and all too real.

Lucy Grantham: "I hated that scene. Even though I'm not a prude, I was really afraid of that scene because I worried that it would set the tone for the whole movie, and I didn't want the film to be like that. I knew it was an important part of the movie, in terms of showing how vicious and cruel the villains were, but I remember thinking that I'd rather not be expressing the cruelty in that way. But that was the way it was, and I didn't question it. To this day, people I know will sometimes hear about the fact that I was in *Last House on the Left*, and my only hesitation in people renting the movie is that particular scene, which is really embarrassing! I guess a lot of actors and actresses have those embarrassing moments in their early films…"

Sandra Cassell: "That was probably the scene that bothered me the most, especially the way it was originally written. The whole thing really freaked me out… in fact, I actually cried a lot during that scene. I don't know how that scene came off, probably horribly, but it was very upsetting for me to do it."

Yvonne Hannemann: "It was funny; there were some things that I didn't even understand in the script, like where they made the girl pee. Lucy couldn't figure out how she was going to do it. I know that when she was rehearsing, working on it, Lucy said 'I just don't know how this is going to come off!'"

Jeramie Rain: "That was one of the worst scenes we had to do, where we made her pee on herself… I mean, how tasteful!"

LAST HOUSE ON THE LEFT

Babes In The Woods

Phyllis attempts to escape the clutches of her captors.

To get the charming effect of a stain spreading across the front of Phyllis' jeans, Grantham simply held a wet makeup sponge between her thighs and squeezed on cue. A note hand-written by Craven in the shooting script reads: "Pissing scene should be covered first as a straight 'take your skirt [sic] off' in case it is too objectionable." While the peeing ultimately passed muster, some softcore footage of the forced lesbianism later hit the cutting-room floor.

Phyllis makes a run for it

When Krug goes off to the car "to get something to cut some firewood with..." Phyllis sees a chance for escape. Whispering to Mari to "go and get help," Phyllis runs off into the forest. Weasel and Sadie give chase, leaving Junior to guard Mari.

Craven experimented with many different approaches to the chase; outtakes reveal that the sequence was directed in a very loose, improvised manner. One discarded piece had Sadie and Weasel crossing over a roaring rapids, balancing on a wire. Another scene had Phyllis hiding under a fallen tree trunk while Sadie obliviously walks over her head as if on a balance beam. The attempted stunt did not work, and the outtakes show Jeramie Rain repeatedly falling off the tree. (See illustration in the first color section.)

Another improvised moment had Weasel stopping in mid-chase to relieve his bladder; this typically-cynical bit of humor hit the cutting room floor. In the finished film, the attentive listener can hear Weasel gasping, 'I gotta give up cigarettes!' as his prey outdistances him.

Lucy Grantham: "It was very scary for me to do the chase scene, because my part was much more physical than I'd realized. There was a lot of running downhill on very precipitous slopes, where there were a lot of branches coming out of the ground, things you could trip on. I remember being very nervous about falling down, and having to do a lot of takes and a lot of rehearsing to work up my courage so that I could run in a way that was realistic."

Jeramie Rain: "The very first day we shot, they had me running down that hill in the woods [during the chase sequence]. As a result, I caught poison ivy on the first day of shooting, and I was all swelled up for half the shooting of that movie! They put me on Prednisone, and I didn't read the directions for taking the medicine correctly, so I didn't understand it and I took like 23 of 'em… I really blew up. There's a scene later in the movie [in Mari's bedroom] where I'm wearing these long black men's socks, and the only reason I'm wearing them is to cover up the poison ivy."

Jim Hubbard: "Vic Hurwitz was always thinking as a cameraman. I remember during the scene where they chase the girl through the woods, we went out to the location, and Sean was just going to do it straightforwardly. But Vic went off into the woods and found places where he could do things with the camera. One time, he found a tree that was leaning over so that it wasn't in the frame, and he swung around on the tree to follow the action around. He came up with two or three of these very imaginative shots for the chase sequence, and they only last a second or two in the final version. But Vic choreographed a lot of things, and it's to Sean's credit that he gave Vic the time to do that."

Jeramie Rain: "My character, Sadie, could have gone either way; she did have a conscience, even if it was just a tiny part of her. There was one moment in that chase where I was going to save one of the girls [Phyllis]… but then she called me a 'stupid dyke' and hit me over the head with a rock! Calling me a dyke, that did it - they had to die!"

Mari and Junior

While Sadie and Weasel are off chasing Phyllis, Mari tries to convince Junior to help her escape by attempting to befriend him. She gives him the name 'Willow' ("…cause you're kinda beautiful and you shake when the wind blows… Krug's the wind…") and promises him methadone from her father's medical supply ("I can get you a fix… My father, he works with addicts… I live across the street…") Torn between his fear of Krug and his desire to help the desperate girl, Junior gives in and reluctantly accepts a gift from Mari: the peace symbol necklace.

Marc Sheffler: "The scene where I'm sitting with Sandra on the edge of a cliff and I have a stick in my hand, and she's trying to get me to let her go, a lot of that was improvised. For some reason, for her that scene was a struggle, and I kind of bullied her a little bit to get a performance out of her. The sequence required a lot of takes, and it was a tricky thing to do because there were two forces working against each other. One was Mari's very powerful will to survive and get out of the

Babes In The Woods

Mari and Junior

situation, and the other was the moral struggle between right and wrong that was going on within Junior."

Sandra Cassell: "I thought I was quite wretched in that scene."

Yvonne Hannemann: "I remember that Sandra was really very worked up about that scene. Enormously worked up... she really believed she was captured. At one point they had her tied to the tree. [*Author's note: Hannemann may actually be describing the death of Phyllis, which was filmed at the base of a tree.*] There was some technical thing, where we ended up not tying her to the tree - whether it took too long for her to get out of the ropes, or it took too much screen time, or something... we did a lot of takes."

Jim Hubbard: "The reason that scene took so long to do was the timing of it. The actors would get up to a key moment in their dialogue, and they would blow the lines."

The Great Westport Disembowelment

The capture and murder of Phyllis form one of the most intensely horrifying portions of the film. Once again, Craven makes effective use of hand-held camera, following Phyllis as she flees through the woods to an old graveyard. Even as she sights a nearby road, the girl is jumped by Krug in what Roger Ebert called "a moment of sheer and unexpected terror."[4] (This time-tested scare tactic prefigures the many similar jolts that characterize latter-day stalk-and-slashers like *Halloween*, *Friday the 13th*, and *A Nightmare on Elm Street*.) Sadie and Weasel lurch from the underbrush like zombies out of *Night of the Living Dead*; the knife-killing which follows is excruciating in its lingering cruelty. Craven's grim, unflinching approach to the murder sequence was later diluted in various stages of editing and by censors, and it

LAST HOUSE ON THE LEFT

seems that some of the footage is lost forever (see Chapter VII.)

Although censors obviously found the sequence gratiuitous, Craven felt there was a psychological point to the excess. "There are obvious parallels between killing someone with a knife, especially in an orgiastic way like the Manson group, and the sexual act," he commented in 1979. "Phyllis' death is very sexual in feeling. The man [Weasel] and the woman [Sadie] stab her repeatedly. But the murderers stop after an intestine loop is pulled out. It was like they were playing with a doll, or a prisoner they thought was a doll, and it had broken or come apart, and they did not know how to put it back together again."[5]

Wes Craven: "I remember the day we shot Phyllis' death… we were all laughing about how we were going to do this horrendous death scene, with her being stabbed and disemboweled. One of the props came up with the solution of sewing together sheepskin condoms, end on end, and then stuffing them with all sorts of mud and blood. There was a lot of joking… it was a morning shoot, and then when we shot it, it was so horrendous, so frighteningly real, in that the actors really got into it. I think Fred Lincoln, especially, brought a tremendous verisimilitude to that… His character could be so chilling; it was really fine acting. And immediately after we finished shooting that scene it was lunchtime… and nobody was able to eat! We all just sort of sat around and laid out staring at the sky in this beautiful, sylvan setting and just thought 'What the hell have we just done?' It was very sobering."

Lucy Grantham: "That was one of the best scenes for me… I loved it! I really did! A scene like that really allows you to go all out as an actress… you can emote to the skies! The blood, by the way, was made from Karo syrup and #2 red food dye, which gave the color and consistency of blood on film. That was one thing I learned, because it was very realistic! In the cemetery, they taped these blood-bags under my shirt, and Fred pierced the bags with his knife. I've never been particularly bothered by [gory] things like that. I'm not sensitive about blood, and I don't get sick to my stomach. So the blood and gore didn't bother me at all; to me it was an opportunity to act."

When asked if the other actors were upset by the gruesomeness, Grantham replies, "I'm not going to say that it was upsetting, but I'm not going to say that we were taking it lightly. I think we were all very serious about what we were doing. There were moments on the set

Fred Lincoln as Weasel.

when we laughed, but generally speaking, I don't remember there being an insouciant attitude on the part of anybody involved. It was hard work, it was tiring, and we really gave our all."

Jeramie Rain: "We spent all morning shooting that scene, and it was just *disgusting*! I think it was towards the end of the shoot that we did it. I was supposed to disembowel the girl, pull out some intestines… So we had her up against this tree, and then we were pulling out those condoms filled with dirt and catsup, or whatever it was… and then, after all of that, they cut for lunch! I was so grossed out, I thought, 'I'll never eat meat again… I'm ruined !'"

Sean Cunningham: "That disembowelment, with that wrecked car and everything, went on right in my backyard! *(laughter)* By and large, the violence in the movie was like playing pretend… I don't know that anybody ever believed the movie would get finished or what it would be in the end. It was like a high school play."

David Hess: "I was kind of numbed at that point. I inured myself to whatever violence there was in the film, and tried to look at it like a detached third person. Bear in mind, I was coming from a background as a musician and a student… I was actually finishing up some graduate courses at Columbia University around the time of *Last House*. I was mostly into a rather artsy-fartsy, post-hippie intellectual world… so beyond the fact that I thought the movie was a really good jumping-off point for an acting career, my whole reason for doing it was that I was convinced that if we pushed the envelope on violence, in a way that nobody had ever seen or heard before, that it would turn out to be an anti-violent statement."

Jim Hubbard: "She [Grantham] was putting up with it. I mean, there was a certain amount of kidding, and so on, but the whole thing was done really professionally. Not only the creation of the disembowelment effect, but the acting and the shooting of it. The feeling was, 'We've gotta do this, so let's get it over with and get out of here.' It was not particularly comfortable to do that scene."

Yvonne Hannemann: "We did a lot of scurrying because the things we made up didn't work. Wes didn't really want a lot of people around during that scene… I remember the fake blood didn't work right, and before we got into the condoms, we were using balloons. And before that, there was also some business about using sheep's intestines… and that didn't work, either they couldn't get them, or the butcher didn't have them, or something like that. Wes would stay up all night trying to work up things, and we would rush around looking for them."

Wes Craven: "With the death of Phyllis in the woods, we shot 7242, a very fast 400 film stock sometimes used in documentaries under very low light conditions, that gave a grainy look to it; it was very strange, almost like old footage from World War II, with the light burned out and the darks very grainy and black. It turned out to be very powerful." The director's notes from the time indicate that he was toying with the idea of using smoke bombs and slow motion in the scene.

Hideous as it is on screen, the death of Phyllis was even worse on paper. The script called for Sadie to gouge out the girl's eyes and tongue, sever her breasts, and carve her vagina into "a glistening pit of formless gore". The written description also included a scene in which Weasel and Krug engage in necrophilia with Phyllis' mutilated corpse. None of these repulsive ideas was ever actually shot.

The sequence was so disturbingly realistic that Hallmark and Atlas International, the distribution company which released *Last House* in Germany, attempted to pass it off as an actual "snuff" film (i.e. a real murder staged for the camera) by editing excerpts from the scene into a pseudo-documentary called *The Evolution of Snuff: Confessions of a Blue Movie Star* (1976). Most of these shots do not appear in any existing version of *Last House on the Left*. (see chapter VII)

K-R-U-G

Junior and Mari flee through the woods, hoping to escape to Mari's house, but the two teenagers run into Krug and his blood-spattered cohorts. Krug tosses Junior aside, and knocks Mari to the ground, holding her at the point of his machete. Mari then asks her captors what has happened to Phyllis ("...did she get away?"). In response, Krug shakes his head slowly, as Sadie drops Phyllis' severed hand on the ground.

The three killers surround the screaming Mari, and Krug uses Weasel's switchblade to carve the four letters of his name into her chest. Following this atrocity, the drooling Krug brutally rapes Mari. While many critics (the late Gene Siskel among them) have asserted that *Last House* glorifies misogynist violence, Craven maintains that he had quite the opposite effect in mind. Indeed, the movie's depiction of rape and its aftermath is anything but glorious; the scene is ugly, harsh, and horrifying.

Wes Craven: "You know, the character of Mari took an enormous amount of abuse. I liked Sandra Peabody a lot; I thought she was very pretty, and very plucky... because she was a very young actress, she wasn't nearly as confident and easygoing as Lucy was, and she had become involved in something that was very, very rough. And she hung in there. When the character was raped, she was treated very roughly, and I know Sandra said to me afterwards, 'My God... I had the feeling they really hated me.'"

Sandra Cassell: "No comment."

David Hess: "That was a difficult scene, because my style of acting is to go over the edge during rehearsal... to push it as far as I can possibly push it, just to see how far I can go. And then I set my parameters. Once I draw that box, once I have those boundaries, then I'm free to do whatever I want within my character. I think I frightened her a few times... I actually got pretty physical with her. She may have been a little bit intimidated, because she couldn't back off when the camera was running."

Yvonne Hannemann: "That one scene was really quite upsetting. I know Sandra had to be consoled; it really got very rough. And I think they [the actors] all got very emotional. Of course, David Hess was just so frightening, that a lot of the acting was sort of method acting."

The carving of the letters K-R-U-G in Mari's chest (which is barely glimpsed in most prints of the film) was done by simply dipping the end of the knife in stage blood. David Hess recalls, "I just drew it on her skin. You saw it being drawn, and then there's a cut back to my face. Then it went back to her and it looked like the letters were cut in. It was just two separate shots, before and after."

Babes In The Woods

The rape of Mari: one of the film's most uncomfortable and shocking scenes.

While he was not present during the shooting of the chest-carving, Marshall Anker vividly remembers seeing the rushes from the sequence: "On one occasion, they gave me a lift back to New York after we'd been shooting, and they said, 'Oh, we're going to look at some of the rushes.' So I asked, 'Can I look?' Sean said, 'Look, we'll show you the rushes, but don't tell anyone what you saw. Act like you never saw any rushes, OK? Nobody's supposed to see them, we'll show you but keep your mouth shut.'

"One of the backers from Boston was there in the editing room with Wes, Sean, and myself. We're looking at the rushes, and these particular rushes showed Krug carving his initials into the girl's breast with a stiletto. The backer was looking on, as all this blood is dripping down, and Cunningham says to him, 'That's what you wanted isn't it? Didn't you want it bloody?' The guy from Boston was really getting sick from looking at it, and he said to Sean and Wes, 'All right, already, you did it, you did it…' He got up, walked out of the room, and went home. I thought it was funny; this guy commissioned it, he asked them to make the movie as bloody and violent as possible, but he couldn't take it himself. It was too much for him, and he got turned off!"

Martin Kove: "I remember seeing the dailies of those scenes in the woods, and they were very graphic and frightening. That was some of the stuff that I didn't like, where they capture the girls, and the rape… It was tough to bite, but it was so realistic that I have to admit Wes did a good job of exposing that element of humanity. It reminded me of *Night of the Living Dead* because it was shot in that newsreel style. *Last House* was so gruesome and so real that these rapists could have been in your backyard. That's what upset me so much… and why *Last House* was never a favorite of mine."

A moment of remorse

After the ordeal of her rape and mutilation, Mari staggers away, drops to her knees, and vomits. She then recites the Lord's Prayer and wades into the pond in a seemingly suicidal trance. At this point, the killers are finally struck by the hideousness of their own actions, looking around guiltily while scraping the bloody blades of grass from their hands.

Wes Craven: "The real essence of the picture was that moment when the characters went so far that they horrified themselves… where they became revulsed and couldn't wait to try to clean up. It was kind of the telling point of the whole story, when everything switched… The bad guys became almost penitent and unsure of themselves, while the parents later became completely ruthless."

Ironically, the shooting script for the film did not describe the villains' remorse; the crucial scene was apparently rewritten during production.

David Hess: "Sean actually wanted me to do that scene differently. He wanted it harder; Sean had some kind of classical ideas about how a bad guy should be, and about the line that Krug should take through the script. And I didn't buy that; I thought that the more wrinkles you show, the more sides of the bad guy's personality, the more people identify with the film. With that scene, I wanted to show just a flicker of humanity in this guy, not that he didn't do what he did, but that he himself was kind of turned off by the grotesqueness of the violence, the unnecessariness of the whole thing."

As a reprise of Hess' ballad "Now You're All Alone" swells up on the soundtrack, the criminals follow Mari down to the pond. In the movie's most emotionally-wrenching moment, Krug grimly shoots her to death. As Mari sinks into the water, she fixes her killers with a final haunting stare.

Sandra Cassell: "The part when I walked into the water and he shot me had to be done over and over again. Initially, I went in the wrong direction from the bullet, and it didn't look real enough. I was jumping in the opposite direction from where I was supposedly shot. Finally, they showed me which direction to go in and we redid it."

At the moment of Mari's death, Craven cuts away to a view of the Collingwood family dog (glimpsed in the beginning of the film under more innocent circumstances) barking frantically in reaction to the sound of the gunshots.

Wes Craven: "I've always been fascinated by animals. I think as beings they have that almost mythological presence in our minds, of creatures that are in some way more attuned to things than we are… sensing danger before we're aware of it. I was very much trying to find things that are primal, that could be watched by a person who came off the veldt of the African motherland 50,000 years ago. I felt that scene was very evocative… the murderers and the alert animal sensing something wrong. I even used birds to that effect, with all of the bird sounds when Phyllis is being chased through the woods."

The criminals' remorse is fleeting. Krug snaps out of his reverie and barks, "Junior! Go up to the car and get the suitcases… let's get washed up and the hell outta here." The three murderers cleanse themselves in the pond and switch identities by donning respectable clothes.

Aside from the symbolic implications of the killers attempting to wash the blood from their clothes, bodies, and consciences, Jeramie Rain claims there was a more practical reason for the inclusion of this scene.

Jeramie Rain: "They spent hours getting my hair out like that every day, and finally I couldn't stand it anymore. I begged them to find a way to stop with the hair, so that's why they wrote that part in where I dunk my head in the pond - so that I could get my hair wet and not have to keep that Sadie hairdo... I couldn't take it anymore!"

The last shot in this sequence is a wide pan away from the killers; in Craven's screenplay, this camera movement was intended to end in a view of Mari... "bloody, mud-smeared, deep in shock, but *alive*."

The Comic Relief: Marshall Anker and Martin Kove

In structuring the film, Craven chose to intercut its most stomach-churning moments of horror with comic sketches featuring the sheriff and his dim-witted deputy. Even the movie's fans seem to dislike these scenes of cornpone humor, and Craven has said he regrets including them. Nonetheless, Craven later used a similar device in *Scream*, with two dumb cops named Sheriff Burke (Joseph Whipp) and Deputy Dewey (David Arquette) appearing admist the onslaught of carnage.

"To me, *Last House on the Left* was almost like two different movies," **Marshall Anker** comments. "When they cut back and forth from the sadistic, bloody stuff to the two dumb cops, it was like putting Laurel and Hardy in the middle of a horror movie. Even *I* thought it was strange, and I liked my scenes a lot. It's known as comic relief, but the comedy was practically 100 percent different from the rest of what was going on in the movie! Here, in the middle of this very heavy, sadistic, gory stuff, they cut away to the two dumb cops on the trail running out of gas, getting a hitch on a chicken truck, and falling off the truck... I mean, what the hell were they thinking when they came up with that?"

Looking back on the movie, **Wes Craven** expresses strong misgivings about the sheriff/deputy shenanigans. "If I had it to do over again, I wouldn't include those scenes with the cops. I think that *Last House* demanded so much from everybody involved in making it, that the humor was a way of distancing ourselves and the audience from the horror of it all. I think that it would have been more honest to leave out the comedy. I don't mind the dark, ironic brand of humor that came from within the key characters, but the broad, farcical stuff between the sheriff and his assistant seems inappropriate to me in retrospect."

Martin Kove takes a different view of his role in the film. "I always thought the film was too gruesome," the actor comments. "I think the comedy helped soften that feeling of ugliness... the movie became a spoof on itself." Likewise, **Marc Sheffler** remarks, "We wanted the humor in there, absolutely... You can't do that kind of horrific violence without following it up with something funny or you take the audience on a complete bad trip; without the humor, it's just a downward spiral. The way to avoid that is through the humor, so that after something terrible happens, you bring the audience up again... and therefore set them up for a bigger fall."

"A lot of people have told me that I stole the movie," Marshall Anker asserts. "It wasn't supposed to be that funny, but some people seemed to prefer the comedy scenes."

Although the crew shot one exterior scene at an actual police station, the interior scenes with the sheriff and deputy (named Frank Boone and Harry Snark in the screenplay) sitting around the stationhouse were shot in Sean Cunningham's office, according to Marshall Anker. When the two overhear a radio broadcast giving a description of the fugitives' getaway car, the announcer's voice sounds quite a bit like Cunningham himself.

"Unless I'm wrong, they just made up one corner of that office to look like a police station, with the ham radio and all," Anker says. "There's one moment when we're playing a game of checkers and, after I win, I wave my tie at the deputy… That bit was an improv which I threw in because Oliver Hardy used to do that, wave his tie around as if to say, 'How d'ya like them apples?'"

Anker and Kove actually rehearsed some of their scenes at the home of David Hess' sister, where Kove lived at the time. By Anker's account, the two actors didn't see eye to eye on how to play the material.

Marshall Anker: "I actually wanted to do something like the Andy Griffith movie, *No Time For Sergeants* [1958], where Griffith was this real hillbilly type who got drafted into the army, and Myron McCormick was his sergeant, a thirty-year man. Griffith's character was always saying, 'Did I do right sergeant?' when he did wrong, and the sergeant would do a slow burn… that whole *schtick*. There were certain things that Martin Kove did off-camera that were very funny… He had these big, stupid, dumbfounded Li'l Abner expressions that were hilarious. He wouldn't do it on camera cause he thought he was overacting; he wanted to be more macho or something. I said, 'Martin, you do it big, and I'll underplay you…' He didn't like that idea… he thought I meant that I wanted to steal the scenes away from him. He said, 'What is this, *Mayberry, RFD* ?! I don't want to do *Mayberry, RFD* !' We never got really close during the making of the movie because of that disagreement."

More comic relief with the deputy (Martin Kove) and the sheriff (Marshall Anker).

"We're Outta Gas, You Idiot!"

After realizing that the car they saw parked near the Collingwood home belongs to the escaped criminals, the cops roar off to save the day. However, their pursuit of the killers is literally stalled out when their cruiser runs out of gas.

Marshall Anker: "We had the cooperation of the Westport Police Department, and I remember shaking hands with a few real cops. The police had loaned one of their cars to the production, and Sean took me

Babes In The Woods

Hippies taunt the sheriff and his deputy; production assistant Steve Miner (pictured in middle), now a prolific Hollywood director, makes a cameo in this scene.

aside and said to me, 'Don't tell any of the officers that the scene we're doing involves the squad car running out of gas and making the police look like jerks.' Well, I spilled the beans, and this cop gave me a funny look. Maybe a New York cop would have gotten angry over it and refused to let us use the car, but these cops were country boys in a way, and they let it go. Sean said later, 'I heard you told the cop that the scene shows their car running out of gas!' I said, 'Yeah, I made a boo-boo! Me and my big mouth!'"

This scene provides a good example of a technical gaffe that ended up working in the film makers' favor.

Steve Miner: "There was no assistant cameraman on *Last House*, so Vic Hurwitz sometimes had me do follow-focus [a job involving the adjustment of focal length within a given shot as an object comes closer or further away from the camera]... which I did very badly! There was one long shot of the police car coming towards the camera, and I screwed it up so badly that Vic Hurwitz was yelling at me, 'You're behind! Catch up! You're too late!" I finally found the right focus just as the car was pulling in. Wes ended up really liking the shot because it went from being totally out of focus to being sharply focused on the flashing lights on the grille. But that shot was a total mistake; it was me not knowing what I was doing."

Later on, the cops try to hitch a ride in a passing car, only to realize that the vehicle is occupied by what the script describes as "hooting hippies" who have no intention of lending a helping hand to the long arm of the law.

Marshall Anker: "They [the crew] were playing a joke on me; it was another one of their tricks. 'Let's see what Anker would do' was a

Ada Washington and Marshall Anker.

game that they would play. I don't remember the exact shot as it came out in the film, but when we rehearsed it, they slowed down the car, and I ran up to them. They got out of the car and they said, 'We hate cops' and they picked up rocks and tree branches and threw them at me. They weren't really trying to hit me, but they were coming close. I turned around and they were all looking for my reaction, like 'What are you gonna do about it?' Wes Craven had told them to do that, that was his big trick… he wanted to see what a normally peaceful guy would do in that situation. So I pulled my gun on 'em… and they reacted like it was a real gun! I remember somebody saying, 'A-ha, push the average American too far and he gets tough with you… underneath the surface, he's just a mean guy with a gun…' You might say that's the theme of the movie, the violence under the surface of the civilized American."

In a 1998 interview, Wes Craven pointed out that Steve Miner makes a guest appearance as one of the hippies.

Ada Washington and the chicken truck

One of the more incongruous bits of humor in the film is the sequence where the sheriff and his deputy attempt to hitch a ride with an elderly black woman (Ada Washington) driving a truck filled with crates of chickens. The two buffoons climb up on the roof of the truck, only to be spilled on the pavement when the vehicle will not start with their added weight. The spunky Ada refuses to unload her cargo to accommodate the lawmen, and leaves the two dolts stranded.

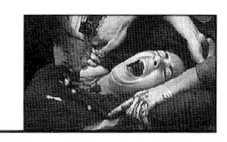

Ada Washington was hardly a professional actress; in fact, she was the Cunningham family's maid and nanny whom the enterprising duo roped into acting in the film. When reminded of the scene, Cunningham bursts into laughter. "I forgot about Ada! She was our maid!" he chuckles. "She was a real character, and Wes thought she was funny, so we wrote a little scene for her driving a chicken truck.[6] But she didn't know how to drive, and we didn't find that out until that morning!"

On the film's posters and newspaper ads, the cast list ended with "...and introducing Ada Washington," a credit which must have provided no small amusement around the Cunningham household.

Martin Kove: "Marshall Anker was always making me laugh during the shoot. There was no difference between his character, the sheriff, and the way he was normally; he was just a funny guy. I had a lot of fun with that chicken truck scene; it's my most vivid memory of doing *Last House*. I've always loved Westerns, and my favorite moment in the movie was that bit where I got down on the ground like an Indian and said, 'I only tell you what the road tells me...'"

Marshall Anker: "Wes Craven didn't want me to do that stunt where I fell off the roof of the chicken truck; he wanted to cheat it by filming two separate shots. But I insisted, 'No, I can do it.' I was so hopped up about doing it that I went out the day before and bought extra frames for my glasses with no lenses, so I wouldn't get my eyes cut up if my glasses broke. I even went to Times Square and bought another sheriff's badge that looked better than the tin piece of shit that they gave me. When I went off the truck, I turned completely around in the air, ass over teakettle... that was a lucky break, because if I hadn't turned in that way, I would have landed on my neck. Afterwards, someone on the crew said, 'The camera jammed; you gotta do it again.' I started climbing back up on the truck again and they said, 'No, no, just kidding. We got it.'"

Steve Miner: "I remember when we had to go and get that truckload of chickens. This was shortly after I came on [as a crew member], and poor Yvonne Hannemann, who was the script supervisor, first assistant director and location manager, she and I ended up having to drive two hours to this chicken farm somewhere out

Belgian poster

in the middle of Connecticut. I wasn't aware of why we were doing this; when you're a gofer, you just do what people tell you to do. So we ended up getting very little shot that day. When I found out the reason we drove two hours was to get chickens, I couldn't believe it, because practically right in Sean's backyard, the next road, maybe two miles away, was a chicken farm. No one was organized or had time enough to know what the hell was going on."

Later, as the two cops trudge down the road on foot, the deputy asks the sheriff, 'You feel like playin' three-thirds of a ghost or somethin'?' Anker's disgruntled reply to the deputy was an improv, as the actor relates.

Marshall Anker: "In the script, the sheriff was just supposed to be silent at the end of that little scene. But during rehearsal, I ended the scene with my own line, 'How'd you like me to put my boot up your ass… sideways?' Wes Craven laughed, and he said, "Do that on screen!" We immediately shot the scene, and afterwards, he asked me, "Where'd you get that line?" I told him that my captain used to say that to me when I was an Army radio operator in Germany; *'Private Anker, did you leave the radio unmanned?' 'I had to take a piss!' 'How'd you like me to put my boot up your ass sideways? What the fuck is this! Get back to the radio!'* Wes got a kick out of that, and I pride myself a little bit on that line, because I improved the script by adlibbing a little bit."

Checking in at the Last House on the Left

The killers' abrupt arrival on the Collingwood family doorstep and the parents' offer to put them up for the night was a longer sequence in the script. Successive drafts of the screenplay show many scribbled revisions of the event - one had Mrs. Collingwood walking down the road and finding the group clustered around the Cadillac convertible - but, in the end, Craven apparently decided to simply cut to the chase.

In an unbelievable gesture of generosity, the Collingwoods offer the criminals use of their missing daughter's bedroom. From some wallet-sized photos in the room, Weasel identifies Mari and alerts the others in the group to the bizarre twist of fate. Later in the film, Krug, Weasel and Sadie lounge on Mari's bed, passing around a bottle of Jim Beam and exchanging drunken banter.

Jeramie Rain: "The bedroom scene where I'm sleeping with the two guys [Hess and Lincoln] was shot in a two-story white farmhouse that Sean had rented out to do some interior shots. That particular scene was done on a very stressful day; I was doing a play at the time, and the people at this theater needed me to come in to New York and do the play that night. Sean and Wes were delaying me, and they were telling me that I wouldn't be able to get back to the city in time for the play. I stormed out to my car and got ready to leave… and then, Sean came out and ordered me to go back in the house like a little puppy… which I did. Finally, after we shot, I got back to Manhattan in time for my play."

Rock trivia-hounds note that in addition to prominently-displayed posters of Mick Jagger and Janis Joplin, a small photo of the great '70s rock band Mountain (from the band's 1971 *Nantucket Sleighride* LP) can be spotted in the background of certain shots of Mari's bedroom.

Dining with Krug and Company

The scene in which the gang sits down to supper with Mari's parents was added in the third draft of the script and parallels a similar sequence in *The Virgin Spring*. The dinner was shot against a flat black backdrop (called 'noseeum' in the trade) because the crew did not have the time or means to arrange a separate room for the sequence. The killers' effort to masquerade as traveling salesmen ("We sell insurance to plumbing companies… in case they steal some toilets or something…") are comically belied by their vulgar behavior and by the telltale traces of their ordeal in the woods (scratches, bite marks, etc.) Again echoing *The Virgin Spring*, the dinner is disrupted by the remorse of Junior, who cries out "I'm sorry!" in his sleep while having a nightmare about Mari.

Craven originally had planned more comedic scenes where the killers attempt to act like upstanding citizens, including one in which Sadie makes Weasel model a fancy dress which she wants to wear to dinner. Another lost bit alluded to the dialogue between the sheriff and deputy, with Krug claiming to be a circus performer from the nearby country fair.

The Moment of Truth

Later that night, Mrs. Collingwood finds a withdrawal-wracked Junior vomiting in the bathroom. She sees Mari's peace symbol ornament hanging around the youth's neck and, sensing that something is rotten in the state of Connecticut, rummages through the killers' belongings. The distraught mom finds the killers' bloodstained clothes and simultaneously overhears an argument between Junior and Krug that reveals the horrible truth (Junior: 'Krug, we gotta get outta here… if they find out we killed their kid…' Krug: 'Shut up, or you'll wind up in the lake with her!'.)

Junior's withdrawal symptoms make for a clever (if perhaps unintended) variation on a moment in *The Virgin Spring* where the young goatherd becomes nauseous with guilt and spits up his soup at the parents' dinner table.

Steve Dwork: " Wes originally wanted to shoot a reverse angle of Junior vomiting *into* the camera! We spent a while in the bathroom with that kid [Sheffler] trying to gag himself, but the reverse shot just didn't work out."

The sequence in which the Collingwoods run to the lake and discover Mari's body was taken day-for-night. Although in most release versions of the film, Mari is already dead when the Collingwoods find her, the scene was originally shot with additional dialogue in which Mari identifies the killers to her parents before dying in her father's arms.

Sandra Cassell: "They wanted to put makeup on me to have me look more 'dead' for that scene. But while we were shooting, the sun was going down, and we didn't have enough time for that."

Doc Collingwood's Plan

The scene in which Doc Collingwood lays a series of booby-traps for the killers (shaving cream on the floor, a trip-wire tied to a fork wedged into a piece of wall moulding, an electrified doorknob positioned over a puddle of water) harkens forward to similar plot devices in Craven's later horror pictures. In *The Hills Have Eyes*, the protagonists use their mother's corpse as bait in a trap for the marauding Papa Jupiter; *A Nightmare on Elm Street* features a particularly Rube Goldberg-like contraption used to snare the diabolical Freddy Krueger. *The People Under the Stairs* takes place in a labyrinthine house filled with hidden trapdoors, and *Shocker* features a kind of elaborate multi-media trap as part of its resolution.

"I do have a fascination with traps," Craven admits. "It goes back to nature… the Venus flytrap, the trapdoor spider. It's just an interesting way to even the odds." Craven has also said that he cribbed the ideas for his traps from an old survivalist manual.

Weasel's Nightmare

Weasel awakens in the middle of the night to find Doctor Collingwood and wife standing over his prone body, dressed in surgical robes and gloves. Handing her husband a hammer and chisel (as a nurse would hand surgical instruments to a doctor), Mrs. Collingwood cautions Weasel, "Don't move," pulling his upper lip back to reveal his teeth. The good doctor places the blade of the chisel directly over Weasel's front teeth and, just as he delivers a bone-chilling hammer blow, Weasel wakes up, realizing it was all a dream.

Wes Craven: "Actually, that dream sequence, which was improvised on the spot, became one of the most powerful things in the film. We shot it on the same day that I wrote it. Time and again, over the years, people have told me, 'That is really the best thing in *Last*

Babes In The Woods

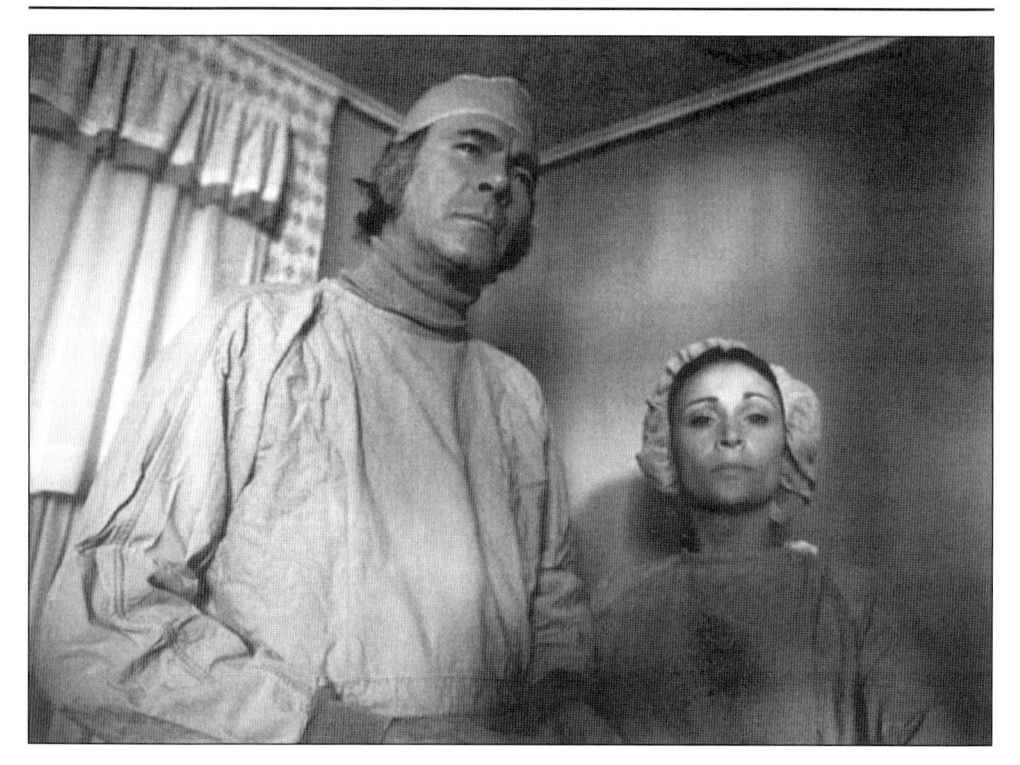

Richard Towers and Eleanor Shaw in the nightmare sequence.

House on the Left because it didn't show that much violence, but I couldn't get the image out of my head.' I realized the power of dream imagery, and I went back to it as I made more films. A lot of my movies had little dream sequences in them, which were interesting to me… one was in *Deadly Blessing,* where we had the spider dropping into Sharon Stone's mouth. Ultimately, it led to me doing an entire film on dreams [*A Nightmare on Elm Street*]. At the time that I made *Last House,* I was living with a PhD candidate in anthropology. I was discussing the primal aspects of the film with her, and she told me that two of the most powerful male fears are of having your teeth broken off and of the *vagina dentalis*, the fear that the vagina is going to eat you, taking away your manhood. So Weasel's nightmare and his death actually touch on two basic fears."

The content of Weasel's nightmare was not specified in Craven's screenplay, and the scene was essentially improvised. The only references to the sequence in the shooting script are a handwritten reminder on the title page stating "NEED WEASEL'S DREAM" and an underlined note in the margin of another page: "TOOTHDREAM."

Weasel's painful demise

Anyone who has attended a screening of *Last House on the Left* can testify to the impact of the sequence in which Mrs. Collingwood bites off Weasel's penis during fellatio; even the most staid audience spontaneously erupts in raucous laughter and screaming. Radio commercials for the film's 1981 re-release touted "The Scene By the Pond" as a highlight. Aside from its Freudian implications (or 'Froodian,' as Craven's characters would have it), the scene also points to the movie's

LAST HOUSE ON THE LEFT

origins as a sexploitation picture. According to the cast and crew of the film, actress Eleanor Shaw had misgivings about doing the scene.

Jim Hubbard: "She [Eleanor Shaw] really was kind of appalled at doing that scene. I remember she talked about it with Sean, about whether she should really do it, how far Sean actually wanted her to go with it. I know there were some highly suggestive scenes between the two of them before they go outside - they both had all their clothes on, but they were feeling each other up. The purpose of all that was to show how she went from not wanting anything to do with him to deciding to seduce him… To simulate the castration, they took an extra leather belt and put it around Fred's hips, with the tongue of the belt coming out through his fly. And she grabs ahold of the belt with her teeth… the belt was the mock-up for his dick. There were no close-ups of the biting. I'm sure there was more shot of that scene than what ended up in the film. Fred practically blew up my microphone when he screamed… he just let out this scream and nearly busted the diaphragm on my microphone."

Steve Chapin: "I remember seeing the film being edited, and there was a shot of the mother spitting something that looked like a hot dog into the lake."

Yvonne Hannemann: "She was quite disturbed at how she was going to carry this scene. And Sean was lecturing her… I remember him being quite anatomical, saying, 'You know, there are no bones down there! It's just like biting into steak! A little gristle, but it's just steak!'"

Steve Dwork: "At the end of the scene, when [Carr] chomped down on the end of the belt we'd tied around Fred's waist and gave this yank, every guy on the set just *cringed*. Any male can empathize with the concepts involved in that scene!"

Fred Lincoln: "They never actually showed that my character was dead… so I want to do "Last House II: Weasel's Back"! A guy with no dick, out for revenge!"

"Blow your brains out!"

In the shooting script for the movie, Junior was to remain alive at the conclusion of the story; after the parents exacted their revenge, Junior was to stagger out into the carnage and remark to Dr. Collingwood, 'You don't look like a doctor to me, mister… you look more like a butcher!' Craven had also written an "alternate ending" for the film which featured Junior killing Krug with the pistol. Somewhere along the line, that ending was reworked so that Krug bullies Junior into putting the gun in his own mouth and shooting himself.

Marc Sheffler: "The movie was basically a compilation of extremes of aberrant human behavior. We had set Krug up as this sort of anti-father, and we thought, 'What's the worst thing a father can do?' And the answer was, 'Kill his kid… or make the kid kill himself.' So that's really how we came up with the scene. I think the decision that was made to have Junior kill himself was a dramatically correct one. It further evolved the evil progression of the Krug character. It had to do with the Krug character's domination and control, and it further led up to Krug's demise. The character of Junior was, in my opinion, extremely pivotal in the film. On the side of the bad guys, he was the only one who wasn't a bad guy. Junior was someone who was not in control of his life; the journey of the film, although it ended in his demise, was a last-ditch effort by Junior to gain some kind of control."

The victimization of Junior by his father is but one example of Craven's ongoing use of a primal fear: the 'bad parent.' Father figures in Craven's horror films are frequently portrayed as monsters; even the silly *Shocker* featured a conflict between a serial-killer Dad and his tormented son. The director has said in several interviews that as a child he was frightened by his own father.

David Hess: "We essentially made that scene up on the spur of the moment. I think that Wes was interested at that point in presenting something that made Krug as crude as possible… just to put a little more shock value in there."

The staging of Junior's death was much gorier than what ultimately appeared on screen. The crew and cast all share vivid recollections of how appallingly grotesque the simulated suicide looked on the set.

Marc Sheffler: "If you recall how the scene is edited, it's done in sequences. There's the sequence that begins it, with David telling me to 'Go ahead, put the gun in your mouth, turn around…', which is after I'm sort of threatening him. There are cutaways to him and then back to me as I put the gun in my mouth, and he continues to taunt me. Then there's another cutaway to my face, and then to David, and then you hear a gun shot. Then it cuts back to me up against the wall. The makeup people had a latex prosthetic filled with fake blood and a brain-like substance that was sewn into my hair, flush up against the back of my head. Wes set it up so that after we hear the gunshot, they cut away to me, I smack my head against the wall and pop this bag of blood and stuff. They go back to another shot, and then the effects people came in and sprayed the wall with blood, and then I slid down the wall."

Jim Hubbard: "When Junior shoots himself, that was a lot gorier than what showed up in the movie. There was a big splat up on the wall, and there was footage of that splat that never made it into the movie. They had a bag of blood off camera that exploded… I don't remember whether it was a squib or just pressure being put on the bag, but it really was very effective… much more effective than I cared for."

Yvonne Hannemann: "I remember we went in and splattered the wall with blood… and it didn't come out right, so we had to move the furniture and do it again. The stuff didn't stick right the first time; it just rolled right off. To photograph properly, the blood had to splatter and stick to the wall for a couple of different takes. We had to move the whole lighting setup around. If we had been able to test the blood out first, like splatter the wall in the bathroom or something, then we would have known. But we were always rushing, so we didn't test things out and got further behind."

Fred Lincoln: "I suggested that they use brains from a Greek restaurant, cause I ate 'em once, and they looked pretty gross."

Steve Dwork: "The brains - now *that* was good. That *really* was gory. The special effects guy built a whole mock-up of Marc Sheffler's head, a whole skull treatment with hair and everything. The whole back of the head was blown out, and there was blood and bits of brain splattered all over the wall. They only showed the view from the front in the final version of the movie, but the whole back view of it was also definitely shot. It was *ugly*."

Krug (out of picture to left) uses a chair to protect himself from Dr. Collingwood's relentless chainsaw attack.

Death by Chainsaw

The climactic fight scene in which Doc Collingwood goes after Krug with a chainsaw presented considerable hazards for the cast and crew. Like all of the stunt work in the film, the chainsaw fight was staged without the benefit of any stunt doubles or other professional guidance. Richard Towers obviously had not been required to wield any life-threatening power tools during his career as a stage actor, and David Hess was left to fend off the advances of his nemesis with a flimsy endtable.

Wes Craven: "The scene was hairy in many different ways; one is that we couldn't put a nick in anything. We had a few things that we brought in [which could be destroyed], like the endtable. But it was a completely functioning chainsaw. David Hess was in stocking feet, and the floor was very slippery. We never knew at any moment whether he would slip into the saw's path. He ended up with the chainsaw right over his face, when he's trapped. In fact, there's a frame of the film where you can actually see Vic Hurwitz's hand come up to brace against Hess' back, to make sure he doesn't fall back into the lens of the camera."

David Hess: "I look back at the chainsaw scene now, after twenty-five years of making films regularly, and it's probably the toughest scene I ever had to do. Since we had no stuntmen, all of us had to figure out what it was that we were doing right from the beginning. I felt that the only way I could protect myself was by my being the aggressor. In other words, they filmed it as if he was being actively aggressive with the chainsaw, but the pressure was coming from me. If you look at the film with that in mind, you'll see that all the pressure on the chainsaw was coming from my chair, or endtable, or whatever I was using to protect myself. I was *guiding* the chainsaw; he [Gaylord St. James] didn't know what the fuck he was doing."

Marshall Anker: "While they were filming the chainsaw scene, I was trying to lie down and rest in the next room. It was a tremendous

Italian poster

noise to be listening to, and I got up to take a look at what they were doing every now and then. I saw David Hess get his finger cut on that portable buzzsaw, when he was holding up that wooden chair; it wasn't terrible, but I saw blood coming down and he was obviously hurt. If they'd really fucked up, David would have lost a finger."

Although Craven intended to imply that Mr .Collingwood actually saws Krug's head off at the end of the fight, the decapitation is never shown. In writing the scene, Craven knew that the production simply couldn't afford a convincing severed-head effect, and the prominently-mixed, moist sound of the chainsaw ripping through flesh had to suffice as the indication of Krug's fate. A shot of Krug after he has been killed is framed so that his head is offscreen.

Jim Hubbard: "I think they winged that whole scene. They didn't have a sure, certain idea what they were going to do for that decapitation. They knew in general what they wanted, but they didn't know how it was going to work out between the actors."

Wes Craven: "We met Steve Miner because of the way that Sean got the location for the interior of the parents' house. Sean found this college kid who was renting a house from a well-to-do family who were out of the country for a while. Steve Miner was friendly with one of the group of young guys that was living in the house, who agreed to rent the house out to us. We were always laughing about the fact that we were filming a chainsaw fight in the living room… because this family had all these nice things, including a grand piano in the living room, and they had no idea what we were doing! Steve Miner was always running around making sure that we didn't nick anything with the chainsaw… he was going crazy wondering how he was going to cover it all up. We were maniacs back in those days!"

Fred Lincoln: "Nobody had really done anything like this chainsaw scene before. And I had done some stunts in the past, so I kind of understood how to cheat camera, and I'd done fight scenes before, so it was fairly easy for me. That's pretty much all that chainsaw scene was; a fight scene. So I helped Sean and Wes a little with the fight scene between David and the father."

The swimming pool bloodbath

The death of Sadie went through a major rewrite during production. The script called for Mrs. Collingwood to drown Sadie in the pond (the same location where Weasel parted ways with his member) after beating her with the severed arm and hand of Phyllis. This outrageous brand of poetic justice was never filmed, and the sequence was ultimately shot at the home of Sean Cunningham's mother, who happened to have a swimming pool.

In the final frenzied minutes of the movie, Mrs. Collingwood chases Sadie into the backyard of the house, where a struggle between the two women ensues. Attempting to flee, Sadie unwittingly takes a running jump into the Collingwood swimming pool. With a savage cry, Estelle slashes Sadie's throat with the switchblade. Spitting blood, Sadie slowly sinks into the pool, paralleling Mari's death in the pond earlier in the film.

Fred Lincoln: "We had a dilemma when we shot the swimming pool scene. We had described Jeramie's character as this wild animal, so a regular housewife would never be able to hurt someone like her. That's why we did the thing with the pool at night [note: the scene was shot 'day-for-night' with a filter over the camera lens] where Sadie is running and *she doesn't know the pool is there*. So then she hits the pool, and when she comes up, if you really look at the movie, the mother's not really aiming the knife like someone who knows what she's doing... she just takes the knife and swings it around, and it catches Jeramie by the throat. We used rubbers [condoms] there too; we put rubbers inside Jeramie's chest. So as soon as the mother went by her like that, Jeramie put her hand up and banged her chest, as if she was going where she was cut. Then, when Jeramie hit the water, the fake blood came out through the top."

The fight between Mrs. Collingwood (Eleanor Shaw) and Sadie (Jeramie Rain).

Jeramie Rain: "I was really strong back then, and I remember the actress who played the mother being angry at me, saying that I really hurt her during the fight in the leaves. That pool that they killed me in was so filthy... it had water in it, but nobody had cleaned it or even gone near it for years! They actually poured a bottle of Lysol disinfectant over me when I got out of the pool... I mean, they didn't know if having been in that pool was gonna kill me! I had a packet of blood inside my leotard, and I had a blood bag inside my mouth. I had to grab my chest to make the fake blood spurt, and make the blood come out of my mouth, and then sink back into that filthy, putrid water (*laughter*)... It was the scariest thing I've ever had to do. "

The Aftermath

The film's concluding moments, in which the shell-shocked Collingwoods are frozen amidst the wreckage of their own living room, were changed substantially from the way they appeared in the script. Along with the decision to kill off the Junior character (see above), Craven's screenplay included an irreverent coda spoofing the miracle which concludes *The Virgin Spring*. In the discarded conclusion, which was to take place by the pond where the rape and murders had occurred, Phyllis' severed hand suddenly springs to life, its clenched fist uncurling and flashing a 'V' for victory sign to the camera.

Another alternate ending for the movie, which was actually shot and used at early screenings of the film, froze on a close-up of the sheriff's blood-spattered face.

Marshall Anker: "When I came in at the ending of the movie, they had to get the blood splattering on my costume in one take. The movie was so low-budget that they only had one sheriff's costume, so they couldn't throw stage blood on my outfit and then do it over again. The original ending was a close up of my blood splattered face looking stunned, blood on my costume and my glasses. I have a clear, visual memory of seeing that ending at a screening of the film for the cast and crew. It was almost saying, 'Look, it's not a joke after all. Look what it came to...'"

Notes

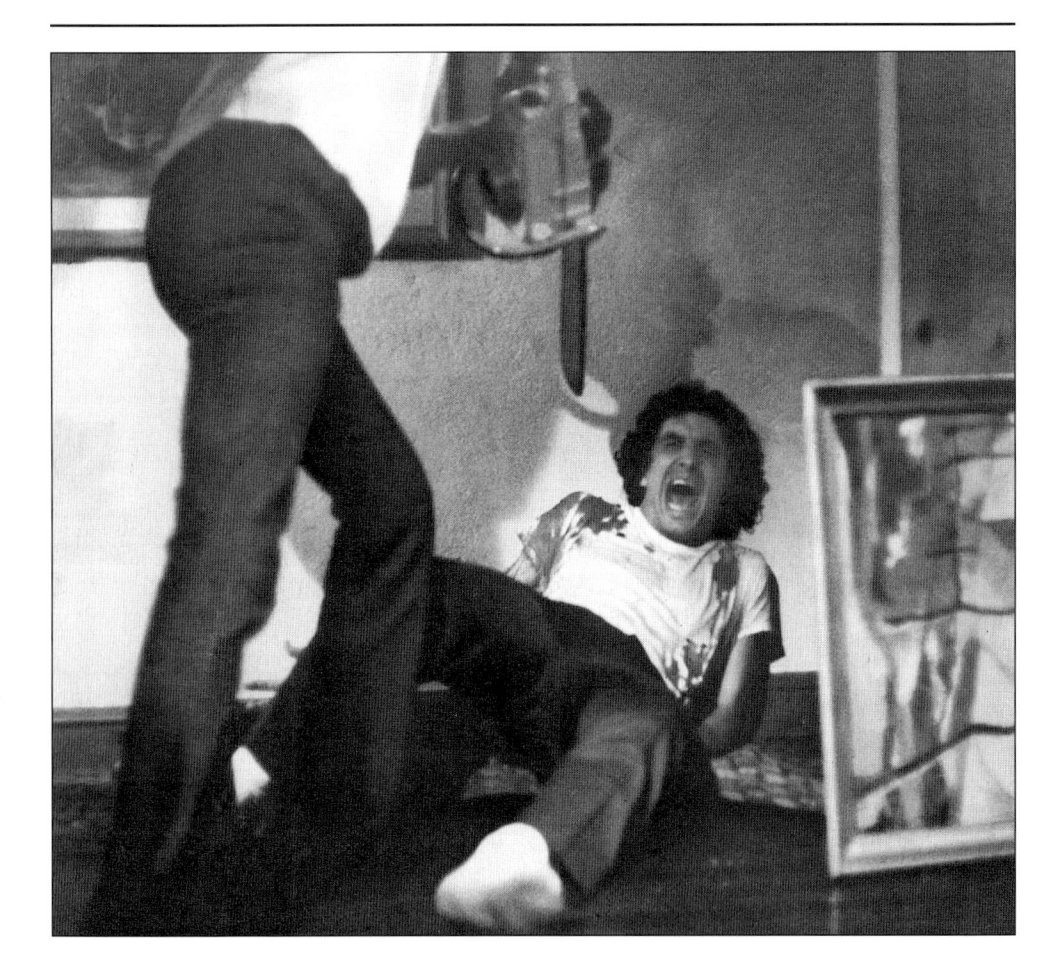

opposite and the following two pages: The film's original ending as shown in the *Night of Vengeance* script.

1   David Hess and Lee Marvin appeared together in *Avalanche Express* (1979).
2   The ice cream parlor scene also filled in a gap in the storyline. At the point where the scene was inserted, a note in the margin of Craven's shooting script reads: "EVENTS? Could use montage on girls, Sean feels. Maybe not here. Hate to break the slide. Maybe include Junior looking for girls, etc."
3   In his book *For One Week Only*, author Richard Meyers suggests that the title *Last House on the Left* derives from a scene in *A Clockwork Orange*. In actuality, there is no reference to any "last house on the left" in Anthony Burgess' novel or in Kubrick's film. See Chapter VI for the real story of the inspiration for the title.
4   Roger Ebert, "The Movies: Last House on the Left", *Chicago Sun Times*, Thursday, October 26, 1972.
5   Tony Williams, "Wes Craven: An Interview," *Journal of Popular Film and Television* 8, no. 3 (fall 1980)
6   The chicken-truck driver is actually described in the original script as an elderly black *man* named Jerome Pickins. Craven's outline of the scene described the chicken truck driver smoking pot and blasting Fats Domino's "Blueberry Hill" as he drives up to the two cops.

SC: 89

CUT IMMEDIATELY TO THE ROARING LIVING ROOM OF THE COLLINWOODS. THERE IS A TREMENDOUS POUNDING ON THE FRONT DOOR AS THE SHERIFF TRIES TO GAIN ACCESS, AND WE SWING TO SEE KRUG PINNED IN A CORNER, THROWING END TABLES, CHAIRS, LAMPS -- ANYTHING -- AT THE ADVANCING SAW. ALL DISINTEGRATE IN THE TEETH, WHICH KEEP ADVANCING.

KRUG: (Losing his composure) Please -- please don't kill me. I didn't know what I was doing!

KRUG BACKS INTO THE COUCH AND LOOKS BACK TO AVOID TRIPPING -- HE SEES MARI, FALLS BACK AND LOSES HIS BALANCE.

SC: 89A

CUT TO THE DOOR AS THE SHERIFF FINALLY BREAKS IT IN, DARTS INTO THE ROOM AND LOOKS IN DISMAY OFFSCREEN, TO WHERE THE DOCTOR HAS KRUG. OUR SHOT STAYS ON THE SHERIFF'S FACE, NOT SHOWING THE DOCTOR. WHAT HAPPENS NEXT HAPPENS VERY FAST.

SHERIFF: John! For Chrissakes don't!

BUT THE SHERIFF'S FACE REGISTERS EXTREME REVULSION IN JUST THE NEXT SECOND -- THERE IS THE SOUND OF THE SAW BITING INTO SOMETHING REALLY HUGE -- A CRUNCHING, WHIZZING SORT OF SOUND WHICH IN TURN IS DROWNED OUT BY A SHORT BUT SHATTERING SCREAM. THEN THE MOTOR STALLS, THE SCREAM SUBSIDES INTO A GURGLE. THEN SILENCE. ABOVE THE HEAD

OF THE SHERIFF A WIDE SPRAY OF SCARLET HAS STRUCK THE WALL, AND IS NOW RUNNING DOWN THE OFF-WHITE SURFACE.

CUT TO A SHOT OF JOHN COLLINWOOD, DROPPING THE DEAD SAW TO THE FLOOR. A FORM LAYS AT HIS FEET.

JOHN: He's all yours, Sheriff.

SHERIFF: (Still panting) Who in the Lord's name <u>was</u> he, John?

SC: 89B

HIS QUESTION IS INTERRUPTED BY THE DEPUTY COMING IN WITH MRS. COLLINWOOD BEHIND. HE TAKES IN THE SITUATION IN THE LIVING ROOM WITH A FACE THAT GOES FROM SHOCKED TO INCREDULOUS.

DEPUTY: Two more down at the lake, Sheriff. And a part of a third, too.

JOHN: That's Phylis Stone, or what's left of her. These three are the ones that had Mari. They --

A NOISE BEHIND THEM MAKES THEM ALL TURN. 'WILLOW', OR JUNIOR, IS ON THE STAIRS, COMING DOWN WEAKLY.

JUNIOR: (Looking towards the fallen form of his father) Is he ... dead?

SHERIFF: If he ain't I sure take my hat off to him -- he ain't got a head no more. Who're you, anyway?

159

JUNIOR SLIDES DOWN THE WALL AND SITS ON THE STAIRS, HIS HEAD BACK AGAINST THE WALL.

JUNIOR: I'm his son (pause) Is she...is the girl... the blond one... is she?

JOHN: She's dead.

JUNIOR: She called me Willow -- she gave me a new name. And...(He pulls the Peace Symbol from his shirt and looks at it weakly) She said her father was a Doctor, and could help me...

HE LOOKS AT DR. COLLINWOOD. DR. COLLINWOOD IS SPATTERED WITH BLOOD.

JUNIOR: You a doctor, mister? You look like a butcher....

FADE TO BLACK

SC: 90

FADE UP ON THE MOONLIT LAKE, PHYLIS'S HAND AND ARM IN THE FOREGROUND. THE MOONLIGHT LAYS ACROSS THE SEVERED LIMB, THE LAKE RIPPLING SILVER IN THE BACKGROUND. AND WE CAN SEE THAT WITH THE BATTERING OF SADIE, THE HAND HAS LOST ITS FIST. INSTEAD, TWO FINGERS HAVE SPRUNG UPWARDS, MIRACULOUSLY FORMING THE 'V' FOR VICTORY SIGN.

'THE END' FADES UP.

THEN ALL FADES TO BLACK.

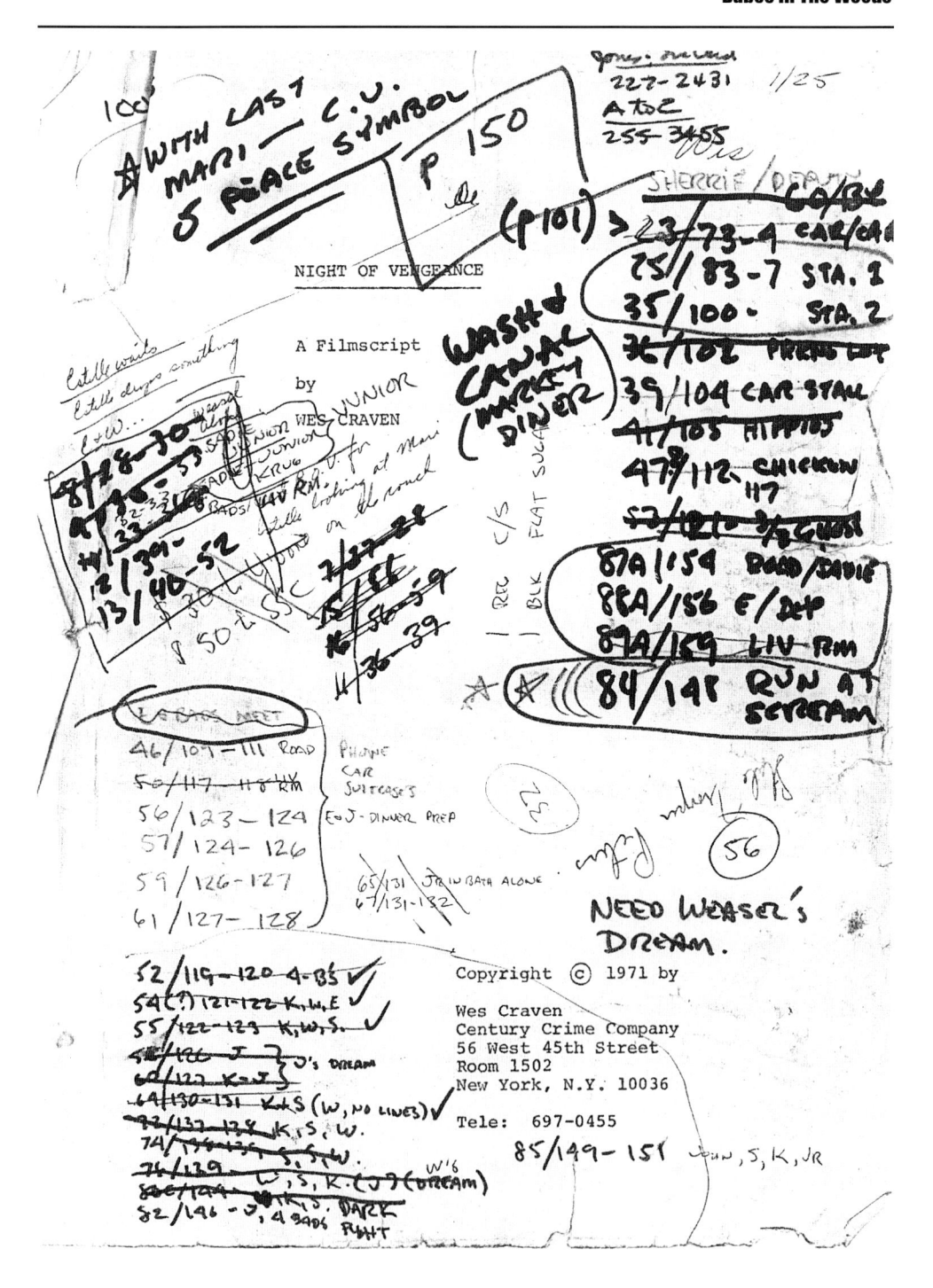

Title page from Wes Craven's shooting script; the numbers refer to scenes and their corresponding pages in the screenplay.

(courtesy Roy Frumkes)

Chapter 4

Cutting, Slashing, Slicing And Dicing

"Especially in the editing room, I began to become aware of how strong it was just for me to work with it. I felt, 'I don't like what's happening to these people, but at the same time, I do like it.' I had to be not only the victim but the murderer, to be the person who could get into somebody being tortured enough to make it sound like she was really suffering. At the same time part of me felt, 'I've been tortured like that, I've felt like that, totally isolated from everybody else. I've seen people take pleasure in my own personal discomfort.' All sides of me were coming in at the same time but there were sides of me I never knew existed, did not recognize or ever want to see revealed. I think that was the key to it."
- Wes Craven, in an interview with Tony Williams, 1979

The *Night of Vengeance* shoot had been such a rushed, improvised affair that Craven and Cunningham were unsure of just what they had 'in the can' when the dust settled. After the shooting wrapped, Craven spent months sequestered in Cunningham's office laboring over a 16mm Steenbeck editing table, and nearly a year elapsed before the final cut was released to theaters as *Last House on the Left*.

Wes Craven estimates that *Last House* took six months to edit, while Cunningham off-handedly recalls a mere twelve weeks. Since the movie wrapped in November, 1971, and was not screened publicly until July, 1972 (see Chapter VI), Craven's would seem the more accurate assessment. Recently-unearthed records relating to the film's musical score show that the first rough assembly of *Last House* was completed on December 7, 1971.

"Since we shot the film without any real plans, it was very difficult to edit," Craven notes. "In some instances, I had taken as many as three master shots of a scene without shooting any cutaways. There was also a great deal of variance between shots in any given scene because, as Sean has said, none of us had any concept of what continuity really was. For instance, there were tremendous variations on how things happened during the scene in the woods involving the humiliation of the girls. We literally had to completely re-invent certain scenes depending on how our footage ended up, rather than according to the script."

One of the few people on the crew of *Last House On the Left* who took any kind of continuity notes was Yvonne Hannemann, who testifies to the fact that the form of many scenes changed radically in the cutting room. "I occasionally dropped by Sean's office to see how they were cutting the film together," the assistant director recalls. "I was struck by how creative they really were when it came to the editing of *Last House*. There were germs and sparks of great things that happened during the shoot, but it was very patchy and needed to be sewn together. Wes is

Cutting, Slashing, Slicing And Dicing

a very good writer, but I think it was his editing craft that really made the film. He spent an enormous amount of time cutting it, and he really worked hard piecing it together."

Craven was assisted in the editing room by the ever-resourceful Steve Miner, whose apprenticeship on *Last House* would later lead to Miner's becoming a key member of Cunningham's production team on films like *The Case of the Smiling Stiffs, Here Come the Tigers, Manny's Orphans,* and *Friday the 13th.* "Steve Miner worked extremely hard during the shooting of the movie, and was terrific to have around," Cunningham says. "He approached me at the end of shooting, and said that he wanted to learn more about film. He asked if he could do anything at all in the editing room, promising he'd do anything it took... so I said, 'OK, we'll see how it works out...' As it turned out, Steve did everything he said he was going to do; he just worked around the clock - he was an absolute sponge. He was an endless supply of energy and good will, even though I paid him very little money. None of us had very much money at the time... when you're that young, you don't need a lot of money to live on. It was all about learning."

"I was with Wes every day in the editing room," Miner recalls. "Wes essentially cut the entire movie himself, and as he went along, he'd show me various techniques and ways to make a scene work. I didn't know anything about editing at the time, so I just tried to absorb as much as possible. It was actually a very exciting time for me. One of the things I remember most about the movie is that it seemed like we cut it for about a year, mostly because nothing matched. In fact, it seemed like five years!"

Several examples of the mismatched footage can be seen in the finished film. The scene in which the killers are tooling down the highway in the Cadillac convertible contains several jump cuts which seem to indicate that Craven lacked enough usable cutaways to cover up the gaps in the master shots. Later, during the scene in which the gang puts the two girls through the paces of a nasty sex-and-violence show, the girls are gagged in one shot and ungagged moments later. When the Collingwoods discover Mari's body, their dialogue is out of sync because Craven chopped out part of the scene where he felt the acting was weak.[1]

Sean Cunningham is fond of telling the following anecdote about the profound level of ignorance that led to the troublesome lapses in continuity: "Shortly after *Last House* was edited, I went out to Los Angeles to watch a movie being made. I noticed that there was a person on the set of this movie who was in charge of continuity, making sure that things matched in consecutive shots. The reason that we didn't have somebody like that on the set of *Last House* was not because of budgetary restrictions, or because I refused to hire somebody, but simply because we really didn't know that there *was*

such a thing as continuity! We kept track of when the camera was turned on and off, but that was it!" The producer is quick to add, "If we had known what continuity was, we would have thought it a darn fine idea… although we wouldn't have hired another body, that's for sure! There just would have been one person who had that much more responsibility."

The above-cited humiliation sequence presented a particularly sticky problem in the editing room because certain moments were too risqué to use in the finished film. Ordering a girl to wet her pants was sick enough, but the simulated scenes of forced lesbianism between Mari, Phyllis, and Sadie were beyond the threshold of acceptability. Thus, not all of the awkward edits in the sequence resulted from simple lack of continuity.

For example, one odd cut occurs after Krug goes off "to get some firewood" from the trunk of the Cadillac. Several shots of Weasel polishing his switchblade and looking off-camera appear in sequence, with no cutaways to the object of his gaze. The conspicuously-absent insert shots, which may have been removed *after* the release of the movie (see Chapter VII) depicted Sadie performing oral sex on the agonized Mari. While Jeramie Rain understandably seems to have blocked this scene from her memory, traces of the offending act remain in the film. Mari's moans of discomfort can still be heard on the soundtrack, and when Phyllis suddenly makes a run for her life, Sadie's head pops up from between Mari's legs.

During the murder of Phyllis, the victim's pants are up in one shot and suddenly down around her calves in the following frame. The missing middle portion of this sequence, revealed in outtakes from the movie, depicts Weasel yanking Phyllis' pants down and handing Sadie his switchblade. Another out take from the Phyllis murder sequence depicts Krug picking his nose (see illustration) and nonchalantly chatting with Weasel and Sadie as the wounded girl crawls off into the woods. There were numerous takes of this dialogue ("How'd she get so close to the road?") that featured Krug digging around in his nostril, none of which made it into even the roughest of rough cuts.

"The movie was remarkably pornographic in its violence, and we cut out an awful lot of it just for our own benefit," Cunningham says. "At a certain point, we said, 'Yecch! We can't do that!' I remember cutting down that one particularly gruesome scene where David Hess is carving his name on the girl's chest for no apparent reason, except to torture her; it was really graphic, and we ended up trimming most of it. I also remember cutting out a lot of that scene where Lucy Grantham's character was eviscerated. They were pulling out the guts, and throwing them around, and it was just awful. It was almost unwatchable. You do it, and you're sort of giggling, like 'This is really naughty,' but, at the end of the day, the scene had to be cut, and in my opinion, it probably wasn't any loss whatsoever." Craven disagrees with Cunningham's opinion on the disembowelment footage. "If I could do it over again, or if I could restore it, I would," he says. "But unfortunately, I'm sure those elements are lost."

"There were some scenes taken out to get the R rating," Steve Miner confirms. "There were also some scenes that were technically terrible which didn't make it into the movie. But my recollection is that Sean and Wes tried to make the film as strong as possible in terms of shock value. I think that was their intent in making the film."

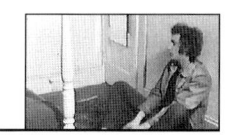

Cutting, Slashing, Slicing And Dicing

The cast cracks up between takes.

opposite:
Last House on the Left was briefly test-marketed as *"Sex Crime of the Century"* in 1972.

(courtesy Greg Herger)

"Sean actually sent *Last House* out to California to get it rated by the MPAA, and went through the agonizing procedure that we all have to complete now," Wes Craven recalls. "The film immediately received an X rating. At a certain point, Sean, who is really one of the toughest, feistiest guys I've ever known, decided that it was just impossible to comply with the MPAA people without cutting the film down to nothing. So he went down the hall to someone else who'd had a film released, and actually snipped the R rating tag from their negative, pasted it on the front of our film, and sent it to Boston. The movie was duplicated and blown up that way… and it 'became' an R rated film! Nothing ever happened… the ratings board never came after us. So we ended up releasing this incredibly violent and shocking film with an R rating, and that was half of its success… it just blew everybody's mind."

Curiously, Craven's tale of the purloined rating symbol does not tally with MPAA records which certify *Last House* as being officially rated R on August 16, 1972. Apparently, a bowdlerized version was submitted to the ratings board, while the uncut film made its way to Hallmark's screens without the MPAA approval. These tactics are certainly consistent with Hallmark's outlaw approach to independent distribution; the company was actually sued by the MPAA for using R and PG rating symbols in their ad campaigns without ever submitting the product to the board. [see chapter VII] Thus, the widely-varying accounts of the movie's shock value and the persistent rumors of an unrated version of the film are not merely the product of hype or over-active imaginations.

"We had one version of the film which we used for the test dates [see chapter VI], and then we got a deal with AIP to release it nationally," Cunningham says. "There, in the intervening time, we had to have the movie rated, which took a great deal of effort because they kept saying, 'No, you can't do that, that's X rated!' I remember making cuts on a Moviola, trying to trying to take things out and put other things back in. During that process, the film became somewhat diluted, but I can't imagine that the cuts really hurt the film."

CUNNINGHAM FILMS presents

SEX CRIME OF THE CENTURY

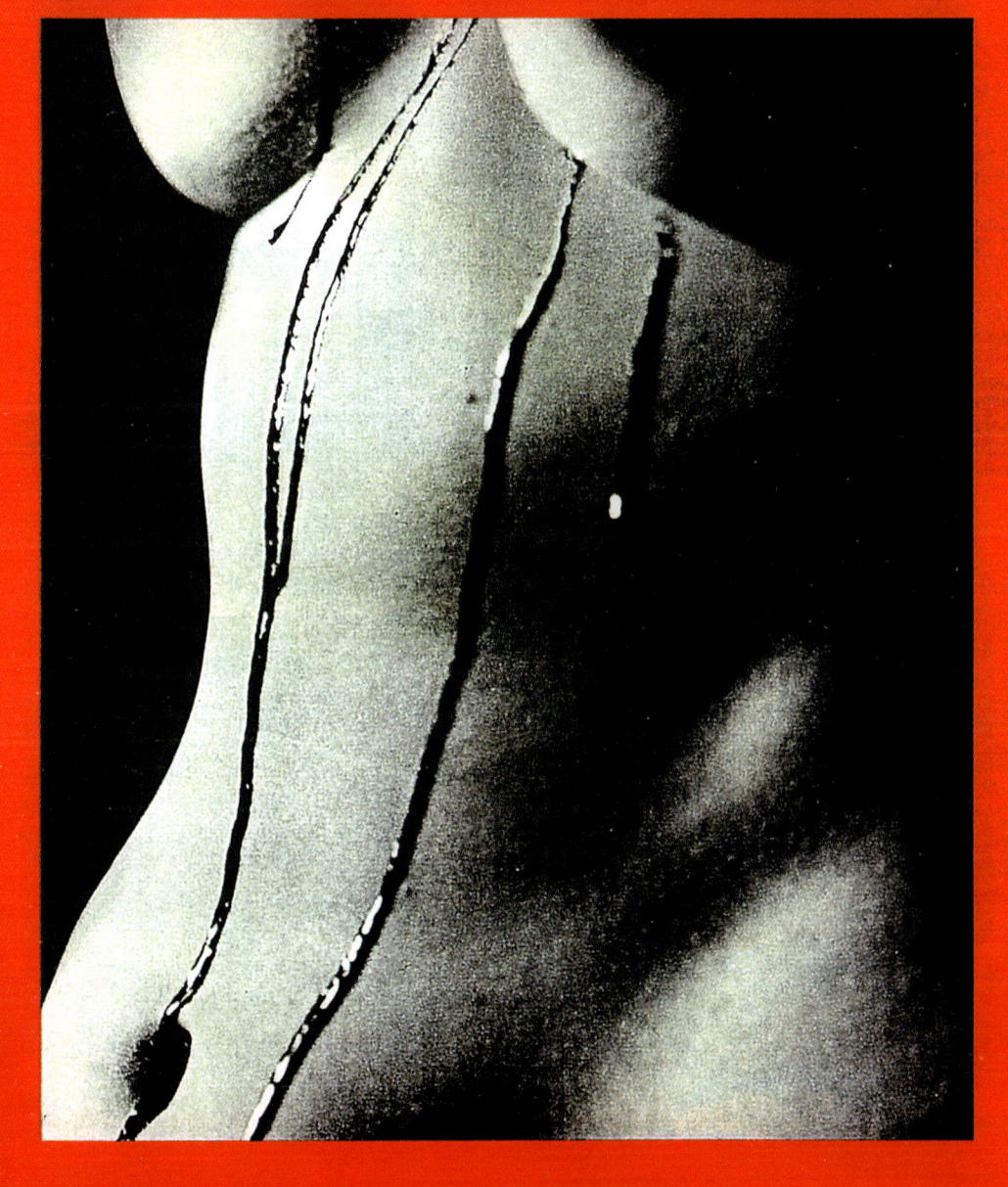

Produced by Sean S. Cunningham
Written and Directed by Wes Craven
Original Score by David A. Hess

Starring David Hess, Jeramie Rain, Fred Lincoln,
Marc Sheffler, Sandra Cassell, Lucy Grantham
with Marshall Anker, Martin Kove, Cynthia Carr,
Gaylord St. James, Ray Edwards
and introducing Ada Washington

above:
Jeramie Rain emerges from the swimming pool.

below: The same moment seen from another angle

above: Wes Craven with son Jonathan (left) and daughter Jessica (right) on the set of Last House on the Left.

below: The cast relaxes between takes - left to right: David Hess, Sandra Peabody, Lucy Grantham, Fred Lincoln.

left: **Crew member Anne Paul paints a throat wound on actress Jeramie Rain. Eleanor Shaw (centre) and Fred Lincoln (left) look on.**

above: **Lucy Grantham as Phyllis.**

below: **Sadie and Weasel.**

opposite: **Krug (David Hess) during the chainsaw attack.**

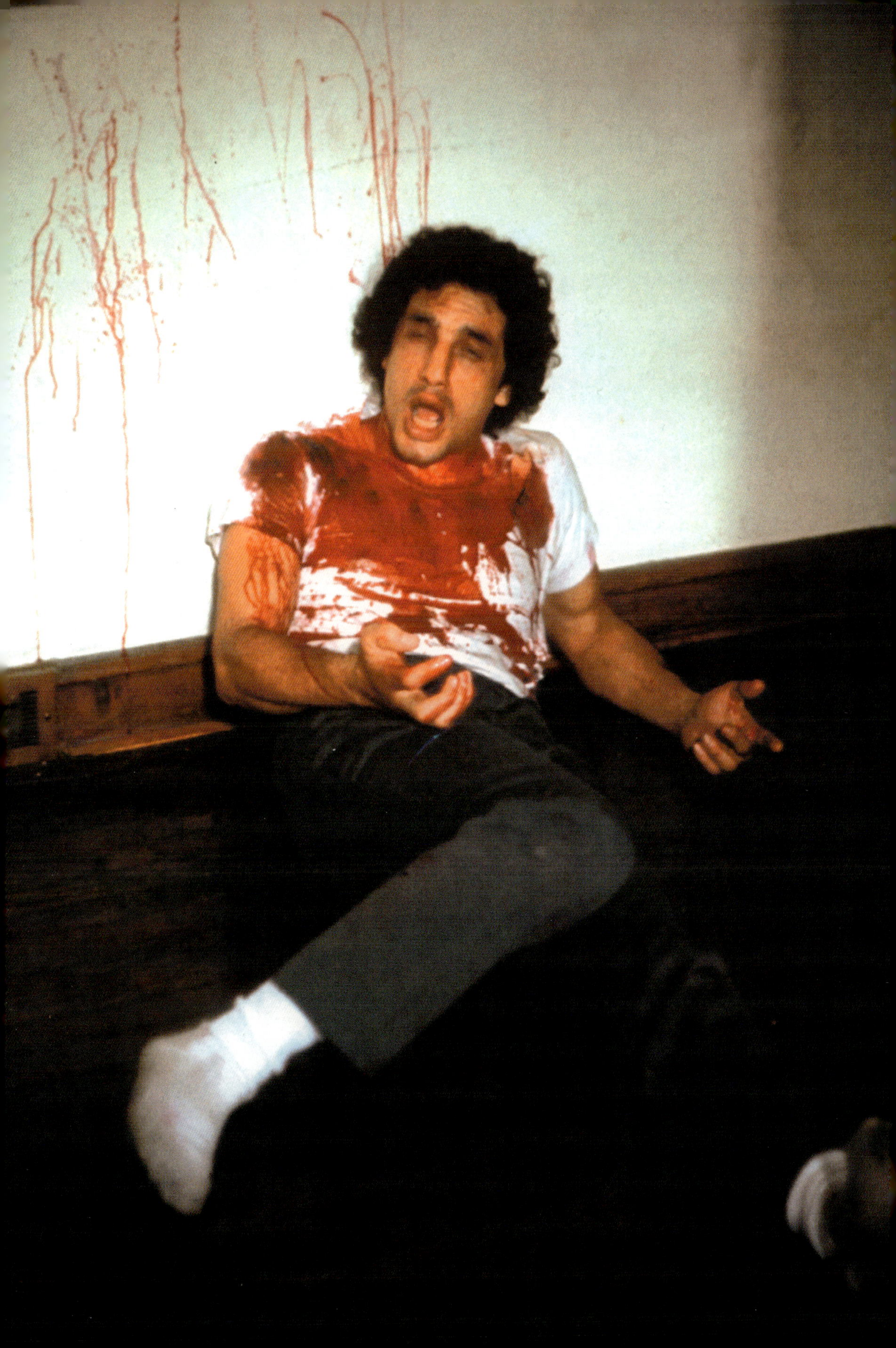

SE NON VOLETE SVENIRE CONTINUATE A RIPETERVI
E' SOLO UN FILM, E' SOLO UN FILM, E' SOLO UN FILM!

L'ULTIMA CASA A SINISTRA

CON DAVID HESS • LUCY GRANTHAN
SANDRA CASSEL • MARC SHEFFLER

REGIA DI WES CRAVEN
UNA PRODUZIONE: THE NIGHT COMPANY NEW YORK

EASTMANCOLOR

The lobby cards and poster shown on this page and opposite were all used to promote the Italian theatrical release of Last House on the Left.

above: Dutch video cover. For many years, this release was arguably the best print available on tape.

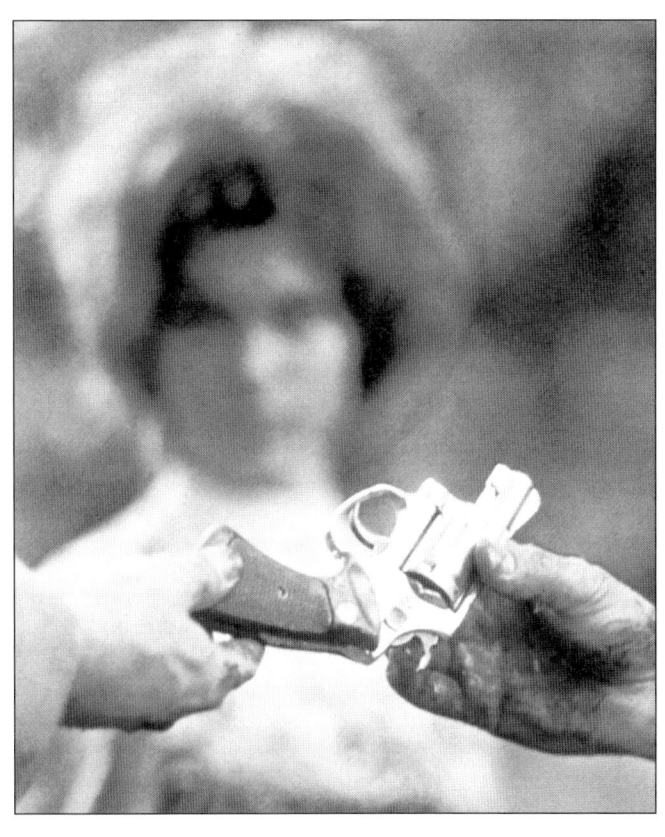

To this day, Craven does not agree with Cunningham about the censorship of the picture. "I had gone out to California to work with Peter Locke on some films that he was making, and I remember getting a call from Sean, saying, 'I think we went too far, and without hurting the picture, we can make some cuts,'" the director relates. "Sean ran down the list of cuts, and I didn't want to be outrageous or irresponsible towards my partner, so I agreed with him, and Sean made the cuts himself. But I was never happy with the cuts as they were actually made, because they were very jumpy... And I really felt that the spirit of the picture was severely compromised by those cuts."

According to one source, the difficult months of post-production sent the project over budget by thousands of dollars. However, the movie still came in at under $100,000, and the added investment in editing and scoring the movie proved to be a wise one. Craven's painstaking efforts in the editing room transformed *Last House* from a disjointed home movie into a fast-paced, hard-hitting narrative film.

Krug takes Weasel's gun in order to shoot Mari.

Craven used the technique of cross-cutting between contrasting scenes to great effect in *Last House*. For example, the sitcom-like skit of Mari's parents baking her a surprise birthday cake was scripted as a separate, uninterrupted scene. This might have dragged on its own, but when the corny buffoonery is alternated with the nerve-wracking scene of Krug, Weasel and Sadie encircling the girls in the sleazy apartment, it makes an altogether different statement. "I wanted to show the parents as being out of touch with the world around them," Craven says of the sequence. "They were preparing this fairy-tale ritual for their daughter, while the reality of what was going on in the world at large was much grimmer than they realized."

Craven placed a strong emphasis on sound during the editing process. Consequently, mixing the film's soundtrack became an involved and elaborate project. "A friend once told me that there were more cuts in the soundtrack for *Last House* than he'd ever seen in any movie," Craven says. "I ran up to thirty tracks at once during the mix... I found a distinct joy in constructing a tangled web of sounds. In addition to the dialogue and music, I kept a very dense group of sound effects tracks running throughout the film. I did a lot of chopping with the music, especially with the electronic noises that David Hess and

Steve Chapin recorded. I layered different sounds on top of each other, and strung together individual sounds which they'd given us. A good example of the 'basket of sounds' that I wove would be all of the bird cries in the background of the scene where Phyllis is being chased through the woods. I selected each bird separately, and ultimately ran about sixteen separate bird tracks. The layers of sound effects became almost a musical track."

"I did all the sound effects for the film, which was a great learning experience," Miner notes. "We had to get ready for the mix, and Sean and Wes simply said, 'Steve, why don't you do the sound effects?' So I said, 'Gee, OK, sure...' I went through the film and made a list of everything from babbling brook sounds to footsteps... basically, all of the foley and sound effects. I didn't know the difference between the two things at the time. I went back to Westport for the weekend, and my girlfriend at the time helped me out with it. I got the idea when Krug was stabbing Phyllis to record the sound of a grapefruit being stabbed - and that's the sound that's in there now. I recorded all the effects and cut them into the film. Now, you'd hire a sound house and a sound editor to do that, but we were too cheap and too dumb for that.

"In that nightmare scene [Weasel's dream], which I think is the strongest scene in the movie, to represent the sound of the hammer and chisel I had recorded the sound of a metal ashtray in Sean's office," Miner recalls. "I took the ashtray and banged it against a filing cabinet or radiator, and it was a great sound effect. It really made you cringe when you heard it. I'd recorded some other effects to put there as substitutes, because there was a lot of 'dirty' sound in the original take, such as buzzing in the background. The original sound was technically poor, but the moment of impact was effective. I prepared the tracks for that scene, and to this day, I feel bad about it, because somehow I lost that [original] sound... and the substitute effect that wound up being used is not nearly as good as that original piece."

Miner's explanation of the sound effects recording for *Last House* sheds light on more than one aspect of the movie's construction: "Because we had such primitive conditions, we would get bad sound effects and use them anyway because they somehow sounded *right*."

Since a fair portion of the film was shot without sync sound (Jim Hubbard estimates that only "between one-half and one-third" of the

top:
Spring 1985 showing of *Last House* at a Dorchester, Massachusetts drive-in which has since been demolished.

above:
Japanese video cover

Cutting, Slashing, Slicing And Dicing

movie was shot in sync) the post-production required certain lines of dialogue to be dubbed in after the fact. This process is known as ADR (Additional Dialogue Recording) or 'looping' and in today's world would be done in a specially-designed audio suite. "We invented our own system for that," Miner smiles. "A lot of the looping was done right in the editing room. We had the actors come in, and we'd play the line we wanted looped back and forth until they got it right. Once they had it, we'd turn off the editing machine so that the fans inside it wouldn't be making noise, and we'd record it right on the spot."

Bizarre promotional montage from the Spanish lobby card set.

LAST HOUSE ON THE LEFT

Cutting, Slashing, Slicing And Dicing

Jim Hubbard remembers another improvised dubbing system used for the film. "One time, we built a box in Sean's office, and lined it with sound blankets and quilts. Two of the actors came in, one of whom was the doctor's wife [Eleanor Shaw], and they got into this quilted box to record some voiceovers that we needed for the film."

One of the most audacious elements added to the movie during post-production was an opening title card declaring that the events depicted in the movie were "based on a true story." This patently false assertion, which remains in the movie to this day, exemplifies the brass

Cutting, Slashing, Slicing And Dicing

balls and black humor of the film makers. Craven laughs when asked about the "true story" label and offers this simple explanation: "We just decided, on top of everything else, 'O.K., now we'll say it's all true.'"

As the film took shape, it was screened as a work-in-progress numerous times for cast, crew and the financial backers. Marshall Anker recalls one such screening, held in Manhattan in the spring of 1972. The reactions of the audience foreshadowed the outrage that the film would inspire during its release. "I was sitting next to Sandra Peabody while we were screening the film," Anker recounts. "She was very upset by what she was seeing, and to top it off, her mother was sitting right there on the other side of her. Sandra was carrying on, 'Oh my God! Oh, it's so horrible! All that blood!' I thought to myself, 'Doesn't she know what she did? What did she think this movie was going to be, a comedy?'"

"I was horrified and upset," Peabody confirms. "It was not at all what I thought it would be. I think the most upsetting scene for me was the one in the woods... but I don't think I ever saw the whole thing. When I went and viewed it, I walked out."

"My friend Perry Gewirtz[2], who had introduced me to Wes Craven, also came to that screening," Anker continues. "Perry's date, a girl named Diane, got up in a huff and walked out halfway through the movie. Diane got this pissed-off look on her face, like she was standing up for the rights of women everywhere. It was really embarrassing, because all the buyers turned around in their seats and saw her exiting the screening room. But, in the end, I think it was exactly that controversial aspect of the movie that made it a commercial success. After the screening, we were all standing there waiting for the elevator. I went over to Martin Kove and I shook his hand, and I said, 'Martin, the comic relief in this movie was terrific.' Fred Lincoln overheard this, and gave me a funny look, like 'What the hell are you talking about?!' So I turned to Fred, and repeated, 'Now, wasn't the comic relief in that movie good?'"

"We had a great time at that cast and crew screening," Cunningham laughs. "We just thought the whole thing was so silly and crazy. People were shaking their heads at us, as if to say, 'Oh, my God, what have you done?!'"

"There were a lot of pre-release screenings of the film during the summer and fall of '72," David Hess recalls. "I went of all of them, and the reactions were amazing! There would be this absolute silence as the audience got up and walked out during the end credits... then they'd get outside, two or three people would break the silence, and, all of a sudden, all hell would break loose! Some people would say they were going to get a petition and protest it, others would say, 'Finally, we see a movie that shows horror in all its graphic reality'... all kinds of bullshit! And I'd just stand there laughing, saying, 'What do they know? C'mon! Just say you liked it!'"

opposite:
On location with Marc Sheffler and Sandra Cassell.

(outtake courtesy of Roy Frumkes)

Notes

1   An alternate take in which the Collingwoods find Mari alive was included in the version of the film released as *Krug and Company*. (see Chapter VII)
2   Gewirtz had a scene-stealing role as the flasher Sonny Williams in Robert Downey, Sr.'s celebrated spoof *Putney Swope* (1969). He also worked as an extra/stunt double in Woody Allen's *Stardust Memories* and *Annie Hall*.

Chapter 5

Krug Plays a Mean Guitar:
The Musical Score

"The toreador leads mesmerized throngs into the violence of the bullring to witness a cruel and meaningless spectacle. The carnival atmosphere surrounding the murder of an innocent creature can be heard as the band marches around the arena..."
- **from the libretto of *The Naked Carmen* (1970), a rock opera co-written by David A. Hess**

David Hess' inimitable portrayal of the villainous brute Krug Stillo was not his only contribution to *Last House on the Left*; the lead actor also composed and performed the movie's musical score. Hess' uncredited partner in crime on the *Last House* soundtrack was Craven's friend Steve Chapin, who assisted in the recording and arranging of the music. In addition to his work on the instrumental portions of the score, Hess wrote and sang several mellow folk-rock tunes which appear in the film, providing an ironic contrast to his threatening presence on screen

Hess' experience as a professional songwriter and musician preceded his acting career. Using the name David Hill, he began writing songs for Elvis Presley, Sal Mineo, Pat Boone, The Staple Singers, Andy Williams, Conway Twitty and others as early as 1957. The most famous of Hess' pop tunes include Elvis' "I Got Stung" (a 1958 hit recently covered by Paul McCartney), Boone's "Speedy Gonzales" and Mineo's "Start Movin'". He also cut two albums of his own for Kapp Records: *David Hill* (1959) and *Wanted* (1960). In the early '60s, Hess performed as a folk singer and briefly shared a Greenwich Village apartment with crooner Bobby Darin (a.k.a. Walden Robert Cassotto).

Initially encouraged by his mother to be an opera singer, Hess attended New York's Juilliard School of Music, where he studied with world-renowned conductor Vincent Perischetti. At the time of his film acting debut in *Last House on the Left*, Hess was pursuing graduate studies in archaeology at Columbia University and working as a writer-producer for Mercury Records. Hess' relationship with Mercury resulted in two albums for which he dropped the 'Hill' pseudonym in favor of his real surname. The first of these now-rare LPs was a collaboration with Malachy McCourt[1] entitled *...And the Children Toll the Passing of the Day* (Mercury Records SR 61258). The second album, released in the summer of 1970, was an ambitious rock opera entitled *The Naked Carmen* (Mercury SRM I-604) on which Hess collaborated with classical composer and conductor John Corigliano, who went on to score Ken Russell's *Altered States*.

Although some of his songs had been featured in two Elvis Presley movies (*Frankie and Johnny* and *Paradise, Hawaiian Style*), Hess had yet to compose a film score when he was hired to do the music for *Last House*. The actor's approach to the task was unconventional by his own admission. "I don't score traditionally, in that I don't wait to sit down and look at the film after it's been made," Hess says. "On *Last House*, I was composing as the film was being shot, and the music evolved as we went along. I was essentially on my own in writing the songs; I would come in and throw ideas at Sean and Wes and they would say 'yes' or 'no.' I feel it's important to be on the set as a composer, because when you're there and you see what's happening, that brings out the organic aspects of the music. You write for the people you're involved with, as opposed to writing for the characters you see on a screen. In my opinion, by writing on the set, you're getting a sense of the characters and the movie one step earlier in their development; the composer becomes a part of the writing team, as opposed to the post-production team."

During post-production, Wes Craven brought in his longtime friend Steve Chapin to assist Hess in arranging and recording the music. "Steve came in as the technical expert at getting the players together and recording the music," Craven says. "David was the artist, the composer of the songs, and Steve essentially produced the soundtrack."

"Wes needed somebody to help weave David's songs in and out of the movie in a way that did the most for the film," Chapin explains. "I was responsible for all of the arranging and the incidental music for the film. I was pretty inexperienced myself at the time; I had done some scoring for short films and for a stage production of Sartre's *No Exit* which Wes directed in 1968, but that was it. David Hess was the guy who had the vision, and my job was to put some instruments behind David's stuff, and to fill in the other gaps of silence in the soundtrack where Wes felt he needed some music as a bridge from one scene to another. David and I worked very closely, especially before we started recording."

When it came time to fit the music to the film, Hess' compositions were edited down considerably; he estimates that only forty percent of the music found its way into the finished film. "David had the idea that *Last House* could have been something of a musical, which, of course,

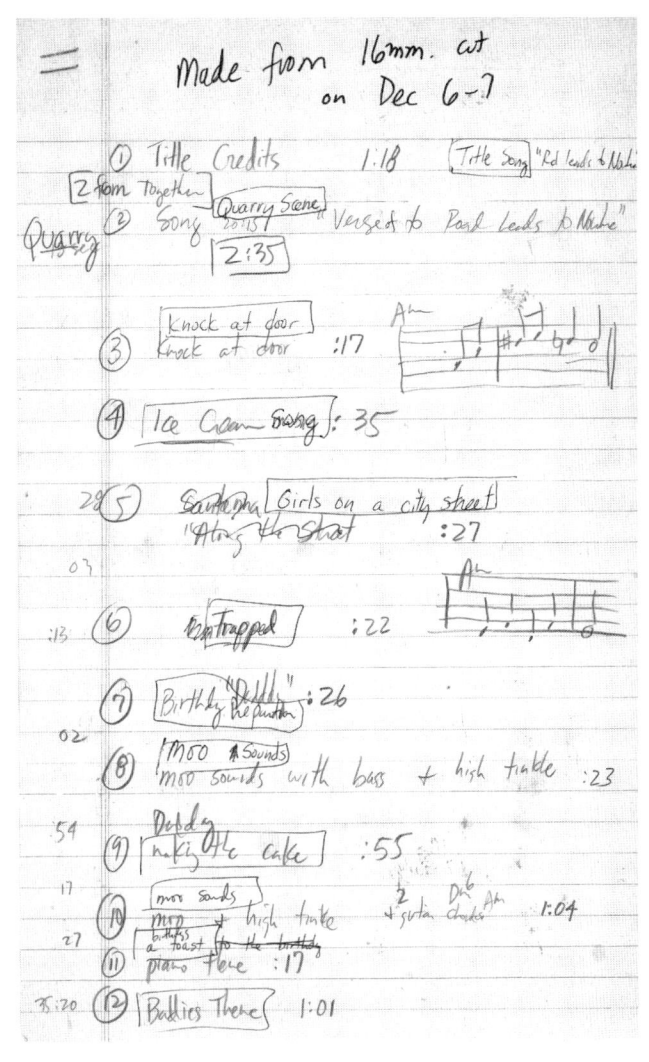

Early editing room notes written by uncredited composer Steve Chapin.

Krug Plays A Mean Guitar

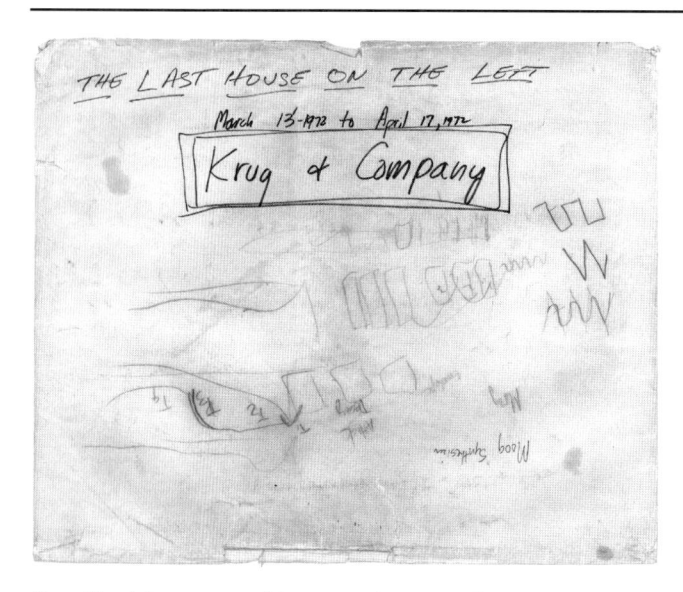

Steve Chapin's music score folder.

it couldn't have been!" Chapin says. "David's songs were really very nice, but the music had to serve the movie; we weren't doing an album. The unfortunate thing is that you can't really tell how a song will sound when you reel off thirty-five seconds of it and then cut back to the movie. We also had to deal with the usual problem that the cuts of the movie were constantly changing. A lot of David's songs were actually much better than they seem in the context of the movie; they built up intensity and steam as they went along, which is a big part of composing music. He wrote some songs with specific characters from the film in mind, and they went through complete storylines musically and lyrically."

One song that hit the cutting-room floor was "Daddy, Put Your Coat of Many Colors On," a folk ballad with lyrics reflecting the film's generation-gap theme. "Daddy" appears in the movie only as an instrumental arrangement (which Chapin calls "The Beatles March") during the scene where the Collingwoods bake Mari's birthday cake.

Hess' mellow vocals on original songs like "Wait For the Rain" and "Now You're All Alone" could not have been farther afield from his abrasive, intimidating presence on screen. Wes Craven praises "Now You're All Alone" to this day, commenting, "It's a really beautiful, haunting piece… I'm surprised that nobody's covered it, because it's really a classic blues song."[2] In addition to the two aforementioned tunes, Hess also wrote and sang a jarringly upbeat ode to the film's villains called the "Baddies Theme." Obviously patterned after the music in Arthur Penn's 1968 film *Bonnie and Clyde* (itself a landmark of cinematic violence), the "Baddies' Theme" was originally subtitled "Sadie and Krug." Accompanied by the down-home sounds of a banjo, piano, and kazoo (!), Hess sings: "Weasel and Junior, Sadie and Krug / Out for the day with the Collingwood brood / Out for the day, for some fresh air and sun / Let's have some fun with those two lovely children and off 'em as soon as we're done!"

"With that particular song ["Baddies Theme"], I guess we wanted to create a bizarre juxtaposition between the carnival raucousness of the movie and the profoundly horrific and sad side of it," Wes Craven comments. "The contrast between that song and the characters was sort of like showing an image of a village getting napalmed and then saying, 'Fuck 'em if they can't take a joke'… that type of humor was very specific to the era of the early '70s, and, I think, terribly cynical."

Responding to criticism of the incongruous hoe-down music, Chapin remarks, "It upset my sensibilities at the time, but what with everything else that was going on in the movie, my sensibilities were already all screwed up, so what did it matter? Who knew how it was going to come off? Nobody had ever done a movie like this before!

Looking back at that song, it almost makes the whole thing seem like a fairy tale, as if none of it ever happened." Chapin's comment on the "Baddies' Theme" is particularly apt in reference to the final minutes of the film, which feature the song happily jangling along to a montage of end credits showing the cast members in humorous poses.

"The 'Baddies' Theme' serves as a counterpoint to the characters," Hess comments. "The song is consistent with the movie; there are so many things about the film that are aberrant. The contrast there was absolutely intentional; to this day, that's the way I approach film scoring. I've always felt that music in movies should be a counterpoint to whatever is going on up on the screen."

The film had already been shot when Chapin became involved with the project; the earliest scoring notes date from a rough cut made in December, 1971. At the time, the music was still in its embryonic stage. "There were about twenty-five cues[3] which we had to work on, ranging anywhere from a minute and a half to twenty-five seconds," Chapin says. "When I first started working on *Last House*, there were only six or seven spots where raw pieces of David's songs had been dropped into the movie. One of the pieces that had already been inserted was the song 'Now You're All Alone,' which comes up when the girls are getting molested in the woods. David played acoustic guitar on that one in addition to singing; he wanted to get as much of himself into the film as possible!"

Steve Chapin recruited most of the musicians heard on the *Last House* soundtrack from his own folk-rock group, known at the time as Mount Airy. At the time of recording, the band included Steve (bass, recorder, backing vocals), his older brother Tom Chapin (acoustic guitar, banjo, backing vocals), Doug Walker (electric guitar), Rich Look (piano), and drummer Ralph D'Onofrio (a.k.a. Kash Monet.) With the exception of drummer D'Onofrio, all of these musicians had previously been in a group called The Chapins, which recorded several singles for Epic Records before being dropped by the label in 1970. In addition to Chapin's group, sidemen Romeo Penque (flute, English horn), Specs Powell (percussion) and Manny Vardi (viola) also played on the *Last*

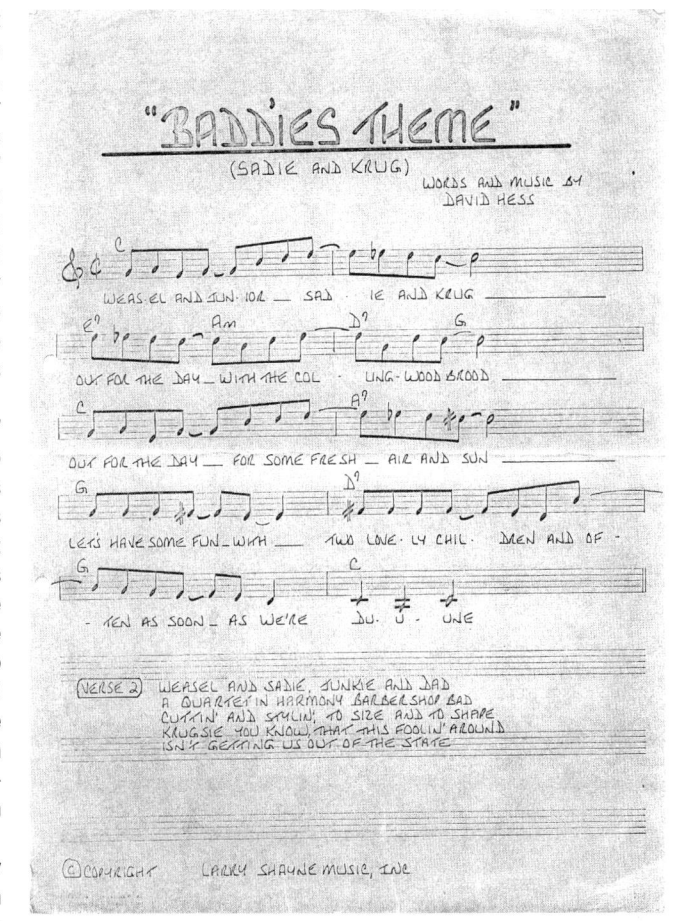

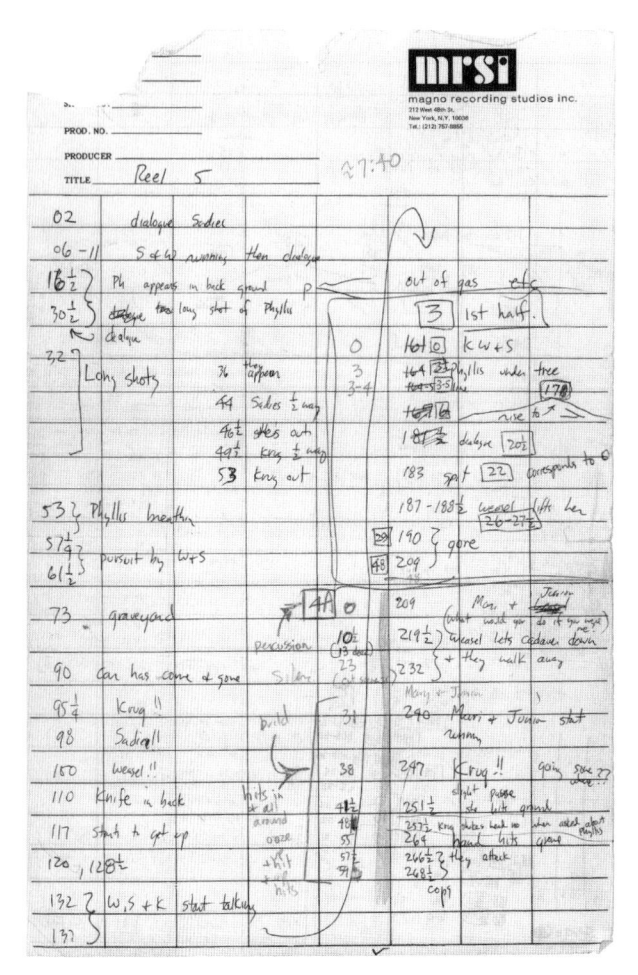

Recording studio sheet.

House sessions. Vardi, a veteran studio musician, composed the music for Sean Cunningham's *Together*.

"It was the type of thing where you end up making about seventy-five dollars for forty hours of work," Steve Chapin says of the soundtrack deal. "The band just did the sessions to help me out... we all lived together, rehearsed together and worked together at the time, so when I said I needed help on a movie score, they said, 'No problem, Steve!'"

Most of the soundtrack music was recorded in the spring of 1972 during two long sessions at New York's Electric Lady Studios, a recording facility originally built for Jimi Hendrix. David Hess speculates that some additional work may have been done at facilities belonging to Mercury Records, with whom he had a working relationship at the time. The experimental electronic sounds heard at various points in the score was recorded in Vardi's home studio on a primitive four track machine.

"The sessions were great," Chapin says. "The only thing that made it bad at any time was the spectre of having to get it all done. The first session was in studio A of Electric Lady, which included the band and the two sidemen... it lasted about eight hours. The second session was in studio B of Electric Lady, where we did all the chase music... it ran shorter, possibly six hours. It was kind of like controlled panic; things moved fast, but we were all relatively inexperienced. I think *Last House on the Left* was a unique challenge because we didn't have a picture to cue the music to. We'd take counts up in the editing room, to see how long the music had to be for a given scene, but the movie was never transferred to videotape. We recorded the music blind, and nobody ever saw it matched up with the film until the music was transferred to mag stock and put up on the Steenbeck. We would go to the editing house to see the sequences after they'd been synchronized, and that was a big deal every time. Towards the end, Sean Cunningham was like the Pope in the Sistine Chapel... 'when are you gonna get this thing done?' He was always on the phone in the next room, and we could hear him through the wall, trying to figure out where his next dollar was coming from."

In addition to the songs *per se*, Hess and Chapin experimented with more eclectic and eccentric means of scoring. "When we recorded the music used for the chase scene, we brought in a percussionist whose name I can't recall," Chapin says. "This guy [Specs Powell] did three or four tracks of percussion by beating xylophone mallets on the leather covering of a stuffed chair. He also created the 'heartbeat' sound [during the hand-held shot of Phyllis staggering through the woods] using the same technique. The guy was amazing, and he really saved our asses when it came to that chase scene."

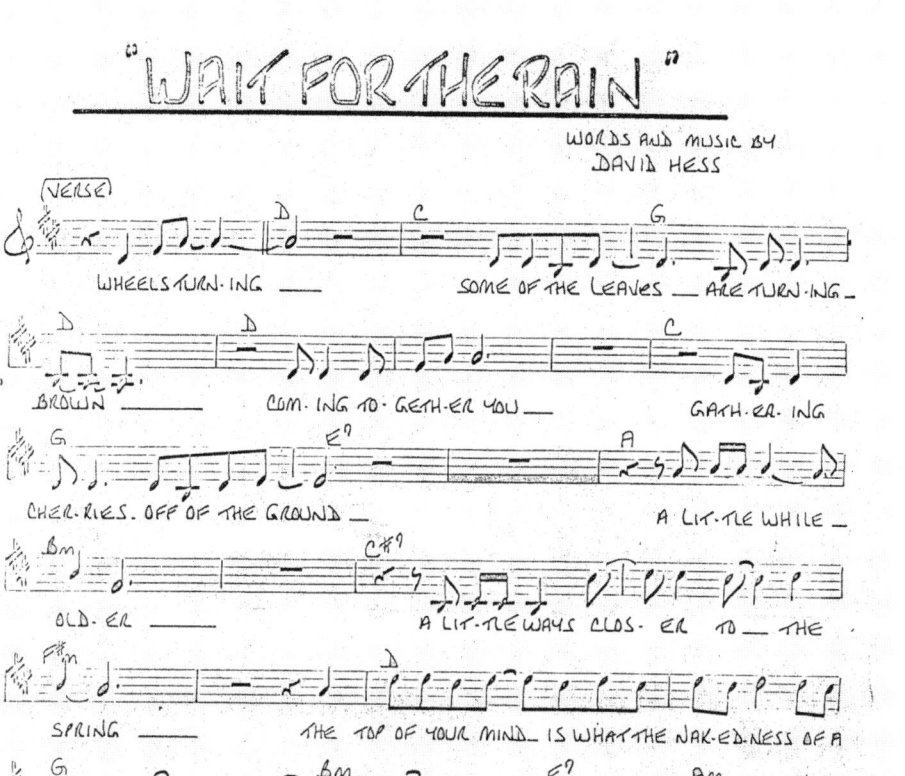

"The electronic music took two days to record, because we didn't know what we were doing," Chapin says. "David and I just went to [Vardi's] house and played; I don't even recall an engineer. We had to come up with about eight cues which went from two and a half minutes to thirty seconds. We churned out a bunch of really ghoulish sounds on a Moog synthesizer, and recorded them on a big, console-style four track machine... I remember using some of those sounds for the scene where David is drooling on that girl in the grass. At the time, I thought that stuff was pretty cool! In the scene where the parents eat dinner with the killers, there was this ill-sounding piece which was written almost like a string quartet. It was like fractured classical music... all the tones in the piece were slightly out of tune and slurping around in the mix. I remember that after Wes heard that music, he recut the dinner scene so that it would fit the music better. He had an image of Fred Lincoln smiling and sucking up spaghetti placed over those sounds... usually, the sound would follow the picture, but Wes rearranged things so that Fred Lincoln's face accentuated the music!"

By Hess' account, an ARP 2600 synthesizer was used for some of this incidental music, including a reprise of the 'Wait For the Rain' theme during the scene where Doc Collingwood sets his trap for the killers. The ARP and Moog synthesizers were also used to create the lurching, queasy sound effect heard in the scene where the killers slowly walk down the hill toward Phyllis' prone body.[4] During the murder of Phyllis, Craven cut in sound effects representing the "shrieks of dying birds."

"I had used the ARP synthesizer before on the *Naked Carmen* album, so I knew approximately what I was doing," Hess recalls. "There weren't a lot of synthesizers being used for film scoring at that time. That electronic music was just a case of necessity being the mother of invention, because we didn't have the bucks... we were under the gun, and we had to get some of those hits and stings for various moments in the film. I said, "Steve, come on, if we go in the studio to do this, we'll be there forever...' so we spent sixteen or eighteen hours just playing around with ideas on the synthesizer, recording little snippets that we knew we could use later on in various places. Cutting those pieces into the movie was the hard part, because we didn't have the film in front of us when we recorded them. We didn't have a finished, edited version of the movie from which we could work; that film was never finished until the moment it got released! Wes was constantly trimming and cutting the film, taking things out and putting them back in, so we thought the best thing to do was to try to emulate the kind of moods we remembered from various parts of the film, without trying to pinpoint the exact part. We did have a list of cues to work off, but that was it."

Although Wes Craven is himself a music lover and classical guitarist, the director's involvement with the scoring was minimal, according to Chapin. "There were financial troubles going on with the movie at the time, and when you're over-budget and behind schedule, you have to work fast. Wes was very much under the gun; he was busy on his end, and we were busy on ours. I'm sure there was a lot of stuff he would have liked to have changed, but he had no options because of the money problems... he just took the attitude of 'Let the boys do their thing'. Wes was young and easygoing back then, whereas David was more like my brother Harry, very insistent and high energy. David wanted to do his songs, Wes had to finish the movie, and I don't think there was a plan either way. It was just a chemistry that worked itself out."

MUSIC CUE SHEET FOR THE FILM
"LAST HOUSE ON THE LEFT"

PRODUCER: SEAN CUNNINGHAM
COMPOSER: DAVID HESS/STEVE CHAPIN
MUSIC PUBLISHER: LARRY SHAYNE ENTERPRISES and/or its foreign assignees
DISTRIBUTOR: HALLMARK RELEASING CORP.

CUE #	CUE TITLE	WRITERS & COMPOSERS	USAGE	TIME
#1	WAIT FOR THE RAIN	DAVID HESS	VOCAL	1:18
#2	WAIT FOR THE RAIN 2	D. Hess	Vocal	2:35
#3	KNOCK AT THE DOOR	D.Hess / S.Chapin	Bkg.instr	:17
#4	ICE CREAM SONG	" "	" "	:35
#5	Girl On a City Street	" "	" "	:27
#6	TRAPPED	" "	" "	:22
#7	DADDY, PUT ON YOUR COAT of many colors	" "	vocal	:26
#8	" " " " "	" "	" "	:55
#9	MOO SOUNDS	" "	Bkg.Instr.	1:04
#10	A BIRTHDAY TOAST	" "	" "	:17
#11	BADDIES THEME	D.Hess	VOCAL	1:01
#12	" "	" "	"	2:52
#13	OUT OF THE CAR TRUNK	HESS/CHAPIN	Bkg. Instr.	:36
#14	now you'RE ALL ALONE	D.Hess	Vocal	1:50
#15	PHYLLIS'ESCAPE	HESS/CHAPIN	BKG. INSTR.	2:55
#16	THE CHASE	" "	" "	:35
#17	WILLOW & MARG	" "		.35
#18	DOWN HILL TO THE GRAVE-YARD	" "	" "	1:15
#19	GOING SOMEWHERE	" "	"	:17
#20	THE BELLS TOLL FOR PYHLLIS	" "	"	:20
#21	PHYLLIS UNDER THE TREE	" "	"	:20
#22	DEATH OF PHYLLIS	" "	"	:07
#23	JUNIOR & MARY RUNNING	" "	"	:20
#24	RAPE OF MARY	" "	"	:34
#25	NOW YOURE ALL ALONE	" "	"	:34
#26	BADDIES THEME	D.HESS	VOCAL	2:15
#27	" "	"	Bkg.Instr	.20
#28	ACROSS THE FIELD	hess/ CHAPIN	" "	:17
#29	Spaghetti Dinner	Hess/Chapin	" "	1:03
#30	Some time later	" "	" "	:05
#31	MARYS LOCKET	" "	" "	:25
#32	WAIT FOR THE RAIN	D.Hess	"	:04
#33	" " " "	" "	VOCAL	1:34
#34	MARYS DEATH	HESS/CHAPIN	"	:17
#35	WAIT FOR THE RAIN	HESS	"	:38
#36	THE WEASEL & THE MRS.	Hess/CHAPIN	"	:53
#37	Collingwppds Traps	" "	"	1:35
#38	WAIT FOR THE RAIN	D.Hess	"	:45
#39	Scene By The Lake	hess/CHAPIN	"	:28
#40	the fight	HESS/CHAPIN	"	:42
#41	THE CLOSING	" "	"	:23
#42	END CREDITS	D.HESS	vocal	2:40

"I never saw the sensitivities or subtleties of that film, no way, no how," Chapin says. "But when I look back at the thing, in terms of the music, there are a couple of sequences which are really nice. I remember one which started out with a babbling brook, accompanied by a whole water theme, which builds up and slam-cuts into the outlaws driving down the road to the 'Bonnie and Clyde theme.' Although there were some things we did which were ungainly and amateurish, David's songs put a funny kind of old-time dressing on top of the movie's modern horror."

Cue sheet for *Last House on the Left*'s original score.

In the opening title sequence of the film, Hess is given sole credit for the score despite Chapin's pivotal role in its creation. "I asked Wes not to put my name on the movie," Chapin explains. "I thought it would be bad for my image at the time, and the movie horrified me to the point where I didn't want my name on it, anyway. I had a real problem watching the film, especially because what I saw was the uncut version, and it was really balls-to-the-wall. I think they've taken out some of that stuff since then; I never saw the whole thing after working on the individual pieces of it. I actually started to watch it once, and I wanted to chuck lunch. It was just a job that I had to do; I got it done, dropped my work off, and I never went to any of the screenings of the finished film. There was no bad blood between me and any of the other people involved; I just couldn't stand to look at the movie anymore."

Unlike Chapin, David Hess is proud of his work on the film and is quick to point out that there is meaning behind all of the shock value. "To me, the whole sense of the film, right from the beginning, is that it's a fairly accurate update of *The Virgin Spring*. Now, on the one hand, *The Virgin Spring* is about a heinous crime, but if you look at it from a spiritual point of view, if you can get into that, it's about rebirth. It's about the young generation that's pushing from underground, striking out to find their own world. *Last House on the Left* is really about the girls, which is why that lyric "the road leads to nowhere" is a central part of the score. The road *does* lead to nowhere, unless we get our act together. But there is always going to be a road, and there are always going to be kids taking that road… the fact that those two girls die in the movie is immaterial."

Post script: David Hess and Steve Chapin reunited in 1999 to produce a limited edition soundtrack CD for Last House on the Left. The compilation includes several songs dropped from the original soundtrack and re-recorded by Hess. Chapin remixed the songs in his home studio.

Notes

1   McCourt appeared alongside Hess in Peter Schamoni's *Potato Fritz* (1975) and played a priest in Sean Cunningham's family film *Manny's Orphans* (aka *Kick*, 1978). He is the author of the memoir *A Monk Swimming* and the brother of prize-winning author Frank (*Angela's Ashes*) McCourt.
2   In the movie, "Now You're All Alone" appears to reflect on the plight of the girls; however, in notes dating from its recording, the song is identified as "Junior's Theme".
3   'Cues' are points in a film soundtrack where music is to be inserted. The score for *Last House on the Left* ultimately comprised 42 cues, the shortest running four seconds, and the longest 2:55.
4   Some of the music which Hess and Chapin wrote for *Last House* was recycled in Sean Cunningham's sexploitation comedy *The Case of the Smiling Stiffs* (1973). In *Stiffs*, the electronic music from *Last House* becomes the mock-scary backing for scenes of simulated fellatio (the premise of *Stiffs* involves a vampiress who kills men through deadly deep throat.) Later in *Stiffs*, the upbeat music heard in *Last House* as Mari and Phyllis walk down the street looking to buy pot ("Girl On A City Street") was placed over footage of a live band whose motions don't come remotely close to the sounds they are supposedly making. The credits of *Stiffs* ascribe the music to Chapin.

Chapter 6

The Launching Of A Thousand Lunches

"Lingering gore, senseless cruelty, sadism and fetishism shock and dismay viewers, particularly those who are unsuspecting witnesses to the disgusting fare. That was the case locally when a movie was judged to be so 'sick' that the audience began walking out after the first fifteen minutes... Predictably, after the theater manager edited out the offensive parts, subsequent customers complained because they paid to see the uncut version."
- Hartford *Courant* editorial on *Last House on the Left*, September 3, 1972

"IT'S A WINNER!"
-*Variety* ad for *Last House*, November 15, 1972

The cult success of *Last House on the Left* came as a complete surprise to its director. Despite Wes Craven's feeling that his movie was not meant to be watched over and over again, *Last House* lingered in theaters for more than fifteen years and continues to play as a revival to this day. If this phenomenon remains baffling to many critics (and even to some of those involved in making the film), *Last House* certainly proved its detractors wrong in their dismissal of its raw, unaffected power.

Whatever the reasons for the movie's ongoing popularity, it is fair to say that *Last House* might never have found its audience if not for the masterful advertising campaign created by its distributor, Hallmark Releasing Corporation. The very title *Last House on the Left* came not from the movie's makers, but from one of Hallmark's business associates. Another key to the movie's success was its irresistible, ingenious advertising slogan: "TO AVOID FAINTING, KEEP REPEATING: IT'S ONLY A MOVIE... ONLY A MOVIE... ONLY A MOVIE..."

David Whitten, who started working for Hallmark in 1970 as a movie theater manager, was one of several publicists involved in the promotion of *Last House*. Over the years, Whitten has stayed true to his roots, playing a role in the release of cult movies such as *Henry: Portrait of A Serial Killer*, *Street Trash*, *Meet the Feebles* and the controversial porn documentary *Sex: The Annabel Chong Story*. Whitten first demonstrated his flair for outrageous publicity in 1972 by working on Hallmark's legendary "vomit bag" campaign for a West

The legendary *Mark of the Devil* barf bag: a Hallmark of quality and good taste.

Voice Fred W. McDarrah

THE MARQUEE OF THE WEEK, without a doubt. Spotted at the RKO Coliseum, Broadway and 181st Street.

The popular press was quick to catch on to Hallmark's *Mark of the Devil* campaign.

German production called *Mark of the Devil*, which had languished in the vaults of a Munich-based distribution firm for several years prior to its American release. "Nobody would touch that film - they just thought it was too repulsive and awful," laughs Whitten's former co-worker George Mansour, now a highly respected booker and consultant for independent films. "Obviously, we didn't think so!"

Both Whitten and Mansour recall that Hallmark's acquisition of European gore films like *Mark of the Devil* influenced the company's decision to finance *Last House on the Left*. "With [*Mark of the Devil*], we discovered gore and sex and violence all worked beautifully," Mansour said in a 1999 interview. "So we thought, let's mix 'em all together!"

A bloody period piece about two witchfinders and the gruesome methods they employ in extracting confessions from accused witches, *Mark* was directed by Michael Armstrong and starred Herbert Lom, Udo Kier, and Reggie (*Salem's Lot*) Nalder. Similar in subject matter to Michael Reeves' *The Witchfinder General* (1969), *Mark of the Devil* was most noteworthy for its crude, graphic torture scenes - one infamous highlight depicted a woman's tongue being torn out with pincers.

The advertising for *Mark* warned the moviegoing public that this was "The Most Horrifying Film Ever Made," and boasted that every ticketholder would be given a free "stomach distress bag" at the box-office. ("After we viewed *Mark of the Devil*, we certainly can assure you that someone will use the Regurgitation Bag" was Hallmark's promise to theatergoers during one early engagement.) Although *Mark of the Devil* had not been officially rated by the Motion Picture Association of America at the time of its premiere, the advertising for the film prominently stated that it was "Rated V for Violence." This deceptive claim annoyed the MPAA ratings board so much that it issued statements to the press denouncing both the movie and Hallmark's tactics. Even newspaper advice columnist Ann Landers jumped into the fray, devoting a 1972 column to the immorality of *Mark of the Devil*'s ubiquitous ad campaign.

Although Whitten was instrumental in the triumph of the barf-bag ballyhoo, he does not claim to have invented the gimmick. As Whitten himself recollects, "One of the partners of the company, I believe it was Steve Minasian, had seen *Mark of the Devil* while on a trip to Germany and decided that he wanted to release the film in the United States. At the same time that this was going on, another German distributor was releasing a Spanish film called *La Semana del Aesino*, or in English, "The Week of the Assassin."[1] *El Semana del Aesino* was the original film that had the vomit-bag gimmick," he asserts.

"The guys at Hallmark brought *Mark of the Devil* back to the U.S. and decided to use that gimmick. They were going to premiere the film in Providence at a brand-new, prestigious cinema they owned called the Four Seasons, but they got nervous that the vomit-bag business might be too aggressive. So they decided to test the film at the Paris Twin Cinema in Worcester, Massachusetts, which I was managing at the time. They gave me a print of the film, and ten cartons of air-sickness bags with a red ad for the movie printed on them. In addition, they gave me about $2,600 to promote the film."

Whitten tackled the assignment zealously. "It was pretty obvious to me that the vomit bag was a neat joke, in the ZAP! comics vein of humor. I got a bunch of local girls to hand the vomit bags out to construction workers and high school kids. Before long, everybody started carrying lunches around in them! We also cut a radio spot for the movie at a little rinky-dink station outside of Springfield, using broken-down, ancient equipment.

"The first night that we opened *Mark of the Devil* [January 26, 1972], the demand was so great that we literally had to stop showing what we had on the other screen and physically run the one print we had back and forth between the two theaters," Whitten continues. "We'd play Reel One downstairs, and then rewind it and bring it upstairs while Reel Two was starting. There was only one print of *Mark of the Devil* in the country at the time, and we had to keep doing this for four weeks until another copy came in."

The Hallmark honchos knew they were onto something immediately. Whitten continues, "The opening night's gross was something like $1,200, which equaled what this theater was making in a week. I called Boston to report the box-office receipts, and five minutes later I got a call back from the same person I'd just spoken to, saying 'I just want to confirm these numbers.' Shortly after that, the three owners of the company came in from Boston, and my immediate boss, Harry Schwab, came in from Springfield. I was sitting at my desk, and they were all standing around me, asking me exactly what I had done to promote the opening of the film. It was almost like I was being interrogated by the police! That night, I was promoted from theater manager to movie promoter. The company sent me and Harry all over New England, setting up engagements for *Mark of the Devil*."

Even the local press had to take note of the movie's phenomenal success. "The Paris Theater canceled the advertised sixth week of *The French Connection* in its upstairs auditorium Wednesday night when an overflow crowd showed up for the opening of the German film *Mark of the Devil*," a Worcester *Telegram* article noted. "At 7 PM, *The French Connection* was pulled out, and *Mark of the Devil* was shown both downstairs (600 seats) and upstairs (300 seats) at 9 PM to full houses…" Another newspaper write-up describes hundreds of youths waiting outside the theater in sub-freezing weather for over two hours to buy tickets. One older patron exiting the theater was quoted: "All I got sick at was the thought that I paid six dollars for me and my wife to see the stupid thing."

The *Mark of the Devil* campaign confirmed Hallmark's instinct that the burgeoning trend of blood and gore was a sure score at the box office. Hallmark would continue to use the same hard-sell approach in promoting *Last House on the Left* and other films of its stripe. "Everyone at the company helped with those ad campaigns," Mansour says. "It wasn't as if we had an official advertising department, or a booking department. Everyone participated; the bosses would ask the

Although one Hallmark employee says that the idea for the *Mark of the Devil* vomit bag originated when one of the company's principals saw an airline-sickness bag on a flight back from seeing the film in Germany, another says that an overseas promotion for Eloy de la Iglesia's *La Semana del Asesino* inspired the gimmick. Hallmark and AIP released *La Semana* in 1973 as *Apartment on the 13th Floor*.

mark of the devil

POSITIVELY THE MOST HORRIFYING FILM EVER MADE

THE MANAGEMENT OF THE PARIS CINEMA WOULD LIKE TO APOLOGIZE TO THE HUNDREDS OF PEOPLE WHO WERE UNABLE TO GET IN THIS WEEKEND TO SEE "MARK OF THE DEVIL". BECAUSE OF THE OVERWHELMING RESPONSE, WE WERE UNABLE TO ACCOMMODATE EVERYONE.

DAVID A. WHITTEN, MGR.

Hallmark's brilliantly opportunistic advertising campaign for *Mark of the Devil* used every trick in the book in order to maintain public interest in their smash-hit success.

kids who did accounting to come in and they'd say, 'What do you think of this?' I think it was on the plane coming back from Germany that someone hit on the idea of using the vomit bags for *Mark of the Devil*. It was a real free for all… Esquire/Hallmark was a very small company, and we all kind of lived out of each others' pockets. I was nominally the booker, and there were publicity people, but everybody sort of overlapped. It wasn't as if every employee had an office and a secretary."

As they had done with Sean Cunningham's *Together*, Hallmark struck a deal with American International Pictures to distribute *Mark of the Devil* nationally. Hallmark was one of several smaller film production and distribution companies with which AIP regularly dealt during the 1960s and '70s. Others included Fanfare, United Producers, and Trans-American.

AIP also had exchanges all over the U.S. and Canada with entrepreneurs who handled bookings of films on commission. One of the liaisons between Hallmark and AIP was a Boston-based independent distributor and Hallmark associate named Jud Parker. Almost immediately after *Mark of the Devil* premiered, Parker passed the word on to AIP that the film was a valuable property which could be exploited nationally. A similar deal would later provide nationwide exposure for *Last House on the Left*.

After the deal with AIP for *Mark of the Devil* was sealed in the early spring of 1972, Whitten was dubbed the company's National Vomit Bag Coordinator in honor of his landmark publicity stunt. One of Hallmark's principals later claimed to have spent $200,000 on vomit bags for *Mark of the Devil*, a sum probably exceeding the cost of making the film itself.

About four months into Whitten's work on the *Devil* campaign, he began to hear talk of a film called *Krug and Company*. "I was in New York City doing work on *Mark of the Devil* when I first met Wes Craven and Sean Cunningham," he explains. "I went up to Sean's office, and they were in there cutting the film. At that time, it was called *Krug and Company*, and we were toying with the idea of adding the catchline *Equal Opportunity Destroyers*. When they finished the movie, we watched a print of it in a tiny cinema that doesn't exist anymore in West Springfield. Harry Schwab was there, along with a guy by the name of Ronnie, who was the head of a New York-based exhibition company. At the time, Ronnie had an older gentleman named George[2] working for him. George reportedly had a serious drinking problem, but he was an advertising genius, and *he* was the guy who came up with the title *Last House on the Left*, along with the ad copy 'It rests on thirteen acres of earth, directly over the center of Hell.'"

Sean Cunningham also recalls being approached about the title change while at a test screening of the film. "This advertising guy said to me, 'You know what I'd like to call this picture? *Last House on the Left*!' I asked him, 'What the hell has that title got to do with anything in the movie?', to which he answered, 'I don't know. I just like it.'"

The Launching Of A Thousand Lunches

In July, 1972, *Last House* was test-marketed at Hallmark's theaters under two different titles, *Krug and Company* and *Sex Crime of the Century*. On July 11, the film opened at two Hallmark-owned drive-ins in Oxford and North Wilbraham, Massachusetts.

On its opening night, the movie was advertised anonymously as a "sneak preview of Sean Cunningham's brand new motion picture." The film then played for one week under the *Krug and Company* title, with a full ad campaign in the local paper. (The U.S. Copyright Office at the Library of Congress has *Last House* registered as "a.k.a. *Krug and Company*.") At the North Wilbraham drive-in, it was shown with a bit of softcore fodder called *The Swinging Stewardesses*,[3] and then on a triple bill with two Westerns, Sam Peckinpah's *The Wild Bunch* (1969) and Don Siegel's *The Beguiled* (1971). At the Oxford Drive-In, the film had an interesting billing-mate in the violent British thriller *Sitting Targets* (1972), which starred Oliver Reed as an escaped con out for revenge.

The advertisements for *Krug and Company* showed a hand holding a long hunting knife, and called the movie "a film you will never forget - ask anyone who's seen it!" Of course, no one *had* seen the film yet, aside from those involved in its making and some personal associates of the financial backers. The brief *Krug and Company* promotion was a flop, and tests of the film at upstate New York venues under the title *Sex Crime of the Century* yielded equally dismal results.

"After *Krug and Company* and *Sex Crime*, for a very brief time, the film was called *The Men's Room*," reveals George Mansour. "That last one was a really odd title that came about for no apparent reason, other than the fact that they decided to use a campaign that depicted a lot of tiles, with *The Men's Room* written in blood on the tile. I guess they thought that the idea of a public restroom would somehow make the movie seem ominous!"

"We had finished the film and we really didn't know what it was or what to do with it," Sean Cunningham recalls. "For whatever reasons, I felt very strongly that, first, a movie about CRIME would be great... and, second, that what kind of crime would be so special, a SEX CRIME... wow, that'd be good, but not just any sex crime, the SEX CRIME OF THE CENTURY. So we thought that this would be one of the greatest titles of all time! We put together an advertising campaign, and tried it out, advertised it just like a regular movie... and it set records for people *not* coming to see it! It was like advertising FREE POISON POPCORN!"

Wes Craven recalls attending several of the test screenings. "The film was released under three separate titles, as an experiment. And the place where it was released as *Last House on the Left* went through the roof, whereas the others didn't. I had gone to two separate screenings at drive-ins, where the reactions were basically that people didn't seem to care one way or the other... So we didn't have a hard idea that it was really going to work."

With Craven's observations in mind, it becomes apparent that the film's title and ad campaign were crucial to its triumph at the box office. "The title *Last House on the Left* is very evocative. Phonetically, it has a certain lilt to it. The use of the word 'left' had a certain significance, because that was back in the hippie days, when so many young people thought of themselves as leftists," David Whitten muses. "Conversely, *Krug and Company* was a bad title; it has a very hard, unappealing sound. *Krug and Company* made the movie sound like a story about a

TONITE — AT DUSK — PRE-OPENING

SNEAK PREVIEW
- of -
Sean Cunningham's
New Major
Motion Picture

OXFORD TWIN
Drive-in theatre - Warc. Screen
Rtes. 12 & 20 W. Oxford - 832-5703

Krug & Company's first showings were anonymous 'sneak previews'.

German industrialist or a Nazi! There are certain people who would go to see any movie with Hitler or Nazis in it, but that's not the audience we wanted. We wanted to tell the public at large, particularly young people, that 'This is your kind of movie.'" In a further pitch to the hippie market, Hallmark warned the public at large that the film was definitely "NOT RECOMMENDED FOR PERSONS OVER 30!" Ironically, the over-30 crowd whom the youth of the day were told to "never trust" included both the movie's director and producer.

Delving further into the less-than-subtle manipulation behind Hallmark's advertising, Whitten mentions some of the other ad copy that helped sell the film. "Just think about that come-on we used: MARI, 17, IS DYING... EVEN FOR HER, THE WORST IS YET TO COME![4] The person reading those words starts to wonder just what happens to this nubile teenage girl in the movie; does she get her clothes ripped off before they kill her, or what? I honestly believe that's what the ad makes people think, whether they consciously form the question or not. The whole thing was very much in the Joe Bob Briggs tradition of 'blood, breasts, and beasts.' Horror is one thing, but if there are a few naked little babes in there along with the horror, that makes it even better!"

Slogans closely resembling the famous warning "To Avoid Fainting, Keep Repeating: It's Only A Movie" had actually been used to sell more than one horror movie years before *Last House on the Left*. Posters for William Castle's *Strait-Jacket* (1964) read: "Just Keep Telling Yourself: It's Only A Movie... It's Only A Movie...It's Only A Movie...". H.G. Lewis' *Color Me Blood Red* (1965) used a similar pitch. Whatever its origins, the tagline reached its mark most memorably with *Last House on the Left*.

Whitten remembers the slogan catching on amongst Hallmark's employees during a horror movie marathon at the Parkway Drive-In Theater. "We used to run dusk-to-dawn movie shows at this particular drive-in, about two or three times a year," Whitten recounts. "On one of these occasions, a group of us were sitting around in the back of the drive-in; I believe it was Ronnie, his friend George, Harry Schwab, Harry's younger brother Bobby, and myself. Bobby and I were left alone around midnight when the other three guys took off. The two of us had to stay at the drive-in until morning, watching the most incredibly bad movies you could ever imagine. We brought out a half-gallon jug of cheap red wine, and guzzled the whole thing during the last couple of movies. We were so disgusted and tired that we started cracking jokes about these rotten films. In the middle of a drunken stupor, one of us yelled out, 'What's the problem? It's only a movie!' We kept getting more irreverent and outrageous, and we came up with lines like, 'To Avoid Puking, Keep Repeating: It's Only A Movie, Only A Movie, Only A Movie...'"

above:
An inauspicious start: some of the very first public screenings of *Last House* were anonymous shows at drive-in theaters. The Parkway drive-in was near Springfield, Massachusetts.

Sean Cunningham gives a different account of the inspiration for the campaign: "The wife of one of the ad people was sitting at a screening of the film, and she kept saying to herself, 'It's only a movie...' The idea of using that phrase as a tag-line developed out of that situation."

Some advertisements for *Last House* carried the legend, "It's Just Across the Street from Joe!", or alternately, "It's Just Across the Street from Joe and Trash!". Whitten says that the reference to John G. Avildsen's sleeper hit *Joe*[5] (1970) was included at the insistence of the late Philip Scuderi, a main partner in Hallmark who perceived a similarity between the two movies. The 'Trash' alluded to in the ad copy was *Andy Warhol's Trash*, which had been successful as a midnight show at some of Hallmark's theaters.

Like the film itself, the ads for *Last House* were so stark and cheap that they proved extremely effective. Despite the arresting graphics of the print ads and posters, David Whitten insists that "...Radio was the medium that sold *Last House*. We never did any television advertising for *Last House*, but we used radio quite a lot. The philosophy behind the radio campaign was to make people say to themselves, 'I don't believe what I just heard!' We would start airing the spots two weeks before the film opened, three to four times an hour on FM rock and roll stations, so that nobody could escape the message we were sending. The audience would then look to the newspaper to find out when and where the film was playing, so we made our newspaper ads as big and lurid as possible. We didn't want to lose that audience we'd cultivated from radio to somebody else's film." The radio commercials featured the deadpan intonations of a narrator who promised listeners "a look into the final, maddening space between life and death," along with a chorus of voices chanting "It's Only A Movie... Only A Movie... Only A Movie" in an ominous mantra

"The slogan 'It's Only A Movie' was the best gimmick we invented, because it was the cheapest one... We didn't have to give anything away like we did during the release of *Mark of the Devil*! Among a lot of people I knew, 'It's Only A Movie' became this kind of sarcastic catchphrase," Whitten laughs. "We'd say, 'It's Only A Pizza,' or, 'It's Only A Volkswagen'..."

Last House on the Left was distributed on a city-by-city basis, a strategy which was common in the U.S. at the time and sometimes called "platforming" or "bicycling" prints. The independent distributor could not afford to release thousands of prints at once, and instead

July 1972: *Last House* is test-marketed as *Krug & Company*, one of several alternate titles.

moved a few hundred prints gradually across the country. Hallmark typically released their movies in their own East Coast theaters, with American International Pictures subsequently handling the rest of the country. This small-scale strategy of distribution would be steadily eradicated in the U.S. as the '70s wore on, with the monster success of pictures like *Jaws* (1975) and *The Exorcist* (1973) shifting the exhibitor's focus towards the major studio blockbuster and away from independently-distributed product.

Last House played for a while as *Krug & Company* at the Parkway drive-in, Massachusetts, on the same bill as Sam Peckinpah's *The Wild Bunch*.

Fear and Loathing... and more Loathing: LAST HOUSE and the Critics

The storm of controversy and criticism that surrounded the release of *Last House* began almost immediately. "From any given theater that showed *Last House on the Left*, we'd get reports of people fainting, getting into fist-fights," Wes Craven says. "We'd get reports of projectionists either cutting the film up or barricading themselves in the projection room because people from the outside wanted to come in and cut it up. It created a really scandalous and sensational debut."

The film opened on August 23, 1972 at two theaters in the Hartford, Connecticut area, and actually inspired public protest at one of the venues. An editorial in the September 3 edition of the *Hartford Courant* offered the following commentary on the protests against *Last House*:

"Incidents such as the local showing of a film billed as a 'horror movie' which instead turned out to be a horrible, sick film add to the mounting pressure brought by the public against the industry to clean house from inside lest the broom of censorship clean up from outside... Lingering gore, senseless cruelty, sadism and fetishism shock and dismay viewers, particularly those who are unsuspecting witnesses to the disgusting fare. That was the case locally in recent days when a movie was judged to be so sick that the audience began walking out after the first fifteen minutes emptying the theater by 9:30 PM. Gathering in the parking lot petition-bound to stop the manager from showing the movie, the main complaint of the people was misrepresentation of advance publicity, coupled with the rating. Apparently, some people thought it should have had an 'X'."

Perhaps the patrons' outrage also stemmed from the fact that they had expected a more polished, palatable 'mainstream' film for their price of admission. For example, the Paris Cinema was showing the Robert Redford vehicle *The Candidate* on one screen while *Last House* was unreeling in the theater next door. A crowd at a rural drive-in or an urban grindhouse might not have been fazed by *Last House*, but a suburban audience at a mainline theater obviously found such fare tough to digest. Thus, *Last House* played a significant role in pushing exploitation movies into the mainstream. Film booker and horror aficionado Rick Sullivan remarked on this aspect of the film's importance in his fanzine *The Gore Gazette*: "Prior to *Last House on the Left*, films of this ilk were confined to skid row theaters where they were co-billed with porno flicks."

David Whitten recalls the circumstances of the Connecticut controversy well: "We had booked *Last House* into a theater in Wethersfield, Connecticut called the Paris 1 & 2. During the first week of the engagement, the Paris theater manager called up Hallmark's Boston office in a state of panic. The man was extremely upset; he said, 'I've got people picketing, I've got people calling up the theater on the phone, I've got people calling me at home... I want to pull this film!' Hallmark sent me over to run the theater until things calmed down. While I was down there, I came up with the idea of an open letter to the parents who were protesting the movie."

The "open letter," which Whitten wrote himself in a tiny back office of a drive-in theater near Worcester, Massachusetts, is a classic piece of exploitation movie hucksterism. Whitten's hastily-penned polemic appeared in the *Hartford Courant* on September 8, 1972, and ran as follows:

An Open Letter to the Critics of "THE LAST HOUSE ON THE LEFT"

The management of the Paris Cinema, Wethersfield is fully aware that since the opening of "THE LAST HOUSE ON THE LEFT" the city officials, police department and news media have been deluged with complaints due to the explicit gore and violence in this film. In fact, demands have been made on this theatre to terminate the engagement of this movie immediately.

However, after carefully considering all the circumstances, management has decided to continue to show the movie. This difficult decision was predicated on the following considerations:

The Film relates to a problem that practically every teen-age girl and parent can identify with, yet does not pander to the subject matter. The story does not justify violence, nor does it glorify the degenerates who perpetrate the violence. In fact, the mainstream of complaints seem to stem from the intense hatred

Original advertising for H.G. Lewis' *Color Me Blood Red*; "It's just a motion picture".

the audience feels for the perpetrators. The Film ends in traditional movie style when all the degenerates are killed and although justice is served by a bizarre and cruel retaliation, the popular reaction is the punishment was commensurate with the crime. Thus we feel the movie is morally redeeming and does deliver an important social message.

This fact is already being borne out by the number of parents who have recently been taking their daughters to see the film. These parents regard this film as a perfect deterrent to this type of behavior."

Hallmark added a slightly revised version of the disclaimer to the top of certain advertisements for the movie in the event that the film ran into further trouble. The adaptation of Whitten's defense added the following:

"LAST HOUSE ON THE LEFT: *CAN A MOVIE GO TOO FAR?* Many people who have gone to see the movie LAST HOUSE ON THE LEFT and many public officials contacted by outraged moviegoers believe the answer to this question is YES! WHY?... LAST HOUSE ON THE LEFT relates to a problem and a situation that practically every teenage girl is vulnerable to and every parent lives in dread of. (Note: The movie is, in fact, a retelling of Ingmar Bergman's Academy Award Winner "The Virgin Spring" in 1972 terms.) A young girl savagely brutalized, killed by a wanton band of degenerates. Revenge of the most horrible kind exacted by the parents of the dead girl - the killers are themselves killed.

Yes, you will hate the people who perpetrate these outrages - you should! But, if a movie - and it is *only* a movie - can arouse you to such extreme emotion then the film director has succeeded.

Violence and bestiality are not condoned in THE LAST HOUSE ON THE LEFT - far from it! The movie makes a plea for an end to all the senseless violence and inhuman cruelty that has become so much a part of the times in which we live. WE DON'T THINK ANY MOVIE CAN GO *TOO FAR* IN MAKING THIS MESSAGE HEARD AND FELT!

With this masterstroke of rhetoric, Hallmark turned a potentially damaging situation around on itself. By overstating the case and playing up the 'controversy', Whitten and his advertising cohorts turned the offended parents' protests into added publicity for the movie. They even managed to work the "It's Only A Movie" slogan into their long-winded rationalization.

Even as Whitten was busy drafting his "open letter", *Last House* opened at two theaters in Boston on August 30. The following day, a writer for the *Boston Herald-Traveler* called *Last House* "an illustration of loathsomeness the likes of which I have never seen…" and summed up the movie as "repulsive." The *Christian Science Monitor* was slightly more charitable, praising the film's comedic elements and "clever photography" but stating that "this sort of thing can do no one any good." The *Boston Globe* chose not to review the film at all. Negative notices aside, one of the Boston theaters reported the film's gross at $20,000 during the first week of its engagement.

LAST HOUSE ON THE LEFT — CAN A MOVIE GO TOO FAR?

Many people who have gone to see the movie LAST HOUSE ON THE LEFT and many public officials contacted by outraged moviegoers believe the answer to this question is YES! Demands have been made to terminate the engagement of this movie immediately. WHY?... LAST HOUSE ON THE LEFT relates to a problem and a situation that practically every teenage girl is vulnerable to and every parent lives in dread of. (Note: The movie is, in fact, a retelling of Ingmar Bergman's Academy Award Winner "The Virgin Spring" in 1972 terms) A young girl savagely brutalized, killed by a wanton band of degenerates. Revenge of the most horrible kind exacted by the parents of the dead girl — the killers are themselves killed.

Yes, you will hate the people who perpetrate these outrages — **you should!** But, if a movie — and it is **only** a movie — can arouse you to such extreme emotion then the film director has succeeded.

Violence and bestiality are not condoned in LAST HOUSE ON THE LEFT — far from it! The movie makes a plea for an end to all the senseless violence and inhuman cruelty that has become so much a part of the times in which we live. WE DON'T THINK ANY MOVIE CAN GO **TOO FAR** IN MAKING THIS MESSAGE HEARD AND FELT!

This fact is already borne out by the number of parents who have taken their daughters to see the film. These parents regard this movie as a perfect deterrent to this type of behavior.

MARI, SEVENTEEN, IS DYING. EVEN FOR HER THE WORST IS YET TO COME!

TO AVOID FAINTING KEEP REPEATING, IT'S ONLY A MOVIE ..ONLY A MOVIE ..ONLY A MOVIE ..ONLY A MOVIE ..ONLY A MOVIE ..ONLY A MOVIE

LAST HOUSE ON THE LEFT

WARNING! NOT RECOMMENDED FOR PERSONS OVER 30!

SEAN S. CUNNINGHAM FILMS LTD. Presents "THE LAST HOUSE ON THE LEFT" Starring: DAVID HESS • LUCY GRANTHAM • SANDRA CASSEL • MARC SHEFFLER • and introducing ADA WASHINGTON • Produced by SEAN S. CUNNINGHAM Written and Directed by WES CRAVEN • COLOR BY MOVIELAB

R RESTRICTED Under 17 requires accompanying Parent or Adult Guardian

...IT'S JUST ACROSS THE STREET FROM "JOE"!

HELD OVER!

PRODUCER'S STATEMENT

"LAST HOUSE ON THE LEFT" is one of the few motion pictures ever to stimulate so much public opinion. People either love it or despise it. Few have no opinion. In this film, unlike so many recent, successful motion pictures violence is not glorified, nor the violators romanticized. All is shown as ugly as it is in real life. For example, in many recent films people are killed in typical "Hollywood" fashion. They do not bleed. They do not suffer. In "LAST HOUSE ON THE LEFT" homicide is portrayed in its true nature; real people dying tragically.

In past films criminals have been shown as glamorous and heroic so that the audience may identify with them in a happy and pleasant manner. In "LAST HOUSE ON THE LEFT" the criminals are shown in true perspective as sick and degenerate people.

Nor does the film make any attempt to glorify or minimize the risks in experimenting with drugs. The portrayed consequences are not only probable but fittingly horrifying.

The purpose of "LAST HOUSE ON THE LEFT" is to bring a true measure of real violence to its viewers. Shock, horror and finally outrage are expected. Our question: Should the outrage be directed at the portrayal on the screen or the conditions that allow such events to occur?

"LAST HOUSE ON THE LEFT" is rated "R" in the best sense of that rating.

SYNOPSIS

On her 17th birthday, while her mother and doctor father prepare a celebration, daughter Mari goes with a less fortunate girl friend to a seamy side of town. They encounter a drug addict member of a criminal quartet (three men and a woman) and are captured to be used bi-sexually by the gang. Fear, perversion, rape and slow torturous death follow for each girl as the gang—its auto broken down—seeks refuge in a forest near Mari's home. The distraught parents seek police help in finding their missing girl while the teenagers are being mistreated and killed in the nearby forest. The gang wanders into the family home where the girl's mother recognizes a birthday gift necklace worn by the addict. The parents find the girl's body, then return home to engage in their own bloodbath, killing the last of the gang with a power saw as the sheriff appears.

Page 3 of Hallmark's press-book for *Last House on the Left*.

"The initial grosses for *Last House on the Left* were spectacular for the places where we played it," George Mansour says. "In some cases the film performed so well that we sold it away from our own moviehouses... There would be times when I had it booked in an Esquire movie theater, and one of the owners of the company would come in and say, 'Wait, you can't do that, we're selling it to a better moviehouse!' I would then have to scramble to find another picture to replace *Last House* in our own theater." When asked to estimate the total gross the film generated, Mansour replies, "To try to gauge what *Last House* grossed would be difficult... but it was a lot in comparison to what it cost, and in those [1972] dollars. I couldn't venture a guess as to what it eventually made."

LAST HOUSE ON THE LEFT

presented by

SEAN S. CUNNINGHAM FILMS LTD.

starring

DAVID HESS • LUCY GRANTHAM • SANDRA CASSEL • MARC SHEFFLER • and introducing ADA WASHINGTON

Written and directed by .... WES CRAVEN
Produced by .... SEAN S. CUNNINGHAM
COLOR BY MOVIELAB • Running Time 91 mins.

• • • • •

PRODUCER'S STATEMENT

Since the opening of the motion picture "Last House On The Left," municipal officials, film reviewers, and theatergoers have deluged the theaters with complaints about the film, and requested that its exhibition be terminated immediately.

The thrust of the criticism is that the film is too violent.

The critics have completely failed to understand this film. It is one of the finest anti-violence films ever made. Here, at last, is a film which puts violence in its proper perspective, as so few films have in the past.

In this film, unlike so many recent, successful motion pictures, violence is not glorified, nor the violaters romanticized. All is shown as ugly and as debauched as it is in real life. For example, we have all seen recently motion pictures in which upwards of 50 and 60 people are killed before the last reel. It is all done in an atmosphere where real people do not die, do not bleed, or do not suffer.

In this film, prior to the last couple of minutes, only two persons have been killed — but they are shown in the true nature of what homicide is, real people dying tragically.

In past films, criminals are made glamourous and heroic. We identify with them in a happy and pleasant manner. In "Last House On The Left" the criminals are shown for what they really are, mean and horrible.

Nor does the film make any attempt to minimize or make pleasurable experimentation with drugs. This is risky business which can only produce consequences as shown in the film.

This, then, is a moral film. A film which has become all the more gripping because we have become so unused to seeing how wicked and unforgivable violence and killing are.

For as long as records for numbers of homicide are broken each week in our urban centers, and the evening news brings us new tales of violence and burning, and we continue to treat these horrors in a nonchalant manner, it will be necessary for films like "Last House On The Left" to bring the true measure of violence to the consciousness of us all.

It is indeed ironic that the criticism which this film has received is because the worth of its message has been improperly assessed. The large numbers of parents now bringing their children to the theater is perhaps illustrative that the true meaning of this film is now being properly received. The film is rated "R" in the best sense of that rating.

— ORDER ALL ACCESSORIES FROM —

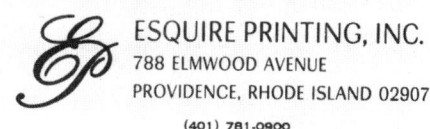

ESQUIRE PRINTING, INC.
788 ELMWOOD AVENUE
PROVIDENCE, RHODE ISLAND 02907
(401) 781-0900

TRAILERS • 1-SHEETS

STILLS • RADIO SPOTS

PRESS • MATS

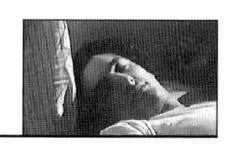

At the Pittsburgh premiere of *Last House* on September 20, 1972, Marc Sheffler made a personal appearance in the theater lobby, signing autographed photos. "Some people loved it, some people hated it, and my father got nauseous during the scene where I stuck the gun in my mouth," the actor recalled in 1991. "I had a relative who worked for that theater chain, and my father, who was a promoter kind of guy, put the whole thing together." Despite Sheffler's valiant effort to meet and greet the public, an entertainment columnist for the *Pittsburgh Press* excoriated *Last House on the Left* in the following day's paper, calling it "a cheap-jack movie of no discernible merit - but considerable tastelessness." The review called the film's plot "tawdry, vicious, and wholly without purpose" and noted incredulously that Sheffler claimed to have seen the film seven times, adding, "...if ever there were a parallel to a child only its mother could love." The headline for this less-than-sympathetic summary named LHOTL as "among the year's worst."

Exactly a month after the Pittsburgh opening, *Last House* had its Midwestern premiere at the Woods Theater in Chicago. The Woods Theater engagement may have been one of the few occasions that the fully uncut edition of the film was shown; the Chicago Censor Board demanded that it be screened as an X-Rated, 'Adults Only' feature.

Along with a writer for the Detroit-based rock and roll magazine *Creem*, Roger Ebert was one of the only critics to give *Last House* a positive endorsement. Ebert's enthusiastic review of the film appeared in the *Chicago Sun-Times* on October 26, 1972. The future *Sneak Previews* host called *Last House* "a tough, bitter little sleeper of a movie that's about four times as good as you'd expect..." and went on to describe it as "a find... one of those rare, unheralded movies that succeeds on a commercial level and still achieves a great deal more." Ebert praised Craven's direction, as well as the unmannered acting and dialogue, and compared the film to *The Honeymoon Killers* and Scorcese's *Boxcar Bertha*. In the week following the publication of Ebert's write-up, *Last House* raked in over $46,000 at a single Chicago theater; the film's exclusive engagement at the Woods Theater continued for a month before spreading out to other area venues.

As patrons rushed to see the movie on the strength of Ebert's praise, the critic found himself deluged with complaints. The backlash became so strong that Ebert wrote a second column addressing the controversy on December 1, 1972. "My review of *Last House on the Left* has brought me more letters and telephone calls of protest than anything else I've ever written," Ebert stated. "Some of my correspondents reminded me that I didn't appreciate the use of violence in such recent movies as *Straw Dogs*, *A Clockwork Orange*, and *The Devils*. How could I possibly give a good review to this uneven little movie with violence that was even more excessive - and certainly more nauseating - than anything by these respected big-name directors? A good question, but I think it suggests its own answer. I did not object to the violence itself in the movies by Peckinpah, Kubrick and Russell, but to the hypocrisy with which it was handled. The violence in *Last House on the Left* is not exhilarating. It does not act as a catharsis. It is not escapist. It is not serious or philosophical. It refuses to allow us any possible avenue of escape; it is just there, brutal and needless and tragic. I still believe *Last House on the Left* is a movie of worth, of a certain dogged commitment to its unsavory content. The fact that so many viewers have apparently been so totally offended by it may prove my point."[6]

Ebert's future *Sneak Previews* co-host Gene Siskel lambasted *Last House* in the *Chicago Tribune* several days after Ebert's original review appeared. "My objection to *The Last House on the Left* is not an

The disc featuring the *Last House* radio spot ads.

objection to graphic violence *per se*, but to the fact that this movie celebrates adult male abuse of young women," Siskel wrote. "Given the similarity of recent crimes in the Chicago area to the events in this movie, I am surprised that any theater owner would want to make a living by playing it. Theater owners who do not control themselves invite others to do so."

Siskel expressed his hatred of *Last House* on numerous occasions in the ensuing years. He named it "the sickest film of 1972" in a recap of the year's most disgusting movies, and even interviewed Hallmark Releasing chairman Phil Scuderi as part of a 1977 column decrying the company's ultraviolent exploitation product. In the wake of *Friday the 13th*, Siskel launched a campaign against what he called "women-in-peril movies," blaming *Last House* as an instigator of the trend. The late critic called Sean Cunningham "one of the most despicable creatures ever to infest the movie business." Although Ebert joined his colleague in the anti-splatter protest, he disagreed with Siskel's criticism of *Last House*

Responding to Siskel's moral condemnation of the film, Wes Craven remarks, "I don't think *Last House* is misogynistic. It really shows a cynicism towards all people. The men, particularly the father figures, certainly don't come off any better than the women. If anything, the Phyllis character shows more strength and dignity than anyone else; she knew what was going on before any of the others did."

"Roger Ebert's review was a big breakthrough for the film," David Whitten notes. "I'll never forget the time when we opened *Last House on the Left* in New York [December, 1972]. The people who ran the RKO/Stanley theater chain where the film was playing didn't want to use Ebert's quote in the advertising! They were a bunch of old-school, cigar-smoking New York businessmen, and I remember them sitting there eating their morning bagels and telling us, 'This is New York. You can't run a quote from the Chicago paper; nobody will pay attention.' We ran the quote anyway, and it really worked. We posted flyers all over the subways and we used that line in the newspaper ads as well."

Although the conspicuously-displayed quote from a major movie critic may have sold a few extra tickets, Ebert's views did not seem to influence New York critics. The *New York Times* reviewer walked out halfway through a screening and subsequently dismissed the movie as "sickening tripe." (A month later, a *Los Angeles Times* critic saw only the *last* ten minutes of the film and made a similar judgment.) The *New York Post* called it "a cheap softcore job," and added, "… the film has enough funny bits to convince a viewer that the people responsible for it knew what they were doing - and should have known better."

David Hess still laughs heartily as he remembers attending the movie's New York premiere. "I took my parents to see it! My mother was so angry that she wouldn't speak to me for a week… I remember her saying, 'What's a nice Jewish boy like you making a film like this for?' I said, 'Mom, you've got to remember, not only did I act in it, I did the music, too! There's some beauty in the music; that's the other side of my personality!'"

Jeramie Rain's memories of watching the finished film are not pleasant ones. "I went to see *Last House* with my room mate, Pam Burton," the actress recalled in 1996. "Pam was horrified at how terrible the movie was, and I think I was too! But there were worse things about the experience than the movie itself. First of all, when my character

LAST HOUSE ON THE LEFT R CAN A MOVIE GO TOO FAR?

THEATRE IMPRINT

died, everybody cheered, 'Yea! Kill the ugly old woman!'… I was twenty-one at the time, so that was not very uplifting to hear. Then, as Pam and I were walking out of the theater in shock, a little girl pointed at me and said, 'I hate you!' The girl's mother said to her, 'No, no, no… she's just an actress. You hate the character she played in the movie!' The girl thought about this for a moment, and reiterated, 'No, I hate *her*!' When we got outside the theater, somebody else recognized me and asked for his money back! I told him that I didn't make any money from the movie to begin with."

The conspicuous advertising for the film caused another embarrassing experience for Ms. Rain. "My father, who worked as a physicist for Union-Carbide, was in New York on business at the time of *Last House*," she relates. "He was absolutely scandalized and horrified by the movie, but for the fact that it was such a huge hit and made so much money. We were walking down Broadway together, and we came upon a theater that was showing the movie. Outside the moviehouse, there was a big display with all these photographs of the cast. A black couple was standing there looking at the display, and my father approached them and said, 'That's my daughter.' The guy turned and looked at my father, looked at me, and then remarked, 'Hey, man… don't say that. That's an insult!'"

In her travels through the New York film scene, Rain encountered one person who viewed *Last House* with enthusiastic appreciation: Andy Warhol. "Andy loved *Last House on the Left*," Rain laughs. "I was in the very first issue of his *inter/VIEW* magazine, and I remember him telling me that."

Unlike Rain, lead actress Lucy Grantham viewed the film's success with pride. "I think that advertising campaign was simply one of the most brilliant marketing maneuvers in history. I literally felt it snowballing; it was palpable, the sense that this movie was catching on and that people were responding to the advertising. I specifically remember listening to those radio commercials and being very excited. The movie had undergone this amazing transformation from something which we all expected would just come and go to having this whole aura of horror around it. The title change to *Last House on the Left* was really, in a nutshell, a metaphor for that transformation, for the idea that suddenly they were turning this movie into something that was really scary. I don't even think any of us knew that we were *in* a 'scary' movie!"

"Strangers started coming up to me in the street, telling me they'd seen me in the film," Grantham adds. "My parents went to see the movie, and although they had some mixed feelings about some of the scenes, those feelings were overridden by the fact that this was a *real* movie that you paid to see at a theater, and not just some student project. This was the Real McCoy, and I know they were very proud of me."

Marshall Anker enjoyed a similar moment in the sun. "When the movie was playing to a mainly black audience on 42nd Street, I was up around there because the actor's union is near there. I would sometimes walk along 42nd Street on my way to the subway and black guys would say, 'Hey, sheriff! How you doin' there, sheriff?' On another occasion, I took a friend of mine to see the film in a Times Square theater, and I remember the black audience applauding at the sight of this honky, redneck sheriff falling off the chicken truck - they loved it!"

"After the movie became so successful, I was able to get a terrific agent," Grantham recalls. "His name was Lloyd Kolmar, and he was a real big shot at the William Morris agency. He wanted to build a career for me; I'll never forget him saying to me that he was going to make me the next Ann-Margret, because I sing and dance in addition to acting. That was what Lloyd envisioned, but I never really gave it a chance. I got this agent because my father said, 'You gotta do it, you're so great!' and there was a part of me that was excited about that but I think at that point even having just gotten the agent I think there was a part of me that needed to let it go."

Anker experienced a dramatically different reaction to his appearance in the film. "There used to be a casting director named Bernie Stiles," the actor explains. "This Stiles was a very nasty character. I remember when I was interviewing with him, I showed him the ad for *Last House on the Left* with my name in it, and I said, 'This film just opened up, and it's making a lot of money.' He looked at the ad and said, 'You're in that *thing*?!' And I'm thinkin', 'Oh, shit.' I wondered, "Am I gonna get this reaction from every casting director, 'What, you're in that shit? Get the hell outta here.'" That discouraged me from being proud of it."

"It was sort of a whiplash," Craven says of the film's unexpected popularity. "Immediately after finishing *Last House*, I had come out to California to cut a film for somebody, and I had no idea what the result would be. I basically was just looking to make enough money to live on. And I called back to check with Sean and see what was happening with the movie. He said, 'Are you sitting down?' A moment later, he said, 'It's a hit! It's a smash… they're lined up around the block to see it!' And I thought he was putting me on… I didn't anticipate that it would make any waves at all."

"At first, when the movie started to make money, there was this thought in my head that, 'Wow, everybody's going to see it as this brilliant, breakthrough film," Craven continues. "And instead, with a couple of exceptions, the reviews were scathing. There was also, just on a personal level, a very sharp reaction from people who knew me and hadn't known what I was working on. A lot of people really hated us vociferously for it… especially among the culture we lived in, middle-class people with kids. When they saw that film, people literally wouldn't leave their children alone with me… They would get up and walk away from the table when I went out to have dinner. There was this powerful feeling that we had done something unspeakable. That sort of ostracism was very difficult to deal with personally."

The nasty reputation stuck to the film over the years. In his popular reference book, *TV Movies*, *Entertainment Tonight* correspondent Leonard Maltin directed some particularly vehement criticism at *Last House*, giving it his lowest (BOMB) rating and calling it "repugnant…technically inept, and REALLY sick." Ironically, one of Maltin's *Entertainment Tonight* cronies did a segment for the show profiling Craven in 1986 and called *Last House* "a walk in the park… but not after dark."

In 1987, television pundit Morton Downey, Jr. devoted an entire broadcast of his syndicated talk show to the debate over the dangers of 'splatter' films. During the debate, Downey used footage from *Last House* to illustrate the case against screen violence. Along with a 1979 episode of *Sneak Previews* devoted to 'Guilty Pleasures' and the above-mentioned *Entertainment Tonight* clip, this constitutes the movie's only exposure on American television.

Canadian critic Robin Wood brought *Last House* to the 1977 Toronto Film Festival as part of a horror film retrospective called "American Nightmares". One of the movie's few defenders, Wood praised the movie at length in the pages of *Film Comment*: "No film is more expressive than Last House of a(n) (inter)national social sickness, and no film is richer in Oedipal references - an extension, in its widest implications, of the minutiae of human relations under patriarchal capitalist culture." Such implications were apparently lost on the festival audience; Wood wrote that "...a number of our customers... even in the context of a horror retrospective, even confronted by a bowdlerized print... gathered in the foyer after the screening to complain to the theater management that the film had been shown at all."

Still, there was a vast audience that received the movie with enthusiasm. Consider the following fan's account of a 1972 showing of the film in Ottawa, Ontario:

"*Last House on the Left* played in Ottawa at a now-defunct venue called the Rideau Theater. The Rideau wasn't exactly known for its *Ben Hur*s or its *Mutiny on the Bounty*s, but chose to offer its clientele somewhat less demanding fare - the *Ilsa*s, *Happy Hooker*s, biker/hot-rod flicks, the occasional Italian muscleman blockbuster, et cetera. The theater proudly hosted a fairly undiscriminating crowd who nonetheless took their entertainment and necking sessions damn seriously. It was a tough room. The thing I remember most about that showing of *Last House* was how still the theater became so quickly into the running time of the movie. Whenever the room went silent and people actually started paying attention to what was happening on the screen - which was almost never - you knew you had a grabber. I can think only of two other films that had the same effect: *The Texas Chainsaw Massacre* and Ken Russell's *The Devils*. Amidst all this rare and unsettling tranquility, there were, however, a few good outbursts:

general groaning at the end of the fellatio scene (male);

general groaning at the sound effect of the organ being spit into the lake (female);

general groaning (all) during the operation/chisel sequence;

and, of course, a collective cheer *à la Death Wish* at the chainsaw climax. Wes Craven obviously knew what buttons to push, and the fact that he was able to push the buttons of such a boisterous and unruly lot as the crowd at the Rideau is quite a testament to his talent."[7]

Although many drive-in patrons and horror fans loved the movie, publications devoted to cult and horror cinema bashed *Last House* mercilessly. In his book *Cult Movies*, writer Danny Peary singled out *Last House* as "absolute trash," declaring it "a sick sexual fantasy for predators that is indeed an incitement to violence" and asserting that the movie "deserves to be banned." (Gerald Peary, brother of the *Cult Movies* author and a noted film critic in his own right, also called for a ban on *Last House* at the time of its release after witnessing patrons cheering on the rape, torture and murder of the two girls.)[8]

Cover of the original US Pressbook.

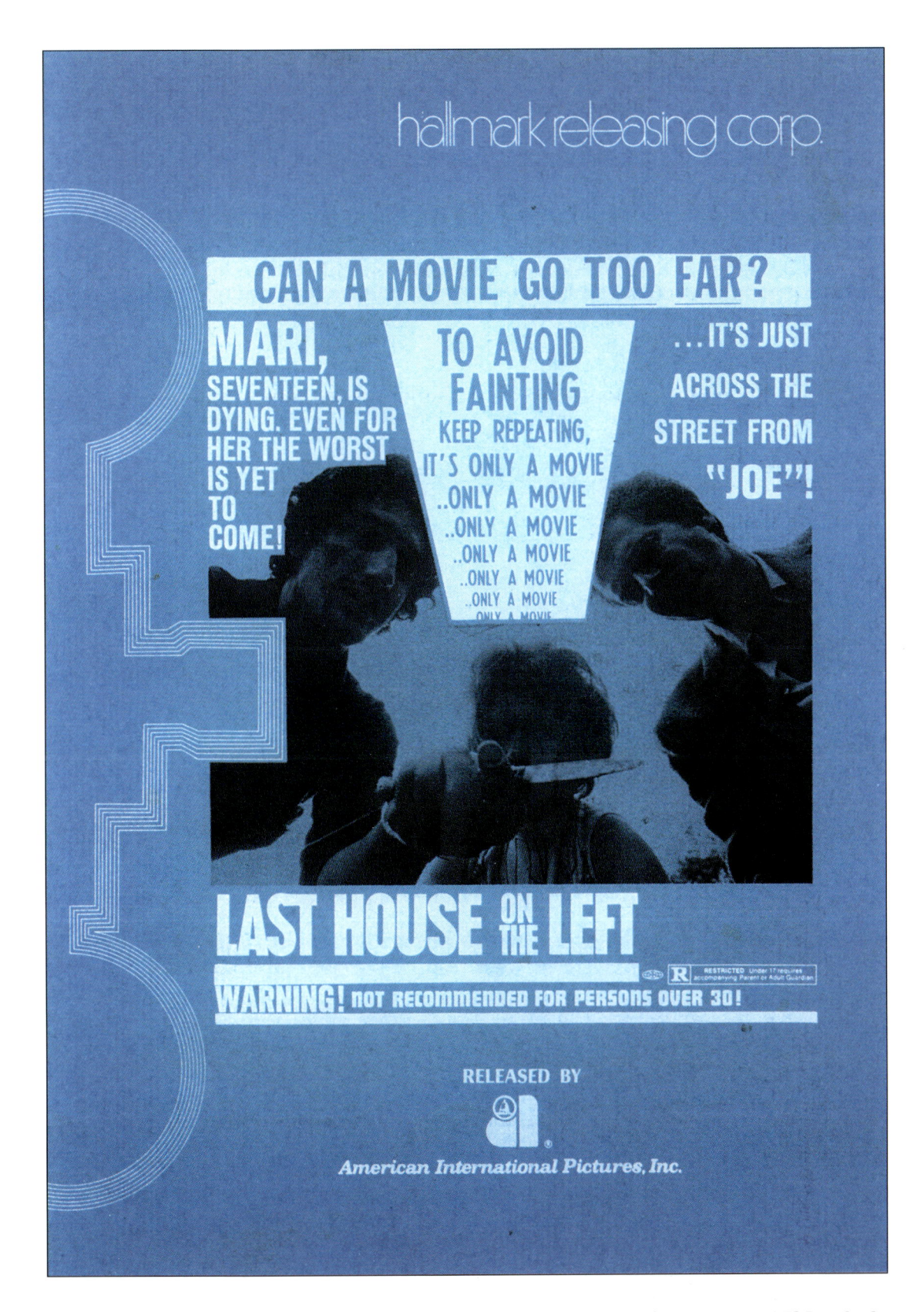

(courtesy Roy Frumkes)

A candid shot of Wes Craven and actress Sandra Cassell on location during the shooting of 'Last House' taken by production assistant / set photographer Steve Dwork.   (courtesy Steve Dwork)

Mari as she is found by the Collingwoods towards the end of the film; in an early cut of the film, Mari survived long enough to identify the killers to her parents.

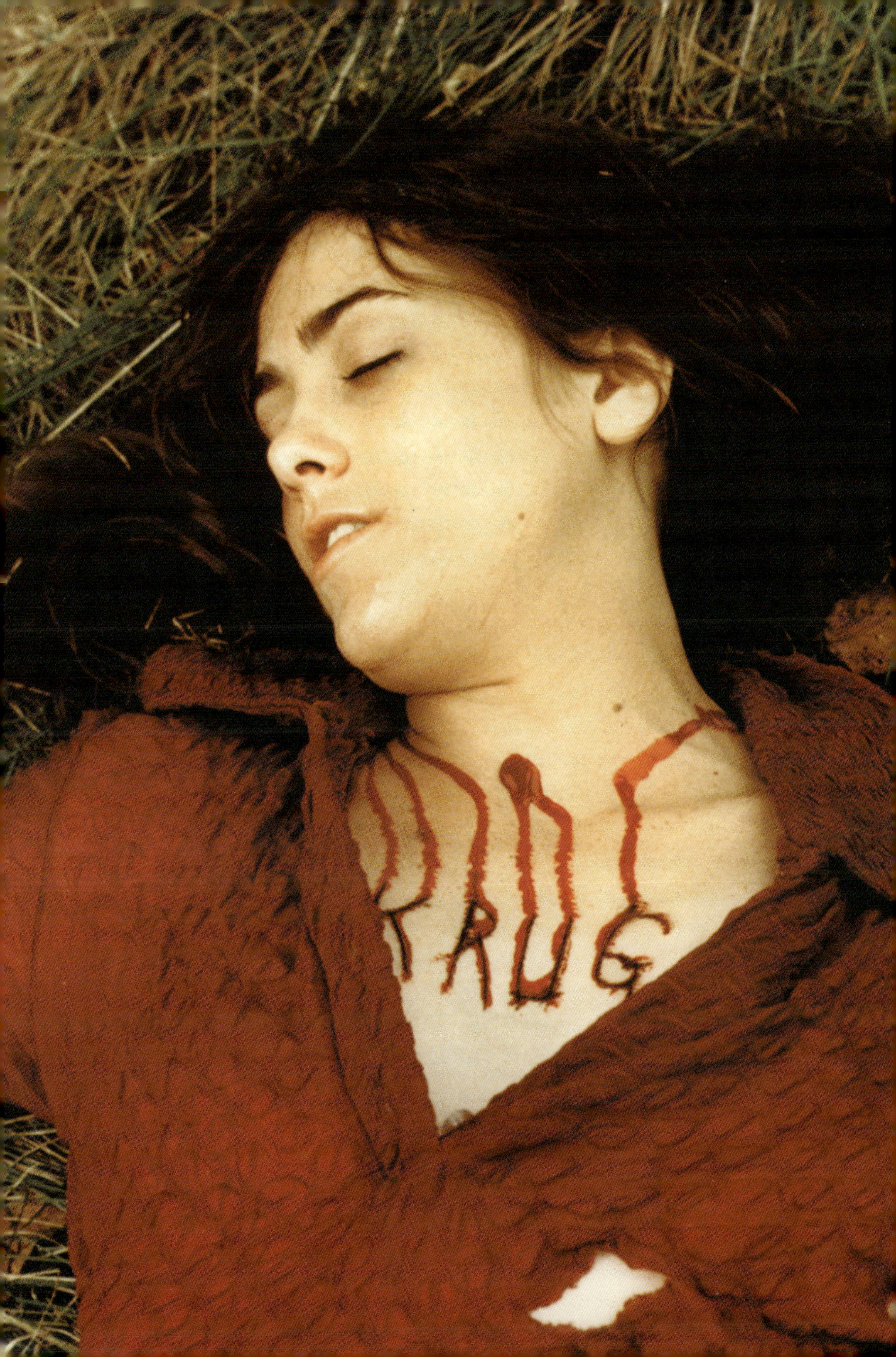
TRUG

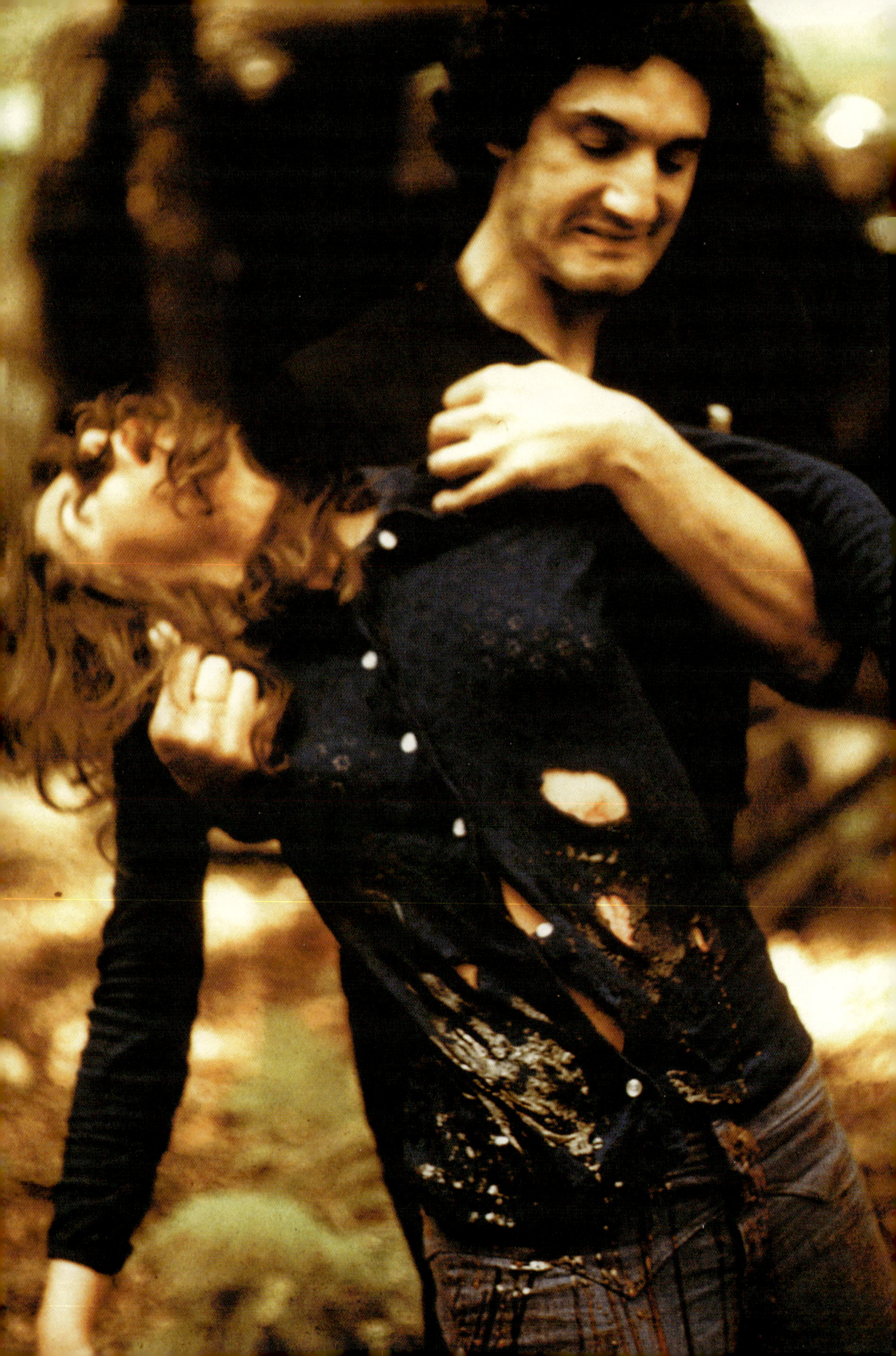

opposite
The often-censored stabbing scene.

top
An out take showing Krug about to drop Phyllis' lifeless body to the ground.
(courtesy Roy Frumkes)

above & right
Krug is apparently unaffected by the stabbing of Phyllis in these out take shots.
(courtesy Roy Frumkes)

Out takes showing the infamous, censored sequence in which Sadie pulls out Phyllis' intestines.

(courtesy Roy Frumkes)

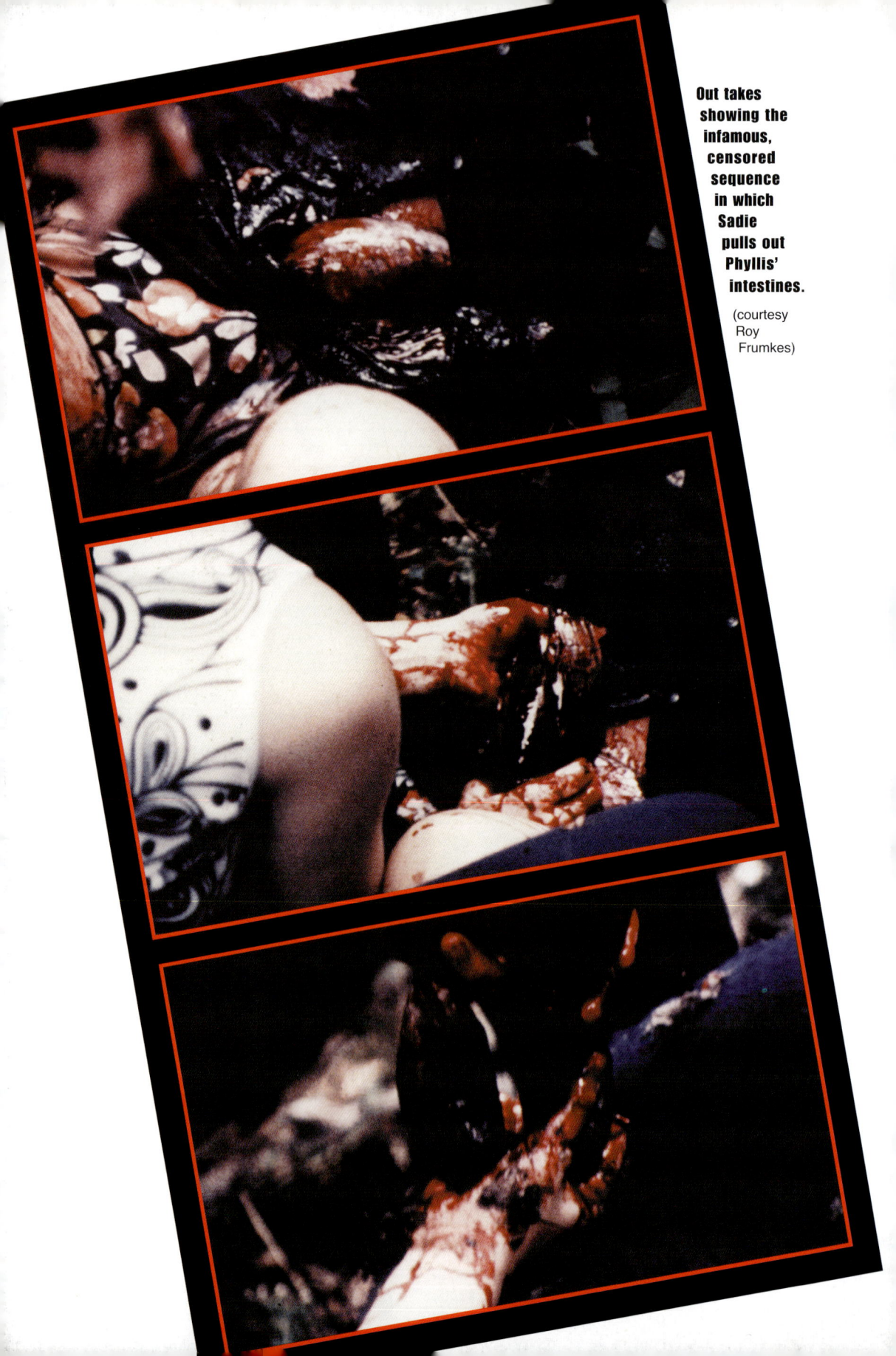

An out take of Jeramie Rain falling off a tree trunk during a failed stunt.   (courtesy Roy Frumkes)

Out take of Jeramie Rain during the murder of Phyllis.   (courtesy Roy Frumkes)

Out take footage from 'Last House On The Left' was spliced onto the end of the German exploitation film 'Confessions of a Blue Movie Star: The Evolution of Snuff'. The excerpts were presented as being from a snuff movie, and were introduced by the film's supposed maker, who is seen wearing a paper bag on his head!
(picture source: Intervision video)

Japanese archivists dug up this outtake shot from the 'chest-carving' sequence for a screening at the 1987 Japanese Fantastic Film Festival.
(courtesy David Beach)

A horror fanzine called *The Monster Times* minced no words in a 1973 capsule review, labeling the film "last year's slice of raw garbage." Even Stephen King made a derogatory comment on the film in his nonfiction book *Danse Macabre*.[9] In their eagerness to vilify *Last House*, certain reviewers have taken it upon themselves to create their own additions to the film's inventory of atrocities. In his compendium, *The Creature Features Movie Guide*, author John Stanley cites the film's appalling scene of "crucifixion".

No doubt the responsible parties were reciting the old rhyme about sticks and stones all the way to the bank. While first-time film makers often get burned by the distributors of their movies, such was not the case with *Last House*. "That was one of the most extraordinary things about it," Craven says of the film's generous financial returns. "The people who ran Hallmark Releasing, to their credit, were extremely honest with us about the profits from *Last House*. There was a period of, I think, about six to eight months when nothing came in, and we thought, 'Well, we'll never see any of that money.' Then, suddenly, I got a check for twenty thousand dollars. You could have floored me! The most I had made in a year teaching college was eleven thousand dollars.

"After that first check, another one came, this time for thirty thousand dollars. In the year following the movie's release, I made close to $100,000 from it. It was like a dream; it was very difficult to process. I had been living semi-communally with a group of people on the Lower East Side, and had virtually no money, and suddenly I was making all of this cash, and had to figure out how to pay taxes. And after about two years of trying to write other kinds of scripts, I was essentially broke again. So, at that point, I was saying to myself, 'Did all that really happen?!' It was very strange, and the beginning of a roller-coaster ride of ups and downs in my financial situation."

"Wes and I made a lot of money from *Last House*, especially considering that he was driving a cab and I was working in a theater," Cunningham chuckles. "My career wasn't progressing at that point,

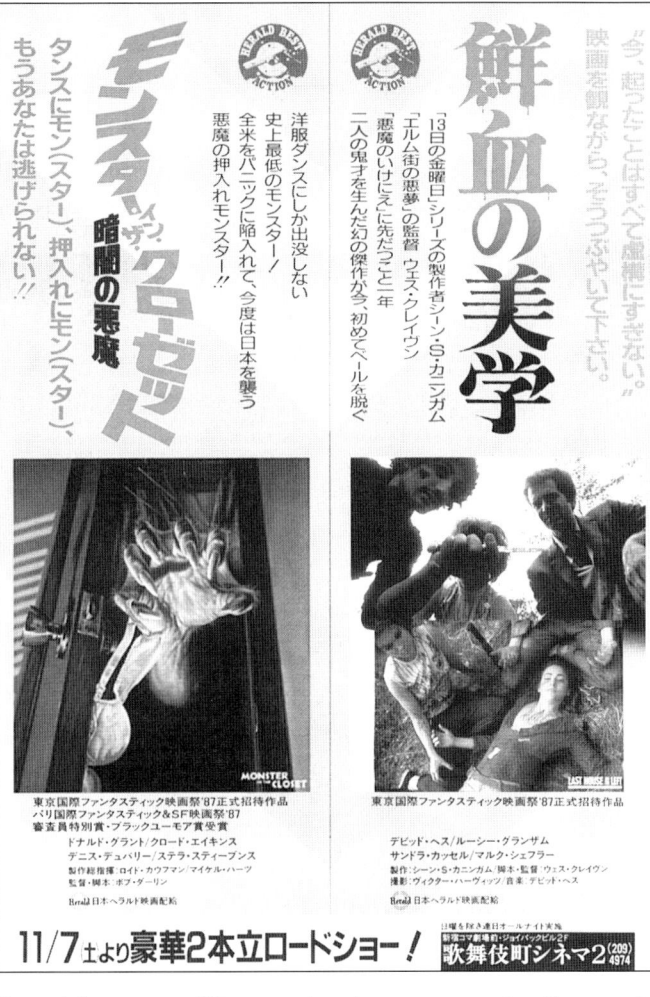

Last House on the Left was given a Japanese theatrical re-release during 1987. It was put on a double bill with *Monster in the Closet*.

anyway, but the backlash against *Last House* had no effect on me. The truth is, all anyone in the movie business cares about is whether or not your picture makes money. They don't care why; if you can get people into theater seats, then you're a desirable commodity."

Although substantial enough to qualify the film as a sleeper hit, the box office returns from *Last House* did not grant its makers the status of "desirable commodity" in Hollywood. Both Cunningham and Craven struggled for years to attract funding for scripts outside the horror genre, attempts which failed repeatedly. Among Craven's projects were an ambitious biopic about Colonel Anthony Herbert (a war hero who had been courtmartialed for reporting American atrocities in Vietnam), a version of *Hansel and Gretel*, and a comedy about beauty contests called *American Beauty*. On his own, Cunningham pitched a *Shaft*-style black action film called *Frog* (which, according to one source, was to star sports hero Walt Frazier) and a script about a divorced father and his child. "Both Sean and I went back to our typewriters trying to write things that were socially responsible," Craven says. "Nothing happened with any of them. We went about two and half, three years that way, at which point I ended up broke because we were devoting all our time to doing that. So that was about a three year period there, from about '72 to '75."

With his "socially responsible" proposals still on hold, Cunningham co-directed a disastrous softcore comedy opus in Miami in 1973. This film, a parody of *Dragnet* in which two stud detectives track down a sexual vampire, was shot under the title *Silver C* (for "Silver Cock") and later released as *Case of the Smiling Stiffs* (aka *Case of the Full Moon Murders*). *Last House* alumni Steve Miner, Fred Lincoln, and Jim Hubbard all worked on *Stiffs*; Lincoln played the movie's 'Joe Friday' cop character opposite Sheila Stuart and porn superstar Harry Reems.[10] Other cast members included Jean Jennings, Ron Brown, and a starlet credited as 'Debbie Craven.'[11] The movie's soundtrack includes recycled portions of the *Last House* score

Sean Cunningham followed up the success of *Last House on the Left* by directing the sex comedy *The Case of the Smiling Stiffs*. The film was received very well in Australia; this illustration shows the Australian video cover.

(see chapter V). Moronic and remarkably un-sexy, *Stiffs* was re-released to US theaters in 1975 with an 'R' rating as *Sex on the Groove Tube*; Cunningham has called the film "a train wreck".

"It was a bizarre experience," Miner says of *Stiffs*. "I got a call at the last minute to go down there, and I worked on the film for three weeks or however long we shot. It was a real mess, and I think I ended up cutting it when we got it back to the editing room. It was supposed to be a comedy, but it wasn't funny… it was just stupid. It was the first time I directed anything though… I shot a bunch of insert scenes back in Connecticut, with the two cops. It got some limited release [in November, 1973] in the U.S., but I've heard that it was a big hit in Australia. They thought it was hilarious down there."

Seeking to escape the stereotype of 'disgusting low-budget producer,' Cunningham departed from sex and horror in the late '70s by directing two family films. The first was a *Bad News Bears* knock-off called *Here Come the Tigers* (1978) which featured Fred Lincoln. The second was *Manny's Orphans* (aka *Kick*,1979), a similar effort about a kids' soccer team that was considered for a time as the potential basis of a network television sitcom. Steve Miner was an associate producer on both films.

Tellingly, it was only upon returning to the horror genre with *The Hills Have Eyes* and *Friday the 13th* respectively that Craven and Cunningham achieved any degree of success. The return to horror was a reluctant one for both the producer and director. "Peter Locke, the producer of *The Hills Have Eyes*, told me for years that I should do another *Last House*, and I resisted his advice for as long a time as I could. I finally gave in and wrote *The Hills Have Eyes* when I ran out of money," Craven remarks.

"*Last House* became a kind of double edged sword," Cunningham reflects. "Since it was very cheap and exploitative, and successful at its own level, people thought of me with the notion that, 'If you want to get puke in a bucket - and get it *cheap* - boy, I've got just the guy for you!' And I just didn't want to do that; I wanted to do other things, and still do. So I was aggressively trying to do other kinds of projects, apart from the horror genre and the sex genre, and none of them met with very much success until 1980, when I said, 'Oh, fuck it!' and decided to do *Friday the 13th*."

The pigeonholing also extended to the careers of the cast. "I couldn't get myself arrested after *Last House*," says David Hess. "No agent would touch me… and *Last House* was a stone cold smash! The production office would get phone calls to the effect of, 'How could you use this guy? Weren't you afraid he was going to blow somebody's head off?' Of course, I *was* a little nuts back in those days, but people really believed that I *was* that character. They gave me no credit for being an actor."

One group of people who did give Hess credit for his talents was Hallmark Releasing. Shortly after the release of *Last House*, the company hired Hess and Marc Sheffler to write a screenplay for a feature called *Sugar Daddy*. "*Sugar Daddy* was a really interesting project… it was a psychological thriller," Hess recalls. "It was about a schizophrenic cop who went around killing young girls, but at the same time was a great policeman… and he had to go after himself! I was going to play the role. At the same time, Hallmark wanted us to do write a horror movie set at a ski resort… so they paid Marc and me to take off and go skiing for three months while we wrote the script. We wrote *Sugar Daddy* during that time, and we also put together the ski lodge script at the same time, although it never came to fruition."

Hess' classic performance in *Last House* and his unique brand of villainy in European shockers (*House on the Edge of the Park*, et.al.) have earned him a lasting cult status among horror fans. "To this day, little old ladies cross the street when they see me coming," Hess laughs.

"I did a film called *Preacher Man Meets Widderwoman* right after *Last House on the Left*," says Jeramie Rain. "*Preacher Man* was a PG-rated family movie, and I played a sweet girl named Willie Mae; the whole thing was 180 degrees away from *Last House*. The producers of *Preacher Man* sent me on a tour of the South to promote their film, and all these reporters wanted to talk to me about was *Last House on the Left*. The producers of *Preacher Man* were very angry about it!"

As Rain's anecdote implies, *Last House* was swiftly becoming something of a legend even as those involved in the film attempted to distance themselves from its bloody, low-budget stigma. The indignant squawks and nauseous groans of censors and critics only added to the mystique surrounding the film.

As of February, 1973, *Variety* reported the gross of *Last House on the Left* at $1,553,392, but this figure does not encompass the total theatrical revenue generated by the movie over the years. Paired with S.F. Brownrigg's Southern-fried shocker *Don't Look in the Basement*,[12] the film shot up to #3 on *Variety*'s chart of top-grossing films in December of 1973. Within two weeks, the gross for the double feature exceeded $1 million.

As anyone who frequented the drive-ins and grindhouses of yore can readily testify, Hallmark Releasing believed in milking its product to the limit. With no cable television or home video to cut into cinema attendance, *Last House* enjoyed a lengthy and lucrative run on the big screen. The movie was continually revived at drive-ins, college campuses and second-run houses throughout the 1970s, and even into the following decade. Even *after* its U.S. home video release in 1985 (the movie has never been shown on television, cable or otherwise) *Last House* was still being exhibited on big screens in Hallmark's home base of New England.

"Going to see films like *Last House on the Left* and *Mark of the Devil* at the drive-in was like a rite of passage for a whole generation of teenagers in New England," remarks David Beach, a New Hampshire native and film archivist who recalls the incessant barrage of Hallmark's radio ads with fond nostalgia. "*Last House* was *the* horror movie to see

above:
One of the many drive-in revivals of *Last House on the Left*; several of the Boston-area theaters listed in this 1978 newspaper ad were owned by Hallmark.

opposite:
The Hills Have Eyes was Wes Craven's triumphant return to the horror film genre; note the film's promotional catch-line!

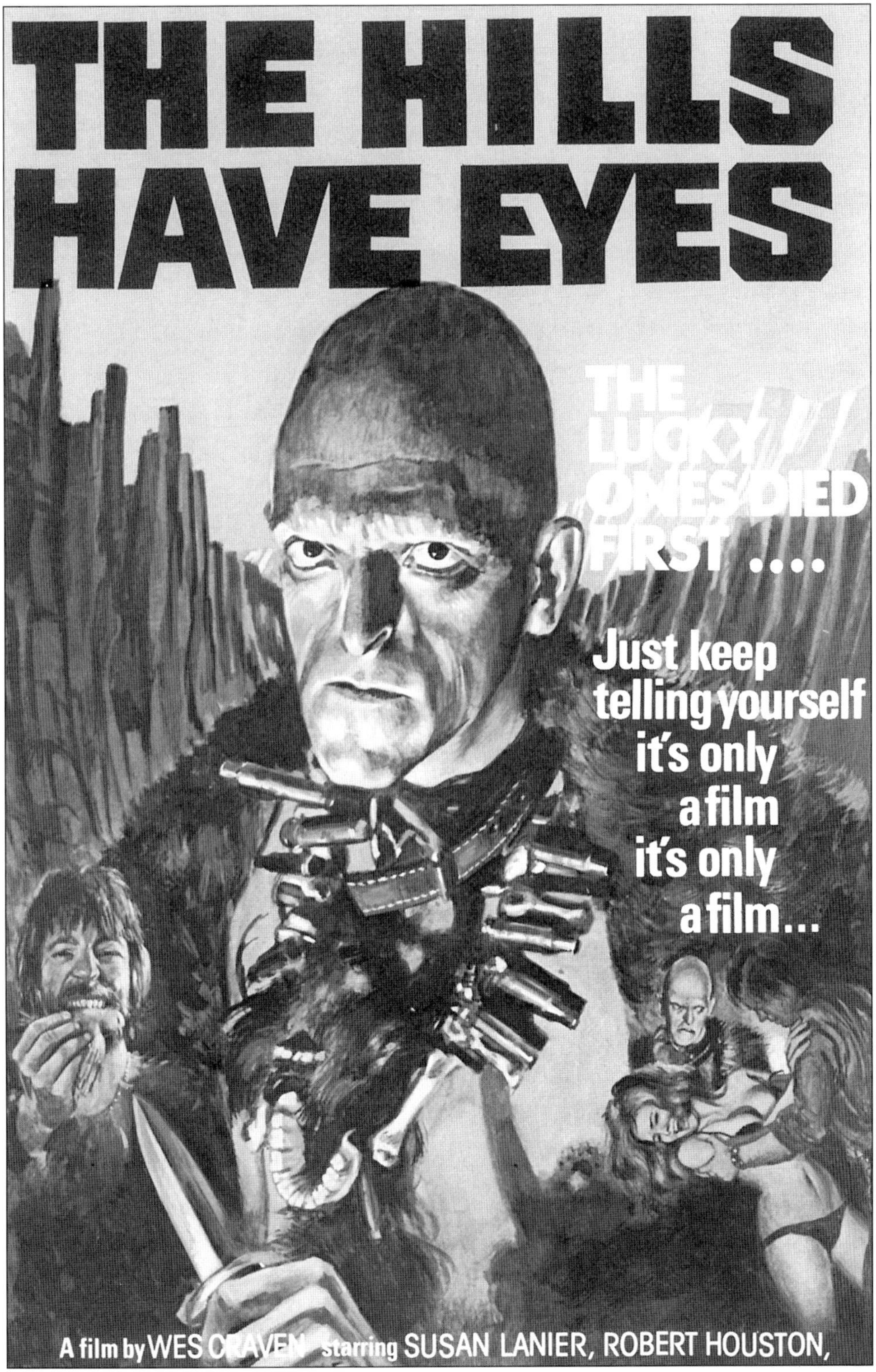
THE HILLS HAVE EYES
THE LUCKY ONES DIED FIRST ....
Just keep telling yourself it's only a film it's only a film...
A film by WES CRAVEN starring SUSAN LANIER, ROBERT HOUSTON,

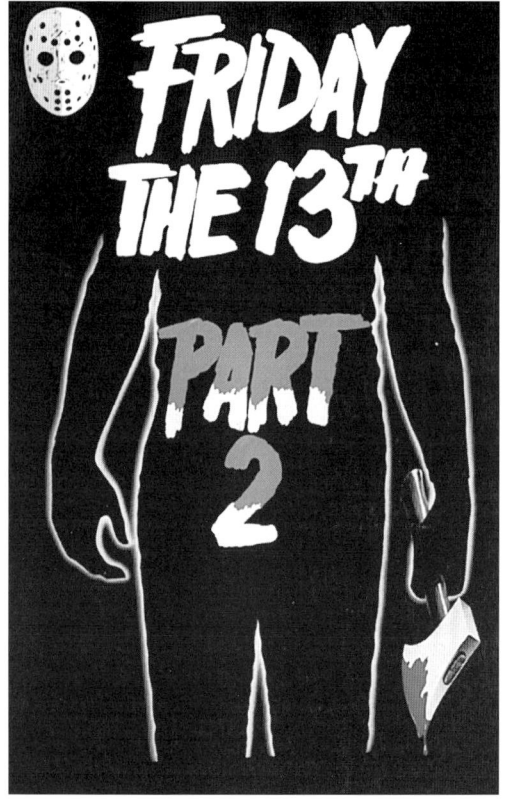

Despite attempts to move into more 'respectable' areas of film making, both Wes Craven and Sean Cunningham have found their greatest success in the horror genre. Cunningham's *Friday the 13th* spawned nine sequels, while Craven progressed from the mediocre *Deadly Blessing* to megahits such as *A Nightmare on Elm Street* and the *Scream* trilogy.

back in the '70s; if you didn't see it one summer, it came back the next summer. I'll never forget seeing a triple-feature *Last House on the Left*, *Mark of the Devil* and Mario Bava's *Shock* at a drive-in theater in 1979. People were honking their horns like mad at every bloody scene… I was blown away!"

"I remember hearing of this one particular drive-in down South where *Last House* just played forever," Jim Hubbard says. "For whatever reason, week after week, all the people down there wanted to see was that movie!"

"It's Only A Movie" proved to be such an effective catchphrase that Hallmark used it to promote subsequent films like *Don't Look in the Basement* (1973) and the Spanish/Italian zombie film *No Profanar El Sueno De Los Muertos* (1974, released by Hallmark as *Don't Open the Window*.) With a catalog including these and numerous other gory epics, Hallmark was able to endlessly repackage its product in varying double- and triple-feature programs.

One of Hallmark's most popular packages was "Three Houses of Hell," a triple bill of *Last House on the Left*, *Don't Look in the Basement*, and a 1974 British thriller that the distributor had dubbed *The House that Vanished* (aka *Scream… and Die!* and *Psycho Sex Fiend*.) The advertising for the "Three Houses of Hell" extravaganza boldly stressed that the trio of films came **"…From *That Company* that reminds you: To Avoid Fainting, Keep Repeating: It's Only a Movie**." Such hype well illustrates that in the world of low-budget horror films, the distributor is often the true star of the show.

Notes

1 *La Semana del Aesino*, also known in the European market as *Cannibal Man*, was an early effort by art-house director Eloy de la Iglesia. The movie told the tale of a deranged slaughterhouse worker who commits a series of bloody murders, later disposing of the corpses via a meat-grinding machine. AIP retitled the film *Apartment on the Thirteenth Floor* and released it to the U.S. in 1974. Under the latter title, the movie also played on drive-in triple-features with *Last House on the Left*. Eloy de la Iglesia has gone on to direct a series of gay-themed films, as well as an adaptation of Henry James' *The Turn of the Screw*.
2 The elusive 'George' referred to by Whitten may actually be Lee Lewis, who Sean Cunningham recently identified as the mastermind behind the *Last House on the Left* title and campaign.
3 *Swingin' Stewardesses* is a German softcore sex film, credited 1972, but probably made in 1971. Original title thought to be *Blutjunge Verführerinnen* (trans: 'Young Seductresses'). It was made by Erwin C. Dietrich (of Eurocine) under his "Michael Thomas" pseudonym.
4 AIP used a variation of the 'MARI' catchline on the posters for the similarly-outrageous shockfest *Deranged* (1974). 'Pretty Sally Mae died a very unnatural death...' exclaimed the legend on top of the provocative ads. Underneath, the copy continued: '...but the worst hasn't happened to her yet!'
5 Like *Joe* and Elia Kazan's novel *The Assassins* (1972), *Last House* dealt with violent conflicts in a middle-class American family divided by the '60s generation gap. At the same time that *Last House* was on the drawing-boards, Sean Cunningham was actually developing an original script called *The Man in the Middle* which was very similar to *Joe*.
6 Ebert, Roger, "In Defense of a Violent Movie that Makes a Statement Against Violence," *Chicago Sun-Times*, December 1, 1972
7 Excerpted from a letter to the author by Grant Dodds, 1992. Reprinted by permission of Grant Dodds.
8 Despite his strong objections to the film, which he has called "scummy and amoral," Peary hosted a benefit screening of *Last House* at the prestigious Harvard Film Archive in 1998. Coincidentally, Mr. Peary went to college with none other than Lucy Grantham, and directed the actress in a campus theater production of W.B. Yeats' *The Green Helmet*!
9 King also made a reference to *Last House* in his "Richard Bachman" novel *The Regulators*.
10 Reems was also the production manager of *Case of the Smiling Stiffs* (credited under his real name, Herbert Streicher) and is rumored to have been up for the role of Junior Stillo in *Last House*!
11 In another homage, a line of dialogue in *Stiffs* refers to 'Inspector Craven.'
12 Posters for *Don't Look in the Basement* stated that the film came "from the makers of *Last House on the Left*." The original title of the film was *The Forgotten*.

Now You See It, Now You Don't: In Search Of The Uncensored

"Our first cut of the film ran 90 minutes and was out in the theaters for about 10 days to two weeks. Sean Cunningham and I became convinced that it was simply too much, that we'd both be sent to Devil's Island if we didn't make some cuts... We'd get prints back where completely different elements of the same film were cut out and thrown away."
- Wes Craven, in an interview with Marc Shapiro, 1990

"Oh, it's all so damned ugly..."
-Sean Cunningham

Last House on the Left established the pattern of an ongoing battle with censorship which Wes Craven has fought throughout his career. Nearly all of Craven's genre films have been compromised or diluted in some way due to the interference of the MPAA ratings board, studios, and other powers-that-be. To this day, *Last House* remains by far the most convoluted and infamous instance of censorship in the director's body of work.

So many different versions of *Last House on the Left* have circulated in theaters and on videocassette that it is truly difficult to establish whether or not a completely uncut version of the film still exists. Although no fewer than five different cuts of the movie have surfaced on video, none of these versions comes close to the running time of 91 minutes reported by *Boxoffice* magazine at the time of the film's theatrical release. The longest available videocassette version of the movie runs just under 85 minutes.

Is the 91 minute running time merely a misprint, or does it reflect a long-lost version of the film? While it is impossible to definitively answer that question, it is admittedly hard to believe that a discrepancy of six minutes exists between all extant prints of the film and the original cut. Nevertheless, an in-depth look at the various versions of the film reveals numerous (if often minor) differences between prints and indicates that several scenes in *Last House* have yet to be completely restored.

Last House on the Left was attacked by censors throughout its U.S. theatrical release. Much of the confusion surrounding the film's running time resulted from the fact that theater owners, projectionists, community censor boards, and distributors all cut the film according to their own standards. It has since come to light that Hallmark screened an unrated *Last House* in some of its own theaters, while American International Pictures generally exhibited a shorter version which had been truncated in order to secure an R rating. According to Wes Craven, the filmmakers initially circumvented the MPAA (who at one point demanded that the movie be cut down to 75 minutes) by simply appropriating an R-rating tag from another film (see Chapter IV).

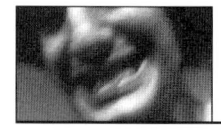

"We always had trouble with the MPAA, but we didn't care," laughs Hallmark's George Mansour. "We didn't care whether these pictures were rated or not. It was really the Wild West. We weren't looking for Academy Awards or respectability, we just we took these movies out and played them. What did we care what these people in Hollywood thought? As I remember, *Last House on the Left* was re-cut several times. Although we finally did get an R rating, we simply put all the censored footage back in *after* we got the R and released it in its complete form. **There were some prints of *Last House on the Left* that were cut and others which were not cut.**"

"Hallmark would take their films and test them out in their own theaters, with their own ad campaigns [see Chapter VI]," David Whitten explains. "And that was how the company got into trouble with the MPAA with a movie called *The Blind Dead* [released by Hallmark in 1972 and aka *Tombs of the Blind Dead*]. The first place I remember them playing that film was the Saxon Theater in Boston. For that engagement, they just simply put these various ads in the newspaper and somebody stuck R and GP ratings on them. The MPAA filed suit in Washington, D.C. on the basis of "unfair trade practices," misappropriating the R rating. They ended up settling the suit out of court… and out of the settlement, some ratings were determined. *Together*, with minimal cuts, got an R. *Mark of the Devil* went from being rated 'V for Violence' to R; that's why the tag-line 'Rated V for Violence' disappeared from the posters. And *Last House On the Left* became an R rated film. As I recall, during the earliest release of *Last House*, the film was unrated [see Chapter VI]."

"Hallmark maintained a full-time editing room someplace where they were re-editing prints of the film," Craven says. "Every time prints of *Last House* came back from theaters to the distributor, they were always hacked up. They would cannibalize footage from one print and splice it into another, so that they could at least have some intact copies of the film."

There were very few completely unexpurgated prints distributed during the movie's final release. In December, 1972, The New York *Times* reported the film's running time at 85 minutes, and according to Jeramie Rain, that version of the film was missing the infamous disembowelment sequence: "I remember shooting it, but when I think about it, I never saw that scene when I watched the movie in the theater," she recalls.

Strangely enough, some rare graphic footage of the disembowelment appeared in an obscure exploitation film called *Confessions of a Blue Movie Star: The Evolution of Snuff* (1976). These brief shots from the murder sequence, which depict Sadie extracting and fondling the bloody viscera, do not appear in any available version of *Last House*, so they are either out takes or part of the fabled 91 minute cut.

Confessions, a ponderous German documentary about the making of a porno film, was originally released in 1974 without the "snuff" subtitle. The film featured an on-camera interview with Roman Polanski in which the director discusses the rumors of "snuff" movies. In 1976, the excerpts from the *Last House* stabbing/disembowelment scene were tacked on to the end of the movie by its distributor, Atlas International, and interspersed with footage of a bogus "interview" with a snuff film maker. The dubbed comments of the impostor (who wears a paper bag over his head and an Iron Cross medallion, resembling a

Nazi biker version of "The Unknown Comic" from *The Gong Show*) include : "At least we were stoned when we did it..."

This splice job was undoubtedly inspired by the success of Monarch Releasing's *Snuff* (1976), which was a similar amalgamation of a shelved 1972 feature called *Slaughter* and a five-minute staged death sequence with bloody special effects by Ed French. Atlas International was the company that distributed *Last House on the Left* in Germany[1], and also sold many foreign films to Hallmark for U.S. distribution such as *Mark of the Devil* and *Born Black* (1970). This seems to explain how the distributor obtained the rarely-seen footage, as well as the "evolution" of an audaciously phony exploitation curio.

Last House was reissued to U.S. theaters in 1981 by Filmways, a distribution company which had taken over the rights to the catalog of American International Pictures. 1981 was the peak of the slasher movie craze inspired by *Friday the 13th*, and Filmways advertised their re-release of *Last House* as "THE ULTIMATE HORROR CLASSIC." However, the prints that made the rounds during this time were all heavily cut. Although a *Fangoria* article on the ratings board suggested that *Last House* had been "trimmed for an R rating upon its recent [Filmways] re-release",[2] it is more likely that the print available to Filmways had already been censored.

Rick Sullivan, editor of the *Gore Gazette* fanzine, commented on the truncated re-release in his self-published "guide to horror, exploitation and sleaze": "Surprisingly enough, 10 years later, the film still seems shocking and packs quite a wallop... Unfortunately, the prints now being shown in area theaters have some of the more gruesome gore scenes missing - the severing [sic] of Phyllis Stone's hand and her graphic disembowelment is nowhere to be seen. Also, Sadie's lesbian attack on the young teen Mari has been excised and is now only hinted at. *Apparently, these scenes have been missing for a number of years now... I know they were all intact as late as 1975.*"[3]

Cover for the long-deleted British video release of *Confessions of a Blue Movie Star: The Evolution of Snuff*, which features otherwise unreleased outtake footage from *Last House on the Left*.

In Search Of The Uncensored

By 1982, the film was already available on video in Europe (see below) but in America, it continued to play in (mostly drive-in) theaters until 1985. In May of that year, Vestron Video released an 82 minute version of the film which was identical to the bowdlerized R-rated print distributed by Filmways.

When it came to Vestron's attention that its video release of *Last House* was significantly cut, the company contacted Wes Craven seeking a complete print of the movie. Craven referred the people at Vestron to film maker and historian Roy Frumkes, who had been friends with the director since the days of *Last House* and volunteered to help with the restoration of the film for a re-release.

The resulting second Vestron version, released in June of 1986 on VHS and laserdisc and advertised on its boxcover as the "uncut" version of the film, runs 83 minutes. This edition of the movie was actually struck from a print which Frumkes had compiled in 1975. At that time, many prints of the film had already been truncated by community censors and theater owners, and Frumkes asked Craven to help him put together an uncut version for posterity.

Craven agreed to the project and helped Frumkes obtain two 16mm prints of *Last House* along with some 35mm footage from a print that, according to Frumkes, came from a shelf in Sean Cunningham's West 45th Street office. The 35mm footage included the following scenes which had been excised from the "R" version of the film:

American video cover

1 - A shot of Phyllis being kicked by Weasel as she crawls through the cemetery;
2 - The bulk of the scene in which Sadie and Weasel repeatedly stab Phyllis, culminating in a brief glimpse of Sadie pulling out a loop of Phyllis' intestine;
3 - The scene of Phyllis' severed hand being dropped to the ground in response to Mari's question "Did she get away?";
4 - A piece of the scene in which Krug carves his name into Mari's chest.

LAST HOUSE ON THE LEFT

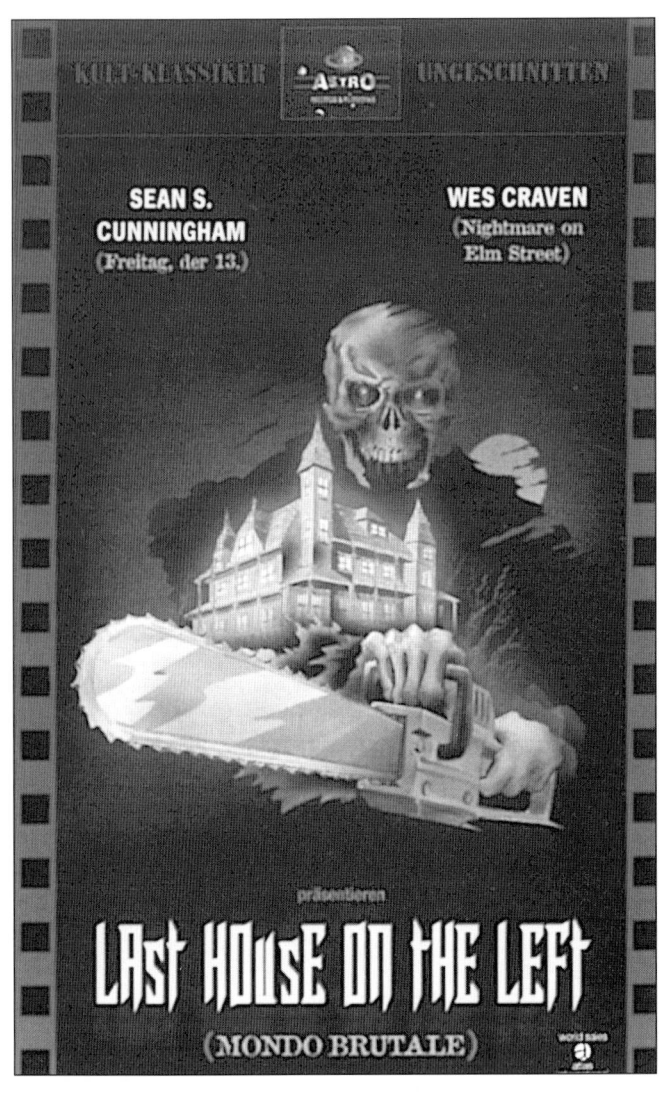

German video cover

Frumkes made a 16mm reduction negative from these 35mm positive clips, submitting the footage to a lab twice in order to match the colors as closely as possible. From the resulting negative, Frumkes struck 16mm positive footage which he integrated into the two prints, one of which was used as the source for Vestron's VHS and laserdisc releases.

The restored footage in the Vestron edition is noticeably grainier than the remainder of the film due to the inevitable degradation of the image involved in reduction from 35mm to 16mm. In defense of the uneven picture quality, Frumkes comments, "I always felt that *Last House on the Left* was meant to be raw, and in that sense, the film really wasn't hurt in the process of restoration." In one case, Frumkes is definitely correct in his assertion, in that Craven intentionally shot the disembowelment/murder sequence to be grainier than the rest of the film.

"We did our best," Craven says of the restoration. "I had saved some pieces of the film from an actual release print... I kept them in a box which I held on to for a while. I gave these little rolls of film to Roy for safekeeping, because at that time he had quite a film archive. So when these people [Vestron] were doing a restoration for videotape, they contacted Roy, and he gave them that footage. But aside from those pieces, I think there were a lot of pieces that had been lost. Unfortunately, the film was just cut a lot... I think the final negative was kind of a hash by the time it stabilized into something that was reprinted or restored in any way. I'm certain there was more footage. Originally, we'd made a *very* strong film."

According to Mr. Frumkes, Craven deliberately did not replace all of the footage which had been cut from the film. "I think Wes' sensibilities had changed in the time since he'd done *Last House*," Frumkes comments. "Some of the scenes *were* actually longer in the original cut of the film, but Wes restored them as he saw fit, and I think the version he put together is, in that sense, a director's cut."

A look at the original 16mm film from which Vestron struck their master tape reveals two spots where footage was left out: the scene of Mari being molested by Sadie in the woods and the scene of Krug carving his name into Mari's chest. During both of these scenes, the imprinted image of a tape splice is visible on the 16mm film, suggesting that the print was duped from another copy which had already been cut. There are also some audible cuts in the soundtrack during these scenes and during the brief glimpse of the disembowelment, suggesting that there was more to both of these scenes.

Confused yet? It gets worse. A Canadian release of the film on the Cinema International Canada (CIC) video label reveals several brief additional scenes which are absent from the reconstituted Vestron edition. This slightly longer print of the film (henceforth referred to as the "CIC" version) was also released by a Dutch company called Empire Video, as well as on Japanese laserdisc. The Dutch and Japanese releases are both letterboxed in the correct aspect ratio of 1.85:1, but the CIC edition is perhaps the most watchable of the three because it does not contain any intrusive foreign-language subtitles. In the Japanese laserdisc, a brief glimpse of full frontal nudity during the scene where Mari and Phyllis are forced to make love is visually 'fogged.'

The CIC version runs approximately eighty-four minutes and nine seconds, as opposed to the Vestron running time of eighty-three minutes, thirty-one seconds. What follows is a catalog of the additional shots in the CIC version:

1 - At the beginning of the sequence where the gang tortures Mari and Phyllis in the woods, Krug instructs Weasel to cut Mari with his switchblade if Phyllis doesn't comply with his orders. While most of this portion was left intact in the Vestron release, a close-up of Mari's bloody fingers accompanied by her voice-over "Phyllis, he cut me!" was edited out, as was a brief shot of the wet patch on Phyllis' pants and a shot of the two semi-nude girls holding each other.

2 - Later in the same sequence, Junior pleads with Krug to stop the sadistic game before things get out of hand. In the Vestron Video version, the scene ends with Junior saying, "…You guys gotta be crazy, man, you gotta be crazy…you're gonna kill someone if you're not careful…" followed by a cutaway to Krug tilting his head back and laughing heartily. The clipped part of this scene which can be seen in the CIC release has Junior go on to say, "…make 'em make it with each other." Sadie exclaims "That's a good idea!", Krug repeats "Make it with each other," followed by a cut back to the aforementioned laughter.

3 - The chase through the woods, while it does not contain any gore, is slightly longer in the CIC print. The short added scene shows Weasel and Phyllis facing each other on opposite sides of a river. Weasel sees her, but can't cross the rapids to get to her; Phyllis raises her middle finger and yells, "Screw, creep!" A close-up of Weasel with an angry facial expression ends the sequence.

4 - Although the chest-carving scene is the same in both the CIC and Vestron versions, the CIC tape features some brief additional shots of the sheriff getting out of the stalled police car and walking along the road.

5 - The dialogue between Weasel and Mrs. Collingwood during the fellatio sequence is lengthier in the CIC edition. The five additional lines at the beginning of the sequence are pure porno-speak:

WEASEL: If you don't watch out, I'm gonna come...
ESTELLE: Then come, sweetie...
WEASEL: Don't you want me to *do* you good and proper?
ESTELLE: You can do both, can't you?
WEASEL: Hell, yeah... I can come five or six times if ya want me to!"

Despite these additions, the CIC version is *missing* one crucial element which appears in all of the other versions of the movie: the titles! As viewers will recall, the movie ends with a montage of each character with the corresponding actor's name optically printed over the scene. CIC's release presents this closing montage *without* the actors' names, and without any of the technical credits which follow. Subsequently, the movie's end theme song ("Baddies' Theme") continues to play over a *blank* screen where the final credit roll normally appears.

French video cover

Similarly, the scene depicting the killers as they carry their captives down the fire escape and into the Cadillac convertible normally includes a superimposed title at the bottom of the screen reading: "...early next morning." In the CIC version this title is absent. Since it is impossible to "undo" such a superimposed image, it may be concluded that this print dates from a time *before* the movie was finished. An alternate explanation is that CIC's print was intended for foreign distribution and therefore struck from elements without English titles.

Further supporting the idea that the bootleg version of *Last House* was struck from an unfinished "workprint" or test-release version of the film is the fact that certain scenes in the video are out of sync. The most glaring example of the gap between sound and picture in this print is the opening dialogue between the Collingwoods, which resembles a dubbed Godzilla movie. These sync problems are not present in the Vestron releases.

A reportedly unauthorized 1982 British release of the film by Replay/VPD video is similar to the CIC and Empire tapes, but inexplicably lacks the 2 minute, 55 second sequence of the sheriff and deputy attempting to hitch a ride on Ada Washington's chicken truck. Replay are assumed to have excised the scene after deciding it did not mesh well with the rest of the film. Nitpickers also note that the Replay tape is missing approximately ten seconds of the opening 'true story' title card, and lacks the final verse of the 'Baddies' Theme' over the blank screen where the end titles normally appear.

The Replay/VPD release of *Last House on the Left* figured prominently in the British "video nasties" scandal of the early '80s, in which police raided video stores seizing copies of grisly horror/slasher movies on the grounds that these tapes violated UK obscenity laws. The "video nasties" debate began in the early months of 1982, touched off by graphic advertising for a ridiculous Italian sleaze picture called *SS Experiment Camp*. Films like *Last House on the Left*, Abel Ferrara's *Driller Killer* (1979), Romano Scavolini's *Nightmares in a Damaged Brain* (1981, aka *Nightmare*) and the notorious *I Spit on Your Grave* (1978) were held up by British censors and politicians as a corrupting influence on society, particularly young children. Soon after the release of the *Last House* cassette, police confiscated copies of the movie from its distributor.

As British writer Harvey Fenton notes, "*Last House on the Left* was a mainstay of [UK] obscenity court cases in the early '80s, and more often than not was found guilty as charged." On June 30, 1983, the video industry was given a list of 52 video nasties, as defined by the Director of Public Prosecutions, including *Last House on the Left*. (Although the list was continually revised over the course of the next few years, *Last House* remained on it even as other titles were removed.) The British censors objected particularly to the sexual nature of the violence in the film, and the movie is still banned in Britain to this day.

British video cover

Canadian video cover

The ban on the movie notwithstanding, in November, 1984, one George Foster of Regency Video in Hull was tried by jury in Beverly Crown Court, whereupon *Last House on the Left* was finally found "not obscene" by the jury. A month later, another video dealer was acquitted in Plymouth Crown Court when the jury failed to reach a verdict on a group of video nasties which included *Last House.*

The rarest version of *Last House on the Left* to surface on video is a British pirated copy of the film under its test-release title of *Krug and Company*[4]. This print was originally submitted to the British Board of Film Censorship (BBFC) in July, 1974 and was promptly classified as 'Rejected' (i.e. banned.) The BBFC logged the film's running time at 83 minutes, 43 seconds. The pirated *Krug and Company* video, allegedly shot when the movie was screened at London's prestigious National Film Theatre as part of a 1982 horror retrospective, features several shots not seen in any other edition of the movie. While most of the added footage in the *Krug and Company* print consists of fleeting cutaways and reaction shots, this version also includes two additional segments:

1 - During the sequence in which the gang tortures Mari and Phyllis in the woods, Krug says, "All right, Sadie, she's all yours... but you'd better not take too long, because Weasel and I are very hungry."

2 - A longer scene in which Mr. and Mrs. Collingwood rush down to the pond and find Mari *alive.* This alternate take runs approximately one minute, and features the following dialogue:

ESTELLE: Oh, God, her chest...
JOHN: Oh, my God... who did this to you, baby?
MARI: Three or four people... two guys and an awful lady... and a guy my age...
ESTELLE: It's them, John, I told you!

TITLE	PRODUCER	COUNTRY	MIN	APPLICANT	REASONS
INQUISITION OF THE MIDDLE AGES, THE	NOT SHOWN	USA	45	FANTASM VIDEO	O(gratuitous sexual violence)
INTERLUDE OF LUST	DIAMOND FILMS	USA	83	CABALLERO HOME VIDEO	O(gratuitous sexual violence)
INTIMATE ENCOUNTERS	W. DANCER	USA	78	PRIVATE SCREENINGS	O(gratuitous sexual violence)
JADE PUSSYCAT, THE	D. CHRISTIAN	USA	51	14TH MANDOLIN	O(gratuitous sexual violence)
JOANNA LA FARFALLA	G. KIKOME	ITALY	160	WFD HOME VIDEO	O(gratuitous sexual violence)
JOY (##)	D. DAVIDSON	USA	70	CABALLERO HOME VIDEO	O(gratuitous sexual violence)
JOY OF FOOLING AROUND THE	J. RAMON	GREECE	90	TABU ENTERPRISES	O(gratuitous sexual violence)
JOY OF FOOLING AROUND THE	J. RAMON	GREECE	94	TABU ENTERPRISES	O(gratuitous sexual violence)
KGA - KIDNAPPED GIRLS AGENCY	HOM	USA	58	LEISUREMAIL	O(gratuitous sexual violence)
KIDNAPPED	M. SCHMIDT	USA	96	HOYTS DISTRIBUTION	O(gratuitous sexual violence)
KRUG & COMPANY	S. CUNNINGHAM	USA	82	VIDEO EXCELLENCE	O(gratuitous sexual violence)
LASSIE IN ACTION	NOT SHOWN	WEST GERMANY	30	J. NASH	O(bestiality)
LAST OF THE WILD	B. BERRY	USA	55	HALLMARK VIDEO	O(gratuitous sexual violence)
LAST OF THE WILD	B. BERRY	USA	55	CABALLERO HOME VIDEO	O(gratuitous sexual violence)
LAST SAVAGE - PART II THE	A. CASTIGLIONI · A. CASTIGLIONI	ITALY	96	PALACE HOME VIDEO	V(i-h-g)
LEATHER PERSUASION	BIZARRE VIDEO PRODS	USA	40	J. NASH	O(gratuitous sexual violence)
LEATHER REVENGE	NOT SHOWN	USA	40	J. NASH	O(gratuitous sexual violence)
LES GRANDES JOUISSEUSES	B. TRANBAREE	FRANCE	90	PRESTIGE VIDEO	O(gratuitous sexual violence)
LES GRANDES JOUISSEUSES	B. TRANBAREE	FRANCE	80	CBS-FOX VIDEO	O(gratuitous sexual violence)
LUST FOR FREEDOM	E. LOUZIL	USA	80	ROADSHOW HOME VIDEO	O(gratuitous sexual violence)
LUST!	MUSTARD FILM	USA	60	VENUS VIDEO	O(gratuitous sexual violence)
LUSTFUL NURSING - LIVE AT THE DOMA CLUB	DOMA-ALL STAR PRODUCTIONS	THE NETHERLANDS	40	W.B. & J.E. WATHEN	V(i-h-g)

Last House on the Left (under the title *Krug & Company*) is one of the many titles listed on the Australian censorship board's official catalogue of banned films.

JOHN: Those people in the house…
MARI: Murderers… murderers…
JOHN: What happened to Phyllis, do you remember?
MARI: She's dead.
ESTELLE: John, we've got to get her to a hospital… Please, John…
JOHN: It's too late.
ESTELLE: (looking at Mari's dead body) Oh, baby….

The melodramatic scene ends with a close-up of Estelle's face, dissolving to Krug, Sadie and Weasel slumbering in Mari's bedroom. All other versions of the film simply show a shot from the end of this sequence (the portion where Estelle is actually saying, "John, we've got to get her to a hospital…") with the overdubbed lines:

ESTELLE: Oh, John… isn't there anything we can do for her?
JOHN: Nothing.
ESTELLE: John…
JOHN: She's dead.

In the final analysis, most of the discrepancies between the various versions of *Last House on the Left* are trivial - only the 82 minute Vestron release of the film is significantly hampered by the cuts. Those whose interest in the film extends only to what writer Chas. Balun has dubbed "the Gore Score" will inevitably be disappointed. A thoroughly uncut version of the film may indeed still exist, but until someone decides to invest time and money in a proper restoration, the remaining "lost" footage will continue to molder on some dark shelf, slowly turning red.

Postscript:

In 1999, *Last House on the Left* was re-submitted to the BBFC by a distributor called Feature Film Company. The censor board handed back yet another list of cuts, defeating the belated attempt to release the movie in the UK. The BBFC press release is reproduced below:

"*The Last House on the Left* is not suitable for cinema exhibition because of the explicit and sadistic sexual violence contained in the film. This is the second time that *The Last House on the Left* has been refused classification by the BBFC. The present version is some four minutes longer than the version offered in 1974, but is still several minutes shorter than the original uncut version. Although the recent resubmission was of a cut version of the film, it was still found to contain elements which are unacceptable under the Board's published Guidelines. The Board asked for further cuts to remove images of the horrific stripping, rape and knife murder of two women. The option of making additional cuts was offered to the distributor in May 1999 and in September they confirmed that the film would be resubmitted with further cuts. After much delay it is now clear that the distributor has declined the option to proceed further. The Board is therefore unable to classify the film in this version."

This is the cuts list which was issued by the BBFC:

Reel 2 - When the two young women are stripped at knife-point, end the sequence before the first victim's knickers are removed.

Reel 3 - Cut at the end of the close-up of villain woman wiping her brow with a bloody hand to the end of shot of the bloody entrails being removed from the body.

Reel 3 - In the stripping and raping of the virgin, remove all knife cuts to her chest and remove side-shot of man lying on partly-stripped woman.

Notes

[1] *Last House* was shown in German theaters under the title *Das Letzte Haus Links* and has been released to video in Germany several times, firstly under the title *Mondo Brutale*.
[2] Suzanne Weyn, "The Great Ratings Debate," Fangoria, Vol.3 Issue 14, p.26.
[3] Rick Sullivan, "Return of a Classic," Gore Gazette #15, 1981. Note that the scene of "Sadie's lesbian attack on Mari" is not shown explicitly in any available version of the film.
[4] *Last House* was also submitted to Australian censors as *Krug and Company* during the '70s, and promptly rejected.

Rip-Offs And Rehashes

One of the most fascinating aspects of the *Last House* legacy is the spate of copycat films which appeared in the wake of the movie's release. Just as the popularity of horror landmarks like William Friedkin's *The Exorcist* and George Romero's *Dawn of the Dead* inspired numerous quickie imitations, so did *Last House on the Left* spawn its own twisted sub-genre of exploitation movies. At least two entries in this cycle of mostly European-made ripoffs were deliberate reworkings of the *Last House* scenario, but most were retitled, previously-shelved features which resembled *Last House* mainly in their blatantly derivative advertising campaigns.

Seeking to cash in on the box-office success of *Last House*, many low-budget distributors and producers simply sought out films that featured a gang of obnoxious, sadistic cretins terrorizing helpless nubiles and used some variation on the "It's Only A Movie!" tagline to promote the product. Although the majority of these rip-off titles were not consciously patterned after *Last House on the Left*, many of them center on a conflict between the insulated world of prim-and-proper bourgeois society and the ugly reality of low-down, dirty criminals. Of course, whatever inadvertent or intentional social implications exist in the likes of *House on the Edge of the Park* or *Last House on the Beach* are secondary to the sensationalistic sexual violence and sleaze... and on that basic level, the *Last House* rip-off films succeed all too well.

The earliest example of the *Last House on the Left* copycat phenomenon is a 1974 Italian production originally called *L'Ultimo Treno Della' Notte*, or, literally, The Last Train of the Night. The film has been known variously as *The Last Stop on the Night Train*, *The Night Train Murders*, *Late-Night Trains*, *Don't Ride on Late-Night Trains*, *Second House from the Left*, *Last House on the Left II*, or, as Central Park Distribution re-christened it for a 1978 U.S. release, *The New House on the Left*[1]. By any name, the film is a Euro exploitation remake of *Last House on the Left*...which is ironic in light of the fact that *Last House* was an American exploitation remake of a European art film

L'Ultimo Treno... was directed by Italian B-movie maestro Aldo Lado, who was credited by the Americanized pseudonym Evans Isle on advertisements for the movie's U.S. release. Lado, who began his career working on spaghetti westerns, has also been known under the pseudonym George B. Lewis. Acclaimed, prolific composer Ennio Morricone (*The Good, the Bad, and the Ugly*) was responsible for most of the movie's original score, including an eerie harmonica theme. Morricone also scored *Hitch Hike* (see below).

Of all the ripoff films, Lado's is the one most closely-patterned on Craven's original. *New House on the Left* copies the basic storyline of *Last House* with one crucial difference: much of the first half of the film is transposed to the setting of a moving train[2]. Boston *Globe* film critic Michael Blowen called *New House* "simply one of the worst movies I have ever seen" and suggested that it might aptly be called *Perverts on a Train*. Though Lado's film is a more professionally-mounted production than *Last House on the Left*, it lacks the sense of humor and the inimitable style of Craven's film.

Rip-Offs And Rehashes

Here's the setup: two schoolgirls, Margaret (Irene Miracle) and Lisa (Laura D'Angelo), are traveling home by rail from Munich to Italy to spend the Christmas holidays with Lisa's parents. Lisa is the "Mari" figure in the story, a virgin whose only vice is the occasional cigarette; Margaret is the more experienced of the two and serves as the movie's "Phyllis." As in *Last House*, the two girls both seem sweet and likable, and thus most undeserving of the nastiness which befalls them.

"Weasel" and "Junior" here become "Blackie" (Flavio Bucci, who appeared in Dario Argento's *Suspiria*) and "Curly" (Gianfranco de Grassi), two young punks on a random spree of robbery and mischief who sneak aboard the train while fleeing the scene of a misdemeanor. The "Krug" and "Sadie" characters are combined in the form of the nameless, decadent "Lady On the Train" (Macha Meril of Argento's *Deep Red*).

Margaret and Lisa run afoul of the trio but manage to escape unharmed when the train is stopped at Innsbruck because of a bomb scare. In order to avoid the resultant delay, the schoolgirls cross the platform and transfer to a deserted compartment on the 'Last Train of the Night'.

The transfer proves to be a fatal mistake, as the three degenerates force their way into the girls' compartment and proceed to make themselves decidedly unwelcome. For openers, the leering Lady forces the girls to watch her have sex with Blackie. After going off to shoot some smack in the bathroom, Curly savagely beats Margaret when she resists his sexual advances. Rape and further perversion ensue, much of it mercifully underlit.

The movie's most disturbing and ironic twist takes place when a drunken businessman notices the goings-on and lingers outside the window of the compartment, silently watching. The criminals spot the middle-aged voyeur and invite him in to join the party. The man agrees, and, after raping the dazed Margaret, goes on his amoral way. (Later on in the film, the briefcase-toting hypocrite makes an anonymous call to the police fingering the three other participants!)

Next, discovering that Lisa is a virgin, the evil, smirking Lady holds Lisa down while the smacked-out, psychotic Curly rapes the girl with a knife... truly a moment which would make the Marquis de Sade cringe. As Christmas Day dawns outside, Margaret flees from her tormentors and jumps to her death from a window in the train's tiny bathroom compartment. Meanwhile, Lisa has died as a result of the

above & opposite:
L'Ultimo Treno della Notte was released in the U.S. by Hallmark under the title *Last Stop on the Night Train.*

hideous switchblade violation, and the criminals throw her body out the window after her friend.

In another parallel to *Last House*, the criminals are briefly overcome by remorse and disgust in the aftermath of their deeds. But here the criminals' guilt only leads them to blame each other. Blackie angrily turns on the manipulative Woman and kicks her in the kneecap, yelling 'It's all your fault!'. Bleeding from the injury, the Woman attempts to placate her accomplices, telling them, 'It was just one of those things…'

The train lets the culprits off at the same stop where Lisa's parents are waiting to meet the girls. The two-faced femme fatale talks Lisa's father - who is, as in *Last House*, a doctor - into harboring the fugitives at his home while he patches up her damaged knee. Subsequently, through a series of equally implausible contrivances (a telltale scarf, a conveniently-overheard radio broadcast) the parents become aware of their daughter's murder and the identity of the responsible parties. After learning of his guests' deeds, the father starts to strangle the Lady in a fit of rage. The Lady, however, convinces the revenge-crazed patriarch that the two "drug addicts" committed the crime, and that she was only a helpless witness.

The Doc actually buys this explanation and goes after the other two criminals. Sneaking up behind Curly while the youth is engaged in the mechanics of a furtive heroin fix, the father breaks the hypodermic needle off inside the addict's arm. The doctor then smashes a handy glass IV bottle in Curly's face, and skewers the villain repeatedly (once through the crotch!) with the business end of the metal IV stand.

Barely missing a beat, the doctor grabs a shotgun and goes off to hunt down the cowardly Blackie, who has fled from the house. As the doc chases his nemesis through the woods, the Lady comforts Lisa's mother. Meanwhile, the bloodied Curly crawls towards the two women, pointing an accusing finger at the Lady. Before Lisa's mother can see this, the Lady repeatedly kicks Curly in the face, and the junkie youth finally expires.

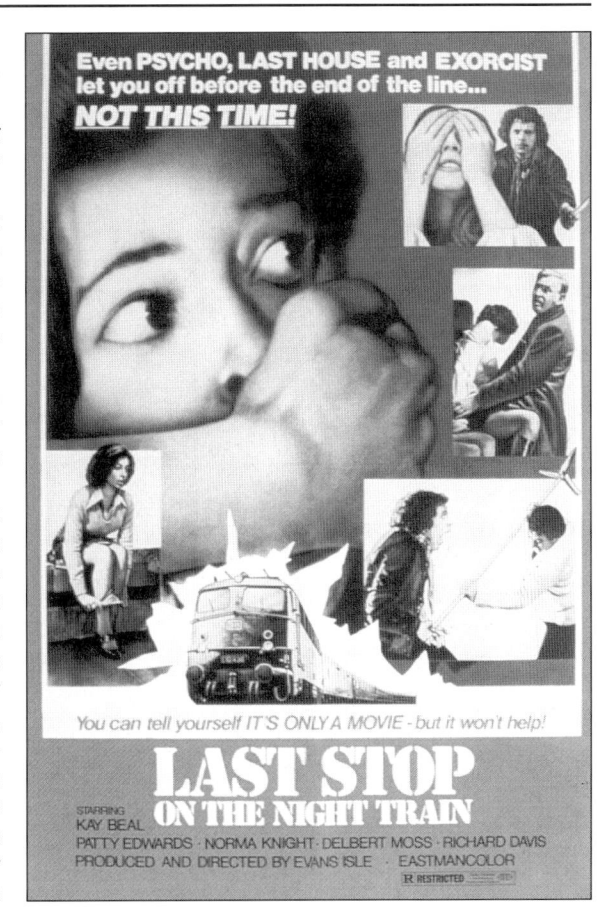

In an ironic ending, the Lady, a veiled hat covering her face, stands unharmed beside Lisa's parents while approaching police sirens wail in the background. Apparently, the Lady's social "veil" of upper-class propriety has ultimately fooled Lisa's father into sparing her. In a final piece of rancid philosophizing, the film's credits are accompanied by a god-awful, warbling theme song by Demis Roussos entitled "A Flower Is All You Need." Roussos previously contributed to bizarro pop culture as a member of the psychedelic rock band Aphrodite's Child, which featured future *Chariots of Fire* composer Vangelis.

Along with the obligatory bloodshed and rape, the makers of *L'Ultimo Treno...* also aped the themes of social and moral malaise implicit in *Last House On The Left*. In two separate scenes of Lado's opus, characters engage in debate over the decaying morals of youth, the rampant spread of violence in modern society, and the responsibility of the State to control its citizens.

The heavy-handedness of these high-minded dialogues is partially redeemed by the ironic context in which they are presented; one such discussion involves the Lady, who exchanges philosophical platitudes with a politician on the train before stepping out for a little rape and murder. In another scene, the doctor and his wife host a Christmas dinner party at which they banter back and forth with their colleagues about the evils of a permissive, jaded society. "Boredom and lack of exercise can lead to violence," opines the complacent, conservative-minded doctor at one point, as the scene cuts away to his daughter being brutalized by the villains.[3]

Yet another re-titling for *L'Ultimo Treno della Notte*.

House on the Edge of the Park (*La Casa Sperduta nel Parco*, 1980), director Ruggero (*Cannibal Holocaust*) Deodato's spin on the *Last House* concept, is perhaps the most entertaining of the rip-off movies, solely by virtue of the fact that the one and only David Hess portrays the lead villain in a singularly abrasive and outrageous manner. Although some shots of New York City appear in the beginning of the film, the remainder of the movie was shot in Rome. "The Italians are very clone-conscious, and although I don't know if *Last House on the Left* was ever released in Italy, they wanted to do an Italian version of it," Hess remarks. "I've worked with Ruggero Deodato a lot, and I wouldn't say he's a great artist. I took the money and ran."

Although Hess is dismissive of *House on the Edge of the Park* in retrospect, he certainly poured himself into his villainous role with gusto. In the Deodato film, Hess plays Alex, a psychotic garage

Rip-Offs And Rehashes

German poster for *House on the Edge of the Park*.

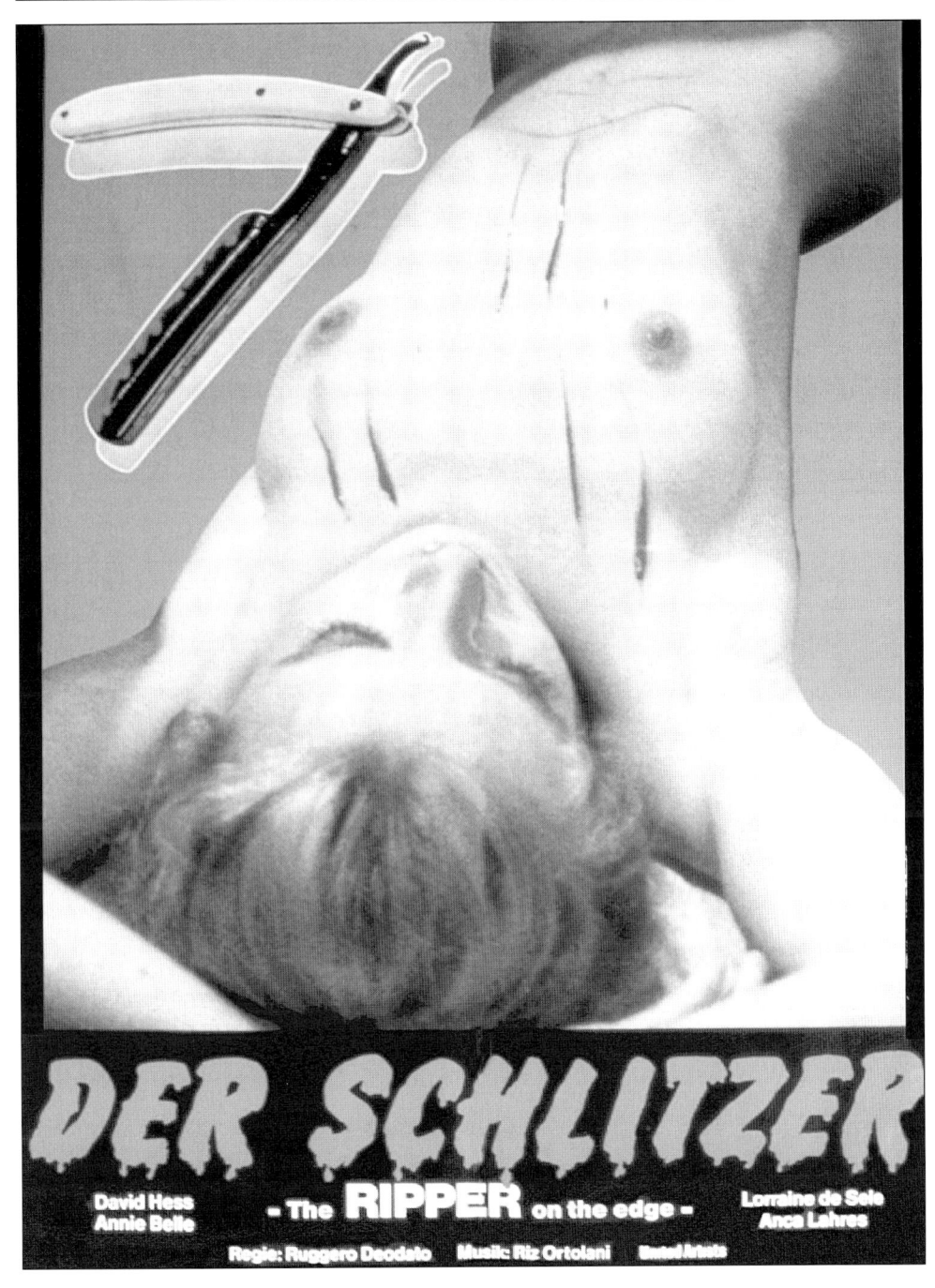

mechanic with an penchant for straight razors and sexual assault. We first meet Alex as he follows a female motorist down a New York City thruway, forces her off the road into a deserted park, and rapes her after crooning the signature line, "Helloooo, Lady!" All of this ugly business occurs even before the opening credits roll.

The film's plot is subsequently set in motion when a *nouveau riche* couple pulls into the garage where Alex works with his seemingly-retarded accomplice Ricky (Giovanni Radice, aka John Morghen of

LAST HOUSE ON THE LEFT   175

Make Them Die Slowly and Lucio Fulci's *Gates of Hell*). Alex and Ricky are getting ready to knock off for the day (to "go boogie") but the yuppies flash a wad of cash at them, imploring the two mechanics to fix the car. After Ricky solves the car trouble, the strangers take the pair of grease monkeys back to their suburban home for a party.

At the party, the couple and their well-heeled, jaded guests amuse themselves by trying to make fools of the two proles. Alex doesn't take kindly to this sort of thing, and, whipping out his trusty straight razor, proceeds to turn the evening into another kind of party. Locking the doors and windows and taking the group prisoner, Alex subjects the captives to a night of sexual assault, beatings, razor slashings, humiliation and endless verbal abuse. Hess' character is truly out of control: he pounds the lead yuppie's face to a pulp in graphic detail, urinates on another man after dumping him in a swimming pool, and croons a love song to one of his female victims during a harrowing multiple-slashing sequence. In another scene lifted from *Last House*, Alex forces two of the female guests to put on a lesbian sex show.

Alex's relationship with Ricky seems to echo that of Krug and Junior in *Last House*. While at first Ricky follows Alex's orders, he develops a conscience and asks Alex to stop; like Junior, Ricky also tries to help one of the women escape but is thwarted by his "father" at the last minute. Finally, as with Krug and Junior in *Last House*, Hess ends up killing his "son" at the end of the film. However, instead of ordering the youngster to commit suicide, here Alex rams a straight razor into Ricky's stomach. In its conclusion, *House on the Edge of the Park* adds an interesting (though not overly believable) twist to the *Last House* formula. Pulling a gun, the party's host reveals that he has intentionally brought Alex to the house to exact revenge for the rape of his sister, the girl in the pre-credit sequence. After shooting Alex in the crotch (Hess' slow motion death throes go on forever) the man calmly phones the police, knowing that he will not be held responsible for the 'self-defense' murder.

Legend has it that one particularly nasty scene in *House On the Edge of the Park* was excised from all videocassette releases but included in the U.S. theatrical version released by Bedford Distribution in 1985. As described in the ever-reliable *Gore Gazette* and by independent producer George (*100 Proof*) Maranville, the offending clip showed Alex pulling a tampon out of a captive girl's panties and exclaiming, "Look what I found!"

As obnoxious and vicious as Alex is, Hess is undeniably a lot of fun to watch in the role of the abusive, hateful villain, and his crude running commentary makes *House on the Edge of the Park* a howler for those with a strong stomach and a warped sense of humor. On the cheesier side, the film might be accurately retitled *Disco Last House*, as

This *Variety* ad for *House on the Edge of the Park* used a likeness of David Hess as seen in *Last House on the Left*!

Rip-Offs And Rehashes

David Hess as the psychopathic Alex in *House on the Edge of the Park*.

left: with Lorraine De Selle.

above: with Giovanni Lombardo Radice (aka John Morghen).

it features a torturous Euro-dance soundtrack and some retina-scorching Studio 54 attire worn by the cast, not the least of which is Alex's canary-yellow boogie vest. Memorable line: Every word out of David Hess' mouth.

Spaghetti auteur Franco Prosperi (*Mondo Cane*, *The Wild Beasts*) made his contribution to the "It's Only A Movie" mythos with an obscure 1977 feature called *La Settima Donna* ("The Seventh Woman") that was renamed *The Last House on the Beach* in 1981. The film has also been distributed under the alternate title *Terror* (not to be confused with Norman J. Warren's British film of the same name.)

In Prosperi's film, three bankrobbers on the lam find themselves stranded near an isolated beach house when their getaway car breaks down. Looking for a place to hide out, the three robbers break into the house, where they find a group of five Catholic schoolgirls and their instructor, a nun (Florinda Balkan). The situation immediately erupts into violence, as one of the criminals (Ray Lovelock) bludgeons a housekeeper to death with an iron as she tries to escape. Another of the thugs tries to molest one of the girls, who thwarts his efforts with a vicious stab wound to the leg.

After this fast-paced opening reel, the movie bogs down into a dreary, interminable morass of misogynist violence similar to *House on the Edge of the Park* but lacking the personality and presence of David Hess. The robbers relentlessly degrade and abuse their captives, making much gleeful sport of the fact that the teacher is a nun. (In one ironic variation on the *Last House* formula, Lovelock's character pretends to be an innocent tag-along caught up in the depravity *a la*

LAST HOUSE ON THE LEFT

Rip-Offs And Rehashes

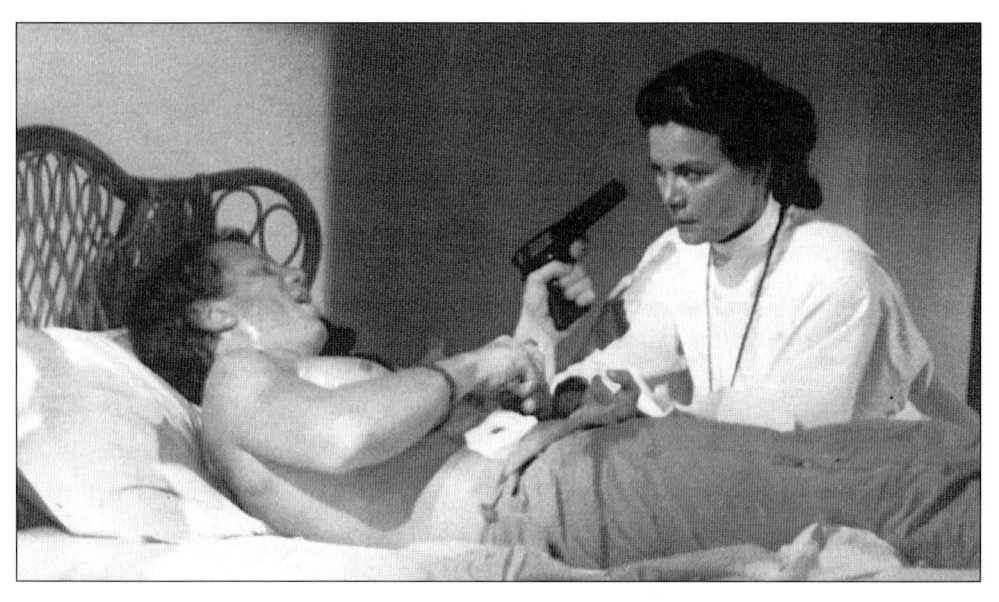

From *Last House on the Beach* (aka *Terror*).

Junior Stillo, but proves even more vicious and manipulative than his comrades.) A scene in which one criminal rapes the nun as his buddy holds her down is quite vile, but the movie's most sickening scene is a slow-motion rendering of sexual assault with a huge wooden stick. Finally, at the end of the film, the pissed-off sister disposes of two of the villains (one by lethal injection, the other by gunshot), and the surviving girls beat the third (Lovelock) to death with an assortment of gardening tools, including a rake. Memorable line: None, but rock and roll aficionados will recognize a portion of AC/DC's 1974 cut "Soul Stripper" as the musical backing for the above-cited slo-mo stick scene.

Last House on Dead End Street (1977) was filmed in Oneonta, NY, reportedly as a student film project for the State University of New York. During production, the film had two other titles: *The Funhouse* and *The Cuckoo Clocks of Hell*. It was briefly released to theaters in 1979 under the *Last House* moniker by Cinematic Releasing, a distributor headed by New Jersey entrepreneur Hank Stern. At the same time, Cinematic also released *The People Who Own the Dark*, a Spanish film co-produced by Sean Cunningham; this may have influenced Stern's decision to use the *Last House* title.

According to Jim Markovic, a New York-based film editor who recut *Dead End Street* for home video in the early '80s, the picture was actually never finished and was disowned by its director, Roger Watkins, who is credited onscreen by the pseudonym Victor Janos. Watkins allegedly appears in the film in the leading role of Terry Hawkins, a degenerate porn film maker and drug dealer who gets out of jail and decides to make snuff movies as a means of getting revenge on his enemies ("I'll show 'em," the greasy-haired, scowling reprobate muses in voice-over, "I'll show 'em all what Terry Hawkins can do!".)

In pursuit of his murderous cinematic vision, Hawkins recruits a weaselly cameraman with a Super-8 rig, as well as a hulking assistant and two slutty Mansonoid henchwomen. The group's first experiment in *cinema vomité* involves the ritualistic strangulation of a blind man. This proves to be such a smashing success on film that the group goes on to stage several more elaborate murders. Luring his enemies (including

LAST HOUSE ON THE LEFT

IT'S BACK! THE EVIL THAT HAD YOU SCREAMING...
IT'S ONLY A MOVIE!

LAST HOUSE ON DEAD END STREET

A Production Concepts Ltd., Presentation • A CINEMATIC RELEASE Starring
STEVEN MORRISON • DENNIS CRAWFORD • LAWRENCE BORNMAN • JANET SORLEY • PAUL PHILLIPS
ELAINE NORCROSS • ALEX KREGAR • FRANKLIN STATZ • BARBARA AMUNSEN • GERALDINE SANDERS
Musical Supervision CLAUDE ARMAND • Written by BRIAN LAWRENCE • Produced by NORMAN F. KAISER
Directed by VICTOR JANOS • COLOR

R RESTRICTED
Under 17 requires accompanying Parent or Adult Guardian

Rip-Offs And Rehashes

a porno movie distributor who has ripped him off) to a cavernous, abandoned house, Hawkins mounts his most hideous, disturbing production.

Last House On Dead End Street certainly doesn't stint on shock value; indeed, the film far surpasses Craven's *Last House* in its violence, especially in one sequence where Hawkins and his gang strap a woman down on an operating table and take her entire body apart with a variety of sharp, nasty implements. This long and brutal sequence, which includes a lingering, full disembowelment, is missing from some video versions of the film.

The film climaxes with a male victim being forced to orally copulate a plastic hoof which is protruding from one of the female attackers' jeans - one simply has to *see* this to grasp the concept. After this kinky humiliation, a power drill is graphically driven into the man's eyeball. (Whether this final touch constitutes a play on the opening razor-blade-to-the-eye shot in Salvador Dali's *Un Chien Andalou* will have to remain a mystery until director Watkins comes out of hiding… in other words, forever.) A somber end voice over announces that Hawkins and his cohorts have been sentenced to life in prison for their crimes.

From its stilted, sardonic dialogue, to the artsy camerawork, lighting, and editing (which give it the quality of a muddled, hallucinogenic nightmare) *Last House on Dead End Street* certainly seems like a student film. By far one of the most freakish and uncommercial movies that ever managed to find its way into a theater, *Last House On Dead End Street* is so relentlessly ugly, disorienting and perverse that it more than deserves the "It's Only A Movie" tagline. Memorable line (said by the above-mentioned smut mogul to a hack film maker who is trying to sell him stag loops): "You sit here showing me tenth-rate porn while your wife is getting her ass whipped in the next room, and you have the nerve to talk to me about your reputation?!"

The Horrible House on the Hill was a retitling of Sean MacGregor's offbeat 1974 film *Peopletoys* (aka *Devil Times Five*), which had nothing whatsoever to do with *Last House on the Left*. MacGregor's film concerns five disturbed children (one of whom is played by a pre-pubescent Leif Garrett) who invade a ski lodge and terrorize its inhabitants. But the advertising for *Horrible House*, created by Jerry Gross and his Cinemation distribution team (who put out drive-in classics like *I Drink Your Blood* and Lucio Fulci's *Zombie*) was a direct knock-off of Hallmark's *Last House* campaign. "To Avoid Fainting, Keep Repeating…It's Only a Movie…" here becomes "If You Get Too Scared, Keep Telling Yourself… It Can't Happen to Me... It Can't Happen to Me… It Can't Happen To Me…"

Hitch Hike (aka *Autostop: Rosso Sangue*, *Death Drive,* 1978) was shot in Italy and Barstow, California by director Pasquale Festa Campanile and featured David Hess in yet another psychotic role. *Hitch Hike*'s story (based, according to the credits, on a novel called "The Violence and the Fury") bears no substantial parallel to *Last House*, but the casting of Hess as a wanted criminal terrorizing a bourgeois couple seems to have been duly influenced by his stint as

Rip-Offs And Rehashes

Krug Stillo. Hess claims that this obscure film (it was never released theatrically in the United States) was the uncredited inspiration for the Rutger Hauer / C. Thomas Howell film *The Hitcher* (1986). Although the actor's assertion is debatable at best, *Hitch Hike* holds up as a nicely plotted, tough little movie in its own right.

Hitch Hike stars Franco Nero as Walter Mancini, a cynical, drunken journalist on vacation with his comely wife Eve (Corrine Clery.) The Mancinis (who spend most of the film bickering and insulting each other) are sucked into a violent ordeal when they make the mistake of picking up a hitch hiker named Adam (Hess) while road-tripping through California. It turns out that Adam is a dangerous fugitive who has just robbed a bank and split from his accomplices with the money. The foul-mouthed, gun-toting psycho takes the Mancinis hostage and demands that they drive him to freedom. Learning of Walter's occupation, Adam proposes that Walter write a memoir of the experience, offering him a cut of the money in exchange for immortalizing Adam in print.

Adam gives Walter plenty of sensationalistic material for the proposed book. First, Adam shoots two cops at a roadblock when Walter tries to pass them a note, and later, at a rest stop, ties the reporter up and forces him to watch as he ravishes Eve. The couple nearly escape the hitch hiker's clutches when the two other bankrobbers return to reclaim the booty, but the wily criminal refuses to say 'die.' Just when the audience is led to think that Hess is out of the picture, he pops up again and disposes of the two accomplices. It is ultimately Eve who rids the couple of Adam's unpleasant presence by shooting him with Walter's high-powered hunting rifle. Interestingly enough, the film doesn't end there; after a few more plot twists, Walter disposes of Eve and hitch-hikes off with the suitcase of money. Nero and Hess are both terrific in the film, making *Hitch-Hike* a must-see for fans of either actor.

House By the Lake (aka *Death Weekend*, 1976) was a Canadian production produced by future Hollywood bigwig Ivan Reitman (*Ghostbusters*, *Howard Stern's Private Parts*) and directed by William Fruet (*Spasms*, *Funeral Home*, *Friday the 13th: The Series*). American International Pictures acquired the film and decided that it made a worthy companion to *Last House on the Left*, booking the two films together[4] with *The House That Dripped Blood* (1971) at drive-ins as "The Three Houses of Horror" (no doubt inspired by Hallmark's "Three Houses of Hell" promotion- see chapter VI.). AIP's ads for the event trumpeted: "Satan Welcomes You to Hellville, USA!... Death! Evil! Terror!"

British video cover for *House by the Lake*.

Rip-Offs And Rehashes

House by the Lake stars Brenda Vaccaro as Diane, a model who goes on an ill-conceived weekend retreat with a wealthy, womanizing dentist named Harry (Chuck Shamata). En route to Harry's sprawling, private lakeside estate, the couple runs afoul of four white trash youths. Diane runs the four punks off the road, humiliating the leader of the gang (Don Stroud) in front of his idiotic friends. Learning the location of Harry's home from a drunken gas station attendant, Stroud and his gang break into the house seeking revenge.

The surly Stroud character and his guffawing, moronic pals spend most of the film getting inebriated, trashing the house (probably the most nerve-wracking part of the movie) and harassing Harry and Diane. In the course of this trial, Harry proves to be a cowardly, materialistic weakling, and after relentless abuse at the hands of the four punks, he is finally killed. In the film's final reel, Diane herself takes revenge on the villains; in this aspect of the story, *House by the Lake* more closely resembles *I Spit on Your Grave* than *Last House*. She slashes one of the group with a piece of a broken mirror (during an attempted rape,) sets another on fire, drowns a third in a bog, and runs Stroud over with a car. The film's odd ending, in which the blank-faced Vaccaro flashes back on images of Stroud, seems to imply that she either feels remorseful for what she has done, harbors a secret romantic attraction for Stroud, or both.

While *House by the Lake* echoes *Last House* with its motifs of rape, home invasion, and class conflict, it was most likely not directly inspired by Craven's film. In fact, an Italian melodrama entitled *The Lonely Violent Beach* (1971) used a very similar premise even *before* *Last House on the Left* was released.

In *The Lonely Violent Beach*, a bourgeois milquetoast and his jaded, unhappy girlfriend (a blonde babe in go-go boots) drive out to an isolated beach house for a weekend vacation. A group of four motorcycle-riding, long-haired miscreants (resembling an acid rock combo - Iron Butterfly, perhaps - with their mod duds and 'dos) invade the house, truss up Mr. Man and violate the girl. As in *House By the Lake*, the girl decides she loves the leader of the gang… oh, the humanity. Memorable line (wistfully offered by one of the rape-happy hooligans): "Once we were just a bunch of happy young hippies…"

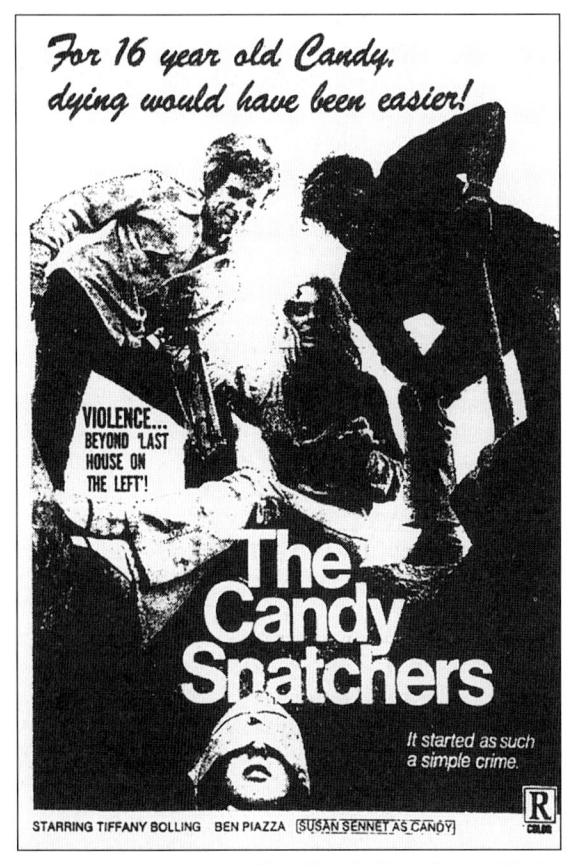

Other '70s films with storylines that coincidentally bear comparison to *Last House* include director Frederick Friedel's underrated neo-noir film *Axe* (1974, aka *Lisa* and *California Axe Massacre*), the biker flick *Savage Abduction* (1972, aka *Cycle Psycho* and *Numbered Days*), Meir Zarchi's notorious *I Spit on Your Grave* (1978, aka *Day of the Woman*) and *The Candy Snatchers* (1973).

Like *The Horrible House on the Hill*, *The Candy Snatchers* stands as yet another case of a low-rent distributor swiping the distinctive look of Hallmark's *Last House* ad campaign. National General Pictures promoted *The Candy Snatchers* with the tag-line "VIOLENCE… BEYOND *LAST HOUSE ON THE LEFT* !" Where the *Last House* ads screamed "MARI, 17 IS DYING… EVEN FOR HER THE WORST IS YET TO COME!" the *Candy Snatchers* campaign blared "FOR 16 YEAR OLD CANDY, DYING WOULD HAVE BEEN EASIER!" To top it off, a still photograph used in certain *Candy Snatchers* ads is very similar to the shot of Krug, Weasel, and Sadie that adorned many newspaper ads for *Last House*.

Downbeat and cynical, *The Candy Snatchers* recalls the misanthropic crime novels of Jim Thompson in its tale of a kidnapping gone wrong. The film centers on the abduction of innocent Catholic schoolgirl Candy (Susan Sennet) by a trio of would-be extortionists. The young criminals (two male, one female) bury Candy alive in a ventilated coffin and demand a ransom of diamonds from their captive's stepfather. The plan soon falls apart when the cold-blooded stepdad refuses to pay up, revealing that he is the heir to Candy's fortune and only too happy to see his daughter disappear. Meanwhile, a mute little boy (who is abused relentlessly by his mother in a sordid subplot) attempts to help Candy escape her premature burial. Much unpleasantness follows (including torture, rape, murder and a home invasion) culminating in a suitably bleak, miserable ending. Memorable line: every word out of the mute boy's mouth.

If *The Candy Snatchers* suggests a lurid '70s TV movie, it's no surprise; director Guerdon Trueblood went on to script several television movies-of-the-week (*SST: Death Flight*, *Tarantulas: The Deadly Cargo*, *The Savage Bees*) as well as *Jaws 3D* (1983). In an odd, coincidental link to the Craven canon, *The Candy Snatchers* features actor James Whitworth as a telephone man who beats up the would-be criminals when they try to steal his truck. Whitworth, Craven aficionados will recall, later portrayed Papa Jupiter in *The Hills Have Eyes*.

The title *Last House on the Left II* has been associated with at least three different ventures, two of them retitled European movies, and the third being an official U.S. sequel that never got beyond the planning stages. Independent distributor Alexander Beck (who served as executive producer on the 1980 slasher classic *Mother's Day*) was apparently selling a feature by that name at the 1982 Cannes Film Festival which may in fact have been yet another retitling of *L'Ultimo Treno Della Notte*. In the mid-'70s, the irrepressible Hallmark hucksters attached the title *Last House-Part II* to prints of Mario Bava's *A Bay of Blood* (1971), which the company had released twice (!) before: as *Carnage* in 1972, and in 1973 as *Twitch of the Death Nerve*. Fans might remember Hallmark's distinctive radio commercials for *Twitch*, which made prominent use of a jawharp ("*Twitch... twang!... of the Death Nerve!*")

Posters for *Last House - Part II* featured a huge photo of David Hess, who was, of course, not in the Bava film. However, Hess' visage may well have appeared in the product which was hawked as *Last House - Part II*. Steve Miner, who worked with the men behind Hallmark on the *Friday the 13th* movies, commented that "the distributor would take a couple of foreign films, mix up the reels with some footage from *Last House on the Left*, and release the result as a sequel."

The 'official' sequel to *Last House* was slated to be shot on location in Wisconsin in April of 1985 by director Danny (*Savage Streets*, *Friday the 13th Part V*) Steinmann. The project, known as *Beyond the Last House on the Left* or simply *Last House on the Left II*, originated with producers Steve Minasian and Philip Scuderi, who had wanted to do a sequel to the film for years. "I wrote a script for a *Last House* sequel for Phil Scuderi, which had Krug and Weasel coming

Rip-Offs And Rehashes

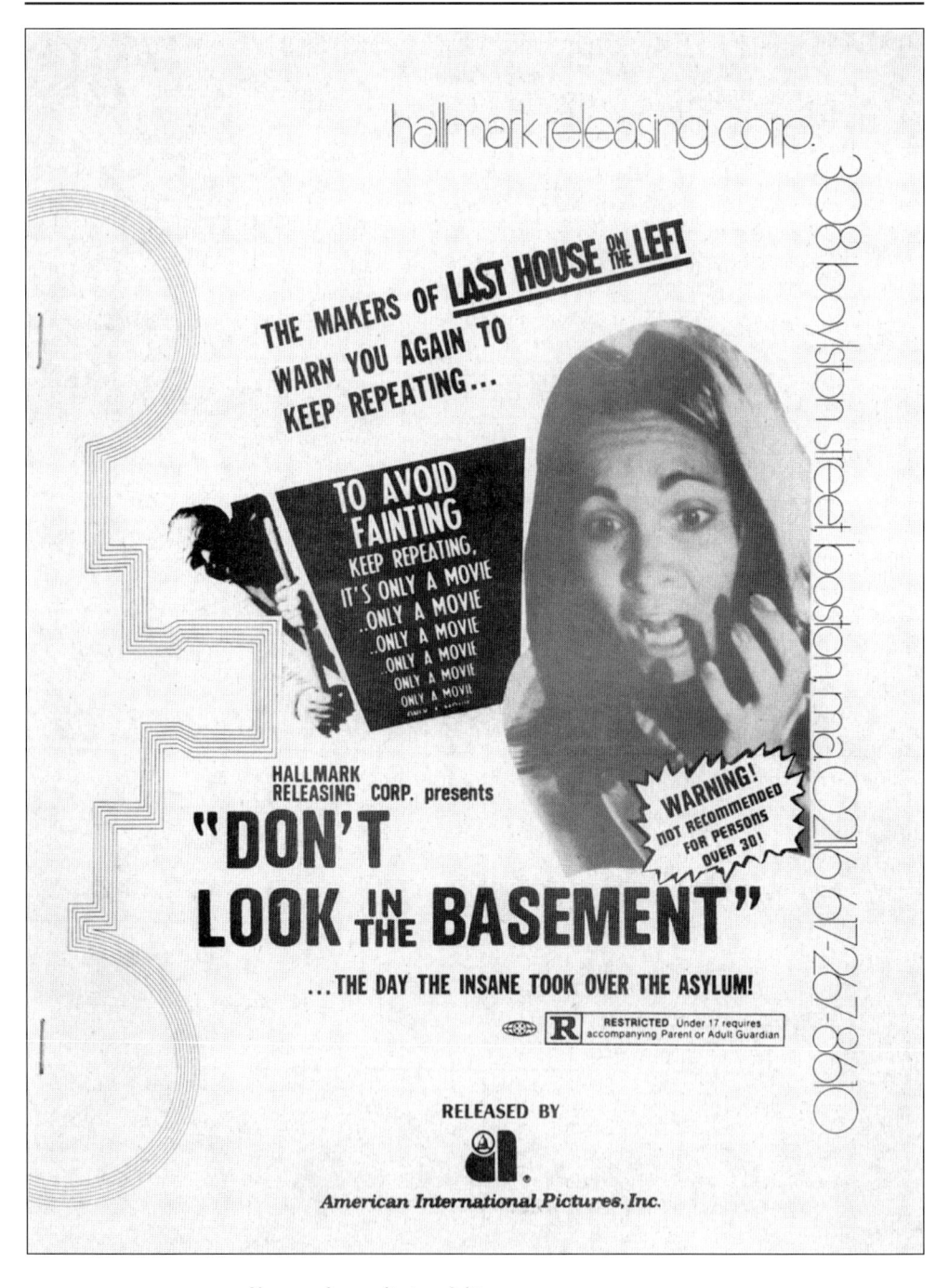

Above and opposite top right:

Hallmark Releasing was one of the first companies to jump on its own bandwagon by hyping S.F. Brownrigg's *Don't Look in the Basement* (1973) as the latest offering from *"THE MAKERS OF **LAST HOUSE ON THE LEFT**."* Trailers for the Brownrigg film even included scenes from *Last House*. Shot in Mexia, Texas in 1972 and briefly released in the South by Cine Globe under its original title, *The Forgotten*, *Don't Look...* is a deranged classic in its own right about inmates who take over an insane asylum. "I've never seen *Last House on the Left*," Brownrigg commented in a 1989 conversation with the author.

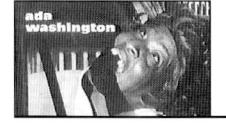

back from Hell," Wes Craven laughs. "But he decided he wanted to go in a different direction." An outline of the script for the proposed Danny Steinmann sequel appeared in Fangoria magazine as transcribed below:

"Krug, the ringleader of the band of sadists in the first Last House picture, returns in the sequel, now making his home on an isolated island with a group of reprobate friends. Krug will be played once more by David Hess. In what Steinmann describes as a Deliverance style situation, a group of kids on a rafting trip gets lost and winds up on Krug's island. Grisly terror no doubt awaits them..."[5]

Cassettes of Vestron Video's heavily-censored 1985 release of Last House on the Left included a series of video titles after the feature announcing that Last House on the Left II ("The House that set the standard for terror... You won't believe your eyes!") was "coming soon". This aborted sequel was essentially the last gasp of the Last House rip-off craze. With the above scenario in mind, perhaps it is a blessing that Steinmann's follow-up never materialized.

Of his involvement with the project David Hess says, "I saw a couple of different scripts, and one was worse than the next... it kind of fizzled. At one time they were going do set it at a summer camp. Danny and I had a lot of talks about it, and we didn't want to make a straight slasher movie... we thought that once we got on the set, we could work with it and make it more interesting. After all, it would seem to me that it would be pretty hard to make a sequel to Last House on the Left; I mean, how are you going to better it?"

Notes

1   New House on the Left was double-billed at American drive-ins with a British film, Terror from Under the House (1971, aka Revenge, Inn of the Frightened People) which starred Joan Collins. New House also played on drive-in bills with Hallmark imports like Don't Open the Window.

2   Lado's film is not to be confused with 1979's Torture Train (aka Terror Express, Ragazza del Vagone Letto), a similarly-themed Italo-sleaze epic directed by Ferdinando Baldi.

3   The editing of the Christmas dinner sequence in L'Ultimo Treno della'Notte bears an intentional resemblance to the scene in Last House where Craven cuts back and forth from the Collingwoods preparing Mari's birthday cake to the girls being abducted by Krug and his gang. (see Chapter IV)

4   House by the Lake was also double-billed with Last House on the Left during a 1981 re-release after AIP became Filmways.

5   David Everitt, "After the Final Chapter: Friday the 13th V", Fangoria, Vol. 3, Issue #44, p.23

Chapter 9

Last Thoughts On The House

Author's Note: At the conclusion of every interview I conducted for this book, I asked the subject for a few summary thoughts about *Last House on the Left*. Their answers reflect the wildly divergent reactions which the film has always provoked.
- D.S.

Wes Craven: "I don't watch *Last House on the Left* very often; I can't remember the last time that I did watch it, but it was quite some time ago. It's a very heavy and dark film, and it's not one that's pleasant to watch. I have noticed, or had to acknowledge, that many times people will say to me, 'That was your best film,' or, 'That was your most powerful film'… that it's the film that has affected them the most out of all the films I've made. It has an intensity level to it that was not easy to attain. It's so raw and horrific… you know, it's not something that I sit down and watch for my own pleasure."

Sean Cunningham: "*Last House* was just fooling around. I'm not even remotely interested in making a movie like that today. You're just there at a particular time, and a door opens, and you walk through it; you don't know what's going to be there on the other side of that door. There's no thought of, 'Is this a career move?' or, 'Is this something I really want to do?' or 'Is this something that I'm even going to be talking about twenty-five years from now?' I can't emphasize enough how far removed *Last House* was from anything like that! The real question at the time was, 'Could this ever be shot and cut into something that looks like a movie?!' I think one of the reasons why the film continued to be so successful, in however limited a way, is that in spite of its clear amateur quality, the story was strong enough to carry it. And also, I think there's something about its lack of polish (that's a kind way of putting it!) that other young film makers can look at it and say, 'I could make a movie as bad as that!' It seems accessible. 'I may not be able to shoot like Bob Zemeckis, but I could shoot *that*!' So I think at some level that's one of the reasons *Last House on the Left* seems to keep perennially popping up in various places. But I'm certainly glad to have made it, because it made a whole bunch of other things possible."

David Hess: "It's nice that the people who started out their careers with *Last House* have, in some cases, remained good friends. There's something about life that's bigger than just making films, or doing any kind of work, and that's the people that you meet, that you have something in common with, and that you maintain a friendship with. And *Last House on the Left* has done that for me. I've always felt that *Last House* was an *other*-driven movie; it wasn't an earth-driven movie, it was created by some other kind of force, because all of us have gone on to do many other things, but none of us have ever made anything that had the initial impact of *Last House on the Left*... it was like we were tools of something else! There has never been another movie like it, nor will there be!"

Lucy Grantham: "My feeling about *Last House on the Left* is that it was a stroke of genius. It was a defining moment in film history, and Wes and Sean had the creative foresight that it takes to break ground. When you talk about breaking ground, you talk about Picasso, or about certain musicians who led the way, who broke with tradition and began a new form of the arts. I put *Last House on the Left* in the same category. Of course, by today's standards, it's not that scary, because these kids have seen so much, with *Jason Goes to Hell* and all that stuff. But when you put *Last House* in its correct time-frame, it's remarkable, it's gutsy, and it has a wonderful combination of humor and horror. I know Wes prides himself on being able to do that, and a lot of people have tried and failed. It almost *took* hindsight to be able to appreciate the vision, the ground-breaking genius behind the concept of *Last House on the Left*. It was almost an out-of-body experience to be part of something that was so revolutionary. We really gave our all."

Sandra Peabody: "I have not seen this film in a long time, so to recollect it is hard. Wes and Sean did a great job considering the limited amount of money that they had... to pull something together like they did took a lot of work. It was really a work in progress... it changed a lot as we were making it. *Last House* was pretty advanced for its time as far as violence... but now I guess it's kind of a funny film. I was really upset and horrified when I first saw it."

Richard Towers: "Some years after we made *Last House on the Left*, a friend of mine came to me and asked me if I would go with him down to the Village, where they were showing the picture to an audience of people who follow these kinds of movies. I said, 'Well, of course!' We went to this room... it was kind of a big room, dark, and there were all of these people, who were kind of weird-looking and out of it, with the whole 'head' thing in those days. So towards the end of the picture, the person I was with had me stand behind a curtain with a chainsaw... and as soon as it ended, I came out from behind that curtain with the saw buzzing and started to walk very menacingly towards one of the girls in the front row. She saw me with the saw and started to scream like nothing you've ever heard in your life... and the whole place broke up!"

Marc Sheffler: "It's still pretty strange! I look at it now with a kind of dual vision, because I'm a lot older now, and I know a lot more... I think that it was definitely a precursor and a pioneer in that genre of films. It's an extremely pure film; it's not cluttered with a lot of nonsense. It's also an extremely frightening film to this day, without relying on a lot of car chases and special effects. It's interesting to balance out the murderous vision that the film is with the fact that we all had a party making it. The negative intensity of the film on camera was balanced by an extremely positive and jovial *laissez-faire* attitude in making it."

Martin Kove: "I don't particularly like *Last House on the Left*. I have two babies, and it's a little horrific for me to digest that kind of madness. I looked at the film about five years ago [1991] and I didn't much care for it… biting off penises and killing people with chainsaws, it's not my cup of tea. I thought looking at the film again, it'd be different… but it is what it was… exactly the kind of movie that five years later I never would have made. But, everybody's got a beginning."

Marshall Anker: "Well, I had fun doing it because I enjoyed the comic scenes and Wes Craven allowed me to improvise and ad-lib. You might say that he was that way because he was a beginner, a neophyte. But except for my scenes, I don't like the movie."

Fred Lincoln: "I would feel so terrible if somebody went out and did something to somebody's daughter because of that movie."

Jeramie Rain: "I believe that *Last House on the Left* is truly the worst movie ever made… and I'm proud to have been a part of it! *(laughs)* Seriously, it's the biggest embarrassment, and I apologize to my children for being in it. It has no redeeming qualities. It does have a cult following, but I'm not proud of it at all… I would hate to think of anyone being harmed or hurt because of something I did. That's not what I want to contribute to the world… I'd rather do positive things with my life."

Yvonne Hannemann: "I never saw the film. It was never anything I was terribly proud of. Nobody I know bought a ticket and went to see it, but everybody I know seems to have seen the title on a marquee, in places like Hong Kong, Peru, and Rio… it was always the subject for a lot of jokes. I always thought it was aimed at the drive-in market, like out *there* in Indiana or New Jersey. It still is amazing to me that it was so successful… I don't quite know why it became this cult movie; I guess it was just the sadistic side of it. The one thing I learned from *Last House* is how much one can do in the editing room."

Steve Miner: "I think the main influence *Last House* had on all of us was that we learned from the mistakes we made, and tried not to make them again."

Steve Chapin: "I have to laugh about the film when I look back on it. The whole thing was a trip, because everybody I met who worked on the movie were such nice, sweet people… and they turned out this fuckin' meatball film with all this blood, guts and gore! It was almost like a joke, like Wes and Sean wanted to see how much they could get away with on people. At the same time, the movie really affected me; it crossed barriers that I didn't think could be crossed. It reminds me of these kids today who strangle each other during sexual intercourse in order to heighten their orgasms… you hear about it, and you say, 'How in the hell could they do that?!'"

Jim Hubbard: "When you're working on the crew of a movie like *Last House*, you're paying attention to business. You just do what has to be done, and you don't stop to think about how the film is going to come

Last Thoughts On The House

across when it's finished. It's therefore sometimes shocking when you see what an editor can do with the footage you've helped shoot; this was definitely the case with *Last House*. It was so much more gruesome and appalling than my impressions of its making that I was amazed."

Ray Edwards (the postman): "I don't care to talk about it."

David Whitten: "*Last House on the Left* is a solid, exciting film. I personally like the story; there's relatively little blood in the film, and there are scenes in it that are still really powerful. The dentist bit still grabs me! And I love standing in the back of a theater when Weasel's death scene comes up; the audience always goes nuts! My definition of a good film is one that gives the audience its money's worth, and I think *Last House* stands up to that test."

Steve Dwork: "Working on Last House was a fascinating experience for me, because it was the first real feature film with which I was involved. But other than the content, it was basically like any other job; it was a typical low-budget film shoot. I never thought it was going to become some kind of *Rocky Horror Picture Show* and I never sat down and watched it in its entirety."

Fred Lincoln: "There are some lessons to be learned here. Number One: Don't ever let anybody shoot a movie like this in your house. Number Two: If you get a girl, don't let her tie you up. And Number Three: If you're copping some dope, don't get it from anybody who looks like a frog."

Wes Craven (right) pictured circa 1981 with *Last House* archivist Roy Frumkes on the set of Craven's *Deadly Blessing*.

(courtesy Roy Frumkes)

LAST HOUSE ON THE LEFT   191

Appendix I

Selected Filmographies

Film titles shown first represent the on-screen title of the most commonly available version. Other commonly-used titles are also shown where appropriate.
The date given for each film represents the year of production, i.e. the year in which the film was ready for general release.

Special Thanks to Julian Grainger for assisting with the collation of these filmographies.

WES CRAVEN
born 2 August 1939 in Cleveland, OH
full name: Wesley Earl Craven

With the release of the acclaimed drama **Music of the Heart** and the publication of his novel **Fountain Society**, Wes Craven made headlines in 1999 for his departure from the genre that made him famous. Craven's emancipation from the mantle of 'horrormeister' is one he has longed for from the outset of his career; still, his fans will forever identify him with all things macabre. **Scream 3**, released in early 2000, will be the last in its series.

1971 **TOGETHER** (aka **Sensual Paradise**) (assistant producer) dir: Sean S. Cunningham
1971 **YOU GOT TO WALK IT LIKE YOU TALK IT, OR YOU'LL LOSE THAT BEAT** (co-editor) dir: Peter Locke
Locke, a producer of **The Hills Have Eyes** and co-founder of the highly successful Kushner-Locke production company, directed this obscure comedy movie which featured Robert Downey, Sr., Richard Pryor, Allen Garfield and Liz Torres. Craven was one of four editors who worked on it.
1972 **THE LAST HOUSE ON THE LEFT** (director/screenplay/editor)
1973 **IT HAPPENED IN HOLLYWOOD** (editor) dir: Peter Locke
1976 **TALES THAT WILL TEAR YOUR HEART OUT** (director of one segment - unreleased)
Craven directed a segment for Roy Frumkes' horror anthology film which was never finished. The piece, which was written by Allan Pasternak, was a horror-western in which Craven, David Hess and Roy Frumkes all appeared in supporting roles. One portion of **Tales** - not Craven's - showed up as a prologue to **Dr. Butcher, M.D.**, the Stateside release version of Italian shocker **Zombi Holocaust** (1980).
1977 **CARHOPS** (aka **California Drive In Girls**) (co-editor - credited as Wes 'hot tracks' Craven) dir: Peter Locke
1977 **THE HILLS HAVE EYES** (director/screenplay/editor)
1978 **HERE COME THE TIGERS** (cameo appearance)
1978 **STRANGER IN OUR HOUSE** (tv movie, aka **Summer of Fear**) (director) [tx 31/10/78 on NBC]
1981 **DEADLY BLESSING** (director/co-screenplay)
1981 **SWAMP THING** (director/screenplay)
1984 **THE HILLS HAVE EYES PART II** (director/screenplay)
1984 **A NIGHTMARE ON ELM STREET** (director/screenplay)
1984 **INVITATION TO HELL** (tv movie, director) [tx 24/5/1984 ABC]
1985 **CHILLER** (tv movie, director) [tx 22/5/1985 CBS]
1985 **A NIGHTMARE ON ELM STREET PART 2 FREDDY'S REVENGE** (original characters) dir: Jack Sholder
1985-86 **THE TWILIGHT ZONE** (tv series, director - 7 episodes)
    A Little Peace and Quiet [tx 27/9/1985 CBS]
    Shatterday [tx 27/9/1985 CBS]
    Word Play [tx 4/10/1985 CBS]
    Chameleon [tx 4/10/1985 CBS]
    Dealer's Choice [tx 15/11/1985 CBS]
    Pilgrim Soul [tx 13/12/1985 CBS]
    The Road Less Travelled [18/12/1986 CBS]

opposite top & right:
Craven directing his segment of
Tales That Will Tear Your Heart Out.

(courtesy Roy Frumkes)

Appendix I

1986 **DEADLY FRIEND** (director)
1986 **FANGORIA'S WEEKEND OF HORRORS** (video documentary) dir: Rex Piano
1986 **CASEBUSTERS** (tv special, director) [tx 25/5/1986 ABC]
1987 **FLOWERS IN THE ATTIC** (screenwriter) dir: Jeffrey Bloom
1987 **A NIGHTMARE ON ELM STREET 3 DREAM WARRIORS** (co-executive producer/co-screenplay/story) dir: Chuck Russell
1988 **THE SERPENT AND THE RAINBOW** (director)
1988 **A NIGHTMARE ON ELM STREET 4 THE DREAM MASTER** (original characters) dir: Renny Harlin
1988-90 **FREDDY'S NIGHTMARES** (tv series, original characters) [tx 8/10/1988-12/3/1990]
1989 **SHOCKER** (director/executive producer/screenplay/acts as male neighbour)
1989 **THE PEOPLE NEXT DOOR** (tv series, executive producer)
1989 **A NIGHTMARE ON ELM STREET 5 THE FINAL NIGHTMARE** (original characters) dir: Stephen Hopkins
1990 **BLOODFIST II** (advisor) dir: Andy Blumenthal
1990 **NIGHT VISIONS** (tv movie, director/executive producer/co-screenplay) [tx 30/11/1990 NBC]
1991 **THE PEOPLE UNDER THE STAIRS** (director/co-exec producer/ screenplay)
1991 **FREDDY'S DEAD THE FINAL NIGHTMARE** (original characters) dir: Rachel Talalay
1991 **FEAR IN THE DARK** (UK, tv documentary) dir: Dominic Murphy [tx 31/10/1991 Channel 4]
1992 **NIGHTMARE CAFÉ** (tv series, creator/writer/executive producer)
    Aliens Ate My Lunch (episode director) [tx 3/4/1992 NBC]
1993 **LAUREL CANYON** (tv pilot, creator/executive producer)
1993 **BODY BAGS** (anthology tv movie) [as pasty-faced man in "The Gas Station" segment] dir: John Carpenter
1994 **WES CRAVEN'S NEW NIGHTMARE** (director/screenplay/acts as himself)
1994 **HALLOWEEN!** (tv special) (cameo) dir: Rob Dustin [tx 29/10/1994 CBS]
1995 **VAMPIRE IN BROOKLYN** (director)
1995 **ANATOMY OF HORROR** (tv documentary) (interviewee) [tx 22/8/1995 UPN]
1995 **MIND RIPPER / THE OUTPOST** (aka **The Hills Have Eyes III The Outpost**) (executive producer) dir: Joe Gayton
1995 **THE FEAR** (aka **Morty**) [as Doctor Arnold] dir: Vincent Robert
1996 **SHADOWZONE THE UNDEAD EXPRESS** (tv movie, act as counsellor) dir: Stephen Williams [tx 27/10/1996 Showtime]

1996 **SCREAM** (aka **Scary Movie**) (director/uncredited act as Fred the janitor)
1997 **WISHMASTER** (executive producer) dir: Robert Kurtzman
1997 **SCREAM 2** (aka **Scream Again** / **Scream the Sequel**) (director)
1998 **DON'T LOOK DOWN** (TV movie, executive producer)
1998 **CARNIVAL OF SOULS** (executive producer)
1998 **HOLLYWEIRD** (TV series, executive producer)
1999 **HITCHCOCK: SHADOW OF A GENIUS** (TV documentary)
1999 **MUSIC OF THE HEART** (director)
2000 **SCREAM 3** (director)

SEAN S. CUNNINGHAM
born 31 December 1941 in New York, NY

Like Wes Craven, Sean Cunningham never intended to become a horror movie director. Nonetheless, his latest venture is the long-awaited **Freddy Vs. Jason**, which pits Craven's Freddy Krueger character against the hockey-masked killer from the **Friday the 13th** films. "For whatever reason, Freddy and Jason have become pop icons... who knows why, but they are," he said in 1997. "If you turn to any... boy [laughs] under 30, and say, 'Freddy Vs. Jason,' they say, 'Cool, man!! Bitchin'!' I don't know quite what they expect, but I think an awful lot of people are going to go see it."

1970 **THE ART OF MARRIAGE** (director/producer)
1971 **TOGETHER** (director/co-producer)
1972 **THE LAST HOUSE ON THE LEFT** (producer / a Sean Cunningham Films Ltd. presentation)
dir: Wes Craven
1973 **THE CASE OF THE SMILING STIFFS** (aka **The Case of the Full Moon Murders**, **Sex on the Groove Tube**; original working title **Silver C.**) (co-director/co-producer - both with Brud Talbot)
1976 **THE PEOPLE WHO OWN THE DARK** (aka **Ultimo Deseo** (original release title), **Planeta Ciego** (shooting title), **Blind Planet**). Cunningham was the uncredited co-producer of this Spanish movie directed by León Klimovsky. Cunningham was also involved during script development.
1978 **HERE COME THE TIGERS** (director/co-producer with Hallmark)
1978 **KICK!** (aka **Manny's Orphans**) (director/co-producer)
1980 **FRIDAY THE 13th** (director/producer)

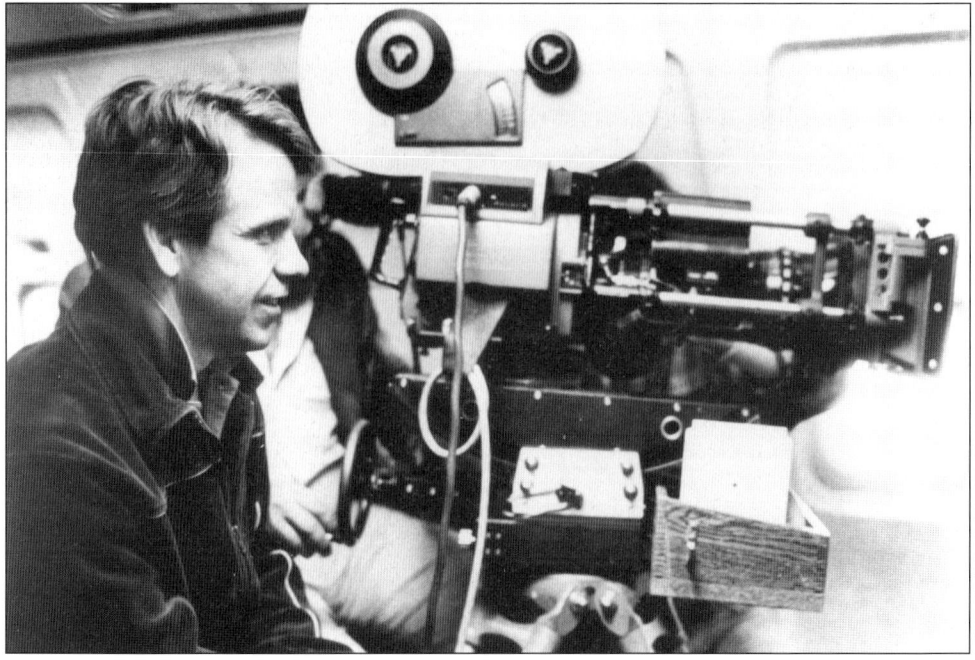

courtesy Cunningham Productions

Appendix I

1981 **A STRANGER IS WATCHING** (director)
1983 **SPRING BREAK** (director/producer)
1985 **THE NEW KIDS** aka **Striking Back** (director/producer)
1986 **HOUSE** (1986) (producer) dir: Steve Miner
1987 **HOUSE II THE SECOND STORY** (producer) dir: Ethan Wiley
1989 **THE HORROR SHOW** (aka **House III The Horror Show**) (producer)
dir: James Isaac, [uncredited] Fred Walton & David Blythe
1989 **DEEP STAR SIX** (director/producer)
1991 **HOUSE IV THE REPOSSESSION** (producer) dir: Lewis Abernathy
1993 **MY BOYFRIEND'S BACK** (producer) dir: Bob Balaban
1993 **JASON GOES TO HELL: THE FINAL FRIDAY** (producer)
dir: Adam Marcus
2000 **FREDDY VS. JASON** (in production)
2000 **JASON X: FRIDAY THE 13th PART 10** (executive producer - in production)

DAVID A. HESS
full name: David Alexander Hess
born: 1942, New York (some sources list 1936)

David Hess moved to Europe shortly after the release of **Last House** to run a record label, and picked up acting again in 1974. "After doing music for two years, I started doing a lot of dubbing for European films as a way to supplement my income," he explains. "I would travel from Munich, to Paris, to Rome, dubbing European films into English. These films were selling pretty well to the United States at the time, so there was a fair amount of money to be made. I got to know a lot of foreign distribution people and a lot of producers. I had been working on dubbing a film for John Derek, and the guy who was producing the movie with John was moving on to another film. He asked me to come and meet the director, who ended up really liking me. So I did that film, **The Swiss Conspiracy**, with David Janssen, and my acting career in Europe was on the way." After ten years of living and working in Europe, Hess moved back to America. He now lives in California with his wife and three children, and continues to be active in music and movies.

as actor:
1972 **THE LAST HOUSE ON THE LEFT**
[as Krug Stillo] dir: Wes Craven
Hess also composed the film's original score.
1973 **THE BATTLE OF MANCHURIA** [voice]
dir: Satsu Yamamoto
This was a condensed 90 minute English language version of **Senso To Ningen** (1970), a film made in three parts of approximately 3 hours each.
1975 **THE SWISS CONSPIRACY** [as Tony Sando]
dir: Jack Arnold
1975 **POTATO FRITZ** (aka **Montana Trap**)
dir: Peter Schamoni
1976 **21 HOURS AT MUNICH** (tv movie shown in cinemas) [as Berger] dir: William A. Graham
1976 **TALES THAT WILL TEAR YOUR HEART OUT** [an outlaw] seg. dir: Wes Craven
Hess played an outlaw in Wes Craven's 'zombie western' segment of this unreleased anthology film produced by Roy Frumkes. (See illustrations on the next page)
1977 **HITCH-HIKE** (Italy, aka **Autostop... rosso sangue** / **Death Drive** / allegedly aka **Never Give A Lift To A Stranger**) [as Adam Konitz]
dir: Pasquale Squitieri

1979 **AVALANCHE EXPRESS** [as Geiger] dir: Mark Robson & Monte Hellman
1979 **HOUSE ON THE EDGE OF THE PARK** (**La casa sperduta nel parco**, Italy) [as Alex] dir: Ruggero Deodato
1981 **SLOW ATTACK** (original title: **Endstazione Freiheit**) dir: Reinhard Hauff
1981 **VALLEY OF THE DOLLS** (tv mini-series) [as Robaire] dir: Walter Grauman
1981 **WHITE STAR** (West Germany, re-released with added footage as **Let It Rock**) [as Frank] dir: Roland Klick
"White Star was an interesting film - it was the story of Jesus put into a heavy metal situation!" Hess says. "I played Judas and Dennis Hopper played St. Peter."
1982 **SWAMP THING** [as Ferret] dir: Wes Craven
Marks the reunion of Hess and Wes Craven.
1983 **SADAT** (tv mini-series) [as an Israeli soldier] dir: Richard Michaels
1986 **ARMED AND DANGEROUS** [as an ice cream vendor] dir: Mark L. Lester
1986 **LET'S GET HARRY** [as mercenary] dir: Stuart Rosenberg
1986 **BODYCOUNT** (**Camping del terrore**, Italy) [as Robert] dir: Ruggero Deodato - Hess maintains that he also co-directed some of this slasher film.
1987 **SURRENDER** [as man at party] dir: Jerry Schatzberg
1988 **14 GOING ON 30** (tv movie) [as host] dir: Paul Schneider
1988 **TO HEAL A NATION** (tv movie) [as anchorman] dir: Michael Pressman
1988 **MAYBE BABY** (tv movie) [as Maitre'd] dir: Tom Moore
1988 **OCEANO** (tv mini-series, Italy) dir: Ruggero Deodato
1989 **VENETIAN SYNDROME** (**Sindrome Veneziana**, Italy) dir: Carlo V. Quinterio
1990 **DIE KALTENBACH-PAPIERE** (tv mini-series, Germany, aka **The Kaltenbach Papers**)
1991 **BUCK AT THE EDGE OF HEAVEN** (**Buck ai confini del cielo**; Italy/Switzerland, aka **The Invincible Buck**) dir: Anthony Richmond [Tonino Ricci] Hess also scored this wilderness story, which co-starred John Savage.
1992 **BLUE LIGHT MURDER** (**Omicidi a luci blu**, Italy, aka **Murder In A Blue Night**) [as a cop] dir: Al Bradley [Alfonso Brescia]
1994 **JONATHAN OF THE BEARS** (**Jonathan degli orsi**, Italy/Russia) [as Maddock] dir: Enzo G. Castellari [Enzo Girolami] This is Castellari's semi-sequel / remake of his 1976 western **Keoma: The Violent Breed**.
1995 **NOI SIAMO ANGELI** (tv mini-series, Italy, aka **We Are Angels**) [as prison captain] dir: Ruggero Deodato

Illustrations above show David Hess in the unreleased *Tales That Will Tear Your Heart Out.*

Appendix I

as director:
1980 **TO ALL A GOODNIGHT**
Having done much to further the cause of splatter in **Last House**, it was only fitting that Hess eventually directed his own entry in the craze. Although Hess does not act in the movie, which concerns a psycho in a Santa Claus getup making mince-meat out of a group of teens, his sister Judy appears in a supporting role.

as producer:
1994 **NIKI DE SAINT PHALLE: WER IST DAS MONSTER - DU ODER ICH?** (aka: **Figuren der Freude**, **Niki De Saint Phalle: Who is the Monster, You or Me?** dir: Peter Schamoni
Hess was one of four producers on this documentary by German art film director Schamoni about Niki de St. Phalle, a controversial avant-garde sculptress and performance artist who first gained notoriety in the '60s.

as ass't producer :
1991 **MAX ERNST: MEIN VAGABUNDIEREN - MEINE UNRUHE** dir: Peter Schamoni

SANDRA PEABODY
aka Sandra Cassell

Sandra Peabody (a.k.a. Sandra Cassell) grew up in the Miami, Florida area where she began acting as a young girl. Her first appearance was in a '60s educational film about drug abuse called **Misfit**. "That film was made by a company from the New York area, and before the shoot, one of the actresses got sick, so they went to all these different schools and auditioned people," she explains. "After that, I started getting roles in low-budget drive-in movies that were being shot in Florida. The first one was called **The Horse Killer**. It was actually based on the true story of a man who castrated horses! It was a really bizarre story, but it wasn't like **Last House**, with sex or murder. It was more of a mystery, where these incidents were happening and they were trying to find this weird guy who was doing it. I was playing the girlfriend, and we had a lot of scenes riding horses and that sort of thing." She later studied acting for two years in New York, and after playing Mari in **Last House** went on to a role in a New York-lensed feature called **The Seven Deadly Sins** (which was later renamed, though she doesn't recall the other title). She appeared on television in commercials and on two soap operas, **All My Children** and **As the World Turns**. Moving to the West Coast, she crossed over from acting into writing and producing children's television, which has been her main avocation for over twenty years. She also teaches acting classes and has worked as a talent agent. Among Sandra's recent producing credits is a series for public television called **Zone In**, which deals with "tough issues for kids."

1970 **THE HORSE KILLER**
1971 **FILTHIEST SHOW IN TOWN** [as Olga in commercials]
dir: Rick Endelson & Robert Endelson
1972 **THE LAST HOUSE ON THE LEFT** dir: Wes Craven
197? **THE SEVEN DEADLY SINS**

STEVE MINER
born 18 June 1951 in Chicago, IL
full name: Stephen C. Miner

Since getting his start as a lowly P.A. on the set of **Last House on the Left**, Steve Miner has risen to become a successful Hollywood director in his own right. His friendship with Wes Craven and Sean Cunningham continues to this day. In addition to directing two sequels to **Friday the 13th**, Miner recently handled the directorial reins for the **Scream**-influenced **Halloween:H20**, the pilot for the TV series **Dawson's Creek**, and the popular killer crocodile horror comedy **Lake Placid**.

1972 **THE LAST HOUSE ON THE LEFT** (production assistant/assistant editor) dir: Wes Craven
1973 **THE CASE OF THE SMILING STIFFS** (aka **The Case of the Full Moon Murders**)
(editor - as Stephen Miner) dirs: Sean S. Cunningham & Brud Talbot
1978 **HERE COME THE TIGERS** (co-producer/editor) dir: Sean S. Cunningham
1978 **KICK!** (aka **Manny's Orphans**) (co-producer/story) dir: Sean S. Cunningham
1980 **FRIDAY THE 13th** (associate producer / unit production manager) dir: Sean S. Cunningham

Appendix I

1981 **FRIDAY THE 13th PART 2** (director/producer)
1982 **FRIDAY THE 13th PART 3 IN 3D** (director / acts as newscaster)
1986 **SOUL MAN** (director)
1986 **HOUSE** (director)
1988 **THE WONDER YEARS** (tv pilot & many episodes over the years) (director / supervising producer) [tx ABC]
1989 **WARLOCK** (director/producer)
1989 **B-MEN** (tv pilot) (director) [tx 27/6/89 CBS]
1990 **ELVIS** (aka **Elvis Good Rockin' Tonight**) (tv pilot/series) (director) [tx ABC]
1991 **MAVERICK SQUARE** (tv pilot) (director/executive producer/story)
1991 **WILD HEARTS CAN'T BE BROKEN** (director)
1992 **FOREVER YOUNG** (director)
1992 **LAUREL HILL** (tv pilot) (director)
1993 **AGAINST THE GRAIN** (tv pilot) (director)
1994 **MY FATHER THE HERO** (aka **Daddy Cool**) (director)
1995 **BIG BULLY** (director)
1997 **THE PRACTICE** (TV Series)
1998 **DAWSON'S CREEK** (TV Series)
1998 **HALLOWEEN H20: TWENTY YEARS LATER**
1999 **LAKE PLACID** (director)
1999 **WASTELAND** (TV Series)
2000 **TEXAS RANGERS**

JERAMIE RAIN
born West Virginia, 1949

Jeramie Rain started working as a production assistant for NBC television shortly after appearing as Sadie in **Last House on the Left**. Around the same time, Rain also had a regular role as "Sam Tolliver" in a popular NBC soap opera called **The Doctors**. She then moved to Los Angeles, where she worked as a writer/producer for NBC and later for CBS. She met actor Richard Dreyfuss at a Hollywood party, and they married three months later in March, 1982. Though currently separated, the couple were married for over eight years and have three children. "I asked Richard not to watch **Last House on the Left**, but he went out and got a copy anyway, and my kids ended up seeing it," Rain groans. "Now, my kids love to tease me about the fact that I was in the worst movie of all time!"

1971 **THE ABDUCTORS** dir: Don Schain
1972 **THE LAST HOUSE ON THE LEFT** [as Sadie] dir: Wes Craven
1972 **PREACHERMAN MEETS WIDDERWOMAN** [as Willie Mae] dir: Albert T. Viola

Appendix I

MARSHALL ANKER

In contrast to his role as the redneck sheriff in Last House on the Left, Brooklyn-born actor Marshall Anker is a self-proclaimed ex-beatnik. He has lived in Greenwich Village for over 30 years. Since **Last House**, Marshall has appeared in over 300 feature films as an extra. He also directed stage versions of Woody Allen's **Play It Again, Sa**m and Moliere's **School for Wives**. His most recent film appearance was in an independent feature film called **Karma Local** which screened at the 1997 Sundance Film Festival

selected filmography:
1971 **FILTHIEST SHOW IN TOWN** (aka **The Maiden Game**) [as bailiff in court case]
dir: Rick Endelson & Robert Endelson
1972 **THE LAST HOUSE ON THE LEFT** [as the sheriff] dir: Wes Craven
1973 **SHAMUS** [as a poker dealer] dir: Buzz Kulik
1988 **COOKIE** [as the head of the parole board] dir: Susan Seidelman
1996 **KARMA LOCAL** [as "The Old Man"] dir: Darshan Parlakian

MARTIN KOVE
born 6 March 1947 in Brooklyn, NY

The most well-known face in the cast of **Last House on the Left**, Martin Kove has enjoyed a steady acting career in both movies and television. His most popular roles include that of Kreese, the evil martial arts instructor of the **Karate Kid** films, and a long-running stint on TV's **Cagney and Lacey** where, as in **Last House**, he played a cop. Born and raised in New York, Kove moved to California in 1974 and began landing parts in numerous theatrical and made-for-TV features. While being interviewed for this book, he was working on a Tarantino-esque film called **Top of the World**, in which he appeared opposite Dennis Hopper.

1969 **WOMEN IN REVOLT** [as Marty] dir: Paul Morrissey
1970 **WHERE'S POPPA** [uncredited, as man in courtroom] (aka **Going Ape**) dir: Carl Reiner
1971 **LITTLE MURDERS** [uncredited] dir; Alan Arkin
1971 **SAVAGES** [as Archie] dir: James Ivory
1972 **THE LAST HOUSE ON THE LEFT** [as deputy]
dir: Wes Craven
1973 **JANICE** dir: Joseph Strick
1973 **COPS AND ROBBERS**
[as ambulance attendant] dir: Aram Avakian
1974 **THE WILD PARTY** [as the editor]
dir: James Ivory
1974 **THE SPY WHO RETURNED FROM THE DEAD** (tv movie) [tx 8/1/1974 ABC]
1975 **WHITE LINE FEVER** [as Clem]
dir: Jonathan Kaplan
1975 **THE FOUR DEUCES** [as Smokey Ross, 'The Deuce of Diamonds'] dir: William H. Bushnell Jr.
1975 **DEATH RACE 2000** [as Nero the Hero]
dir: Paul Bartel
1975 **CAPONE** [as Pete Gusenberg] dir: Steve Carver
1976 **KINGSTON THE POWER PLAY** (tv movie)
[as Deeley] dir: Robert Day [tx 15/9/1976 NBC]
1976 **THE NOVEMBER PLAN** (tv movie - originally shown as 1st three episodes of series "City of Angels") [as Stan] dir: Don Medford
1976 **THE CAPTAINS AND THE KINGS**
(tv mini-series) dirs: Douglas Heyes & Allen Reisner
[tx 30/9 - 11/11/76 NBC]

Appendix I

1977 **WHITE BUFFALO** (aka **Hunt to Kill**) [as Jack McCall]
dir: J. Lee Thompson
1977 **MR BILLION** [as Texas gambler] dir: Jonathan Kaplan
1977 **"CODE R"** (CBS tv series) [as George Baker]
1977-78 **WE'VE GOT EACH OTHER** (CBS tv series)
[as Ken Redford]
1978 **DONOVAN'S KID** (tv special for "Walt Disney Presents")
[as Kelso] dir: Bernard McEveety [tx 14+21/1/1979 NBC]
1978 **SKYTRAP** (tv special for "World of Disney")
dir: Jerome Courtland [tx 13/5/1979 NBC]
1979 **SEVEN** [as Skip] dir: Andy Sidaris
1980 **TROUBLE IN HIGH TIMBER COUNTY** (tv pilot for "The Yeagers") [as Willie Yeager] dir: Vincent Sherman
[tx 27/6/1980 ABC]
1980 **LABORATORY** [as Jerry Hanson]
dirs: Robert Emenegger & Allan Sandler
1980 **BLOOD TIDE** (aka **Red Tide**) [as Neil Gries]
dir: Richard Jeffries
1982 **CRY FOR THE STRANGERS** (tv movie) [as Jeff] dir: Peter Medak [tx 11/12/1982 CBS]
1982 **THE EDGE OF NIGHT** (ABC tv series) [as Romeo Slade]
1982 **PARTNERS** dir: James Burrows
1982-88 **CAGNEY AND LACEY** (CBS tv series) [as Det. Victor Isbecki]
1984 **THE KARATE KID** [as Kreese] dir: John G. Avildsen
1985 **RAMBO FIRST BLOOD PART II** [as Ericson] dir: George P. Cosmatos
1986 **THE KARATE KID PART II** [as Kreese] dir: John G. Avildsen
1987 **STEELE JUSTICE** [as John Steele] dir: Robert Boris
1988 **HIGHER GROUND** (tv movie) [as Rick Loden] dir: Robert Day [tx 4/9/1988 CBS]
1989 **THE KARATE KID PART III** [as Kreese] dir: John G. Avildsen
1989 **HARD TIME ON PLANET EARTH** (tv series) [as Jesse]
1991 **WHITE LIGHT** (Canada) [as Sean Craig] dir: Al Waxman
1991 **VOICES THAT CARE** (tv pilot) dir: David S. Jackson [tx 28/2/1991 Fox]
1992 **SHOOTFIGHTER FIGHT TO THE DEATH** [as Lee] dir: Pat Alan [actually Robert Ginty]
1992 **PROJECT: SHADOWCHASER** (UK/Canada) [as Michael DaSilva dir: John Eyres
1993 **WITHOUT A KISS GOODBYE** (tv movie) [as Cecil Harding] dir: Noel Nosseck [tx 21/3/1993]
1993 **TO BE THE BEST** [as Rick] dir: Joseph Merhi
1993 **THE OUTFIT** [as Agent Baker] dir: J. Christian Ingvordsen
1993 **LIGHTNING IN A BOTTLE** [as Duane Furber] dir: Jeff Kwitny
1993 **FUTURE SHOCK** [as Doctor Langdon] dir: Eric Parkinson
1993 **FIREHAWK** [as Stewart] dir: Cirio H. Santiago
1993 **PRESIDENT'S TARGET** dir: Yvan Chiffre
1994 **WYATT EARP** [as Ed Ross] dir: Lawrence Kasdan
1994 **SAVAGE LAND** [as Jabal] dir: Dean Hamilton
1994 **GAMBLER V PLAYING FOR KEEPS** (tv movie) [as Black Jack Ketchum] dir: Jack Bender
[tx 2+4/10/1994 CBS]
1994 **ENDANGERED** (aka **Uncivilized**) [as DeVoe] dir: Nick Kellis
1994 **CAGNEY AND LACEY THE RETURN** (tv movie) [as Det. Victor Isbecki] dir: James Frawley
[tx 6/11/94 CBS]
1994 **WITHOUT MERCY** (Indonesia, aka **Outraged Fugitive / Respect!**) [as Wolf Larsen] dir: Robert Anthony
1994 **DEATH MATCH** [as Paul Landis] dir: Joe Coppoletta
1994 **WYATT EARP RETURN TO TOMBSTONE** (tv movie) [as Bad Jack Dupree] original footage
dirs: Frank McDonald & Paul Landres [tx 2/7/1994]
1995 **BABY FACE NELSON** [as John Dillinger] dir: Scott Levy
1995 **FINAL EQUINOX** [as Torman]
1996 **MERCENARY** (cable movie) [as Phoenix] dir: Avi Nesher [tx 17/1/1997 HBO]

Appendix I

1996 **JUDGE & JURY** dir: John Eyres
1997 **ASSAULT ON DEVIL'S ISLAND** (Canada) dir: Jon Cassar
1997 **DEADWOOD** dir: Michael Mileham
1997 **GRIZZLY MOUNTAIN** [as Marshall Jackson] dir: Jeremy Haft
1997 **THE MARKSMEN** [as Samuel J. Weber] dir: Steve Kanaly
1997 **TOP OF THE WORLD** [as Carl] dir: Sidney J. Furie
1998 **HYACINTH**
1998 **ILLUSION INFINITY** [as cabdriver] dir: Alan Smithee (anonymous)
1998 **JOSEPH'S GIFT** [as Parker] dir: Philippe Mora
1998 **NOWHERE LAND** [as Hank] dir: Rupert Hitzig
1998 **SHADOW WARRIORS II: HUNT FOR THE DEATH MERCHANT** [as Andy Powers] dir: Jon Cassar
1998 **THE THIEF AND THE STRIPPER** [as Face] dir: John Sjogren
1998 **TRANCE** dir: Gary Dean Orona and Rafal Zielinski
1998 **THE WATERFRONT** dir: Jesse Dell

opposite:
Martin Kove as Kreese in *The Karate Kid*.

FRED LINCOLN

Fred Lincoln (aka Fred Perna, or, as he is credited on many of his films and videos, F.J. Lincoln) has directed, produced and acted in adult films for over twenty years. His credits are too extensive to list here; for example, in 1993 alone, Fred directed over 30 (!) X-rated videos, many of which were fetish/bondage tapes. Sometimes appearing onscreen in cameo appearances, Fred now sports a wild mane of long silver hair and a beard, nearly unrecognizable from his appearance in **Last House**. At one time he was married to porn starlet Tiffany Clark, and the dynamic duo were described in one publication as "the kinkiest couple on the East Coast porn scene... running the now closed Plato's Retreat swing club. They often commented on how their life together was a non-stop party - swinging, porn films, and hosts of a cable television show on matters erotic." He has since remarried several times and is, like many of his **Last House** co-stars, a proud parent. He offers no regrets or apologies for his involvement in the porno business, but says that "Last House on the Left is the only movie I'm ashamed of doing." Fred was inducted into the Adult Video Hall of Fame in 1993.

Fred Lincoln's credits as a stunt man include **The French Connection**, **Shaft**, **Cotton Goes to Harlem**, **Little Murders**, **Hercules in New York** and Otto Preminger's **Such Good Friends**.

as actor (selected):
1971 **FLESHPOTS ON 42ND STREET** dir: Andy Milligan
1972 **THE LAST HOUSE ON THE LEFT** [as Weasel] dir: Wes Craven
1973 **THE CASE OF THE SMILING STIFFS / The Case Of The Full Moon Murders** [as Joe]
dir: Sean S. Cunningham
Lincoln did an unlikely impersonation of Jack Webb's 'Joe Friday' character from the TV series DRAGNET in Sean Cunningham's slapstick sex film.
1973 **A GAME OF LOVE** [as the man] dir: James Wood
Softcore feature from the man who went on to direct **Dr Jekyll's Dungeon of Death**
1974 **DEFIANCE** (aka **The Defiance of Good**) dir: Armand Weston
Hardcore S&M extravanganza. Fred has directed several shot-on-video sequels to **Defiance** and did cameos in a few of them.
1978 **HERE COME THE TIGERS** dir: Sean Cunningham
Fred appeared in this wholesome, **Bad News Bears** styled family film.

As director:
Too many X-rated films to count (1976-present).
1988 **TERROR NIGHT** dir: Nick Marino
Fred is credited as the sole second unit director on this horror film although Fred Olen Ray, David DeCoteau and veteran Andre De Toth all worked on the film. The cast features Cameron Mitchell, John Ireland, Aldo Ray and 'scream queen' Michelle Bauer (aka Pia Snow of **Café Flesh**).
1989 **WILD MAN** (director/actor as the old indian)
Cast features former porn queen Ginger (Lynn) Allen.

MARC SHEFFLER

When asked if he pursued acting after his stint as Junior Stillo in **Last House on the Left**, Marc Sheffler drily replies, "I pursued cab-driving." His professional activities since doing **Last House** have mostly been in television writing and producing. Marc started working in television circa 1976 when he wrote a movie-of-the-week about killer snakes called **The Unseen**. "The script was never produced, but I got paid for it and that moved me to California," he explains. His behind-the-scenes TV credits include the Scott Baio/Willie Aames sitcom **Charles in Charge**, **Harry and the Hendersons** and the 1992 **Happy Days** reunion special. He lives in Los Angeles and is currently gearing up to direct a feature film called **Kid 58**.

Television
"Sister, Sister" (Writer) Paramount/UPN
"Harry and the Hendersons" (Writer/Consulting Producer) Amblin.Universal
"The Hard Hats" (Writer) Danny Arnold/ABC
"Everything's Relative" (Co-producer) Columbia/CBS
"Chicken Soup" (Writer) Carsey-Werner/ABC
"Who's the Boss?" (Writer) Columbia/ABC
"Charles in Charge" (Executive Story Consultant) Universal/Syndicated
"Lewis and Clark" (writer/Co-Creator) Carson Productions/NBC
"Brady Brides" (Executive Story Consultant) Paramount/NBC
"Co-Ed Fever" (Producer/Writer) Ranoshoff/CBS

Pilots and Made-for-Television
"Every Other Week" (Creator, Executive Producer) Paramount Television
"The Ringers" (Writer/Producer/Director) Bell Atlantic Corp.
"Grace Gets Lucky" (Co-writer/Co-exec. Producer/Co-Creator) Columbia/ABC
"Little Shop of Horrors" (writer) Lorimar/ABC
"Rosey's Rockets" (Exec. Producer.Writer/Creator) Paramount/NBC
"Like Father Like Son" (Creator/Writer) Bud Austin/Burt Sugarman Prod./NBC
"Beetle Bailey" (Writer) Chuck Fries/NBC
"Duarte" (Producer/Co-writer) Alan Sacks/NBC
"The Unseen" (Writer) Lee Lacy Prod./NBC

Specials
"1994 People's Choice Awards" (Writer)
"The Best of the Hollywood Palace" (Writer/co-producer) Malcolm Leo Prod./ABC
"More of the Best of the Hollywood Palace" (writer) as above
"The Happy Days Reunion Show" (Writer) Malcolm Leo Prod./ABC
"Miss Hollywood" (Producer/Creative Consultant) Proctor &Gamble/ABC
"ABC Presents Tomorrow's Stars" (Writer) Pasetta Productions/ABC
"How Bugs Bunny Won the West" (Writer) Warner Bros./CBS
"Us Against the World" (Producer/Writer) Carolyn Raskin/NBC

Feature Films
1972 **THE LAST HOUSE ON THE LEFT** (as Junior Stillo) dir: Wes Craven
1983 **DU-BEAT-E-O** (writer) Alan Sacks Productions
Marc Sheffler wrote the screenplay for this punk-rock comedy feature based on an original idea by producer-director Sacks (best known for his work on the popular TV series **Welcome Back, Kotter**.) The story concerns a zany punk moviemaker (Ray Sharkey), and his attempts to patch together a film starring Joan Jett (who appears as herself, performing several songs) with the help of his cough syrup-swilling assistant (Derf Scratch of the band Fear.) At some point during the editing of **du-BEAT-e-O**, degenerate L.A. rock band the Mentors were called in to put their perverted spin on the production, which apparently had run low on funds. The result was a stream of demented, obscene narration - "written and performed by Alan [Sacks] with [Mentors vocalist] El Duce and friends" - along with randomly inserted footage of pornographic polaroids, miscellaneous insanity, and H.G. Lewis-style gore effects. It's hard to believe that this aborted meta-movie (which features drive-in starlet Cheryl "Rainbeaux" Smith as well as character actor Len Lesser of the 1971 gem **Blood and Lace**) was ever released.

Appendix I

LUCY GRANTHAM

1972 **THE LAST HOUSE ON THE LEFT** [as Phyllis]
dir: Wes Craven

"**Last House on the Left** was my big moment," Lucy Grantham reflected in a 1996 interview. "I never really did anything else worth mentioning, and that was due to the fact that I didn't pursue acting in a serious way. I wanted to do it, but I didn't have enough focus at that time in my life. And it was scary to be in the movie business in particular at that time because the people it attracted were very wild. And when I was around wild people, I was wild too. I never really gave acting a chance after **Last House**, even though I did have an agent at one time. I couldn't handle that sort of life. The good part about **Last House on the Left** was that it gave me a sense of fulfillment, because I had been involved in a project that was a major success. I didn't walk away [from acting] with this feeling of 'coulda, woulda, shoulda, maybe, can-I' I never felt that those years acting were lost or wasted in any way. I learned so much from **Last House**, and I felt that I did what I set out to do. A lot of kids who go into the field never even get to feel that. I felt very fortunate to have been a part of it.".

RICHARD TOWERS
aka: Gaylord St. James

Prior to playing the role of Mr. Collingwood in **Last House on the Left**, Richard Towers worked as a talent agent for a New York firm which represented Tom Jones and Englebert Humperdinck. As an actor, Towers' first love was theater; his stage credits include Broadway productions of **The Death of Odysseus** and **The Male Animal**, as well as a two-year stint at Radio City Music Hall in **A Night in Venice**. He also appeared on television in episodes of **The Defenders**, **The Bell Telephone Hour**, **The Bobby Clark Comedy Hour**, and **The Doctors and the Nurses**. In **Last House**, he used the pseudonym 'Gaylord St. James' as a means of avoiding conflicts with the Screen Actors Guild. He later moved to Las Vegas, where he continued his show business career managing musical groups and acting in plays. He currently lives in New York City.

1962 **PRESSURE POINT**
dir: Hubert Cornfield
1965 **MURDER IN MISSISSIPPI**
dir: Joseph P. Mawra
1972 **LAST HOUSE ON THE LEFT**
[as Doctor John Collingwood]
dir: Wes Craven

LAST HOUSE ON THE LEFT　　203

FILMS DISTRIBUTED BY HALLMARK RELEASING CORPORATION

Hallmark Releasing, a Boston-based group of movie theater owners, served as the uncredited executive producers of **Last House on the Left**. If not for the canny exploitation instincts of Hallmark, Wes Craven and Sean Cunningham might never have gone into making horror movies. The main partners in the company were Steve Minasian, Phil Scuderi, and Robert Barsamian. They commissioned and financed **Last House**, came up with its title, and exhibited it in their own theaters before selling it to American International Pictures for nationwide release. In the '80s, Hallmark's principals played a key role in funding and developing the **Friday the 13th** films. Some of the murder sequences in the **Friday** sequels were inspired by scenes in '70s exploitation flicks distributed by Hallmark. After Hallmark dissolved, Minasian teamed up with Dick Randall to produce three '80s slasher films: **Pieces** (**Mil Gritos Tiene La Noche**, 1983), **Don't Open Till Christmas** (1984), and **Slaughter High** (aka **April Fools Day**, 1985). Under the banner of Melrose Entertainment, Minasian distributed a reissue of **Phantom of the Opera** in 1993.

The following filmography is included as a tribute to the '70s drive-in horror market that helped make **Last House on the Left** possible. Commentary in quotes is taken from an interview with former Hallmark theater booker George Mansour.

George Mansour of Hallmark Releasing Corporation

The years cited reflect the U.S. theatrical release dates, not necessarily the years of production.

1971 **TOGETHER** (Aug. 70 mins, rated X)
(US, 1971, dir: Sean Cunningham)
See Chapter II

1972 **MARK OF THE DEVIL** (Jan. 95 mins, unrated)
(**Hexen bis aufs Blut gequält**, West Germany, 1969, dir: Michael Armstrong)
See Chapter VI

1972 **BORN BLACK** (April) (**Der verlogene Akt**, West Germany/Italy, 1969, dir: Rolf von Sydow)
"This was another one we bought while in Germany. I believe its original title was **Misconception**. It was a very mild movie, it really had nothing to do with anything black, but we put it out as a blaxploitation movie. It was this very lugubrious German movie, about a man who was cheating on his wife with a white prosti-tute. The prostitute had a black pimp, and she had engaged in sexual relations with this pimp just before the white guy came over and had sex with her. Then the married guy went back and had sex with his wife, impregnating her, and then she had a black baby... hello?! The highlight of the movie

is when this white woman gives birth on screen to a black baby. Of course, the title **Born Black** and the campaign made it sound like it's some sort of gritty, **Shaft** kind of movie. This black audience came in looking for an action film and sat through 90 minutes of dubbed German softcore sex. People practically rioted when they saw the movie. It made a lot of money."

1972 **CARNAGE** (May. 90 mins, rated R) (**Ecologia del delitto**, Italy, 1971, dir: Mario Bava; aka **A Bay of Blood**, **Blood Bath**, **Twitch of the Death Nerve**)
This Mario Bava picture about a succession of murders surrounding a real estate inheritance was one of the original "splatter" epics. Hallmark first released it as **Carnage** in the spring of 1972, with the following warning to viewers: "If your idea of horror is Frankenstein or Dracula, or if you are a Shirley Temple fan, CARNAGE is not for you. But if you are interested in the horror of the '70s, which is filled with violence, brutality, and unbelievable shock, you can't afford to miss Mario Bava's CARNAGE!" Towards the end of 1972 they retitled it **Twitch of the Death Nerve**, under which moniker the film often played with **Last House on the Left**. Later on, the movie was given the title **Last House - Part II**.

1972 **DEEP END** (West Germany/US, 1970, dir: Jerzy Skolimowski)
Hallmark regionally released this Jerzy Skolimowski art picture about a sauna attendant. According to the following amusing anecdote from Mansour, the film also played under other titles. "I bought a film from Paramount, a very interesting little art film called **Deep End**, directed by Jerzy Skolimowski, with Diana Dors... it took place in a seedy London bath house. Phil Scuderi came to me and said he had a great idea for a title for a softcore sex film, **Steam Room Girls**. So he said, 'Find me a movie that I can call **Steam Room Girls**.' So I looked around, and Paramount did have this picture [**Deep End**] and you could buy it flat in other words, you didn't have to report a gross, because the film was considered so unplayable that you could buy it for fifty dollars! So I bought **Deep End** for fifty dollars from Paramount, and we clipped off the title and manufactured a little header that said **Steam Room Girls**, or **Steam Bath Girls**. Then we'd play it in the drive-ins, and if a lot of people came, we knew that the title would work and then maybe we'd go over to Germany or some other place in Europe and actually find a film that fit the title."

1972 **ASYLUM EROTICA** (97 mins, rated R) (**La bestia uccide a sangue freddo**, Italy, 1971, dir: Fernando Di Leo; re-released in 1973 as **SLAUGHTER HOTEL**)
An Italian import, originally entitled **La Bestia Uccide A Sangue Freddo**, Hallmark initially released it as **Asylum Erotica** in Summer 1972. By Summer 1973 it had been re-released under the title **Slaughter Hotel**. Although Hallmark's **Slaughter Hotel** campaign implied that the film was a dramatization of the real-life Richard Speck murder case ("SEE: The Slashing Massacre of 8 innocent nurses! Torn from today's headlines!") the movie was actually a trashy, gory whodunit set at an insane asylum and starring the inimitable Klaus Kinski.

1972 **THE BLIND DEAD** (July. 86 mins, rated PG) (**La noche del terror ciego**, Spain/Portugal, 1971, dir: Amando de Ossorio; aka **Tombs of the Blind Dead**)
Amando de Ossorio's celebrated 'Knights Templar' zombie movie was on theatrical release in the US from July 1972, under two separate titles: **Tombs of the Blind Dead** and simply **The Blind Dead**. It was re-issued to theaters in October 1972 to take advantage of the Halloween trade ("Makes 'Night of the Living Dead' and 'Mark of the Devil' look like a kids' pajama party!")

1972 **THE LAST HOUSE ON THE LEFT** (Aug. 85 mins, rated R) (US, 1972, dir: Wes Craven)
Last House on the Left was also financed by Hallmark.

1972 **WHY** (Nov. 102 mins, rated PG) (**Detenuto in attesa in giudizio**, Italy, 1971, dir: Nanni Loy; aka **In Prison Awaiting Trial**)
"This was really quite a good movie. It opened in New York, and it got good reviews, but we lost money on it. It was one of the only times that Hallmark tried out a so-called art film."

Appendix I

1973 **APARTMENT ON THE 13TH FLOOR** (June. rated R) (**La semana del asesino**, Spanish, 1971, dir: Eloy de la Iglesia; aka: **The Cannibal Man**) - See Chapter VI

1973 **DON'T LOOK IN THE BASEMENT** (Sept. 89 mins, rated R) (US, 1973, dir: S.F. Brownrigg, original title **The Forgotten** (note that there is a spoken reference to this title in one of the opening scenes of the film.)
In June of 1973, Hallmark briefly tested out this S.F. Brownrigg classic under the title **Death Ward #13** before hitting on the 'Don't' appellation which spawned a splatter sub-genre of its own with low-budget horror titles like **Don't Open the Window** (see below), **Don't Go in the House**, **Don't Go in the Woods** and **Don't Answer the Phone**.

1973 **THE HAMMER OF GOD** (**Longhu Dou,** 95m, Hong Kong, 1970, dir: Jimmy Wang Yu; aka **The Chinese Boxer**)

1973 **SHANGHAI KILLERS** (Sept. rated R, 83m)

1974 **DEADLY WEAPONS** (April. 72 mins, rated R) (US, 1974, dir: Doris Wishman)
While most of the company's releases with the notable exception of **Last House on the Left** were all acquisitions, Hallmark actually produced this Doris Wishman epic about Chesty Morgan and her 73 inch breasts. Wishman was unhappy with the deal, so she made the sequel, **Double Agent 73**, on her own later during the same year.

1974 **KARADO, THE HONG KONG CAT** (Hong Kong, aka **Super Kung Fu Kid**)

1974 **DEEP THRUST** (May, 88 mins, rated R) (Hong Kong, 1973, dir: Heang Feng; aka **Deep Thrust Hands of Death**)
"On our second trip to Germany, we bought a bunch of karate films. The whole karate craze was just starting, and we really rode that wave. We changed the titles around a lot - we called one **Deep Thrust**, because **Deep Throat** was popular at the time, and there was a woman in it. we all participated in retitling these movies. **Karado, The Hong Kong Cat** was another and then we had some other movies that we advertised as 'Starring Bruce Li' this was all very profitable."

1974 **LIZARDS** (**I basilischi**, Italy, 1962, dir: Lina Wertmüller)

1974 **THE HOUSE THAT VANISHED** (July. 95 mins, rated R) (**Scream... and Die!** / **Psycho Sex Fiend**, United Kingdom, 1973, dir: José Ramón Larraz)

1974 **SUMMER OF '69**

1975 **MARK OF THE DEVIL PART 2** (Feb. 90 mins, rated R) (**Hexen geschändet und zu Tode gequält**, West Germany, 1972, dir: Adrian Hoven)

1975 **COMPUTER KILLERS** (April, 88 mins, rated PG) (**Horror Hospital**, United Kingdom, 1973, dir: Antony Balch)

Appendix I

1975 **THE CATAMOUNT KILLING** (Nov. 93 mins) (**Pittsville Ein Safe voll Blut**, US/West Germany, 1975, dir: Krzysztof Zanussi)

1975 **MAN EATERS** (Newport, July, aka **Shark**)
Hallmark quickly capitalized on the success of Steven Spielberg's summer 1975 blockbuster **Jaws** by retitling Samuel Fuller's 1969 film **Shark** as **Maneaters** and luring audiences in with the tag-line "Burt Reynolds is the bait!"

1976 **ANONYMOUS AVENGER** (Feb. 88 mins, rated R) (**Il cittadino si ribella**, Italy, 1974, dir: Enzo G. Castellari [Enzo Girolami] aka: **Street Law / Vigilante 2 / Revenge**)

1975 **DON'T OPEN THE WINDOW** (Newport, 88 mins, rated R) (**No profanar el sueño de los muertos**, Spain/Italy, 1974, aka **Breakfast At The Manchester Morgue**, **The Living Dead At The Manchester Morgue**. dir: Jorge Grau)
One of the better **Night of the Living Dead** ripoffs, Jorge Grau's gory zombie movie featured Arthur Kennedy and was heavily cut when Hallmark released it to drive-ins as **Don't Open the Window**. The advertising for **Don't Open the Window** featured a photo of a screaming actress taken from S.F. Brownrigg's **Don't Look in the Basement** and a shot of Linda Hayden taken from **The House on Straw Hill**!

1976 **PHAROAH** (May, 134 mins, rated R) (**Faraon**, 1965, Poland, dir: Jerzy Kawalerowicz; re-released in June 1977 in an unrated version, @ 140 mins)

1976 **MANSON MASSACRE** (Newport, aka **House Of Bondage** (1980 re-release title)
The made-for-TV movie **Helter Skelter** got a big ratings share in 1976, so Hallmark quickly unleashed this exploitation flick. Although it has eluded most movie reference guides, it's a fair bet that **Manson Massacre** was made in the early '70s and retitled by Hallmark.

1977 **LAST HOUSE - PART II** (Newport, June)
Although many sources claim that this was another retitling of Bava's **A Bay Of Blood**, film archivist David Beach saw this film at a drive-in in 1978 and maintains that it was actually **L'Ultimo treno della notte / Night Train Murders** (Italy 1974)   (see 'Ripoffs and Rehashes.'). [Also released in April 1978 as **The New House on the Left** by Central Park Distributing Corp.]

1977 **THE SCHOOL THAT COULDN'T SCREAM**
Actually a retitled version of the 1971 Italian/West German film **What Have You Done to Solange?** - a 'giallo' murder mystery directed by Massimo Dallamano and photographed by Joe D'Amato.

Appendix II

The Shooting Schedule

Fri. Oct.1   Postman, Montage & at mailbox
   Mari in Shower + dressing in room
Sat. Oct.2   Kitchen, Morning
   "Cake" scene
   First Living Room
   Master Bedroom

Sun. Oct.3   Girls' Car
Mon. Oct.4   First Living Room [rescheduled from 10/2?]
   Second Living Room
   Sheriff looks at car
   Doctor Rigs Traps

Tue. Oct.5 / Wed. Oct.6 : Rushes & Prep.
Thur. Oct.7   Girls out of car
   Walk to Lake
   Lovemaking through escape
   Junior & Mari
   "Dressing"
   Mari from Lake at night

Fri. Oct.8   Chase and death of Phyllis
   Mari's death, Mari's shooting
   P.U. [pickup] Collingwood exteriors
   [dog barking, Estelle]
   Note P.U. [pickup] - John
   Mari on couch
Sat. Oct.9 / Sun. Oct.10   Rain days

Mon. Oct.11   "Freud" scene
   Krug bedroom (all 4)
Tue. Oct.12   Back up and Rushes

Wed. Oct.13   More Phyllis chase if needed
   Bads meet Estelle
   Bads meet John
   Dinner scene
   TV scene
   Weasel and Estelle, interior
   Krug, doctor fight in bedroom
   Hallway pickups
Thur. Oct.14   Police Station
   Car and Road Pickups (Sheriff)
   Chicken Truck

Fri. Oct.15 / Sat. Oct.16 / Sun. Oct.17
   Rushes & Prep. Police Station,
   Car and Road, Cars (Krug/cop)
Mon. Oct.18   Estelle & Weasel, Exteriors
   Estelle & Junior, Bath & Hall
   Estelle, Third Bedroom

Tues. Oct.19   Fight and End
Wed. Oct.20   Technical Setup for New York [crossed out and replaced by continuation of previous day's scenes]

Thur. Oct.21   New York Interiors
Fri. Oct.22   New York Interiors & Street

Sat. Oct.23 / Sun. Oct.31   Hold open for retakes and pickups

Appendix II

Following is a list of entries made by sound man Jim Hubbard in a 1971 slim-line diary which he used to keep track of the hours he worked on the set of Last House on the Left (Night of Vengeance). Although he may not have been present on every single day of shooting, Hubbard's sparse notes show that the shoot proceeded differently than the pre-production schedule indicates.

Sat. Oct.2	Night of vengeance- Day 1
Sun. Oct.3	off
Mon. Oct.4	Day 2. Doctor's living room
Tues. Oct.5	off
Wed. Oct.6	off
Thur. Oct.7	Day 3. Ext. Redding Glen

(refers to shooting woods scenes in state park in Redding, CT)

Fri. Oct.8	Day 4. Convertible
Sat. Oct.9	Day 5. Rain day. <u>Glen</u>. 8:30. Girls and wine.
Sun. Oct.10	off (rain.)
Mon. Oct.11	Day 6. Chase and cable-crossing.

('Cable-Crossing' refers to failed stunt in which Weasel and Sadie walk hand over hand on a wire suspended over a river during the chase through the woods. Footage of these stunt scenes appears in outtakes from the film - see colour section.)

Tues. Oct.12	Day 7. Woods across the road- (Bottles) 2-3
Wed. Oct.13	Day 8. 3-4. Sean's house, cemetery, death of Phyllis.
Thur. Oct.14	Day 9. 3-4. Rape and death of Mary [sic] Pondside.
Fri. Oct.15	off?
Sat. Oct.16	off
Sun. Oct.17	off?
Mon. Oct.18	off
Tues. Oct.19	Day 10. 3 + 2. Mari death.
Wed. Oct.20	Day 11. 3+4. Pick ups with Don Morales [an uncredited production assistant].
Thur. Oct.21	Day 12. 4+2. Chicken truck.
Fri. Oct.22	Day 13. Interiors. 3-2
Sat. Oct.23	Day 14. Weasel and Estelle in and out. 2-

(Refers to outdoor scene of blow-job / oral castration and preceding indoor dialogue scene in living room.)

Sun. Oct.24	Day 15. 8:30
Mon. Oct.25	Day 16. Bedroom scene Doc and Krug. 8:30-11:30

(Doc sneaks into Mari's bedroom with shotgun, awakening Krug - their dialogue, etc.)

Tues. Oct.26	Day 17. 9:00 AM.
Wed. Oct.27	Day 18. 2+5
Thur. Oct.28	off.
Fri. Oct.29	Day 19.
Sat. Oct.30	Day 20.

339 W 87th. 4th. Snyder. 799-9562
(This is the address of the apartment building which provided the interior of the criminals' hideout. Filming there probably continued into Oct.31)

Sun. Oct.31	Day 21.

(LAST HOUSE shooting appropriately concludes, with the exception of one "make-up day", on Halloween night.)

Tues. Nov.2	Day 22. Make-up Westport.

(This notation is scribbled over; the make-up day was postponed to Nov.4)

Thurs. Nov.4	Day 22. Westport make-up.

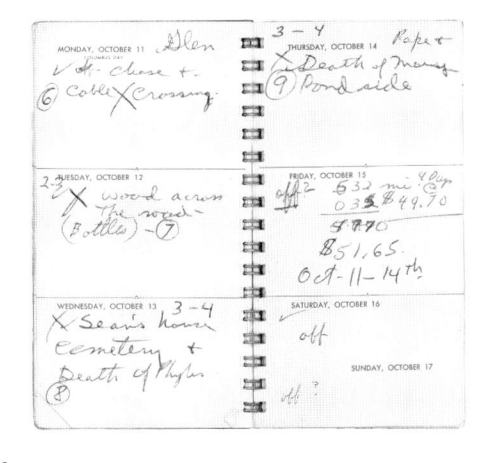

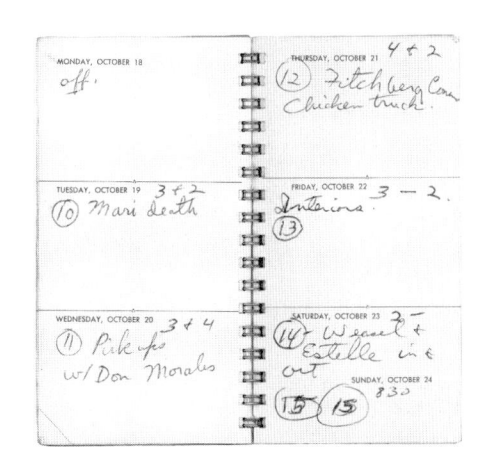

The Ballad

*"...with **The Virgin Spring**, my motivation was extremely mixed. The God concept had long ago begun to crack, and it remained more as a decoration than anything else. What really interested me was the actual, horrible story of the girl and her rapists, and the subsequent revenge. My own conflict with religion was well on its way out."*
- **Ingmar Bergman** [1]

Ulla Isaakson based her screenplay for Ingmar Bergman's *The Virgin Spring* on a fourteenth century Swedish ballad called *Tore's Daughter in Vange*. Bergman's rendering of the legend later became the inspiration for *Last House on the Left*. The English translation of *Tore's Daughter* shown here appears courtesy of the Swedish Film Institute.

Tore's Daughter in Vange

Tore's daughter, of Vange town,
She sleeps too long in her bed of down
She oversleeps the morning mass,
May God have mercy on this churchgoing lass!

Lady Mareta climbs up to the loft
–The forest was wet and cold–
Her daughter Karin she wakens so soft
–And the buds on the trees unfold–

"Rise up my daughter, be not slow;
Thou shalt to church in Kaga go."

Noble Karin sat on her bed,
Binding her locks with a ribbon red.

Noble Karin donned her silken shift,
The work of fifteen maidens' fingers swift.

Noble Karin slipped over her head
The lovely skirts with the golden thread.

Noble Karin donned her cloak of blue,
Now to leave for church she was due.

In the midst of the forest gloom
Three herdsmen in her path did loom.

"Either thou serve as our herdsmens' wife
Or thou shalt lose thy young life."

"Do not try thy force on me,
Or my father will deal with thee."

Neither thy father nor thy kin do we fear,
After we slay thee we shall not be here."

First she became the herdsmen's wife
Then she lost her budding young life.

They led her by her golden hair
Into a grove of birches fair.

By her golden hair so free
They pinned her against a fallen tree.

From her body they cut her golden head,
A spring welled forth where the girl lay dead.

Appendix III

They stripped her body of clothes and gold,
Filled their bags with all they could hold.

In a shallow grave they lay her down
And took her clothes to the nearby town.

By chance they followed the same way
That Noble Karin had taken that day.

They walked so long and the path was the same
That to Vange the herdsmen came.

They came to the house on Sir Tore's lands.
Waiting at the door Sir Tore stands.

"You look so warm in your coat of fur,
We herdsmen are cold, can you shelter us, sir?"

Into his house of stone he did lead
The herdsmen, and offered wine and mead.

Sir Tore for his daughter yearned
Why has his Karin not returned?

Before Lady Mareta went up to bed
She turned to look when a herdsman said:

"Do you want to buy a silken shift,
Surely the work of nine maidens swift?"

When the garment he did show
The mother's heart was filled with woe.

Lady Mareta went to her husband's room
To bring him tidings of Karin's doom.

"Wake up my lord, I tell of slaughter
The herdsmen have slain thy beautiful daughter.

"Her bloodied shift the herdsmen possess
Anguish upon my heart does press."

Into the hall ran the noble lord,
Under his cloak a naked sword.

He killed the first, and the second too,
And then the third he also slew.

Then Sir Tore threw down his sword
"Have mercy on my deed, dear Lord."

"How shall I atone for the deed so gory?
I shall build a church of stone to Thy glory."

"That, we shall willingly do,"
–The forest was wet and cold–
"Let the Karna church be my penance true."
–And the buds on the trees unfold–

Notes

1   Ingmar Bergman, *Images: My Life in Film.*
Translated from the Swedish by Marianne Ruuth (New York: Arcade Publishing, 1994), p.244

Appendix IV: Props and Equipment list for Night of Vengeance shoot

Note: *This appendix is transcribed from a list handwritten by Wes Craven on his shooting script for Last House on the Left (Night of Vengeance). Annotations in italics have been added by the author for reference purposes.*

EQUIPMENT

1. Containers, bulbs, and tubing for blood
2. Ingredients for blood
3. Smoke bombs   *Possibly intended to stylize the Phyllis murder sequence.*
4. Glycerin + sprayers/atomizers   *To make the characters look sweaty.*
5. "shock" sparker for doorknob
6. Car rig up
7. Firecrackers?   *Possibly to represent gunfire.*
8. Seamless black for windows 12' x 50'
9. Sheets of cardboard

CLOTHES

1. During "cake" scene, John should wear full arm cover
2. Weasel wears a tie from dinner to lake
3. Mari needs 3-4 changes of this set, all alike:
a) white bellbottoms
b) whitish peasant blouse or Indian shirt
c) sandals (one or two pair)
d) leather b [elt?]
4. Phylis: large purse for wine bottle. Shirt. Maybe should be anti chic a la tennis shoes- two or three pair. Ring. Blouse that unbuttons down front.

PROPS AND OTHER STUFF

1. A mailbox, or an old one repainted
2. A car rooftop sign reading "U.S. Mail"
3. (3) ?? portable radios.
4. Two or three knives, one a switchblade
5. A gun or two, one which fires
6. Envelopes addressed to Mari
7. Peace symbol and box. Ring for Phylis? - *The ring was used to distinguish Phyllis' severed hand.*
8. Decorations of birthday, esp. banner
9. A portrait of Mari in living room
10. A shot [photo] of John, Mari and Estelle
11. Capsules for "reds". Boone's apple wine. - *"Capsules for 'reds'": In the script, Phyllis was popping pills while driving to the Bloodlust concert.*
12. Guitars, etc. - *For the aborted fantasy sequence where Mari and Phyllis 'make it with Bloodlust'.*
13. "Works" for Junior
14. Cigars for Krug and Sadie
15. Helium balloons
16. Weasel's "heart" underwear - *In the scene where the killers are lounging around their apartment hideout, Weasel was supposed to be wearing underwear emblazoned with little hearts!*
17. Women's lib buttons, "smile" button
18. Blanket
19. Sash cord - *Blanket and sash cord were intended for the scene where the girls are thrown in the car trunk.*
20. Six packs of beer - *Krug, Sadie and Weasel were supposed to be swilling beer during the scene where they torture the girls.*
21. Something for Krug's car to distinguish it - *In one early draft, Craven had written that Krug's car was distinguished by a bullet hole. A note written by Cunningham in the margin reads: "I doubt we can afford a bullet hole."*
22. Sheriff's office props- radio, safety posters, etc. Small TV. Checkers game, Classics Illustrated
23. "rock" sponge - *For the scene where Phyllis bludgeons Sadie over the head with a rock.*
24. Card deck - *For the scene of Mr. Collingwood playing solitaire.*
24. Card deck
25. Chicken truck, pipe
26. [Phylis' severed] Arm.
27. Suitcase
28. Pandas, dolls, etc
29. Dinner dressing
30. Fake dong for Weasel ?
31. Shotgun
32. Chain saw

INDEX

This index of film titles refers to the main text (chapters 1 to 9)

100 Proof	176	Friday the 13th, Part V:		Paura nella città dei	
2000 Maniacs	8	A New Beginning	185	Morti Viventi	176
A Bay of Blood	102, 163, 177, 178	Funhouse, The	see Last House on	Paradise, Hawaiian Style	118
A Clockwork Orange	15, 59, 96, 140		Dead End Street	Peopletoys	see Horrible House on
A Nightmare on Elm Street	8, 9, 19, 76, 89, 90	Gates of Hell	see Paura nella città dei		the Hill, The
Altered States	118		Morti Viventi	People under the Stairs, The	19, 20, 89
Andy Warhol's Trash	see Trash	Ghostbusters	182	People Who Own the	
Apartment on the 13th Floor	see Semana del	Godfather, The	29	Dark, The	178
	Asesino, La	Good, the Bad & the Ugly, The	33, 171	Potato Fritz	126
Around the World in 80 Days	27	Halloween	20, 76	Preacherman Meets	
Art of Marriage, The	27, 44	Halloween: H20	46	Widderwoman	156
Assault on Precinct	13 20	Happy Hooker, The	144	Psycho	57, 116
Autostop... Rosso Sangue	see Hitch Hike	Hard Gore	36	Psycho Sex Fiend	see House that
Avalanche Express	96	Henry: Portrait of a Serial Killer	17, 127		Vanished, The
Axe	184	Here Come the Tigers	102, 149, 155	Putney Swope	117
Beguiled, The	131	Hills Have Eyes, The	8, 16, 19, 20, 21, 25,	Ragazza del Vagone Letto, La	164
Behind the Green Door	27		43, 89, 92, 155, 156,	Revenge	187
Ben Hur	27, 144		157, 185	River's Edge	19
Beyond the Law	25	Hills Have Eyes III:		Salemıms Lot	128
Blind Dead, The	see Tombs of the	The Outpost	see Mind Ripper	Savage Abduction	184
	Blind Dead	Hitch Hike	171, 181, 182	Savage Bees, The	184
Blood Feast	8	Hitcher, The	182	Savage Streets	179
Bloodthirsty Butchers	37	Honeymoon Killers, The	140	Savages	37
Bonnie and Clyde	17, 61, 120, 125	Horrible House on the Hill, The	180, 181	Sex: The Annabel Chong Story	127
Born Black	162	House by the Lake	182-184	Scream	8, 9, 16, 82
Boxcar Bertha	140	House on the Edge of the Park	156, 171, 174-177	Scream... And Die!	see House that
California Axe Massacre	see Axe	House that Dripped Blood, The	182		Vanished, The
Candidate, The	134	House that Vanished, The	158	Searchers, The (short film)	24
Candy Snatchers, The	184-85	Howard Stern's Private Parts	182	Second House from the Left	see Ultimo Treno della
Cannibal Ferox	176	I Drink Your Blood	41, 181		Notte, L'
Cannibal Holocaust	174	I Spit on your Grave	167, 183, 184	Semana del Asesino, La	128, 129, 159
Cannibal Man	see Semana del	Ice Storm, The	22	Settima Donna, La	see Last House on the
	Asesino, La	Inn of the Frightened People	see Revenge		Beach, The
Carnage	see A Bay of Blood	Is There Sex after Death?	153	Sex on the Groove Tube	see Case of the Smiling
Case of the Full Moon Murders	see Case of the Smiling	It Happened In Hollywood	25, 44		Stiffs, The
	Stiffs, The	Jason Goes To Hell	183	Sex Psycho	see Widow Blue
Case of the Smiling Stiffs, The	102, 116, 126, 154-55,	Jason Lives: Friday the 13th VI	178	Shaft	154
	159	Jaws	134	Shivers	20
Chariots of Fire	174	Jaws 3D	184	Shock	158
Chien Andalou, Un	180	Joe	133	Shocker	55, 89, 92
Chinatown	29	Kick	see Manny's Orphans	Sitting Target	131
Color Me Blood Red	132, 135	Lake Placid	46	Slaughter	see Snuff
Confessions of a Blue Movie		Last House on the Beach	171, 177-78	Snuff	162
Star: The Evolution of Snuff	79, 154, 155, 161, 162	Last House on Dead End		Spasms	182
Count Yorga, Vampire	41	Street	178-81	SS Experiment Camp	167
Cycle Psycho	see Savage Abduction	Last House on the Left II	see Ultimo Treno della	SST: Death Flight	184
Dawn of the Dead	171		Notte, L'	Strait-Jacket	132
Day of the Woman	see I Spit on your	Last House Part II	see A Bay of Blood	Strangers on a Train	57
	Grave	Last Stop on the Night Train	see Ultimo Treno della	Straw Dogs	15, 140
Deadly Blessing	90, 144, 158		Notte, L'	Suspiria	172
Deadly Friend	19	Late Night Trains	see Ultimo Treno della	Swamp Thing	19
Death Drive	see Hitch Hike		Notte, L'	Sweet Savior	41
Death Weekend	see House by the Lake	Legendary Champions	25	Swingin' Stewardesses	131, 132, 159
Death Wish	144	Lisa	see Axe	Tarantulas: The Deadly Cargo	184
Deathmaster	41	Little Murders	37	Terror	170
Deep Red	172	Lonely Violent Beach, The	183	Terror Express	see Ragazza del
Deep Throat	29, 30	Love-Thrill Murders, The	see Sweet Savior		Vagone Letto, La
Deliverance	187	Make Them Die Slowly	see Cannibal Ferox	Terror from Under the House	see Revenge
Deranged	159	Manny's Orphans	102, 111, 126, 155	Texas Chain Saw	
Devil in Miss Jones, The	29	Mark of the Devil	102, 128, 129, 130,	Massacre, The	7, 20, 21, 22, 144
Devil Times Five	see Horrible House on		133, 156, 158, 161, 162	To Kill A Mockingbird	23
	the Hill, The	Meet the Feebles	127	Together	27-32, 40, 114, 122,
Devils, The	140, 144	Mind Ripper	57		130, 161
Diamonds are Forever	31	Mondo Cane	177	Tombs of the Blind Dead	161
Don't Look in the Basement	20, 106, 156, 158, 159,	Monster in the Closet	153	Torture Train	see Ragazza del
	186	Monterey Pop	25		Vagone Letto, La
Don't Open the Window	see No Profanar el	Mother's Day	185	Trash	133
	Sueno de los Muertos	Mutiny on the Bounty	144	Turn of the Screw	159
Don't Ride on Late Night Trains	see Ultimo Treno della	Natural Born Killers	17	Twitch of the Death Nerve	see A Bay of Blood
	Notte, L'	New House on the Left, The	see Ultimo Treno della	Ultimo Treno della Notte, L'	171-174
Driller Killer, The	167		Notte, L'	Virgin Spring, The	7, 10, 11, 34, 88, 89,
Evil Dead, The	20	Night of the Living Dead	20, 22, 76, 80		91, 95, 100, 118, 126,
Exorcist, The	20, 134, 171	Night Train Murders	see Ultimo Treno della		131
Fleshpots of 42nd Street	37		Notte, L'	Widow Blue	36
Forgotten, The	see Don't Look in the	Nightmare	167	Wild Beasts	170
	Basement	Nightmare Café	57	Wild Bunch, The	131, 133, 134
Frankie and Johnny	118	Nightmares in a Damaged		Witchfinder General	128
French Connection, The	37, 129	Brain	see Nightmare	Wizard of Gore, The	7
Friday the 13th	8, 9, 21, 76, 102, 133,	No Profanar el Sueno		Woodstock	26
	141, 155, 158, 162	de los Muertos	158	You Gotta Walk It Like	
Friday the 13th, Part 2	46, 178	No Time for Sergeants	83	You Talk It	25, 44
Friday the 13th, Part 3	46	Numbered Days	see Savage Abduction	Zombie	181

ART OF DARKNESS
the cinema of Dario Argento

Order this book direct from FAB Press for
only £16.99
including p+p within the UK.

Europe:
£20 inc. Airmail delivery.
Eurocheques preferred.

USA:
$35 inc. Airmail delivery.
US$ Cash & standard US$ Checks accepted!

Grisly ultra-violence collides with fairytale logic and the aesthetics of European art house in the films of Italy's **Dario Argento**. An unending source of fascination for horror fanatics and academics alike, his films compel scrutiny, inviting their audiences to search beyond their weird, multicoloured facades, and enter a dangerous world of obsession and gruesome, violent death and torment.

Art of Darkness is lavishly illustrated with many ultra-rare posters in full colour. Plus a multitude of stunningly reproduced stills, most of which have never been seen in print anywhere before!

Every film is reviewed in depth by a team of the world's very best genre writers. This, the second book in the **FAB Press directors series**, is the definitive Argento career over-view - engaging, incisive, brimming with fresh ideas, highly readable and beautifully presented. Order today!

Art of Darkness:
the cinema of Dario Argento
edited by Chris Gallant

ISBN 0 9529260 9 1

£16.99 (UK)
£20.00 (Europe)
$30.00 (USA)

Also available... the first book in the FAB Press directors series: **Cannibal Holocaust and the savage cinema of Ruggero Deodato**. Full filmography, career-spanning interview, reviews of every film. "Sets a new standard of excellence" (Fangoria).

Order it direct from FAB Press for only **£14.99** including postage and packing within the UK.

Europe:
£17 inc. Airmail delivery.
Eurocheques preferred.

USA:
$30 inc. Airmail delivery.
US$ Cash & standard US$ Checks accepted!

To order these books please send your name, address and a cheque or postal order payable to **FAB Press** to:

**FAB Press
PO Box 178
Guildford
Surrey
GU3 2YU
England, UK**

email enquiries: harvey@fabpress.com

...and you will face the sea of darkness, and all therein that may be explored...

Master of the Macabre Lucio Fulci is celebrated in this lavishly illustrated in-depth study of his extraordinary films. From horror masterpieces like **The Beyond** and **Zombie Flesh-Eaters** to erotic thrillers like **One On Top of the Other** and **A Lizard in a Woman's Skin**; from his earliest days as director of manic comedies to his notoriety as the man behind the banned slasher epic **The New York Ripper**, every detail of his varied career is explored.

Stephen Thrower embarks on a journey through the wilder reaches of Italy's fertile film culture, taking a close-up look at the cinema's most daring and anarchic horror specialist - **Lucio Fulci** - a man willing to go ever further in search of the ultimate horrific set-piece.

'Beyond Terror' is a deluxe collector's item - no expense has been spared to bring you what is universally acclaimed as being the most beautiful book on horror films ever published.

Copies can be ordered direct from the publishers for only **£24.99**.
No hidden extras - this price is inclusive of delivery within the UK.

Quality guarantee - all books securely packaged to prevent damage in transit.

UK: **£24.99** inc. delivery.
Europe: **£30** inc. Airmail delivery. Cash or Eurocheques accepted.
USA: **£50** inc. Airmail delivery. US$ cash & checks accepted.

312 large-format pages, luxury binding
*
40 full colour pages, over 800 illustrations in all
*
Introduction by Fulci's daughter Antonella
*
Complete credits for all 52 films
*
Filmographies for all of the major stars

To order this book please send your name, address and a cheque or postal order payable to **FAB Press** to:

**FAB Press
PO Box 178
Guildford
Surrey
GU3 2YU
England, UK**

MAKING MISCHIEF
The Cult Films of Pete Walker

by Steve Chibnall

ISBN 0 9529260 1 6

£12.95

Britain's Greatest Exploitation Film Director!

No other British film-maker achieved the level of transgression that Walker regularly delivered to cinema-goers in the 1970s. Beginning his career by making 'skinflicks', Walker went on to direct a trio of bona fide horror classics. **House of Mortal Sin**, **Frightmare** and **House of Whipcord** probe beneath the glossy surface of the permissive society to expose a malevolent underworld of madness, obsession and vindictive violence. The author, Steve Chibnall, teaches Film and Cultural Studies and co-ordinates the British Cinema and Television Research Group at De Montfort University, Leicester. *Making Mischief* is the only major critical study of the controversial director, and it received the full cooperation of Pete Walker and his screenwriters. 224 profusely illustrated pages.
"The highest possible compliment" (EMPIRE)

Order this book direct from FAB Press for only **£12.95** including p+p within the UK.
Europe: **£15** inc. Airmail delivery. Eurocheques preferred.
USA: **$30** inc. Airmail delivery. US$ cash & standard US$ Checks accepted!
FAB Press, PO Box 178, Guildford, Surrey GU3 2YU, England, UK

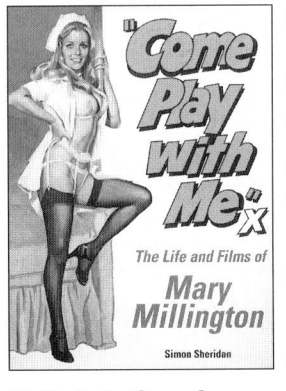

COME PLAY WITH ME
The Life and Films of Mary Millington

by Simon Sheridan

ISBN 0 9529260 7 5

£14.99

Britain's Sex Superstar of the 70s!

Mary Millington was the girl next door who became the sex superstar of the 1970s. Her rise was meteoric, controversial and scandalous. Glamour model, cover girl and hardcore porn actress, Mary was an outspoken opponent of the Obscene Publications Act, and a forthright bisexual who promoted her ideals of sexual openness and equality. She starred in numerous British sex comedies, all of which are reviewed in depth here. Simon Sheridan's heavily illustrated, widely-acclaimed book re-visits the Seventies cycle of celebrity excess and casual sex (her lovers included PM Harold Wilson and actress Diana Dors) that would eventually lead to Mary's downward spiral through prostitution, kleptomania, a celebrated trial at the Old Bailey, and cocaine abuse, to her tragic suicide at the age of 33.

Order this book direct from FAB Press for only **£14.99** including p+p within the UK.
Europe: **£17** inc. Airmail delivery. Eurocheques preferred.
USA: **$30** inc. Airmail delivery. US$ cash & standard US$ Checks accepted!
FAB Press, PO Box 178, Guildford, Surrey GU3 2YU, England, UK

Cult Movies from the Margins to the Mainstream

UNRULY PLEASURES
the **Cult Film** and its **Critics**

Showgirls
From Dusk Till Dawn
David Cronenberg
Starship Troopers
Enter the Dragon
Snuff Movies
Lucio Fulci
Rollerball
Russ Meyer
The Exorcist
Roger Corman
and much more !!!

edited by
Xavier Mendik
and
Graeme Harper

- **The Rocky Horror Picture Show** and **Starship Troopers**: Radical Messages in Cult Cinema

- **Rollerball**: Cult Visions of a Not Too Distant Future

- **Squirting and Gushing**: The Female Body in Hardcore Porn

- **Enter the Dragon**: Transnational Cult Kung-Fu Movie

- **Shivers**, **Crash** and the Cult Cinema of **David Cronenberg**

- **Thunderbirds**: Cult Marionation across Film and TV

- The Cult Cinema of **Russ Meyer**

- Cult Stars: **Celebrity Deaths**

- Cult as Hysteria: the lasting Impact of **The Exorcist**

- **The Snuff Movie** as Cult Phenomenon and Media Scapegoat

- **Showgirls**: Fandom and Cult Experiences

- **From Dusk Till Dawn** and Contemporary Cult Viewing

- **Fulci's Waste Land:** Cinematic horror and the dreams of modernism

...and much, much more

Unruly Pleasures: The Cult Film and its Critics
edited by Xavier Mendik and Graeme Harper
256 heavily illustrated pages - ISBN 1 903254 00 0

Whether we look at genres such as **horror, science fiction, action/thriller, pornography** or **camp musical**, the cult film has come to attain an important place in cinema culture. **Unruly Pleasures** is the first British volume dedicated to the critical consideration of cult movie making from the margins to the mainstream. In a series of beautifully illustrated, innovative articles by leading film critics and theorists the book deals with aspects of the medium including the cult film's definitions, genres, film styles and gender depictions.

This book should be available in all good book stores, alternatively it can be ordered direct from **FAB Press** for only £14.99 (UK), **£17.00** (Europe), **$30.00** (USA). All prices include post and packing. Payment in the form of cheques or postal orders made out to 'FAB Press'. *Europe:* We accept Eurocheques and International Money Orders. *American customers note:* cash and standard US dollars checks accepted! (Please only ever send cash by Registered mail.)

To order this book, or to receive details of other books in the internationally acclaimed range of FAB Press publications, write to us today. Alternatively check out the FAB Press website at: **www.fabpress.com**

FAB PRESS

PO BOX 178
GUILDFORD,
SURREY, GU3 2YU
ENGLAND, U.K.